Picking Winners?

Picking Winners?

From Technology Catch-up to the Space Race in Japan

SAADIA M. PEKKANEN

Stanford University Press
Stanford, California
2003

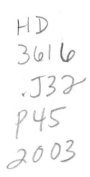
Stanford University Press
Stanford, California

Library of Congress Cataloging-in-Publication Data

Pekkanen, Saadia M.
    Picking winners? : from technology catch-up to the space race in Japan /
Saadia M. Pekkanen.
        p.   cm.
    Includes bibliographical references and index.
    ISBN 0-8047-4732-6
    1. Industrial policy—Japan.   2. Japan—Economic policy.   3. Japan—
Economic conditions.   I. Title.
HD3616.J32 P45 2003
338.0952—dc21   2002154093

Original printing 2003

The last figure below indicates the year of this printing:
12   11   10   09   08   07   06   05   04   03

Designed and typeset at Stanford University Press in 10.5/12 Bembo

For my mother and father

Contents

Figures and Tables

Acknowledgments

THIS BOOK HAS HAD a lot of support, and I gratefully acknowledge the help of many individuals and organizations during its completion. It is to my dissertation committee at Harvard, under whom this book was started, that I owe my real training in graduate school. My profound thanks to the chair, Susan Pharr, for getting me interested in Japan and to Lisa Martin, Andrew Moravcsik, and Lawrence Broz for keeping me focused on the field of international political economy. Apart from my dissertation committee, I owe a debt of gratitude to Richard Samuels and Ellis Krauss for their support of many aspects of this book. I am also very grateful to two economists, David Weinstein, who graciously shared data and ideas, and Yishay Yafeh, who helped crystallize parts of this research early on. Finally, as econometricians and methodologists, both Nada Eissa and Robert Franzese deserve special thanks for providing expert advice on the quantitative analyses.

I also wish to thank the following individuals who have helped me during both the course of research and in commenting on this work in different ways: Robert Bates, Marc Busch, John Coatsworth, Gerry Curtis, J. P. Gownder, Bill Grimes, Ehud Harari, Samuel Huntington, Saori Katada, Ed Lincoln, Greg Noble, Masahiro Okuno-Fujiwara, Hugh Patrick, Robert Pekkanen, T. J. Pempel, Jane Prokop, J. Mark Ramseyer, Henry Rosovsky, Ulrike Schaede, Frank Schwartz, Mireya Solis, Mark Tilton, Steve Vogel, and Kozo Yamamura.

At the Ministry of Finance in Japan, I wish to thank Yano Kaji for his help in assembling some of the industry data in the summer of 1993. At the erstwhile Ministry of International Trade and Industry (MITI, now the Ministry of Economy, Trade, and Industry [METI]), I was helped by far too many gracious individuals to name and to all of whom I remain grateful for their time during hectic schedules. For the kind of input that made a qualitative difference, my warmest thanks go to Shimpei Ago, Yukiko Araki, Takahiro Hagiwara, Takashi Hattori, Sota Kato, Shigeru Matsushima, Takeshi Miki, Hiroki

Mitsumata, Sataoshi Miura, Naoko Munakata, Toru Nakayama, Akihiro Sawa, Shigeaki Tanaka, Shuichi Wada, Shin Yasunobe, and Yasuhiko Yoshida. I owe a special thanks to Yuji Hosoya, the Director at MITI's Research Institute, for kindly allowing me access to the resources and facilities at the institute during 1997.

For their comprehensive help at very short notice, I also thank some high-ranking government officials involved in Japan's space policy efforts, especially Yasunori Matogawa, Director of the Kagoshima Space Center, and Masayuki Shibata, Director of the Space Policy Division Research and Development Bureau at MEXT. Takashi Ishii, in the President's Office at IHI Aerospace, has long been able to offer me his unique private-sector perspective. Paul Kallender, a Tokyo-based journalist specializing in Japan's space efforts as a whole, was tremendously generous in sharing with me his expertise and resources. All of them answered endless questions patiently and thoroughly. Last but not least, for their very helpful research assistance at different stages at Middlebury College, I thank Kartik Raj, Vinay Jawahar, Cori Loew, and Linda Booska.

Finally, I thank also Muriel Bell at Stanford University Press for her unflagging support of this project, as well as Carmen Borbon-Wu and Tony Hicks for making the production process run so smoothly at the press.

I most gratefully acknowledge the financial support for this project from different sources. Early research was made possible by awards from the Radcliffe College Research Grant for Graduate Women, Harvard Graduate Student Council Graduate Summer Research Grant, and the Edwin O. Reischauer Institute of Japanese Studies Graduate Summer Research Grant. Subsequent research and writing at the dissertation stage were funded by the National Science Foundation Doctoral Dissertation Improvement Grant (SBR-9422822), the Andrew W. Mellon Dissertation Completion Fellowship at the Graduate School of Arts and Sciences at Harvard University, and the Social Science Research Council/American Council of Learned Societies' Joint Committee on Japanese Studies Dissertation Write-up Fellowship. For funding that allowed me to turn the dissertation into a book and do additional research in Japan, I remain grateful to the very generous support provided by the Harvard Academy for International and Area Studies. Chet Haskell, the former Executive Secretary of the Harvard Academy, deserves special thanks for accommodating so many of my wayward requests. I hope, above all, that this book does some justice to the academy's vision of combining theory and area studies.

Finally, I dedicate this book to my parents, who made it possible because of all that they have done for me for so long with love, patience, and inspiration. To my brother and especially my sister I give my heartfelt thanks for always being there and encouraging me. To my daughter, Sophia, I am deeply thankful for teaching me what matters in life in a way no one else could. To my husband, Robert, at each step I truly owe much more than I can say.

S.M.P.

Abbreviations

AIST	Agency for Industrial Science and Technology
AST	Office of the Associate Administration for Space Transportation (USA)
BM	Basic Metals
BOJ	Bank of Japan
BOR	Subsidized Borrowing
CE	Ceramics
CH	Chemicals
COMSTAC	Commercial Space Transportation Advisory Committee (USA)
EIAJ	Electronics Industry Association of Japan
EM	Electrical Machinery
ESA	European Space Agency
FD	Processed Food
FILP	Fiscal Investment and Loan Program
FM	Fabricated Metals
GEO	Geostationary Earth Orbit
GM	General Machinery
GTO	Geostationary Transfer Orbit
ISAS	Institute of Space and Astronautical Sciences
JAMA	Japan Automobiles Manufacturer Association
JDA	Japan Defense Agency
JDB	Japan Development Bank
JECC	Japan Electronic Computer Corporation
JEIDA	Japan Electronics Industry Development Association
JISF	Japan Iron and Steel Federation
JMBTA	Japan Machine Tool Builders Association
LDP	Liberal Democratic Party
LEO	Low Earth Orbit

MEO	Medium Earth Orbit
METI	Ministry of Economy, Trade, and Industry (formerly MITI)
MEXT	Ministry of Education, Culture, Sports, Science, and Technology (MEXT, formerly MOE)
MITI	Ministry of International Trade and Industry (presently METI)
MOE	Ministry of Education (presently MEXT)
MOF	Ministry of Finance
MOT	Ministry of Transport
NAL	National Aerospace Laboratory
NASA	National Aeronautics and Space Administration (USA)
NASDA	National Space Development Agency of Japan
NTR	Net Transfers
NTT	Nippon Telegraph and Telephone
PC	Petroleum and Coal
PCSE	Panel Corrected Standard Error
PI	Precision Instruments
PP	Paper and Pulp
QTA	Quotas
RDS	R&D Subsidies
RLV	Reusable Launch Vehicle
RSC	Rocket System Corporation
SAC	Space Activities Commission
SBFC	Small Business Finance Corporation
SBS	Net Subsidies
SCAP	Supreme Commander of Allied Powers
SJAC	Society of Japanese Aerospace Companies
SME	Small and Medium-sized Enterprise
SSTO	Single Stage to Orbit
STA	Science and Technology Agency
TAR	Tariffs
TAX	Tax Rates
TE	Transport Equipment
TEPCO	Tokyo Electric Power Company
TIPs	Trade and Industrial Policies
TSCS	Time-Series Cross-Sectional
TX	Textiles

Picking Winners?

Introduction

AS IT DOES almost without fail every Wednesday, on 19 June 2002 Japan's highest policy-making body in the space industry, the Space Activities Commission (SAC), met for discussion and debate in full view of an assortment of government officials, industry representatives, foreign agencies, journalists, and academics. On the meeting agenda, among other things, were two policy concerns that stand to have a significant impact on the future substance and direction of Japan's space-related ventures: the domestic development of satellites and especially launch vehicles. The discussion was lively, at times contentious, and basically frank. The overall tone was one of concern about the future of the fledgling space industry in Japan and the necessity of indigenizing it through a variety of means.

The question is why? Why this emphasis on technology acquisition in a sector long dominated by established foreign players like the United States and the European Union? Japan's present endeavors in the space industry cannot be viewed in isolation. Instead, they need to be understood, examined, and analyzed in the context of the nation's historical efforts at industrial development and technology catch-up. Given Japan's swift industrial ascension and its present rank as the world's second-largest economy, there is to this day a great deal of controversy about the sources of Japan's efforts.

In the past, some of these controversies have bordered on the mythical, particularly with respect to the role of the Japanese government. During the 1970s and 1980s, for example, Japanese industries seemed unbeatable and the Japanese economy invincible. One after another, from steel to automobiles to semiconductors, Japan seemed poised to take over key industries and technologies around the world. Japan's major trade partner, namely the United States, became deeply concerned about an industrial onslaught that seemed to strike at the very heart of America's economic prowess. As much as the global competitiveness of its firms, Japan's model of capitalism challenged long-held Western ideologies by its success. For many, the dazzling speed with which Japanese industries moved to positions of global competitiveness confirmed the view that their home government had successively chosen national industries for promotion and support. Engulfing an entire generation of academics and policy-makers, the debate boiled down to arguments about how the Japanese government went about selecting industries or, more popularly, picking winners.

Then the winds of empirical fortunes shifted against Japan. The Japanese financial bubble burst, and Japan entered a recession. There was no more talk of a Japanese economic miracle or the prescience of Japan's bureaucracies that had allegedly chosen all the right industries and thereby engineered the miracle. In conflating its financial problems with manufacturing ones, many proceeded to write off Japan's economic, industrial, and technological prospects altogether. Reminiscent of the gloomy "declinism" debate in the United States in the 1980s, some observers now see Japan's economic growth prospects as negligible. In fact, most now believe that the Japanese developmental state is in shambles and has no relevance to Japan's industrial or technological future.

How wrong they are. There are several concrete reasons for continuing to pay attention to Japan's industrial and technological development. First, current depictions of Japan's decline, like those of the 1980s in the United States, are premature and historically shaky. Sudden reversals of national economic fortunes, as epitomized by the recent rise of the United States in the international economic system, are the norm, and we should fully expect a reinvigoration of Japan's economic muscle. Second, by its own account, the Japanese government takes a keen interest in the industrial and technological future of its manufacturing base. Despite the recession, this interest has not changed and may even have been fortified further under the present economic doldrums.

Third, perhaps most important of all, the logic of Japanese government choices still stands as an important lesson for developing and emerging economies. The fact that Japan became an industrial powerhouse so fast and so impressively remains one of the greatest development success stories of our time, no matter which way the winds of empirical fortunes happen to be blowing. Whatever Japan's travails now, governments around the world, especially in the developing countries, still assume Japan got rich and powerful because bureaucrats favored key industries for support. Perhaps less obvious but no less true, Japanese government officials still believe in alternative paths to industrial and technological catch-up and therefore retain an interest in promoting their brand of economic development at theoretical and policy levels.

But drawing on the core lessons from Japan's industrial development story requires a thorough analysis of Japanese government choices that breaks through the myths and perceptions about the government's industrial strategies and that focuses as much on the possibilities as the realities of its actions. How do we do this?

The Bigger Picture

In retrospect, it is clear that a key question was overlooked both in the intense controversy of the 1980s that reinforced the idea of the Japanese developmental state and the conventional wisdom of the 1990s that dismissed its relevance altogether. This oversight continues to be as true in the general industrial policy literature as in the Japan-specific literature even today. The question, simply put, is this: How do governments choose which industries to favor?

Despite the distinguished pedigree of this question and its relevance to the whole issue of industrial strategies, it is astonishing that there has never been a single, systematic attempt to answer this question empirically. This is not to say, however, that we do not have some ideas about whether governments should do such choosing and, in the event that they are able to do so, whether it is of economic benefit to their countries. From Adam Smith to Alexander Hamilton and down to contemporary theories of endogenous policy and strategic trade, one idea after another has underscored the importance of government choice. But there is little agreement on any of these very good ideas. What some seem to think pivotal, others dismiss as nonsense. In the meantime, there is also little by way of empirical evidence that would allow us to judge the efficacy of these ideas with any confidence.

This book attempts to answer the single question above by first probing theories for clues as to how to get a handle on the problem and then testing these theories' predictions in the real world to see whether they have any relevance. And there is merit in this methodical approach. It means that we do not simply have to continue the debate over the ideological appropriateness of government intervention or the causal effect of trade and/or industrial policies (what I call "TIPs" for short) such as subsidies and tariffs that governments use to tamper with industrial outcomes. Instead, the question above forces, first and foremost, an analytical consideration of the criteria for selection that are deemed important.

By what criteria are some industries chosen over others? Due in large part to the theoretical respect given to TIPs by the new strategic trade policy literature, there is some rationale for picking industries characterized by economic criteria, such as rents and external economies. In contrast, the endogenous policy literature leads us to expect political realities, such as reelection concerns and campaign contributions, to hold sway in the choice of sectors to be favored. Both of these views make crucial, and opposing, assumptions about government motivations, such that we can expect to see radically different outcomes in terms of government choices. If we rely on theories that assume governments are inevitably captured by political factors, for example, then the whole picture of government choices in industrial policy looks very different than if we believe governments are out to maximize national economic welfare.

In Chapter 1, I make these different assumptions explicit in an effort to flesh out the motivations behind government choices. By closely tracing the thinking in major works, my purpose is to then draw out the economic and political criteria for selection. Together, the motivations and the criteria lead to very precise causal hypotheses about why governments choose the industries they do. At the core of this book is a methodology that pits these competing explanations against one another, draws out their testable propositions, and then uses three research strategies to assess their relative empirical importance in government decisions across industries and over time. The crucial case in which to do this is postwar Japan. Moreover, this seemingly simple exercise has enormous implications not just for the schools of thought that constitute the point of departure but also for the theory and policy of industrial selection.

Back to Japan

Japan is crucial as a test case in large part because its rapid industrialization has added fuel to such theories and made history in the process. For this reason, I bring the single initial question from the abstract to the specific: How did the Japanese government choose which industries to favor during the postwar period? In Chapter 1, I also show how much of the more formal theory is echoed in the works by political scientists who examine Japanese economic policy-making. On the purely economic side, some Japan specialists and policy-makers argue that the Japanese government has plotted the course of its industrial future, strategically choosing and promoting future industrial winners. This idea of a meritocratic Japanese state—in which enlightened and unencumbered bureaucrats direct the course of industrial selection based on some economic calculus—is an attractive vision.

But this vision is not without its critics. Not only dismissed by market proponents as empirically improbable, it is also increasingly ridiculed by advocates of choice-theoretical principles whose arguments are based on the key assumption of rationality. Taking their cue from deductive models of political motivations for economic policy, these recent choice-theoretic works on the Japanese political economy place elected officials at the center of policy-making in a representative democracy. The implication here is not only that politicians govern, which the Japanese bureaucrats are conventionally thought to have done. It is also that the politicians' motivations for allocating TIPs across sectors has little to do with national industrial selection and far more to do with personal aggrandizement.

Only one of these equally logical views on industrial selection can be right. But which one? The evidence we have to date does not allow us to say. This is because, unfortunately, scholars holding either the political or economic viewpoint tend to talk past each other, if at all, in existing political science works on Japanese economic policy-making. Case studies are frequently used to prove that either one or the other view is relevant to the allocation of TIPs, with virtually no regard for the null hypothesis (that the view does not matter) or the alternative hypothesis (that the other view has at least some credence). As a result, there is no systematic evidence on the hypothesized and conflicting criteria that together make up a testable model of government choices. So, then, what is the best way to provide this evidence?

Preview of Answers and Implications

Although the central question is simple and theoretically tractable, the problem is complex at an empirical level. In this book, I shift levels from a very aggregate to a more detailed analysis in steps and then weave back and forth between these steps to come to a general answer. In Chapters 2 through 5, therefore, I bring a range of empirical techniques to bear on this question, namely econometrics, structured data analysis, and case studies. As the successive buildup to the final answer shows, the core of this book is very much about evidence—about the social scientific tools with which we attempt to gather it and about the scope and limits of exactly these tools for general inference.

The book is careful and neutral in its treatment of the evidence—a necessity if one is to test such highly contested theories. Each of the three methods used here contributes a unique perspective to the question at hand. Each also serves as a powerful check on the biases associated with the use of any one of the other methods alone. The econometrics analysis gives us a swift overview of the importance of each criterion in government choices. The structured data analysis complements this basic analysis by making clear which sectors were most favored by the government. Finally, the case studies add historical and perceptual factors to the picture of actual government policy choices

Just what is the answer? How did the Japanese government choose which industries to favor, and what does that mean for the theoretical frameworks with which we began? In weaving together the cumulative evidence from the three approaches in the end, we can make some pertinent generalizations about the logic of Japanese industrial selections, both in terms of motivations as well as the method of implementation. In Chapter 6, I conclude that the Japanese government chose industries on the basis of economic criteria—that it made a conscious and deliberate effort to choose industrial winners wholesale from the 1950s to the late 1980s. Moreover, despite recent constraints and setbacks, it is still concerned with acquiring niches in what it deems to be strategic high-technology sectors of the future. That is certainly the answer given by the government officials involved directly in the selection process, and, to a remarkable extent, their rhetoric is backed up by the aggregate quantitative results across the postwar period.

The evidence also allows us to judge the theories that helped define the core of the project. While hardly monolithic in terms of its choices, the Japanese government has made a deliberate effort to support some industries over others on the basis of high value-added and the potential for externalities up until the early 1980s. Again, the quantitative evidence, as well as the qualitative assessment that comes through in the interviews, helps lead to this conclusion. The amazing part of the story is that such selections were carried out not in the absence of pressures from politicians and interest groups but in their full presence. In fact, much about the industrial selection process in Japan can be understood in the good old-fashioned political sense. Yet by and large what we find is that, at an aggregate level, Japanese TIPs moved to the tune of broad economic dictates for most of the postwar period.

Why have these outcomes prevailed in Japan when our mainstream political economy theories lead us to expect otherwise? Why do we not find overwhelming evidence in support of theoretical claims that government economic policies, or TIPs in this case, are almost always and everywhere determined by political factors? Moving beyond my initial research agenda, I present some major explanations about what may have made a difference in the selection process in Japan. The conventional answer is that institutional arrangements in Japan, and specifically the way the Japanese state relates to industry, refracted the expected outcomes to a great extent. Here industries engaged in extensive political lobbying, politicians were concerned with their electoral standing, and bureaucrats were acutely sensitive to political pressures all around. But both formal and informal institutions held the actors in check, constraining their behavior and their interactions. Drawing on the research of Japan scholars, I set out some notable institutional features in the Japanese political economy that may well have led to the unexpected outcome we observe in Japan. In addition to the institutional factors, I argue further that the widespread perceptions about the importance of technology for the very survival of Japan have led to a core ideological consensus among government officials, as well as the wider public, about maintaining the technological edge despite concerns with economic cost and efficiency.

Of even greater interest, what lesson does this evidence offer other countries? It is not that other governments should charge out to pick winners, which—as I demonstrate in detail—is a process fraught with great complexity even in the Japanese case. For one thing, we still have a long way to go to establish empirically whether some sectors are deserving of more favorable TIPs, whether what is supposed to make such sectors special is indeed consistently unique to them in time and space. For another, counterfactually, it is far from clear what the Japanese industrial economy would have looked like had most-favored selection not taken place.

Instead two far more subtle features about the logic of industrial selection or picking winners stand out as potential lessons—one could even say warnings—from postwar Japan. First, perhaps the most important generalization with respect to industrial strategies is not just about the selection of industries, it is about their deselection. By "deselection" I mean the reduction or gradual withdrawal of wholesale TIPs to an industry. As Japanese government officials maintain, and as part of the aggregate quantitative evidence shows, there is a distinct selection-deselection pattern across the manufacturing industries in postwar Japan. As I discuss in some detail, this crucial evidence on the implementation of Japanese TIPs goes to the heart of debates about "market-conforming" industrial policies as well as controversies about the limited role of governments in the industrial economy. This point has not been analyzed comprehensively because of a methodological focus on examining industry cases rather than analyzing TIPs across all industries over the postwar period and, in addition, tends to be ignored due to prevalent views that deselection happened rarely, if at all. If other governments really wish to emulate the logic of industrial selection in Japan, however, they would do well to try to learn just what it takes for a government ultimately to let such industries go their natural way.

Second, in the real world of industrial selections or picking winners, it appears that perceptions about the nature of technology matter considerably. The qualitative evidence suggests there are distinct themes with respect to the "why" of industrial selection. The more than one hundred interviews I conducted with government officials exposed me to core beliefs and perceptions about technology that permeate the fabric of Japanese governmental institutions. Most salient among such perceptions are those about benefits brought about by spillovers and linkages in key economic sectors, about the importance of cutting-edge technology for the very survival of Japan, about Japan's standing with respect to its competitors, and even about the future of industrial evolution as a whole. As officials discuss—sometimes directly, other times implicitly—much about the selection process with respect to future industrial winners is hard to pin down, and sometimes even very self-conscious selections are determined by intangibles. It was also easier when Japan had catching up to do and much harder now that it has caught up. This should make other governments wary of going after key sectors in a grand, wholesale manner based just on hard criteria as theories would have us believe.

There are as yet no easy solutions, no magic combinations that allow governments, or even firms for that matter, to determine confidently why one sector should be favored over another based on some foolproof criteria for selection. And this is why the real, messy, and still ongoing logic that emerges from Japan is as much a constructive recognition of how governments might choose industries to favor as it is a sobering reminder of why they might ultimately be constrained in doing so.

The Logic of Industrial Selection

HOW MIGHT GOVERNMENTS pick winners? Is there any theoretical logic behind actual government decisions to favor some industries over others? The reason why such questions continue to be controversial is because they go to the heart of rival debates about why governments choose to do the things they do. The rivalry in all such debates boils down to whether governments can escape the straitjacket of political pressures and thus act in the national economic interest. The dominant view in political economy is that the rules of the electoral game make a government highly susceptible to sectoral pressures and thereby motivate it to act more concretely in the interest of its own political survival than on the basis of some abstract concept of national economic interest.

Here is the reality, however: Even though they are based on different assumptions and come to radically different predictions about government choices, there is a great deal of credibility to both the economic and political logic. My major goal in this chapter is to detail how and in what ways that is the case. Although much of this terrain is familiar to political scientists, it is nevertheless useful to revisit it in the specific context of trying to understand the logic of industrial selection or, popularly put, picking winners. This chapter unites the disparate perspectives on government actions in an integrated analytical framework that can then be tested in a real-world case like Japan.

Specifically, in this chapter I identify and draw out the criteria for selection based on two conflicting but equally valid assumptions about government motivations in both the strategic trade and endogenous policy literatures. Going a step further, I also show how the same theoretical logic echoes resoundingly in key works by Japan specialists, although it is not as systematic or as explicit as posited in the more formal models. The remainder of this chapter is in two major parts, each of which focuses on deriving rival hypotheses about the determinants of and motivations behind industrial selections. In order to extract testable hypotheses on government choices, I confine my examination of the scholarly works strictly to their discussions on the criteria for selection, which means leaving out nuances in some of the arguments. Moreover, my focus is not on supporting or criticizing bureaucratic dominance or choice-theoretical frameworks, which so often, as traced closely below, is an implicit part and parcel of the works. Rather, in analyzing the major scholarly works, every effort is made to draw out the criteria in a neutral fashion without privileging the two sets of logic.

With this in mind, the first part of this chapter turns to the logic of economic motivations, in which governments are assumed to be benevolent and strong and in which bureaucrats and technocrats play a leading role. It clarifies the criteria deemed important in the new international economics, namely rents and external economies as a basis for choice. It also shows how a similar, though often far more indiscriminate, reasoning pervades the work of some very influential scholars concerned with economic policy-making in Japan. The second part sets out the logic of political motivations behind industrial selections, in which governments act in their own narrow interest rather than in the interest of the national economy. It also shows how this same deductive logic has increasingly been brought to bear on the subject of government policies in Japan by yet another set of scholars. For ease of comparison, both the general and Japan-specific hypotheses are set out in Figure 1.1.

In Chapter 6, I will return to assessing these and other related scholarly works on Japanese economic policy-making in far greater detail. In the meantime, in the next four chapters I will bring evidence to bear on the efficacy of the hypothesized criteria for selection, specifically by examining the evidence at different levels of industrial aggregation and with different methodological approaches. But first to deriving the criteria themselves, because this allows us to understand the fundamental basis for government choices: Who chooses? And why?

The Logic of Economic Criteria

THE VIEW FROM THE NEW INTERNATIONAL ECONOMICS

Classical trade theory suggests that there are no "strategic" sectors. This is because perfect competition eliminates the difference between what equivalent quantities of labor and capital can earn in sectors of equal risk. In such a world, rents can always be competed away because higher returns in some industries cannot last for long due to competition. Put simply, all sectors are or become equal over time.

FIGURE 1.1

Derived Criteria for Industrial Selection

	General	Japan Specific
Economic Hypothesis	The higher the rents and external economies, the more economically strategic the sector and therefore the more concerted the government efforts to allocate resources to it. The government is both willing and able to direct TIPs as it chooses, and it acts out of a keen concern with national economic welfare in the long run.	The higher the prospects for growth, wages, value-added, and, especially, spillover potential, the more economically strategic the sector and therefore the more concerted the Japanese government's efforts to allocate TIPs to such sectors. The Japanese government—specifically the bureaucracy in the elite economic ministries—is, by and large, both able and willing to direct TIPs as it chooses, and it acts out of a concern with a view to the national economic welfare in the long run.
Political Hypothesis	The greater the potential an industry offers for both incumbents and challengers to maximize their electoral support, particularly in the form of campaign contributions and votes, the more concerted the efforts of such politicians to promise or provide TIPs to such industries. Regardless of the preferences of the bureaucracy, politicians are both willing and able to direct TIPs to such industries, and they act largely out of a keen concern with their own political fates.	The greater the potential for LDP incumbents and challengers to cultivate personal votes and campaign contributions in an industry and/or the greater the number of institutional channels for influence from industry to government, the more concerted politicians' rhetorical and actual efforts to allocate TIPs to any such industry. Regardless of the preferences of the bureaucrats in such decisions, politicians are both willing and able to direct TIPs to such industries, and they act largely out of a keen concern with their own individual electoral fortunes.

In direct contrast, the view from the new international economics suggests that there are indeed "strategic" sectors in which rents may not be competed away because of the importance accorded to economies of scale, the advantages of experience, and the potential for innovation as explanations of trading patterns. By pointing to such noncomparative advantage-based sources of specialization, this new view has not only legitimized imperfect competition in policy debates but has also left the door wide open for governments to attempt to create comparative advantage.[1]

The simple idea, then, that governments can use trade and/or industrial policies (TIPs) to improve the position of national industries that are engaged in international oligopolistic competition has become theoretically credible.[2] Based on the assumption that government policy seeks to enhance the welfare of the nation as a whole, the new theories suggest that government TIPs can help transfer potential monopoly rents from foreign to domestic firms and thereby also increase the external benefits associated with the activity.[3] The more blunt, and also the more exciting, implication is that winners can be picked in sectors where there are higher "rents" and higher "external economies" and that if these two criteria characterize certain sectors, TIPs can raise national income by securing for a country a larger share of such strategic industries. The most controversial implication of these works is that to "profit shift" through government TIPs is advantageous both for the industrial sector and the economic welfare of the nation. Let us look at these ideas—specifically the criteria for selection—more closely, for as we shall see shortly, they have had a powerful impact on advocates who base their case for TIPs on postwar Japan.

The most commonly cited criterion for selection in the theoretical literature is the presence of potential rents in a sector.[4] Rent means that capital and labor in the sector will themselves earn exceptionally higher returns than they could elsewhere in sectors of equal risk. This is a key criterion for many advocates of TIPs, and in the real world it means generally that sectors with high rents are those that are, relative to other sectors in the industrial structure, characterized by higher levels of growth, supernormal profits, value-added, productivity, and/or wages.[5] To the extent that the idea of rents is viable as a criterion, it has been criticized severely. This is because if there is competition for scarce resources among what a government thinks are equally strategic sectors, it is extremely complicated to devise a welfare-improving policy of intervention.[6] Despite these caveats, rents, or extraordinarily high returns, remain compelling because of the importance accorded to economies of scale, advantages of experience, and innovations as explanations, all of whose presence means that rents will not be fully competed away because of significant barriers to entry.

The second theoretical criterion for discriminating among industrial sectors is even more powerful. Virtually everyone cites external economies as a criterion for selection (positive externalities or spillovers). The presence of external economies means that some sectors will yield high returns because in addition to their own earnings, they provide benefits to capital and labor employed elsewhere in society. In the real world this means that some sectors generate higher levels of beneficial research and development (R&D), which leads to higher knowledge and experience and which, in turn, can potentially spill over into other industrial sectors, thereby benefiting them as well.[7]

While all this sounds good in theory, external economies as a criterion present a daunting empirical challenge. For one thing, there are no satisfactory measures of this criterion since by definition it does not leave a price trail that can be followed. Moreover, external economies offer an almost post hoc justification for selection because it is only later, if at all, that their effects can be seen across the entire industrial range. Yet even today, the thinking that somehow one sector's benefits spill over into another remains the foundation for the idea of external economies, which is widely considered to be the pivotal element in strategic sectors and a far more important argument for TIPs and against free trade in the new strategic trade policy literature.[8]

In short, measurement of either variable is daunting, external economies more than rents, which would suggest that no government could select strategic sectors systematically. Problems of measurement are further complicated by the idea that picking winners depends both on past and projected measures of these two criteria (assuming they can be measured at all). In this case, even past averages for the criteria cannot necessarily be extrapolated forward into the future with the assumption that the same trend will continue. Moreover, given the difficulties of measuring past or present external economies, it is almost impossible to estimate precisely how knowledge spilled over in the past or, even more difficult, how it may spin off in the future.

But despite problems of measurement and accuracy, no amount of empirical work can detract from the theoretical elegance of the two criteria. This point is crucial. Whether right or wrong, both rents and external economies are ultimately the most systematic set of criteria with which to identify strategic sectors. In part, the two criteria—and external economies in particular—remain influential precisely because of their ambiguity and their promise of a tremendous prize for the whole economy. Even if government intervention itself remains dubious in practice, there is no question that the presence of these criteria opens the possibility, at least in theory, that a government could use TIPs to shape the industrial base of the future.

Insofar, then, as the presence of these theoretical criteria designates strategic sectors in the literature, the logic of industrial selection is very clear. But since industrial selection represents a decision, it also forces attention on the assumptions about the government doing the selection, which is not really an explicit part or concern of the economic models. The only real emphasis on the government is that it commit credibly to some TIPs in a strategic sector, and the key enabling assumption is that such a government is the sum of benevolent agents seeking to maximize aggregate economic welfare.[9] This view of the government as a benevolent social guardian has a long history, with some even pointing out that the debate over TIPs today has its roots in the development literature of the 1940s and 1950s.[10] Then the argument was that the unique problems of the underdeveloped countries justified government intervention, whether in the case of infant industries or in allocating scarce resources.[11] Now the argument is that the unique characteristics of some industries—their economic "strategicness"—justifies government intervention. In both cases, the government has solid information about an industry and further has both the willingness and the ability to allocate TIPs exactly as it would prefer to without being unduly influenced by political pressures from any faction. In addition, while there is a scarce supply of resources, their forced allocation to certain sectors has few welfare costs and generates little political turmoil.

If the key assumption is that governments are primarily concerned with economic optimization, then it stands to reason that they will make choices based on the twin economic criteria of rents and external economies. This leads to a very clear general economic hypothesis about industrial selection, as presented in Figure 1.1. At the very least, the theoretical rigor behind this hypothesis has had a profound impact on policy debates, particularly with reference to Japan. It is not an exaggeration to say that the key criteria in this hypothesis have both affected and been affected by a singular interpretation of postwar Japanese economic policy-making. In fact, as shown below, the hypothesis has an almost equal empirical counterpart in some highly influential studies of the postwar Japanese political economy. Given their long understanding of Japanese economic policy-making, many advocates of government TIPs believe that it is actually the theory that has finally caught up with the real world, not the other way around.[12]

THE JAPANESE BUREAUCRATS AND INDUSTRIAL SELECTION

The theory from the new international economics certainly made the general debate over the usefulness and desirability of industrial selection more respectable than ever before in academic and development policy communities. But several scholarly interpretations of the postwar Japanese political economy had already made the case for TIPs quite compelling with a focus on the Japanese government's activities. Very often, the assumption in this literature was, and still is, that Japanese selections were based on a set of sound economic criteria.[13] This basis for the celebrated Japanese "development model"—a meritocratic state guiding the general and specific workings of the economy—was made doubly attractive, given Japan's industrial prominence in so short a period of time after the Second World War.

State-centric theories have, in fact, always held a privileged position in studies focused more narrowly on Japan. By some accounts, the Japanese state has never had to be brought back in, given that it has loomed large in the marketplace since at least 1868. What exactly does state-centric mean, though, in matters of industrial selection? Virtually the first systematic, and certainly the most influential, answer came in the guise of the Japanese "developmental state," with the Ministry of International Trade and Industry (MITI) as the central agent in directing strategic industrial transformations.[14] In this view, as well as in its variants, the primary institution of governmental policy-making in Japan has not been the ruling Liberal Democratic Party (LDP) or private interest groups but rather the central state bureaucracy, typically MITI and the Ministry of Finance (MOF).[15]

Whether right or wrong, the concept of the "developmental state" set the terms of debate for further work on economic policy-making and development in general. Since then, the precise contribution of the Japanese state—and MITI in particular—has become a subject of great controversy. Some of the later works on the debate over Japanese industrial strategies are influential precisely because they either agree or disagree with this statist viewpoint. While, for example, the Japanese state was accorded a central role in matters of development policy, some shifted the locus of state power, according greater importance to the Bank of Japan at the top of the government hierarchy because it controls almost the entire credit supply and can therefore easily channel resources to priority sectors.[16] Others proclaimed sweepingly that, in Japan, the bureaucracy *is* the government, less a director than a player with its own purpose of achieving some future industrial vision of the Japanese economy.[17] Still others argued that since 1868 the Japanese government has shown a historical determination to mastermind certain types of industrial structures to benefit the nation in the long run—a determination borne out of the belief that some industries are more important than others in the Schumpeterian sense, that is, competition in the long term is based on changes in technology and innovations in some industries rather than on price.[18] Those with a direct interest in economic policy-making also stressed the importance of the Japanese state's role in pursuing concentrated development strategies. In direct contradiction to traditional economic thinking, they used the Japanese case to argue that there could be no a priori assumption that national economic welfare is better served by "free" market signals than by government intervention, which "distorts" such signals.[19]

There is also a significant critique of the statist approach that takes on the statist arguments directly by positing it vis-à-vis the market or the private sphere. Although the critiques share some key assumptions with the statist ones they seek to modify, they suggest clearly that the Japanese state—specifically as led by the bureaucrats—has not been very successful in imposing its preferences, is porous at many points, and is not all-powerful in any event. One critique suggests rightly that the Japanese developmental state is itself a useful notion but that it has been unfairly exaggerated. Instead of a Japanese state unilaterally choosing industries for intervention, the argument is that any such intervention is a result of the "reciprocal consent" between the state and private sector. In addition, the state's ability to discriminate between firms and sectors is determined by historical coalitions and conflicts.[20] Nor do these constraints disappear completely in the face of a distinct set of beliefs about the development of technology and national security in the long run—beliefs that can be captured in the formal ideological slogan of the Meiji era, *fukoku kyohei* (rich country, strong army), which underpinned efforts to develop technology and industry. But even this emphasis on a "technonational" ideology that permeates and fosters Japanese institutions for development purposes imparts more coherence to the idea of an overarching developmental strategy than actually exists.[21] Others also find a monolithic and supremely strategic Japanese state unrealistic, likewise stressing the interdependence between MITI and the private sector that binds them to each other. Both or one can be equally strong depending on the issue, leading to depictions of a "societal," "relational," or "network" state.[22]

While it is masterful as a concept, even the pioneers of the developmental state idea are suitably cautious of its implications for countries that wish to follow in Japan's footsteps.[23] But there is another reason for caution. These central works are so intent on conceptualizing the Japanese state that they touch upon but never directly address the real controversy over TIPs. Put succinctly, "The heart of the policy is the *selection* of the strategic industries to be developed or converted to other lines of work."[24] This is the issue that brings us back neatly to the broader theoretical concern about some general criteria for selection. What exactly was the logic of industrial selection in postwar Japan? Was there some foolproof set of criteria that allowed the Japanese government to determine which sectors should get more shifts of resources than others? Here was a gaping empirical hole in the literature, though to most minds the key assumptions about industrial selections based on sound economic criteria and a government making choices in the interest of long-term national economic welfare remained largely incontrovertible in the Japanese case.

A few examples concerning assumptions about the Japanese criteria for selection are worth pointing out since they cut across agreements or disagreements about the statist focus and since they also echo the more formal ideas in the new international economics literature discussed earlier. The departure point for these assumptions came from Japanese bureaucrats themselves, who did not deny that they identified and selected certain industries for preferential promotion—industries that, at a broad level, were strategic enough to be of vital importance to Japan's technological development and future economic welfare.[25] To many minds, this left no doubt that the specific criteria that MITI consciously used to select potential winners were clearly economic ones, with a long-term focus on creating comparative advantage in high value-added, capital- and technology-intensive industries that would affect industrial activity throughout Japan.[26]

In evaluating whether an industry is strategic, some suggested that only two criteria clearly dominated Japanese selection in a self-conscious way: perceived potential for economic growth and technological change.[27] In pointedly stating that some of the criteria of the Japanese may be useful in choosing projects and industries for promotion in other countries such as the United States, others moved on to suggest that industries characterized by high knowledge intensity, rapid growth, high income elasticity of demand, extensiveness of uses, and a disproportionate contribution to economic growth and productivity were central to the Japanese choices and would therefore suffice universally.[28] Even those who disagreed with the idea of industrial policy per se pointed to some official criteria that MITI used, such as productivity growth, income elasticity, and employment relatedness.[29] In all this selection, there was even less doubt that technology intensity was key or, more generally, that a "technonational" ideology was pervasive in Japanese government institutions. The story was that the Japanese were playing an intense game of catch-up with the more advanced West and selected those sectors that were crucial sources of technology, regardless of military or civilian applications. While high rents, and especially high value-added, were key criteria, the more important criterion was the potential for technological change and extensiveness of uses of the sector. In practice, this meant an emphasis on selecting industries on the basis of nonproduction benefits, especially learning and diffusion that by definition do not leave a price trail.[30] As we saw in the previous section, this argument was based on the more general concept of spillovers or externalities, which many pioneers of the new international economics continue to consider vital in identifying strategic sectors and a far more potent argument in favor of TIPs.

In all, while the issue of state leadership remains controversial in the key Japan works cited above, two things clearly unite these studies. Almost singularly, these works suggest that there are criteria that distinguish economic winners from their lesser cohorts and that, more often than not, refer more to the potential for technological spillovers than straightforward growth or value-added levels. In doing so, they clearly echo the widely esteemed criterion of external economies in the formal theoretical literature above. More important, they suggest that the choices made by the Japanese state—which is itself presumed to give top priority to the long-term industrial base—have by and large been motivated by such criteria. Like the works in the new international economics, the works on Japanese industrial strategy also lead to an explicit hypothesis as set out in Figure 1.1, the major difference between the two being that the latter works do so in the concrete case of Japanese industrial selection.

But the importance of these criteria to Japanese industrial selections remained more assumed than tested across the entire manufacturing range. As if the lack of systematic empirical evidence were not in itself troubling, the very idea of a Japanese state crafting an industrial vision and then selecting industries to implement that vision has been laid siege to by an equal and opposite view whose central tenet is that politics matters and self-interest even more. The logic that motivates industrial selections in this "new" view is a very old one, but its application to Japan has only just begun seriously, and already it has turned the conventional understanding of Japanese industrial selections on its head. It has deflated the image of a prescient Japanese bureaucracy and placed elected officials squarely at the heart of economic policy-making. In making Japanese politics as "normal" as in other advanced industrial countries, it has also dealt a severe blow to the singular idea of economic motivation or strategy behind the Japanese development model. But first to the theory that informs this latest round of arguments concerning the selection choices of the Japanese state.

The Logic of Political Motivations

POLITICAL ECONOMY IN GENERAL EQUILIBRIUM

Economists have long suggested that free trade and unfettered markets are almost always the best policy. In fact, one of the strongest conclusions from neoclassical trade theory is precisely that unless a country has a trade volume so huge that it can affect international prices, any protection of domestic industries from import competition is likely to lower average income, and consequently economic welfare, in that country. By the early 1990s, the pioneers of the new international economics—who had punctured some of the central tenets of this very theory by pointing to the importance of non-comparative advantage sources of specialization (economies of scale, increasing returns, or external economies), as we saw above—also pointed out that free trade was still the best policy. Moreover, so that it might not be disputed, they also went on to point out that economists were right and the general public wrongheaded on this particular issue.[31]

Back in the real world, however, governments clearly have not and do not maintain a laisser-faire attitude to either trade or markets. Given that the theoretical claim above is akin to a gospel truth of sorts for some economists, governments' choices to pursue inefficient TIPs seemed irrational for a long time. At the same time, economists maintained that decision-makers in the market who confronted the dilemma of selection made superior choices compared to those in the state who were grappling with the same issues. That is, the acumen of persons in the market was superior to the ineptness of government policy-makers. This very idea, however, led to the exact and embarrassing paradox in which people could display both economic shrewdness and political stupidity at the same time.[32] Nevertheless, economists blamed something baffling called politics, which did not imply much beyond the obvious; the economists, in turn, were blamed for not understanding the nuances of politics and institutional constraints.

In the early 1970s, however, it was largely a particular set of economists who began to bring politics into the marketplace, using the same assumptions and rigor reserved for economic models. When the dust settled, what had hitherto been perceived as the irrationality of government choices became deductively rational. A pioneering piece of work suggested a pervasive phenomenon called the rent-seeking society. This analysis focused attention on the entrepreneurs—the potential rent-seekers—in society who would compete to obtain import licenses that guaranteed them large economic prizes. More generally, by possessing the means to have TIPs allocated in their favor, such special interests helped maintain a trade control system that earned them extraordinary profits at the expense of both economic efficiency and welfare to the rest of society.[33]

These central ideas were echoed in the more general literature on directly unproductive profit-seeking activities.[34] These new theories incorporated lobbying and related policy-influencing activities by interest groups into formal economic models. Since economists are always concerned with economic efficiency, the result worthy of interest was that TIP seeking, and particularly tariff seeking, by special interests had the effect of diverting resources from productive to nonproductive activities. Directly unproductive profit-seeking activities, in other words, imposed an additional cost on the conventional cost of protection to national economic welfare. This was clearly not desirable because the distortions brought about by TIPs, and specifically trade protection via tariffs, were perceived to be economically inefficient from the standpoint of the whole economy.[35]

The idea that interest groups participated in the political process to influence or demand policy outcomes in their favor, however, did not say much about the black-boxed government doing the supplying, except to imply that government should not be doing the supplying. From the perspective of trying to understand the determinants of TIPs in a representative democracy, the emphasis on TIP-demanding special interests was clearly crucial, but so was the government-supplied TIP that remained exogenous to the theorizing. This issue was dealt with specifically by bringing governments—and, more specifically, political parties and voters—into the picture under the rubric of endogenous policy theory, which has had extraordinary consequences for our understanding about representative governments and redistributive TIPs in what is clearly and ultimately a political economy.[36]

An endogenous policy is one in which the explanation is deduced from the assumption that all actors pursue their narrow self-interest. Nowhere is there place in this framework for benevolent agents, such as enlightened bureaucrats, seeking to maximize, say, aggregate economic welfare. Instead, the focus is on the objective functions of politicians and the organized special interest groups, both seen as maximizing agents who pursue their individual selfish interests at the cost of the rest of society. Simply put, special interest groups lobby to have TIPs that are favorable to themselves. Politicians want to get elected or stay in power. The average voter is imperfectly informed about both the policy positions of the politicians and the dealings between special interest groups and politicians. Challengers and incumbents are therefore able to use the resources obtained from the special interest groups to sway the voters in their respective favor. Things are not so simple, however. Even with the dominant assumption of self-interest, there are two distinct approaches to political optimization behind the endogenous determination of TIPs.

One approach stresses incumbents' concern with maximizing political support; and the other, more subtly, political competition among competing candidates.[37] In the former approach, which laid the microfoundations of endogenous explanations of TIPs, regulation is by and large actively acquired by the industry and is designed and operated primarily for its benefit.[38] The industry "pays" for the regulation through the two things that candidates or parties need most: votes and campaign contributions (or resources). Given the rationality and goals of the incumbents, the allure of this "payment," in turn, allows us to deduce what they will do. Very plainly, they pursue their self-interest by choosing a position on TIPs that maximizes their chances of reelection, subject to the political weights placed on the support of gainers and losers resulting from that very TIP.[39] What later became known as the political support Stigler-Peltzman model was also further extended to declining industries, where social justice considerations in protecting and compensating structural difficulties had hitherto been seen as motivating government policies. Even in this case, compensatory TIPs, and the consequent acceleration or retardation of a declining industry, could arguably be determined by the assumption of political expediency on the part of the politicians-cum-policy-makers.[40]

Political-support motivation for TIPs does not take into account the fact that the TIPs themselves are subject to competition from potential challengers, which is precisely the merit of the second approach. In models of political competition, candidates for political office actively announce competing policies in response to industry-specific lobbying efforts. A differentiated TIP not only distinguishes one candidate from another, it also allows lobbies to evaluate the alternative TIPs available and then make the decision to contribute to the party whose candidates promise them the highest level of direct benefits.[41] Just as the lobbies maximize their expected returns from their respective political investments, each party also pledges those TIPs that maximize its probability of election.[42] The only thing that constrains the parties' positions on TIPs is the possibility of general voter dissatisfaction with the dispensation of favors to special interest groups. But the parties can potentially use the acquired funds to sway voters who are, in any event, presumed to be imperfectly informed about the incumbents' or challengers' specific agendas.

Both of these approaches contribute to our understanding of the political optimization underlying the endogenous determination of trade policy but illuminate different aspects of the puzzle.[43] Political-competition models, for instance, generally give more weight to differentiating the individual party's position on TIPs, which in essence is then used to form a campaign platform from which to convince special interest groups and also voters of each party's respective merits. More important for the purpose of this project, however, is the alternative emphasis on models of political support. This approach focuses attention on the extent and implications of specific TIPs chosen by the incumbent or even challengers. In addition, it also forces consideration of some of the characteristics—specifically, the political power or influence—of the industries selected over others.

Even as these two approaches brilliantly deduced the reasons for certain behaviors and outcomes, one thing remained puzzling because of its absence. The assumption of self-interest had clearly focused attention on the basic units doing the acting—that is, politicians, special interest groups, voters. This was a neat world, but surely not the whole one as far as policy-making was and is concerned. Curiously, or perhaps conveniently, most models of endogenous policy theory disregarded the fact that elected representatives are not the only aspiring policy-makers within a government and that endogenous policies that result theoretically from all of the actors pursuing their self-interest still have to be mediated through the calculations of the comparatively more permanent presence of the bureaucracy, to whom, in the end, the politician-cum-aspiring-policy-maker must delegate responsibility for implementation of his or her preferences. In short, politicians may have the comparative advantage in raising money for getting votes but not in administering programs or TIPs, which is exactly what is so crucial for challengers to be elected or for incumbents to stay in office.[44]

On this front, the earlier advances made in public choice theory by another set of economists played a crucial role for theories of bureaucracies. As yet another economic explanation of the political arena, this theory also was premised on self-interest or utility maximization of the actors, an assumption that continues to generate testable hypotheses as readily as extreme controversies.[45] Here, too, politics was seen as a set of arrangements in which actors with different objective functions interacted to generate a set of outcomes that were not necessarily economically efficient. By definition, the focus was on the governmental sector, but specifically with a methodological focus on the behavior of persons as voters, as politicians, and as bureaucrats. Only by incorporating the bureaucracy, which is ultimately responsible for supplying, say, the TIPs, into the picture could an effective model of the government arguably be obtained. Since the implementation of TIPs, or the actual process of government, remained with the bureaucracy, the issue of legislative control over what could be extreme discretionary powers of the bureaucracy was and is a central one.[46]

On this score, the more immediate point of focus has been on the nature of the relationship between the politicians, who have clearly derived preferences in the analytical models above, and the bureaucrats, who potentially stand in the way of those preferences being implemented. It is important to show that the preferences of the politicians are by and large being implemented, for if they are not, the theoretical raison d'être for politicians being in office becomes shaky. Both of the political optimization models above implicitly rely on the idea that the politicians-cum-aspiring-policy-makers can have their preferred TIPs pushed through the government apparatus, and not just on paper; otherwise no matter which model is taken, their tenure in office is doomed to be brief, if it materializes at all. Special interest groups are not likely to woo the favors of any such candidates or incumbents but might turn to cultivating relations with the bureaucrats who are running the show—a point that invalidates some of the neat results of the deductive models.

It is no small task, then, as considerable effort and debate on the subject make clear, to show whose preferences exactly—the politician as principal or the bureaucrat as agent, or vice versa—are being implemented in the end. The premise here is that politicians specifically attempt to fashion legislation—which is meant to provide the legal basis for any government TIPs—that maximizes their electoral gains, constrained only by the opposition created by such legislation. To ensure the provision of legislation that is directly in their interest, politicians are shown to have a direct, but not necessarily visible, stake in the design and guidance of administrative procedures as a means of controlling agencies that are ultimately responsible for policy outcomes.[47] Agency compliance, then, with the policy preferences of the politicians is quite crucial for sustaining the assumptions and the theories above.

Whatever the merits of fine-tuning theories that stress the optimization problem, the deductive logic of political motivations remains clear, even if controversial.[48] In contrast to the general economic hypothesis above, the major alternative explanation for the allocation of TIPs, or industrial selection in general, points both to political pressures in a representative democracy and a commanding policy-making position for politicians as laid out in

Figure 1.1. Once again, the premises and conclusions of this theoretical literature, and specifically the resulting political hypothesis above, are almost unilaterally shaping the debate over Japanese economic policy-making. Until recently, the application and testing of this key hypothesis were limited almost exclusively to the American case. But no more. For a growing number of influential scholars, the broad electoral logic applies equally to Japanese institutions and actions. As discussed below, it is also increasingly being defended with empirical evidence from Japan, though this very process continues to generate extreme controversies among Japan scholars.

BRINGING JAPANESE POLITICIANS BACK IN

No matter what the focus or force of the economic hypothesis in Japan, some Japan scholars and observers disagree with its approach altogether. Contrary to the statist viewpoint, and in keeping with the behavioral assumptions of the public choice approach, new interpretations of the Japanese political economy suggest bluntly that there are clear political motivations for Japanese industrial selections. The main bone of contention is this: Whereas the bureaucratically dominated state acts in the national economic interest, the politically dominated one is motivated out of an interest in political self-preservation and aggrandizement. On this point, it closely resembles the state of the public choice literature, as the choices made by the state in terms of industrial selection have less to do with economic criteria than with (at least) the instrumental concern of politicians to stay in office. The starting point for these critiques is that they all find bureaucratic leadership in economic policy-making to be problematic, if not practically unrealistic in a representative democracy. But there are two distinct sets of critiques, one taking issue with the lack of politics, the other with the sources of the industrial miracle. Both cast a pall over the very idea of strategic industrial selection.

In the first set of critiques, the departure point is that the politician-bureaucrat interaction, and particularly the issue of their relative power in policy-making, has been key in interpretations of postwar Japanese politics.[49] In an effort to bring politics back in, the emphasis is on a state-centered but pluralistic policy-making process, where a strong state may well have patterned interests but interacts with and is influenced by pluralist elements. Altogether, this imparts a nonstrategic element to the Japanese state by showing that development goals were hardly consistent and were themselves nothing more than key strategies designed to accomplish political goals. Moreover, there are myriad ways in which industries could seek to influence policy choices, both directly via contact with bureaucrats or indirectly via politicians.[50] All this has the ultimate effect of making it difficult to assert that the Japanese state can unilaterally come up with and impose its own policy preferences in sectors, whether in terms of industrial selection or otherwise.

Such an assertion becomes even more difficult as the emphasis on the political has been recast in the tradition of the more formal endogenous policy theories above.[51] In almost one fell theoretical swoop, these latest works show how, given a basic principal-agent framework in the Japanese case, the arrow of influence could be reversed, with the preferences of the legendary bureaucrats at the mercy of those of the elected politicians.[52] In fact, these works have come to represent the most significant and pointed critique of bureaucratic dominance and industrial development to date and have generated a heated controversy in the process.[53] The controversy is not about the fact that the works have placed elected officials at the center of economic policy-making and, by specific extension for our purposes, industrial selection. The activities of politicians have been studied widely, and the blend of politicians, pork, and particularistic policies is not startlingly new to Japan.[54] Even those works that stress the efficacy of the Japanese bureaucracy in playing a dominant, competent, and far-sighted role leave that very bureaucratic structure open historically to a myriad of political influences and interests.[55] If the point of this so-called new approach in interpreting Japanese economic decision-making is banal, then that is precisely the point: As far as the general disbursement of TIPs is concerned, in Japan the electoral logic is as relentless as elsewhere.[56] What differentiates this approach in Japanese political economy analyses is merely that the politics-as-usual argument uses the distinctive logic of a standard choice-theoretical framework. Just as consumers and producers in the neoclassical economic world are assumed to act in their own self-interest, so, too, the argument goes, it is logical to impute self-interested behavior to politicians and policy-makers in what is increasingly perceived as a neoclassical political-economic world. Long-time scholars of Japan find the assumptions and predictions of exactly this theoretically structured world highly dubious, ahistorical, and indefensible in the case of Japan and, frankly, elsewhere as well.[57]

Whatever the merits of such controversies, their real virtue is that they force us to contend with the debates over Japan's industrial selections in the context of mainstream theories concerning government policy choices. As elsewhere, the tradition of rational-choice approaches suggests that political actors in Japan maximize their electoral standing subject to institutional constraints or the rules of the game. The rules of the political marketplace in Japan led to a clear set of electorally driven policy preferences for the LDP, whose tenure in office between 1955 and 1993 no doubt also further institutionalized the very corruption that was creating the incentives or preferences for both the principals and agents in the first place. The combination of a single, nontransferable vote with multimember electoral districts forced the

LDP to even out its votes among its candidates, who were necessarily pitted against each other. This could be done most competitively if the LDP candidates cultivated personal support networks (*koenkai*) promising pork, services, TIPs, and so on in an even exchange for votes and campaign funds. In turn, those networks could be cultivated most effectively if the aspiring candidates could credibly demonstrate they could manipulate the party's control over the government, and especially the bureaucracy, which would thereby guarantee the delivery of promised pork in the future for votes or financial contributions now. Voters or funders, therefore, presumably prize politicians who can control bureaucrats. Essentially, in the tradition of models of political support in the formal theory above, this setup is seen to have been the essence of Japan's competitive political marketplace in the postwar era.[58]

Of particular interest for this project is the relationship between the politicians and bureaucrats and the clear implications that basic principal-agent theory has for the logic of industrial selection in Japan. "Implicit contracts" between the agents and principals within the Japanese government take on added importance, the argument goes, because these two sets of actors do not necessarily have similar interests or preferences across issue-areas. Simply put, the idea is that politicians would make bureaucrats disburse TIPs in a way that consistently maximizes their electoral fortunes, which has consequent, and negative, implications for industrial selections in line with bureaucratic visions. The same logic has also recently been empirically defended by other observers. By examining expenditures on particularistic programs as a tool for maximizing individual electoral fortunes or by asserting that the LDP has been a key player in budgetary policy-making long considered the sole preserve of the MOF, these new works suggest the relevance, and dominance, of politicians to economic policy-making.[59]

The importance of the role of politics and political factors in assessing the debates over industrial selection is supported further by works that debate the very source of the Japanese industrial miracle. In this second significant set of critiques, the major works point either implicitly or explicitly to the Japanese private sector as the major force behind Japan's industrial transformations. In doing so, they also fundamentally suggest the weakness of bureaucratic dominance and therefore a state-led model of industrial selection.[60] Although the debate is dominated by economists, there are also some notable political scientists in this camp. In most instances, their works shunt aside the role of the state, and particularly the bureaucracy, by showing that it is not strategic, foresighted, or omnipotent in selecting sectors or divining the wave of the industrial future.

Some have suggested bluntly that rather than accounting for any economic miracle, Japanese TIPs are not only insignificant in comparison to other nations belonging to the Organization for Economic Cooperation and Development (OECD) but also that their major function is to serve as a substitute, and not an unfair complement, for the market allocation of capital.[61] Methodological critiques have similarly provided a useful empirical antidote to works that impart an overwhelming strategy to the behavior of the Japanese state, with the criticism that the advocates of TIPs generalize from narrow empirical bases, case studies, and anecdotal evidence. Moreover, the emphasis on the causal role of TIPs in enhancing competitiveness or productivity remains in doubt, since there is some proof to show that industrial selection per se did not induce or change the course of Japanese industrial development.[62] Added to this negation of industrial selection is the damning conclusion that the Japanese government did not select potential winners, that is, the sectors characterized by high growth. Instead, over a roughly forty-year period, it seems to have allocated resources to losers such as textiles and mining. Based on the negligible role of the economic variables, the assumption here is that the major criteria must have been political, either lobbying pressures or employment considerations in declining sectors.[63] But there is a tremendous leap in inference. Showing that the economic criteria were ineffectual does not constitute proof that political ones were systematically of import in their stead. Yet this is an assumption that is carried over into other works that are again more concerned with characterizing the Japanese state than in proving systematically the basis for its policy choices. Some, for example, argue that the Japanese state is characterized by hesitancy and clientalism and that it allocates more resources to declining sectors for political reasons.[64] Moreover, from the perspective of industrial selection, it is less an issue of the Japanese government choosing industries to favor and more one where it follows the inherent dynamism and farsightedness of the private sector.[65]

Finally, what unites these two sets of critiques is their stress on the ineptness of the Japanese state in terms of economically based selection, not out of stupidity but rather due to the dictates of a political balance between politicians, bureaucrats, industries, and voters.[66] In this view, Japanese economic policy-making is both highly politicized and dominated by politicians who are simultaneously principals (as bureaucrats) and agents (of the voters). Despite the presence of institutions and structures that have been specific to Japan, particularly under the LDP, which dominated Japanese politics for much of the postwar period, the interpretations of the Japanese political economy above are more universalistic in their theoretical premises. In fact, regardless of their conclusions or cases, they take their cue from the same underlying logic that informs the more formal works and which, unsurprisingly, leads to a similar hypothesis about industrial selection in Japan as shown in Figure 1.1.

Let me sum up. Based on key works in both the general political economy literature as well as Japan studies, this section has set out the criteria for government selection of industries to favor. It also showed how different assumptions about government motivations lie behind the different kinds of criteria that are thought to be important.

With respect to how governments choose industries to favor, then, we find that the general answers in theory and the more specific ones from Japan tend to be the same. On the one hand, there is a set of economic criteria that presumably motivate governments with the promise of some larger prize to the nation; on the other, a set of political criteria that motivate them largely on the basis of a narrow electoral logic. This exercise leads to two precise and, more important, testable hypotheses that predict radically different outcomes in terms of government choices. As also discussed, some deride the relevance of economic dictates or vent against the political reasoning, but there is absolutely no a priori reason to dismiss any criteria on rhetorical grounds alone. They all deserve equal, neutral, and empirical investigation.

This brings us to the issue of whether these criteria have actually mattered in government choices to favor industries in the Japanese case. If so, how much exactly? Do some criteria matter more than others overall and do so consistently over time? In the final analysis, were Japanese patterns of industrial selection determined more by the economic nature of an industry or by political factors?[67] How do we find out?

Plan of the Book

In an effort to provide evidence for and against the hypotheses, the next four chapters move from a macro quantitative approach, through structured data analysis, and finally detailed case studies to answer the questions at hand. Using both aggregate and detailed approaches helps us to get a more solid grip on a difficult empirical problem through different angles and also compensates for the weaknesses of any one of the research methods alone.

In Chapter 2, the econometric analysis helps us to test the efficacy of the political and economic criteria simultaneously. The time-series cross-sectional (TSCS) regression analysis allows us to see which criteria mattered more on average across all industries for the postwar period and thereby allows us to say whether a proposed causality can be accepted or rejected with some degree of statistical confidence. More than any of the other approaches, the multiple regression analyses of TSCS data for each of the eight TIPs across all the manufacturing industries tell us explicitly whether, how much, and which criteria, if any, affected Japanese government choices. In providing the broadest check on the rhetoric and reality of Japanese government decisions across the postwar period, the aggregate econometric results set the stage for the investigation that follows and thereby greatly complement the detailed evidence from the other two approaches.

The structured data analysis in Chapter 3 is a middle ground between the econometrics and case studies and a valuable step in terms of a more comprehensive picture of Japanese government decisions. It provides a systematic appraisal of where the postwar Japanese TIPs went and why, thereby helping to establish both the most-favored sectors and a side-by-side evaluation of the criteria that made these sectors more favored than others. It also gives us a broad overview about the consistency of Japanese government choices across the entire industrial range, and it represents an aggregate check on whether the econometrics evidence has any bearing on the reality of the allocation of TIPs in the postwar period.

Finally, the case studies in Chapters 4 and 5 offer an in-depth look at the criteria, as well as any ideas, beliefs, or perceptions, that play a critical role in actual decisions to choose industries. In Chapter 4, I reexamine ten key industries that have become the basis for a great many generalizations about the efficacy of postwar Japanese selections. Combing through the extant literature reveals that while much has been written about these industries, little attention has been devoted to why these industries were selected for support in the postwar period. That is the lacuna I seek to fill.

In Chapter 5, I bring the issue of industrial selection up to date by conducting a more detailed case study of a high-technology sector about which relatively little is known or written. This is the commercial space launch industry that the Japanese government has been attempting to indigenize, still unsuccessfully by international comparisons, since the 1970s. An examination of this industry gives us an in-the-making guide to the politics and economics of industrial selection in a fully industrialized Japan—an exercise that may well serve as a benchmark for actions of the Japanese government in other leading sectors in the future.

The process of examining specific industry cases is an inductive, bottom-up, and contextually sensitive way to approach the central question of interest about the criteria for selection. It is also a vital means of squaring the aggregate and quantitative evidence with the actual realities of policy-making in Japan. Since there is virtually little recorded or reported information on the role of possible criteria in government choices, I utilized interviews as my primary source of information and supplemented them with information from government, industry, and secondary sources whenever possible. The more than one hundred interviews I conducted with Japanese government officials between 1997 and 2002 speak directly to the motives of bureaucrats and politicians in the process of government choices, and this causal link in the real world is key in the overall analysis.

Additionally, this method allows us not just to take the historical and institutional context properly into account but also to consider other factors that are not allowed for by the rigid theoretical framework. Most important of all, this is the only way to know to what extent, if at all, the theoretical criteria play a role in the actual decisions to choose and favor industries. To some extent, it also allows us to judge where Japanese industrial policy is headed, whether its raison d'être is really changing as many like to believe or whether there are significant continuities in the thinking of Japanese government officials concerning any criteria. Additionally, it moves us beyond just tangible criteria and reminds us of the importance of perceptions and beliefs that also greatly affect government choices.

Chapter 6 concludes by summarizing the analytical and empirical terrain in the book and drawing out implications. To the simple question of how governments choose industries to favor, the Japanese case offers up a general answer. The evidence, both longitudinal and cross-sectional, suggests that the choices of the Japanese government were moved more by economic considerations than political factors across the full range of industries in the economy for most of the postwar period. Finding a solid answer to our simple question in the context of Japan is invaluable on two counts, both of which are set out and discussed in detail in the conclusion. First, it helps us to evaluate rival theories in political economy, to test their scope and limitations in a real-world case. Second, at a more practical level, it also helps to inform later developers whose governments may well still think of emulating the industrialization patterns of the world's second-largest economy.

CHAPTER 2

Quantitative Arts and the Criteria
for Selection

THIS CHAPTER and the following one focus on different quantitative methods to analyze the realities of industrial selection in postwar Japan. Both of them allow us to assess whether the Japanese government was motivated by economic or political criteria as suggested by the rival hypotheses in Chapter 1. But they give us two very different angles on the choices made. In the econometric analysis, we learn whether, how much, and which criteria affected the Japanese government choices. In the structured data analysis, we find out which sectors were the most-favored ones in Japan and whether the criteria affected their favored status overall.

Both methods use a single aggregate data set, consisting of time-series and cross-sectional components. The time-series component stretches from 1955 to 1990 and thereby covers most of the postwar period. The cross-sectional component, based on the two-digit Standard Industrial Trade Classification (SITC), covers the major TIPs disbursed and the political and economic characteristics of all major manufacturing industries in Japan. To put it simply, the analysis uses data on eight measures of TIPs and twelve industrial sectors for each year between 1955 and 1990. Using this time-series cross-sectional (TSCS) data set, this chapter takes the first and broadest cut at testing the rival political and economic hypotheses.

Why Econometrics?

One of the main reasons for analyzing Japanese industrial selections at a high level of industrial aggregation is that we want to see what is true on average across the whole of the Japanese industrial economy and not just one or two sectors. Since this book concentrates on the manufacturing sector in the postwar period, which was almost entirely under the jurisdiction of MITI, the merit of this bird's-eye approach is that it allows us to see whether there are any meaningful and consistent patterns across all the industries in the Japanese economy over time.[1] The facts on the Japanese economy give us some perspective as to why this aggregate view may be necessary.

Over the postwar period, the entire Japanese manufacturing sector, compared to agriculture, construction, services, transport, communications, and so on, has averaged about 28 percent of the total Gross Domestic Product (GDP). It has, however, undergone structural changes in terms of composition. In 1955, textiles dominated the picture with 22 percent of the entire manufacturing range, followed by steel (basic metals) with 18 percent, chemicals with 14 percent, and processed food with 11 percent. By 1995, the picture had changed substantially, with electrical machinery dominating the industrial economy picture with 14 percent, followed closely by general machinery with 11 percent and transport equipment with 10 percent. While textiles was out of the picture with a mere 1.96 percent, both basic metals and chemicals, though far less than before, continued to comprise about 6 to 7 percent of the manufacturing output.

If the entire manufacturing output is nowhere near the whole story behind the Japanese industrial economy, then focusing on selection in one or two subindustries—say the very large scale integration (VLSI) project in semiconductor process technology—seems a little absurd. This is because, individually, the subindustries, whether cars, aircraft, semiconductors, or machine tools, do not constitute the entire manufacturing output. We therefore cannot use them to generalize about the remaining industrial economy, much less the entire nature of the Japanese political economy. So what to do? Given the scheme of the book, stability in terms of inferences requires that we begin with the entire manufacturing base and then incorporate more detailed evidence to come up with a realistic picture of industrial selections.

With the level of industrial aggregation here, an econometric analysis is the most appropriate method to begin the investigation. By allowing us to weigh the economic and political hypotheses against each other in a way that is simply not possible with other methods, such an analysis can swiftly establish whether a proposed causality can be accepted or rejected with some degree of confidence.[2] But we should be mindful of some caveats. For one thing, causality itself is not an explicit specification of the classic regression model, although the very idea of causality still remains a requirement for evaluating theory, as is the case here.[3] An even more sobering point is that the very process of an econometric analysis is an art that requires judgments and decisions at every stage, from the specification of the model to its final estimation. Even though theory provides us with a needed specification of the model—though unfortunately in this case, only in terms of the variables to be included and not the functional form to be estimated—there may be different reasons for estimating the same parameters of a given model in different ways.[4] Finally, perhaps the most troubling problem is the one that also afflicts more qualitative approaches—we stop looking for the answer when we find the one that we esteem, the one that accords with our vision of how things work back in the real world.

This small detour should therefore remind enthusiasts and critics of econometric analysis that it is only one small step forward in shedding light on a real-world problem. Thus while overall the econometric results support the economic hypothesis comparatively more than the political one, we should remember that they have to square with the remaining quantitative and qualitative sets of evidence that follow before we can come to any final conclusions about what the Japanese government did or did not do.

Testing the Rival Hypotheses

The central issue of interest can be put simply: What determined industrial selections in postwar Japan? To reiterate briefly: If the economic hypothesis—which is really about enlightened bureaucratic leadership—is true, then we can by and large expect to see that government policies in Japan were affected largely by economic considerations such as high growth, high value-added, high wages, and the potential for technological spillovers. However, if the political hypothesis—which is basically about good old-fashioned politics—is true, then we can largely expect to see that policies in Japan were controlled by political dictates such as votes, lobbying pressures, and campaign contributions. The latter hypothesis is the dominant viewpoint among economists and political economists—namely, that government choices are almost always and everywhere more likely to be determined and corrupted by political factors than not.

Rather than give a privileged position to one or the other, the remainder of this chapter essentially pits these economic and political hypotheses against each other in an attempt to see which one actually dominates on average in the case of Japan. It sets out the three major stages of the econometric analysis from the specification of the model to its final estimation. The first section briefly describes the dependent and independent variables, as well as the industry cases chosen for study. The second section presents the main equation or model estimated for the TIPs, along with a consideration of some of the econometric problems and remedies that bear upon the results. The third part sets out the actual findings for each of the TIPs used by the Japanese government as an instrument of industrial selection, and an overall summary of the results is presented at the end. If we focus on those criteria for selection that emerge as influential across all the modeling techniques, the results suggest that the economic criteria have been comparatively more important in the selections made by the Japanese government across industries and over time. A concerted effort is made at the end to discuss the general pattern emerging from this analysis with regard to the logic of industrial selection in postwar Japan.

DEPENDENT VARIABLE

Table 2.1 outlines each of the eight dependent variables as measured by individual TIPs at time t.[5] Ranging from subsidies to taxes and on to tariffs, these TIPs represent the most comprehensive and tangible means of measuring the industrial selection process. A focus on several TIPs helps avoid the common fallacy of looking at only one or two government policies as the main tools of industrial selection. Rather than compounding all of the TIPs together into a single measure of selection, each of the TIPs in Table 2.1 is treated in isolation as a full model by itself.[6] Although this presents us with a very clear estimation for an individual TIP, it has the effect of reducing the entire world of selection to that one TIP, whereas the reality is that a simultaneous selection is going on through all the other TIPs as well. For this reason, rather than focus on only part of the picture, an overall assessment is made about the logic of industrial selection based on all the TIP results in the end.

Why focus on hard measures alone? This requires some defense up front. Two types of measures have not been included as TIPs in the quantitative measures, which come up in the case studies. First, nontariff barriers, such as product standards or testing requirements (using Japanese subjects) as in the pharmaceutical or biotechnology sectors, have not been considered as it is virtually impossible to standardize them in a coherent way across the entire manufacturing range. Second, the analysis does not include "soft" measures of TIPs, implemented specifically through the practice of administrative guidance (*gyosei shido*), which according to some has been key in Japanese industrial policy.[7] Administrative guidance refers to the practice whereby a government ministry can issue any number of a combination of directives, requests, warnings, or suggestions to actors within a particular ministry's jurisdiction.[8] There are several reasons for not including measures of administrative guidance. To begin, administrative guidance is issued informally and is a legally nonbinding means of issuing provisions. Since by definition there are few if any formal indications about its existence, it is difficult to measure systematically and consistently across all the industrial sectors used in this study. In addition, administrative guidance would be used in conjunction with other policy instruments, and it alone can hardly compensate for or stand in stead of the many tangible TIPs with which the Japanese govern-

TABLE 2.1

TIPs as Dependent Variables

TIP[a]	Operationalization
Subsidies (SBS)[b]	Annual real net subsidies (subsidies less indirect taxes) in billions of yen by sector
Net Transfers (NTR)[c]	Annual ratio of real net subsidies divided by real gross output by sector
Tax Rates (TAX)[d]	Annual ratio of corporate income taxes received divided by taxable corporate income by sector
JDB Loans (JDB)[e]	Annual real JDB loan allocations in billions of yen by sector
Subsidized Borrowing (BOR)[f]	Annual ratio of real JDB loans divided by total loans by sector
Tariffs (TAR)[g]	Annual estimated effective rates of protection by sector
Quotas (QTA)[h]	Annual quota coverage by sector
R&D Subsidies (RDS)[i]	Annual real R&D subsidies divided by real gross output by sector

[a]Except for tariffs and quotas, which are expressed as percentages, data are deflated by the sector-specific wholesale price index to a base of 100 for 1985.

[b]Data on subsidies is from the *Annual Report on the National Accounts* from the Economic Planning Agency. The data are normalized as reported in the text.

[c]NTRs are useful to examine because subsidy allocation by itself may be governed just by the size of a sector. Estimated NTR is then multiplied by 100. Data for the gross output by sector are from the *Annual Report on the National Accounts* from the Economic Planning Agency. All data are deflated by the appropriate sector-specific domestic wholesale price index available in the *Price Indexes Monthly of Japan.*

[d]Refers essentially to the ratio of taxes paid by each industry divided by the profits made by the same industry across the period. The virtue of using actual taxes paid is that all special tax treatments (such as lower sector specific tax rates, accelerated depreciation, special deductions, and so forth) should be captured in the numerator, which should reflect any substantive discrepancies in the levels of taxes paid across the sectors. In addition, since we are calculating the taxes paid by an industry to its own level of profits, it gives us a good sense for what proportion of the income was being given special treatment. By getting around the obvious problem that higher-profit industries had higher tax rates, this also then allows us to compare the ratios across the sectors. Data are from the *Kokuzei-cho Tokei Nenpo-sho* (Annual statistics of the National Tax Office). In some instances, tax rates are identical because the tax data were classified along broader categories than the ones used in this study.

[e]Refers to Japan Development Bank (JDB) disbursement of outright cash loans to the private sector. Founded in 1951, the JDB was originally thought of as one of the two key centers (the other being the Japan Export Bank in 1950, which later became the Export-Import Bank) for government loan allocations to industrial sectors. Data on JDB loans by the twelve industrial sectors are from the *Economics Statistics Annual* of the Bank of Japan. These data were normalized as reported in the text using data on total sectoral loans and the wholesale price index from the same source.

[f]Refers to rates that show which sectors received more or less government credit as a proportion of their total loans. Total loans include commercial loans, as well as some loans from eleven government institutions such as the Small Business Finance Corporation, Japan Export-Import Bank loans, and so forth.

[g]Refers essentially to the extent to which import tariffs or other quantitative trade restrictions increase the domestic value-added price of goods in the relevant sector relative to the world market value-added price. Data on effective rates of protection are based on an earlier study done by Yatsuo Shouda, "Effective Rates of Protection in Japan," *Nihon Keizai Kenkyu*, no. 11 (March 1982). Shouda estimated effective rates of protection at five-year intervals to 1987 based on the

TABLE 2.1 *(notes, continued)*

liberalization gains from the Tokyo Round (1973–79). For this reason, tariff data between Shouda's years have been extrapolated, and tariff data before 1963 and after 1987 were calculated by adjusting the effective rates of protection by the weighted average tariff rate as reported in the *Annual Report on the National Accounts*. Since the tariff data for most years are based on estimations or calculations rather than on directly reported observations, the results discussed in the text should also be taken as the best possible estimation of the empirical evidence.

[h]Quota coverage for each of the twelve industrial sectors is estimated as the ratio of total number of individual items subject to quotas in a sector divided by the customs product classification. Data on quota coverages are from *Genko Yunyu Seido* (Present Import System). The same caveats as for the tariff data apply to the data on quota coverages. Official data for quota coverage ratios begin in 1965, and the entire TSCS data set is reduced to an analysis between 1965 and 1990.

[i]Refers to the amount of subsidies disbursed by both local and central governments in millions of yen divided by sectoral gross output. Even in its raw form, the data on R&D subsidies show dramatic differences from year to year. Sometimes the data across sectors are not released for confidentiality reasons (as indicated either by X or .). Some observers suggest that there is a hidden budget for R&D subsidies and that therefore official figures do not tell the whole story on any such TIPs in particular. No correction is made to a few observations on official data on R&D subsidies that are given as 0. The only correction made to the data is to use an average based on 1972 and 1975 observations to fill in the 1973 and 1974 observations in the petroleum and coal (PC) industry, for which no data are reported at all. Data on R&D subsidies is from *Kagaku Gijutsu Kenkyu Chosa Hokoku* (Report on the survey of research and development) published by the Somucho Tokei-kyoku (Statistics Bureau, Management and Coordination Agency, Government of Japan) from 1953 onward.

ment can favor some sectors over others. Finally, if the tangible measures of TIPs have an ambiguous relationship with selection and competition, it is hard to know the extent to which administrative provisions alone are likely to have an impact on the selection, performance, or direction of sectors.

INDEPENDENT VARIABLES

Table 2.2 identifies the independent variables or regressors with respect to each TIP. As we saw in Chapter 1, there are two broad categories or sets of variables, one economic and the other political.

In the set of economic criteria for selection, the categories of both rents and external economies have to be operationalized. For rents, growth rates, average value-added, and wage levels for each of the twelve industrial sectors are used as proxies in this study. For external economies, total R&D expenditures are used as a proxy for spillovers with the reasoning that this measure suggests the potential for spinning off knowledge in the future and thereby providing benefits not just to capital and labor employed in an industry but also elsewhere.[9]

In the set of the political criteria for selection, the focus is on tangible political variables such as votes and campaign contributions, as well as on institutional links that can serve as a conduit for lobbying pressures. Unlike most of the economic variables on which data are directly available, these require some indirect estimation. For votes, sectoral employment levels, which refer to the actual number of people employed within a sector, serve as a proxy.

TABLE 2.2

Criteria for Selection as Independent Variables

Criterion	Operationalization	Anticipated Effect and Hypothesis
Growth (GRO)[a]	Annual growth rates calculated as the percent difference of real output by sector	*Positive:* The higher the growth rates the higher, and thereby more favorable, the TIPs.
Value–added (VAL)[b]	Annual figure calculated as production value less raw material expenses in millions of yen by sector	*Positive:* The higher the value-added the higher, and thereby more favorable, the TIPs.
Wages (WAG)[c]	Annual figure calculated as the average of monthly cash earnings in thousands of yen by sector	*Positive:* The higher the wage level the higher, and thereby more favorable, the TIPs.
Spillover Potential (SPL)[d]	Annual figure estimated via the total R&D expenditure in billions of yen by sector	*Positive:* The higher the spillover potential the higher, and thereby more favorable, the TIPs.
Votes (VOT)[e]	Annual figure estimated via employment levels as the number of persons engaged at year's end by sector	*Positive:* The higher the number of potential votes the higher, and thereby more favorable, the TIPs.
Amakudari (AMA)[f]	Annual figure for informal lobbying channel estimated as the total number of government officials approved for retirement by sector	*Positive:* The higher the number of *amakudari* positions the greater the informal means of influence by sector and the higher, and thereby more favorable, the TIPs.
Dantai (DAN)[g]	Annual figure for electorally sensitive channels for lobbying pressures estimated as the total number of groups, organizations, and associations existing by sector	*Positive:* The higher the number of *dantai* that offer a basis for electoral/vote-splitting strategies and related political pressures the higher, and thereby more favorable, the TIPs.
Lobbying Amount (LOB)[h]	Annual figure for donations/contributions in yen amount estimated via the lobbying power function as the product of industry concentration and industry sales by sector	*Positive:* The greater the potential contributions the higher, and thereby more favorable, the TIPs.
TIP Legacies	Annual figure for one-unit lagged TIP	*Positive:* The higher the presence of a favorable TIP at time $t - 1$ the same or more of the TIP at time t (primarily a control for serial correlation.)

Where appropriate, data are deflated by the sector-specific wholesale price index to a base of 100 for 1985.

All expected effects are positive for all TIPs except tax rates whose model works in reverse to the other TIPs. That is, a lower tax rate is obviously a preferred TIP, and therefore negative coefficients are signs of preferential treatment.

[a]Refers to estimations based on total value of manufactured goods shipments, which also includes receipts from processing or repairing, sales of scrap and waste, and other receipts. Data are based on the *Census of Manufactures* as of 31 December of the year stated, as reported in the annual volumes of the *Japan Statistical Yearbook*, 1955–93. The survey covers the manufacturing establishments, excluding those owned by the central or local governments.

[b]Also subtracted are domestic excise taxes and depreciation. Data are based on the *Census of Manufactures* as of December 31 of the year stated, as reported in the annual volumes of the *Japan Statistical Yearbook*, 1955–93. Domestic excise taxes refers to the taxes included in the value of manufactured goods shipments. Until the late 1960s, value-added figures were recorded without depreciation. Value-added is technically part of all the TIP models and is included in the estimations even though it is highly correlated with the other economic variables.

[c]Refers to the monthly sum of contract earnings and extra payments of regular workers. Data are based on the *Monthly Labor Survey*, as reported specifically in the 1955/56, 1960, 1969, 1975, 1982, 1985, 1989, and 1992 annual volumes of the *Japan Statistical Yearbook*. The nationwide survey has several categories for the manufacturing establishments for each industry broken down by the number of people employed, that is, establishments with 30 or more regular workers, establishments with 5–29 workers, and all establishments with 1–4 workers. In this analysis, I only use the cash earnings for establishments with 30 or more regular workers. The cash earnings include both fixed and temporary payments, representing the amount before income tax, savings, labor union fees, and disbursement of purchases. Regular workers refer to laborers regularly employed, including production workers as well as administrative, clerical, and technical workers. After 1968, the cash earnings for both the processed food and tobacco-manufacturing sectors are reported together. To retain consistency in comparing the figures before 1968 to those after, I average the separate figures for processed food and tobacco to obtain one general figure for cash earnings between 1955 and 1967.

[d]Data on sectoral R&D expenditures is graciously provided by David Weinstein.

[e]Data are based on the number of persons engaged at year's end (31 December) as reported in the annual volumes of the *Japan Statistical Yearbook* from 1960 onward. Persons engaged refers to the regular workers, working proprietors, and unpaid family workers. Data on persons engaged between 1960 and 1969 is broken down by (a) establishments with fewer than 10 persons engaged, and (b) establishments with 10 or more persons engaged. To get the total number engaged, I have summed the figures for these two categories. All other data on the level of employment are as reported in the total number engaged, influding both men and women.

[f]Data are based on information provided on those officials approved for *amakudari* as found in *Jinjiin* (National Personnel Authority), *Eiri Kigyo e no Shushoku no Shonin ni Kan Suru Nenji Hokokusho* (Annual report on approval for employment in private enterprise). The publication of this report begins in *Showa* 38 (1963), from which time the data series is taken. Although obviously government officials have descended into a great variety of private sectors, such as transport & communication, wholesale & retail trade, real estate, notably financing and insurance, and even more notably construction, as well as other general sectors in the economy, they are disregarded. For the purposes of this analysis, *amakudari* refers strictly to descent into manufacturing industries, whose operations are further classified into production, planning, sales, repairs, R&D, exports, and imports, all of which are simply (and also generously) taken as part of manufacturing as a whole. The breakdown for the twelve industrial sectors themselves is obtained by classifying and coding each official's data given in the entry entitled *togai eiri kigyo no eigyo naiyo*,which refers directly to the principal type of industry into which the government official stands to descend. Several points should be noted: (1) if, as often happens, an enterprise has more than one type of industrial venture identified, the first one listed is taken as the principal one, or the most frequently occurring one is taken as the principal one, or a judgment is made as to the principal one out of a combination of all those listed; (2) there is one and only one *amakudari* into an industry at any given instance as coded for the single official doing the descending; and (3) the principal types of operations listed in the *Hokokusho* have been used to classify the entry under the industrial aggregation used in this analysis, for example, software, data processing machines and so forth have been assigned to electrical machinery (EM) and so forth. The entire stream of data points for *amakudari* between 1955 and 1962 inclusive is officially unavailable. An estimate of the missing data during this period is calculated using the average of seven-year sets beginning 1963–69 for 1955, 1964–70 for 1956, and so forth. Subsequently, any missing data between data points are filled by taking the average of the latter two points.

[g]Data are based on the classification provided in the three volumes of the 1995 *Zenkoku Kakushu Dantai Meikan* (Comprehensive directory of all Japan organizations 1995). All the industries included for analysis in the subsequent case studies are under one of these categories. For a detailed listing of the principal types of industries whose associations, groups, and organizations are classified within the sectoral aggregation used in this study, see Pekkanen 1996. Since new *dantai* do not come into operation every year it is reasonable to assume that the same number of *dantai* continue operating over the years, and therefore the data points for each successive year are calculated by adding all the previous number of *dantai* before it.

[h]Refers to the product of a concentration measure (Herfindahl index) and the total value of the industry sales. The Herfindahl index ranges from 0 to 1, with 1 representing a perfect monopoly and 0 representing perfect competition. Data for the Herfindahl index in this study are calculated using the total number of corporations (n) in a sector within each year such that $H = 1/n$. Data on the total number of sectoral corporations between 1955 and 1990 is from *Okurasho Zaisei Kinyu Kenkyusho Chosa Tokei Bu* (Ministry of Finance, Institute of Fiscal and Monetary Policy), *Zaisei Kinyu Tokei Geppo: Hojin Kigyo Tokei Nenpo Tokushu* (Monthly fiscal and monetary policy statistics: Annual financial corporate statistics [special edition]). Data on the total volume of sales by sector between 1955 and 1990 is also from *Okurasho Zaisei Kinyu Kenkyusho Chosa Tokei Bu* (Ministry of Finance, Institute of Fiscal and Monetary Policy), *Zaisei Kinyu Tokei Geppo: Hojin Kigyo Tokei Nenpo Tokushu* [Monthly fiscal and monetary policy statistics: Annual financial corporate statistics [special edition]). In Showa 34 (1959), the term *to keigyo shunyu* becomes *uriagaridaka*, both of which mean sales.

Employment levels can also be a proxy for job-related concerns that have political repercussions and to which politicians are presumably sensitive in a representative democracy.

For campaign contributions made by the industries to the government, direct information is virtually impossible to obtain, if not often suspect when available.[10] This leaves us with the task of coming up with a proxy that provides a reasonable estimation across all the sectors, and in this study use is made of the "lobbying power function," which allows us to guess how much a protectionist lobby would be willing to contribute for TIPs. The key empirical focus in the lobbying power function is not just on the number or size of firms in a sector that comprise the "total" lobbying group potential but also more specifically on the idea that total contributions should move in tandem with the size of the industry (total sales) in question. In essence, the total estimated contributions should reflect each member firm's gain in the passage of a given TIP, and therefore the higher the estimated sectoral contribution, the more the sectoral firms stand to gain.[11]

For institutional links, which refer to the existing channels between the public and private sector that afford opportunities for influence and lobbying, there are the observable features of both *dantai* and *amakudari*.[12] Here *dantai* refers to the number of all listed national, regional, and prefectural industry or business associations (*kyokai*), federations (*renmei*), committees (*iinkai*), export associations, import associations, general trade associations, and research institutions that exist within an industrial sector. On the face of it, Japanese industries are formidably well organized by sector and by specific sub-industries. Because of the detailed industrial level at which they are organized, they serve as one coherent channel of communication between the interests of their firm members and the government at a wider industry level.[13] From the perspective of party politicians, these *dantai* could have been a useful basis for splitting the vote in multimember districts with the single nontransferable vote in the old electoral system.[14] They could thus become the conduit for different kinds of political pressures on the bureaucracy. *Amakudari* refers to the well-known practice whereby bureaucrats retire or "descend from heaven" into private industry or private associations. Presumably, the allocation of TIPs is affected when the bureaucrats have official jurisdiction over industries into which they hope to retire and also, equally important, when they continue to maintain exploitable contacts with relevant ministries once they have actually retired into industries.[15]

Table 2.2 also shows explicit hypotheses about the relationships between the dependent and independent variables that, coupled with the structural form of the model, determine the expected signs of the coefficients. The hypothesized signs of the coefficients for each of the set of variables are based on the economic and political variables outlined above. If the economic hypothesis is to be borne out, we should by and large see that the coefficients on the economic variables are positive and significant. Alternatively, if the political hypothesis is to be supported, we should expect to see the coefficients on the political variables, especially votes and campaign contributions, to be positively and statistically significantly related to each of the TIPs. In addition, a one-unit lagged value of the dependent variable or TIP is also used in the individual TIP models where appropriate. While this notion of TIP legacies has not been a central hypothesis in this work, its usefulness both in terms of modeling the inherent temporal dynamics in the data as well as capturing the notion of institutional history where MITI's policies are concerned makes it a desirable regressor.

INDUSTRY CASES

The industries chosen for analysis refer to twelve standardized sectors, which together constitute almost the entire manufacturing range at the two-digit SITC level of industrial aggregation.[16] The sectors are processed food (FD), textiles (TX), paper and pulp (PP), chemicals (CH), petroleum and coal (PC), ceramics (CE), basic metals (BM), fabricated metals (FM), general machinery (MA), electrical machinery (EM), transport equipment (TE), and precision instruments (PI). Why is it important to analyze all these sectors? In addition to the arguments set out at the beginning of this chapter, there are three additional reasons for concentrating at this level of industrial aggregation. First, official data on all variables are consistently available across all of the twelve sectors. Second, the inferences concerning the central hypotheses will be drawn from an analysis that introduces the greatest possible variation in terms of industrial sectors as well as time. And third, the breadth of the analysis will allow us to extract any major patterns in Japan's postwar development path.

Main Model

Explicitly, then, given a set of theoretically specified economic and political criteria, we have to model the determinants of TIPs across the entire range of manufacturing sectors. Given that the maintained hypothesis of interest is a strong positive relationship between TIPs and the economic criteria, what we are testing to see is whether this holds across all the TIPs or whether, alternatively, political factors have mattered more in the determination of TIPs. How exactly will these hypotheses be tested? To begin, there are twelve industries, each of which has observations on eight measures for economic and political variables between 1955 and 1990. In addition, there are eight different dependent variables, namely the individual TIPs at time t, used as measures for government preferential selection across the same time period. The general model to be estimated with these data is given as

$$\text{TIP}_{it} = \alpha + \beta_1\text{TIP}_{it-1} + \beta_2\text{GRO}_{it} + \beta_3\text{VAL}_{it} + \beta_4\text{WAG}_{it} + \beta_5\text{SPL}_{it} +$$
$$\beta_6\text{LOB}_{it} + \beta_7\text{AMA}_{it} + \beta_8\text{DAN}_{it} + \beta_9\text{VOT}_{it} + \text{DUM} + \varepsilon_{it}$$

where

TIP_{it}	=	Annual Real TIP for industry i at time t
TIP_{it-1}	=	Annual Real TIP for industry i at time t - 1
GRO_{it}	=	Annual Real Growth Rates for industry i at time t
VAL_{it}	=	Annual Real Value-Added for industry i at time t
WAG_{it}	=	Annual Real Wages for industry i at time t
SPL_{it}	=	Annual Real Spillover Potential for industry i at time t
LOB_{it}	=	Annual Real Amount of Lobbying Funds for industry i at time t
AMA_{it}	=	Annual Number of *Amakudari* Positions for industry i at time t
DAN_{it}	=	Annual Number of *Dantai* for industry i at time t
VOT_{it}	=	Annual Number of Votes for industry i at time t
DUM	=	Industry Dummies

While this general specification holds across all TIPs and criteria, including the lagged criteria, the final judgment about the most influential criteria for selection is made after testing their validity across different models. I now turn to some other issues that bear upon the estimations before presenting the actual results.

GENERAL CONSIDERATIONS IN POOLING AND ESTIMATION OF MODEL

The central unit of analysis in this chapter is an industry year. The rationale for this marriage of convenience between time and space is twofold. First, since the data are arrayed across industrial sectors and over time, they allow us to tap both cross-sectional and cross-temporal variation. Second, if, in addition to the existing regressors, the number of regressors has to be increased for reasons of time correlations as explained below, combining the cross-sectional data (twelve industrial sectors) with temporal data (thirty-six years) more than compensates for problems. This is because it produces a data set of 432 observations, which greatly increases the degrees of freedom necessary for enabling more precise estimates than would result using data sets based on either alone.[17] Estimating parameters from pooled data is, however, potentially fraught with statistical difficulties.[18] In particular, the most commonly used ordinary least squares (OLS) regression estimates become inappropriate, as the resulting errors from the pool almost always violate central OLS assumptions.

Three such violations, as discussed briefly below, are typically to be expected even in the most well-specified TSCS models.[19] First, regression errors from time-series data are usually serially correlated, and this is likely to occur in temporally dominated pooled data as well (in this case, we have thirty-six years [T] for twelve industries [N]). This means that temporally successive values, such as those for the political and economic characteristics of the industrial sectors, are not likely to be independent over time. The wages in the electrical machinery sector in 1975, for instance, are sure to be serially correlated with wages in the electrical machinery sector in 1976. An examination of preliminary residuals, coupled with the data analysis in Chapter 3, suggests that the residuals are positively correlated for almost all the individual TIP models. A reasonable enough approximation to this serial correlation process proves to be the first-order autoregression, or $AR(1)$, process. For purposes of estimation, I will assume that this form of serial correlation exhibited in the stochastic process is not only constant across time but also across the industries. Two basic corrections are used where appropriate. First, the dynamism in the pooled data is modeled directly by including lagged values of the dependent variable, which refers specifically to a lagged value of the TIP being modeled. Second, where a lagged dependent variable proved insufficient, the Cochrane-Orcutt procedure is used to eliminate the serial correlation in the model and is further used as a benchmark for the other estimations.

Second, errors tend to be contemporaneously correlated in pooled data. That is, for example, a large error for the electrical machinery industry in 1973 may be associated with a large error for the transport equipment industry in 1973. Such associations are entirely possible across all industrial sectors at particular points in time because they are all operating in the same economy and under the same macroeconomic conditions. Any shock to the economy, such as the oil price shock in 1973, is likely to affect all sectors at the same time, although it may be unequal in the magnitude of its effect across the sectors. An interesting consideration is that the error term in the high-growth industrial sectors may well be tied together but remain independent of the low-growth industrial sectors in the economy. Again, for purposes of estimation in this data, I will assume that the contemporaneous correlation is fixed over time. Finally, the errors from the regression may also show panel heteroscedasticity. That is, the variance of the error term may differ from industry to industry. In the data at hand, this is very likely because the level of each TIP to a particular industry, as well as the characteristics of each industry, differs greatly. Although it is also entirely possible that the error variance differs within the industry over time, for purposes of estimation I assume that the errors differ only across the industries but remain constant within a particular industry.[20]

Despite the complicated error structures expected in TSCS data, I will attempt to model potential causes and effects in the most straightforward manner possible across the twelve industrial sectors between 1955 and 1990. As pointed out earlier, TSCS data lead to a far greater number of observations, which helps to mitigate the problem of restricted degrees of freedom, thereby allowing the inclusion of a larger number of regressors. One such regressor of concern, however, is that of TIP legacies, which refers more broadly to the idea that the sheer history of a government policy determines its continuity in the future. That is, the level of a TIP given to an industry at time t is potentially also determined by the level of the same TIP given at time t-1 (or t-2, t-3, and so forth). Thus including a one-unit lagged dependent variable (effectively last year's TIP) as a regressor addresses this concern while also allowing us to model the temporal dynamics of the TSCS series.

In general terms, to deal with the time-series problem of autocorrelation among the residuals (typically removed or at least ameliorated by including a lagged TIP) and the cross-sectional problem of error variances among the industrial sectors, I proceed as follows.[21] I begin with the assumption that the parameters of interest—the coefficients on the political and economic criteria—are constant across the industries. But the assumption of constant intercepts entails a serious misspecification as the average allocation of TIPs differs greatly by industry. In short, then, the assumption that the slope coefficients are constant does not mean that the intercepts for each industry will be the same for each TIP. The justification, therefore, for including the N-1 dummy variables (pulp and paper industry excluded) is that we can reasonably assume that each industry may have factors peculiar to it that affect the determination of each TIP.

While we do not know exactly what these factors are (thereby admitting ignorance of specific causal processes) and the exact interpretation of these dummy variables is entirely vacuous, this constant slope–different intercept specification of the model turns out to conform with the qualitative evidence, both with respect to TIPs and the criteria for selection across the postwar period. Known better as the Least Squares Dummy Variables (LSDV) or Fixed Effects model, the upshot of this method is that it assigns the between-industry variance to the intercept dummies and uses only the within-industry variance (time-series variance) to estimate the equation in hand. Assuming, then, that this LSDV model is a reasonable approximation of reality, we can hypothesize about the general direction of the effects of each of the explanatory variables, keeping the central argument about the influence of economic or political dominance in matters of allocating TIPs. If MITI selected sectors on the sole basis of strategic economic concerns, the distribution of TIPs should be positively and significantly correlated with the economic criteria and negatively or weakly correlated with the political ones.

Major Findings

It would be quite a feat to achieve such singularly clear results, however. Because we are dealing with eight measures of TIPs and not one aggregate measure of all of them, we should expect beforehand that TIP-specific results may well be contradictory, thereby complicating the overall acceptance or rejection of the central hypothesis. The reason for this expectation, as borne out later in the other sets of evidence as well, is the sheer complexity of the selection process.

How, then, will we decide whether there is evidence in favor of either the economic or political hypothesis? Certain decisions made in advance can help toward this task. There are four economic and four political variables that are present in each TIP model. Ideally, we would like to have all of the variables in one set both positive and significant, with those in the other set near zero and/or insignificant. Realistically, however, evidence in favor of either hypothesis will be based on finding a minimum of significant findings for two variables in the set. Preferably, both should be positive and significant, but if not at least one of the two must be significant, and both should be positive to constitute evidence in favor of the set hypothesis.

SPECIFIC CONSIDERATIONS IN ASSESSING THE RESULTS

This section discusses the problems and procedures involved in the estimations for each of the eight TIPs, followed by the regression results. Two sets of results are presented for each TIP as shown in Table 2.4 at the end of the chapter: (1) a levels model based on the natural logs of the variables, in which a percentage unit increase in a criterion affects the TIP by the percent amount of the estimated parameter of the criterion;[22] and (2) a differenced model based on the first differences of the natural log of the variables, in which the unit growth rate of a criterion affects the unit growth rate of the TIP by the amount of the estimated parameter of the criterion.[23]

Several things that bear upon a discussion of the results need to be pointed out. First, the augmented Dickey-Fuller (ADF) unit root test on all the series (natural log, differenced natural log) is carried out to determine their stationarity in order to be more certain that any resulting correlations are not spurious. With the exception of quotas, the Mackinnon critical values allow us to reject the hypothesis of unit roots in all the individual series at the 1 percent or certainly at the 5 percent level. Second, the major problem to be dealt with in temporally dominant data is serial correlation, and throughout this analysis the test used for its detection in the presence of a lagged dependent variable is a modification of the Breusch-Godfrey (BG) test, which is equivalent to the Durbin m test in cases of first-order autoregression.[24] The results from the BG test are reported only in the event that the serial correlation persists.

Third, since we remain unsure of the precise nature of heteroscedasticity in the TSCS pool, robust (White's) standard errors are used throughout. As a check to the inference, the TSCS models are also estimated using feasible generalized least squares with panel corrected standard errors (PCSEs).[25] In the event that it is not possible to reject the null hypothesis that the industry dummies are equal under the posited LSDV model, the estimations are also checked against single constant models to make sure that they are not completely out of line.

The fourth point concerns the general assumption behind the models. A simple correlation between TIPs and the criteria for selection may well be misleading, as the TIPs may be causing the higher levels of the (especially economic) criteria at earlier points in time. In other words, the independent variables may well be endogenous, as it is reasonable to expect that government TIPs affects all of them at some level.[26] To overcome this potential problem and to determine whether the criteria for selection actually do "cause" the selection, the models are also estimated throughout with (one year) lagged values so that the independent variables are from a period before the observations of TIPs.[27] In short, we have two general sets of results for each model. One posits a contemporaneous relationship between the dependent and independent variables—that is, the observations on both sets of variables occur at the same point in time. Another begins with the assumption that past or lagged values of the criteria affect future observations of the TIPs.

In drawing final inferences, both the magnitude and the direction of the effect of each variable in each set will be taken into at least as much account as its statistical significance across all the estimations. Joint hypotheses tests for each set, while not reported below, are also taken into account. In a strict sense, of course, neither the R^2 nor the slope coefficients from the levels and differenced models can be compared. This is because the models have different dependent variables, natural log of a TIP in the former and a differenced log of a TIP in the latter. In addition, their slope coefficients also have entirely different interpretations, percentage change in the former and rate of growth in the latter. While they are clearly not equal in any sense, the justification for examining the influence of the criteria across different models is simply that it allows us to assess whether the influence, if present, actually holds across equally valid estimation techniques. By reporting all possible sets of estimations, we get a better sense of the difficulties in deciding on the "correct" model. On the issue of the correct model, this also allows us to guard against the danger of reporting only those estimations that accord well with any a priori expectations that we may have.

TABLE 2.3

Overall Econometric Evidence for Rival Hypotheses by Individual TIP

TIP	Economic Hypothesis	Political Hypothesis
Net Subsidies (SBS)	Supported (value-added, wages)	Rejected
Net Transfers (NTR)	Supported (wages)	Rejected
Tax Rates (TAX)	Supported (value-added)	Rejected
JDB Loans (JDB)	Rejected	Supported (votes)
Subsidized Borrowing (BOR)	Rejected	Supported (votes, lobbying contributions)
Tariffs (TAR)	Rejected	Supported (*dantai*)
Quotas (QTA)	Supported (value-added, spillovers)	Rejected
R&D Subsidies (RDS)	Supported (value-added, spillovers)	Rejected

Criteria that are consistent in the direction of their hypothesized effects across both the levels and differenced models for the respective TIP are shown in parentheses.

RESULTS FOR ALL TIPS

The most salient results from the estimations are summarized in Table 2.3, and the formal results are presented in full in Table 2.4 at the end of this chapter. More specific details from the estimation process are discussed briefly below for each of the eight TIPs.

Net Subsidies

Net subsidies, the sum of real net cash transfers to an industry, represent the most straightforward means of government selection. The subsidies model is estimated in both levels and differences, and the results are broadly compared across the different models.

The levels estimates shown suggest that, as a whole and across the various estimations, the economic variables conform to the expected direction of effect. That is, if any one of the economic variables changes by 1 percent unit, then, while the other variables are held constant, the level of subsidies changes positively by the relevant coefficient's percent. In the contemporaneous levels estimations, the economic variables have a very strong positive showing, becoming even more so under PCSEs. At the same time, with the exception of *dantai*, the political variables do not have either the expected effect or statistical significance. Votes actually emerge as negative under the PCSE-based estimations.

The differenced log model estimates turn out to be a little more mixed. Here the idea is that a unit growth rate in these criteria affects the unit growth rate in the TIP in a positive direction. The notable fact in the results is that generally both the size and direction of the coefficients and the standard errors tend to be similar, giving us more confidence in the stability of the estimations. Under robust standard errors (SEs) and PCSEs, both high value-added and high wages turn out to be statistically significant. Votes also emerge as significant in the differenced model with PCSEs.

In the lagged levels estimations, the economic variables generally hold the direction of their effects very strongly, with all of them statistically significant. On the other hand, again, the political variables in the levels models do not conform to the expectations laid out in the political hypothesis. Moreover, whereas both *amakudari* and *dantai* are substantively positive, with the latter also statistically significant under PCSEs, both votes and especially lobbying contributions appear to change subsidies by a negative percent. In the lagged models, therefore, according to the initial setup on assessing evidence, the overall results on net subsidies favor the economic hypothesis and particularly the criteria of high value-added and high wages.

Net Transfers as a Percentage of Output

Net transfers refer to the sum of real net subsidies divided by gross output, and the results are presented here as a check to the net subsidies estimations above. The BG test reveals no serial correlation in the residuals throughout, but it should be noted that we cannot reject the unit root hypothesis completely at the 1 percent critical value, which may have a bearing on the estimations.

In the levels estimations, the economic variables generally hold the expected direction of effect, but they do not emerge as statistically significant. Under PCSEs, however, wages do show a strong positive effect on percentage increases in the disbursement of the TIP. The political variables, on the other hand, do not conform to the expected results at all. In the differenced estimations, the test for equality of industry dummies [$F(11,386) = 0.73$; $P > F = 0.713$] suggests that a constant coefficient model is more appropriate. Since the estimations from both the LSDV and constant coefficient model do not vary much, only the latter estimates are shown for the differenced models. Again, the estimations for economic variables are generally similar, with wages emerging as statistically significant in the set. The political variables fare badly, showing contrary direction of effect, at statistically significant levels, than those expected.

In the lagged levels estimations, the economic variables have the expected effect, though they are not statistically significant. The one exception is growth rates, which have a positive and significant effect on the disbursement of net transfers. As in the other estimations, the political variables fare badly, with negative effects at statistically significant levels, especially for lobbying efforts and votes. Only *dantai* or the potential pressure groups conform to the prior expectations. Once again, the overall evidence on net transfers favors the economic hypothesis and particularly the criterion of high wages.

Tax Rates

The tax rate is calculated as the ratio of taxes paid by each industry divided by the profits made by the same industry across the same period of time. This essentially means that all special tax treatments (such as lower sector-specific tax rates, accelerated depreciation, special deductions, and so forth) are captured in the numerator of the ratio. As in the models before it, a final assessment of the influential criteria for selection is made after several different estimations are obtained for the same set of tax rates data.

One important point to remember about the tax model is that it works in reverse to the other TIPs. That is, a lower tax rate is obviously a preferred TIP, so we have to take negative coefficients as signs of preferential treatment in the case of the economic variables (that is, the higher the presence of economic criteria, the lower the tax rate and therefore the more preferential the tax treatment). Conversely, for the political variables, negative coefficients mean more political clout leads to lower taxes.

A test of equality of industry dummies [$F(11,399) = 0.66; P > F = 0.7721$] reveals that the single constant model is more appropriate for the levels model. The BG test reveals no first-order serial correlation. Looking across both the robust and panel-corrected standard errors, the estimates show that high-growth and especially high value-added sectors received preferential treatment. Among the political variables, sectors characterized by potentially higher votes or lobbying contributions did not receive preferential tax treatments, and both *dantai* and *amakudari* are inconsistent in the direction of their effect.

In the differenced estimates, the constant coefficient model is once again more appropriate [$F(11,386) = 0.37; P > F = 0.9654$]. Here value-added continues to hold its direction of effect but is not statistically significant. These estimates suggest definitively that high-wage sectors received preferential tax treatment but that high-growth ones did not. While we find that votes have the expected significant effect under the robust SEs, this washes out under PCSEs. Lobbying also appears to have an extremely adverse effect on tax rates at statistically significant levels.

The lagged levels estimations are also presented from the constant coefficient model [$F_{(11,397)} = 0.86; P > F = 0.5819$]. The presence of high value-added continues to mean preferential tax treatment, although the statistical significance is not consistent across the two estimations. Here the effect of high wage levels contradicts the differenced model findings, leading us to discount its importance. To a lesser degree, the same holds true for growth rates. The estimates in the political set show that sectors with high voting potential are definitively not the recipients of preferential tax treatments. Although *dantai* has the anticipated effect, it appears almost negligible and statistically insignificant. Based, then, on the expected direction of effect, and to a lesser degree on statistical significance, the overall evidence on tax rates favors the economic hypothesis and particularly the criterion of high value-added.

Japan Development Bank (JDB) Loans

Although including a lagged dependent variable usually helps to model the temporal dynamics directly into the equation, the BG test for the levels model of Japan Development Bank (JDB) loans shows that there remains significant first-order serial correlation in the residuals [$t\text{-}stat = 4.182$; $p > abs(t) = 0.0000$]. Several different autoregressive specifications (one-unit to five-unit lags) were also modeled successively into the equation, but the serial correlation in the residuals continues to be dominant in every specification. Assuming, then, that serial correlation in fact derives from the error structure of the model, I correct for it by using the iterative Cochrane-Orcutt procedure.

In the levels estimates, high wage levels emerge as having a significant positive effect on the disbursement of JDB loans, with both value-added and spillovers having the expected direction of effect. However, it is absolutely clear negative growth rates, as in declining sectors, have prompted favorable JDB loan disbursement. In the political set, high voting potential is immensely important at statistically significant levels, with *dantai* emerging as influential under the PCSEs as well.

In the differenced model, the BG test reveals first-order serial correlation, and use is made again of the Cochrane-Orcutt procedure. Once more, high wage levels turn out to have a positive and statistically significant effect on the disbursement of JDB loans. Similarly, high growth rates have a negative effect on increases in JDB loans, which is the same as saying that declining sectors have been more favored through such loans. In the political set, votes emerges again as being a tremendously influential determinant of JDB loans, with both lobbying contributions and *amakudari* also having the expected positive effect.

In the lagged levels estimations, the pattern noticed in the estimations above continues to hold. Because of the persistence of first-order serial correlation, the Cochrane-Orcutt procedure is used for the estimations. Growth levels are, once again, negatively and significantly correlated with percentage increases in JDB loans. The other economic variables generally have the expected positive effect, though none are statistically significant. Among the political criteria, both votes and *dantai* emerge as hugely influential in the disbursement of JDB loans.

Because of the technical standards set up earlier in deciding which hypothesis is more favored than the other, both the economic and political hypotheses are equally favored in this case. But it is difficult to believe that JDB loans are not disbursed for political reasons and are geared especially toward declining industries. In fact, interviews with JDB officials confirm the emphasis placed on supporting declining and high employment/vote sectors, like coal and textiles, for reasons of political stability well into the 1980s. Although this support has slowly decreased, with an emphasis now on supporting high-technology sectors, it has been a key feature of JDB policy until very recently.[28]

Therefore, there is some evidence in favor of the economic hypothesis and specifically the criterion of high wages as expected. However, in comparison, the overall evidence favors the criteria in the political hypothesis, and especially votes, as far more important determinants of JDB loans.

Subsidized Borrowing Rates

Subsidized borrowing rates are expressed as the ratio of total government loans (as roughly measured by JDB loans) to total loans across the industries. These rates are, therefore, an indication of the percentage of loans that are subsidized by the Japanese government to a particular sector. Not surprisingly, here, too, the levels model using a lagged dependent variable, or specifically a lagged subsidized borrowing rate, is beset with remaining serial correlation in the residuals. This holds true for different autoregressive specifications that were tried successively (for the one-unit lag, the lagged residual in the BG test has a $t\text{-}stat = 4.242$; for the two-unit lag, the lagged residual in the BG test has a $t\text{-}stat = 9.421$.

Once again, then, inference is based on the levels estimations from the iterative Cochrane-Orcutt procedure, followed by those under PCSEs. Among the economic variables, growth rates are again negatively and significantly correlated with subsidized borrowing rates. The remaining economic variables are all statistically insignificant and, with the exception of value-added, tend to have a negative effect. Conversely, the political variables generally have the expected direction of effect, and votes and *dantai* turn out to be statistically significant.

In the differenced estimates, there are no problems with serial correlation under either set of estimations. Notably, growth rates continue to hold their negative effect throughout, while both value-added and wages have the expected positive effect. None of the estimates for the economic variables, however, are statistically significant. The estimates for the political variables fare far better in that they generally have the expected direction of effect, especially for lobbying contributions and votes, which also turn out to be statistically significant in turn.

In the lagged levels estimates, growth rates have both a negative and statistically significant effect on the subsidized borrowing rates. Although high value-added turns out to have a significant positive influence, it is the only economic variable that conforms to the expectations in the economic hypothesis. The political variables do not fare as well under these estimates, with only *dantai* emerging as having a positive and significant effect. While lobbying contributions hold their positive effect, votes do not, and neither emerges as statistically significant. The overall evidence on subsidized borrowing rates then favors the political hypothesis and specifically the criteria of lobbying contributions and votes.

Tariffs

Tariffs refer to the effective rates of protection, that is, the extent to which import tariffs or quantitative trade restrictions increase the domestic value-added price of goods relative to the world market value-added price. In the levels estimation, the BG test immediately detects a first-order autocorrelation problem in the lagged residual [*t-stat* = 7.219], and different autoregressive specifications of the tariff (two-unit, three-unit, and five-unit lags) do not ameliorate the problem. Assuming, then, that serial correlation is the most important problem, the estimates for the levels model are obtained using the iterative Cochrane-Orcutt procedure. Under robust SEs, each of the political variables—lobbying contributions, *amakudari*, *dantai*, and votes—has the hypothesized positive effect, with votes and *dantai* being statistically significant as well. Conversely, the economic variables are contrary to the hypothesized direction of effect; each of them is negative, and wages and spillovers are also statistically significant with respect to their negative effect. Under PCSEs, the estimated economic criteria do not change much in terms of direction of effect or significance. Among the political criteria, the results are much weaker, with both lobbying contributions and votes now showing negative effects that are nevertheless statistically insignificant. *Dantai* remains both positive and hugely significant.

In the differenced estimations, the presence of first-order serial correlation remains, and use is made again of the Cochrane-Orcutt procedure as well as PCSEs. The test for the equality of industry dummies in both cases also suggests strongly that a constant coefficient model is more appropriate. Although none of the criteria, either in the economic or political set, emerge as statistically significant, it is immediately notable that the political criteria all have the anticipated direction of effect, whereas the economic ones do not.

In the lagged levels estimates, the economic variables again have the opposite direction of effect than anticipated in the overall economic hypothesis. Higher levels of growth, wages, and spillovers all have a negative effect on tariff protection, with the latter two being statistically significant. Only value-added has the anticipated effect, but it is statistically insignificant. The political criteria do not fare much better, with only *dantai* emerging as statistically significant and both lobbying contributions and votes showing inconsistency in terms of effect.

While there is no overwhelming evidence in support of the political hypothesis, it is comparatively more favored by the evidence than the economic one. Therefore, the overall evidence on tariff protection favors the political hypothesis and specifically the criterion of *dantai*.

Quotas

Quotas refer to the import quota coverage across the sectors and are estimated as the ratio of the total number of individual items subject to quotas divided by the number of product classification. Data on import quotas begin in 1965, reducing the usable data to 1965–90. Four of the twelve industries, namely pulp and paper, ceramics, fabricated metals, and electrical machinery, are dropped from the analysis, as they have erratic observations or, in the case of at least one, no observations at all. Reduced observations are not, however, as significant a problem as the fact that the measurement of this variable is the least reliable of all the other economic series analyzed and is characterized by extreme positive skew and kurtosis, which no standard transformations ameliorate. Additionally, we cannot reject the null hypothesis of a unit root for the natural log quota rates at even the 10 percent level. The first-differenced log quota rate series fares better, but here the null hypothesis cannot be rejected at the 1 percent level.

For the sake of consistency with the analyses of the other TIPs, the estimations are carried out thoroughly. But given the problems above, it would be prudent to recognize the fragility of inference in this one case. I will assume that first-order autocorrelation is the major impediment to inference, and the BG test confirms this. The iterative Cochrane-Orcutt procedure is used to produce estimates, followed by estimations using PCSEs. The economic criteria, specifically high growth, value-added, and spillovers, all generally have the expected direction of effect. The opposite is true for the political criteria, which are all negatively and significantly correlated with quota coverage ratios.

In the differenced estimates, the economic criteria fare a little better than the political ones in terms of expected direction of effect, though none of them appear as statistically significant. Under PCSEs, the estimates show that none of the politically powerful sectors, particularly those with high lobbying contributions and votes, have enjoyed corresponding levels of import quota protection. Although the BG test does not detect first-order autocorrelation, the estimates are checked against those from the Cochrane-Orcutt procedure, and they strongly favor the economic hypothesis. Under PCSEs, the test for the equality of the industry dummies suggests that a constant coefficient model would be more appropriate, but since the results are essentially the same in both cases, only the LSDV estimates are shown. Comparatively, both favor the economic criteria over the political ones.

In the lagged levels estimates, the BG test detects severe first-order autocorrelation, and use is made again of the Cochrane-Orcutt procedure, followed by estimates under PCSEs. As before, with the exception of wage levels, the economic criteria fare slightly better than the political ones. The persisting problems mentioned earlier with respect to the quota series should sound a warning note about the stability of the inferences. However, based largely on the expected direction of effect, the overall evidence on quotas favors the economic hypothesis, particularly the criteria of high growth, value-added, and spillovers.

R&D Subsidies

R&D subsidies refer to the cash subsidies disbursed by both local and central governments divided by gross output. Note that for the natural log of R&D subsidies series, we can reject the hypothesis of a unit root at the critical values of 10 percent and 5 percent levels but not at the 1 percent level. As the BG test detects serial correlations [t-stat $= -2.237$ for the first-order autocorrelation lag], I simply use the iterative Cochrane-Orcutt procedure and PCSEs to produce estimates for the R&D levels model. For the economic criteria, only value-added and spillovers consistently have the expected positive effect, with the latter also being statistically significant. Conversely, the political variables have negative coefficients, suggesting that unit changes in them affects the disbursement of R&D subsidies adversely. This is especially true for votes, which is the only one of the political variables to be statistically significant.

In the differenced estimates for the R&D subsidies, there are no problems with unit roots or first- and second-order serial correlation in the residuals. The estimates show that all the economic variables, namely growth rates, value-added, wages, and spillover potential, tend to have the hypothesized positive effect, although none of them is significant. Importantly, the political variables all have negative coefficients, with *dantai* being statistically significant as well.

Given the potential problem with unit roots in the levels series for R&D subsidies, the lagged estimates were carried out using both levels and differenced series. Because the differenced estimates did not alter the overall results from those of the levels models, only the latter results are shown. Among the economic criteria, it is clear that neither growth rates nor wage levels have the expected positive effect. Value-added and spillovers, however, do have a positive effect, with the latter being statistically significant as well. Here, too, the political criteria fare badly, with lobbying contributions and especially votes having a negative effect on the disbursement of R&D subsidies. Of the remaining three criteria, none is statistically significant, though both *amakudari* and *dantai* exhibit consistent positive effects. While not overwhelmingly supportive, the overall evidence on R&D subsidies favors the economic hypothesis and specifically the criteria of high value-added and spillovers.

Summing Up the Econometric Evidence

What does this first round of evidence on Japanese industrial selections suggest about the viability of the economic and political hypotheses respectively? Let me begin with some caveats. At the outset, it was made clear that the expectation of finding a neat answer that favored one or the other hypothesis consistently across all the eight TIPs was clearly unrealistic. In large part, this would hold true for investigating any complex real-world phenomenon like industrial selection. In part also, we have to assume a great deal about the nature of the data in order to use the statistical techniques. For these reasons, as the previous section showed, each TIP was modeled in both levels and differences, using both robust and panel-corrected standard errors. This was not just as a means to remedy statistical problems that were potentially an impediment to valid inference but also as an effort to see whether the effects of the criteria actually held across equally valid estimation techniques.

What do the results generally suggest with regards to the logic of industrial selection in Japan? To be sure, politics has had a conventional and consistent effect on the allocation of Japanese TIPs. This much cannot be denied. And this very consistency in effect is important, given the fact that, unlike the economic variables that can be measured almost directly, the political variables have to be measured through proxies that might attenuate their statistical influence. It is noteworthy, therefore, that the political variables such as votes emerge as significant in their own right, particularly where the conventional wisdom expects them to, as in the case of tariffs. Although not always statistically significant, other political variables such as *dantai* and lobbying contributions also had the expected hypothesized effect. There is very little doubt, then, that politics has been influential in industrial selections.

But this influence is limited, as both tariffs and subsidized borrowing rates are really the only TIPs that appear to be captured wholly by political interests. Overall, as Table 2.3 shows, the economic hypothesis is favored for at least five of the eight TIPs examined, namely net subsidies, net transfers as a percent of output, tax rates, quotas, and R&D subsidies. On average, the presence of criteria such as high wages, value-added, and spillover potential has led to a favorable increase in each of these TIPs.

The conclusion, therefore, is that the econometric evidence points to the relatively greater importance of the economic hypothesis compared to the political one. Given the setup of the hypotheses, we then also have to concede by a leap of inference that bureaucrats have generally been at the helm of industrial strategy for much of the postwar period in Japan and that politicians have not mattered as consistently in the process of industrial selection as the newer choice-theoretical works suggest. As will soon be clear, the evidence from the econometrics analysis above does not stand in isolation. In fact, it foreshadows the complex realities of industrial selections that emerge as the investigation moves closer to the actual policy-making realm. Like the other methodological approaches to which I turn next, the econometric analysis here acknowledges the relevance of politics but suggests the comparative dominance of the economic criteria for selection. And this emphasis on an economic logic also comes across in the next two rounds of evidence, namely structured data analysis and case studies.

TABLE 2.4

Estimations for All TIPs with Robust and Panel-Corrected Standard Errors

(a) Net Subsidies

Levels, LSDV

	Robust SE n 420			Panel-corrected SE (XTGLS) n 430		
	Criterion	Coefficient	*t*-stat	Criterion	Coefficient	*z*
ECON	lgro	0.653	6.013	lgro	0.012	1.056
	lval	0.118	1.578	lval	0.499	7.464
	lwag	0.019	0.284	lwag	0.483	5.802
	lspl	0.034	1.400	lspl	0.103	2.785
POL	llob	-0.008	-1.895	llob	-0.018	-1.860
	lama	0.013	0.630	lama	0.003	0.278
	ldan	0.027	1.411	ldan	0.103	3.247
	lvot	-0.135	-1.995	lvot	-0.224	-2.157
	Adj-R^2 0.995					

Differenced, LSDV

	Robust SE n 408			Panel-corrected SE (XTGLS) n 408		
	Criterion	Coefficient	*t*-stat	Criterion	Coefficient	*z*
ECON	dlgro	-0.003	-0.025	dlgro	0.023	0.347
	dlval	0.344	3.998	dlval	0.342	5.260
	dlwag	0.451	3.503	dlwag	0.455	4.923
	dlspl	0.059	1.464	dlspl	0.049	1.462
POL	dllob	-0.005	-0.677	dllob	-0.003	-0.332
	dlama	0.009	0.642	dlama	0.010	1.013
	dldan	-0.017	-0.425	dldan	0.008	0.196
	dlvot	0.238	1.361	dlvot	0.316	2.213
	Adj-R^2 0.341					

Lagged Levels, LSDV

	Robust SE n 418			Panel-corrected SE (XTGLS) n 418		
	Criterion	Coefficient	*t*-stat	Criterion	Coefficient	*z*
ECON	lgro1	0.047	5.917	lgro1	0.035	2.546
	lval1	-0.035	-0.449	lval1	0.276	2.961
	lwag1	0.080	1.466	lwag1	0.612	5.895
	lspl1	0.046	1.676	lspl1	0.106	2.330
POL	llob1	-0.010	-2.019	llob1	-0.022	-1.892
	lama1	0.005	0.362	lama1	-0.007	-0.418
	ldan1	0.009	0.441	ldan1	0.140	3.670
	lvot1	-0.018	-0.269	lvot1	-0.039	-0.312
	Adj-R^2 0.994					

TABLE 2.4 (b) Net Transfers

Levels, LSDV

| | | Robust SE n 420 | | | Panel-corrected SE (XTGLS) n 430 | |
	Criterion	Coefficient	*t-stat*	Criterion	Coefficient	*z*
ECON	lgro	-0.090	-0.993	lgro	-0.005	-0.418
	lval	-0.021	-0.331	lval	0.043	0.709
	lwag	0.058	0.884	lwag	0.246	3.135
	lspl	0.016	0.625	lspl	0.010	0.286
POL	llob	-0.011	-2.357	llob	-0.028	-3.021
	lama	0.009	0.470	lama	-0.001	-0.079
	ldan	0.024	1.278	ldan	0.035	1.147
	lvot	-0.155	-2.349	lvot	-0.744	-7.439
	Adj-R² 0.987					

Differenced

| | | Robust SE n 408 | | | Panel-corrected SE (XTGLS) n 408 | |
	Criterion	Coefficient	*t-stat*	Criterion	Coefficient	*z*
ECON	dlgro	-0.014	-0.188	dlgro	-0.033	-0.504
	dlval	-0.0004	-0.005	dlval	0.004	0.058
	dlwag	0.303	2.723	dlwag	0.314	3.452
	dlspl	0.011	0.289	dlspl	0.010	0.306
POL	dllob	0.004	0.230	dllob	0.003	0.307
	dlama	0.002	0.138	dlama	0.002	0.211
	dldan	-0.037	-1.003	dldan	-0.032	-0.787
	dlvot	-0.415	-3.203	dlvot	-0.388	-2.814
	Adj-R² 0.090					

Lagged Levels, LSDV

| | | Robust SE n 418 | | | Panel-corrected SE (XTGLS) n 418 | |
	Criterion	Coefficient	*t-stat*	Criterion	Coefficient	*z*
ECON	lgro1	0.032	3.114	lgro1	0.003	0.289
	lval1	-0.028	-0.481	lval1	0.098	1.354
	lwag1	0.042	0.862	lwag1	0.128	1.476
	lspl1	0.033	1.263	lspl1	0.017	0.447
POL	llob1	-0.010	-1.900	llob1	-0.039	-3.763
	lama1	0.004	0.365	lama1	-0.010	-0.820
	ldan1	0.024	1.296	ldan1	0.069	2.141
	lvot1	-0.153	-2.548	lvot1	-0.703	-6.528
	Adj-R² 0.987					

TABLE 2.4 (c) Taxes

Levels

	Robust SE n 420			Panel-corrected SE (XTGLS) n 430		
	Criterion	Coefficient	*t-stat*	Criterion	Coefficient	*z*
ECON	lgro	-0.036	-1.172	lgro	-0.001	-0.273
	lval	-0.023	-2.012	lval	-0.020	-1.186
	lwag	0.031	2.833	lwag	0.031	1.466
	lspl	0.003	0.950	lspl	0.010	1.300
POL	llob	0.001	1.147	llob	0.012	4.819
	lama	0.001	0.510	lama	-0.003	-0.906
	ldan	-0.001	-0.184	ldan	0.005	0.582
	lvot	0.019	2.492	lvot	0.004	0.206
	Adj-R^2 0.887					

Differenced

	Robust SE n 408			Panel-corrected SE (XTGLS) n 408		
	Criterion	Coefficient	*t-stat*	Criterion	Coefficient	*z*
ECON	dlgro	0.074	3.132	dlgro	0.049	2.303
	dlval	-0.026	-1.148	dlval	-0.016	-0.893
	dlwag	-0.124	-3.461	dlwag	-0.071	-2.561
	dlspl	0.005	0.454	dlspl	0.003	0.275
POL	dllob	0.014	5.146	dllob	0.015	5.415
	dlama	-0.003	-0.925	dlama	-0.003	-0.896
	dldan	0.008	0.638	dldan	0.016	1.147
	dlvot	-0.091	-2.194	dlvot	-0.056	-1.345
	Adj-R^2 0.140					

Lagged Levels

	Robust SE n 418			Panel-corrected SE (XTGLS) n 418		
	Criterion	Coefficient	*t-stat*	Criterion	Coefficient	*z*
ECON	lgro1	-0.003	-2.22	lgro1	0.0002	0.065
	lval1	-0.023	-2.093	lval1	-0.0325	-1.74
	lwag1	0.037	3.362	lwag1	0.0792	3.656
	lspl1	0.002	0.715	lspl1	0.0051	0.665
POL	llob1	0.000	0.293	llob1	0.0020	0.639
	lama1	0.003	1.078	lama1	0.0008	0.231
	ldan1	-0.0003	-0.097	ldan1	-0.0093	-0.992
	lvot1	0.021	2.758	lvot1	0.0368	2.055
	Adj-R^2 0.889					

TABLE 2.4 (d) JDB Loans

Levels, LSDV

	Cochrane-Orcutt n 429			Panel-corrected SE (XTGLS) n 430		
	Criterion	Coefficient	*t-stat*	Criterion	Coefficient	z
ECON	lgro	-0.105	-4.182	lgro	-0.138	-4.365
	lval	0.091	0.636	lval	0.253	1.381
	lwag	0.914	4.402	lwag	0.620	2.865
	lspl	0.007	0.085	lspl	0.002	0.017
POL	llob	0.039	1.507	llob	0.051	1.478
	lama	-0.023	-1.002	lama	-0.038	-1.282
	ldan	0.012	0.143	ldan	0.301	3.535
	lvot	1.538	4.966	lvot	1.103	3.830
	DW_{Orig} 0.4415					
	DW_{Tran} 1.5557					
	Adj-R^2 0.899					

Differenced, LSDV

	Cochrane-Orcutt n 407			Panel-corrected SE (XTGLS) n 408		
	Criterion	Coefficient	*t-stat*	Criterion	Coefficient	z
ECON	dlgro	-0.469	-3.210	dlgro	-0.440	-3.025
	dlval	0.178	1.264	dlval	0.164	1.153
	dlwag	1.111	5.291	dlwag	1.125	5.452
	dlspl	-0.006	-0.086	dlspl	-0.001	-0.016
POL	dllob	0.025	1.011	dllob	0.025	0.941
	dlama	0.005	0.253	dlama	0.002	0.116
	dldan	-0.072	-0.738	dldan	-0.077	-0.721
	dlvot	1.668	5.255	dlvot	1.559	4.715
	DW_{Orig} 1.671					
	DW_{Tran} 1.985					
	Adj-R^2 0.148					

Lagged Levels, LSDV

	Cochrane-Orcutt n 417			Panel-corrected SE (XTGLS) n 418		
	Criterion	Coefficient	*t-stat*	Criterion	Coefficient	z
ECON	lgro1	-0.062	-2.798	lgro1	-0.068	-2.508
	lval1	0.187	1.453	lval1	0.320	1.915
	lwag1	0.099	0.531	lwag1	0.235	1.208
	lspl1	-0.001	-0.019	lspl1	0.015	0.181
POL	llob1	0.036	1.551	llob1	0.046	1.414
	lama1	-0.040	-1.914	lama1	-0.048	-1.863
	ldan1	0.344	4.774	ldan1	0.510	6.917
	lvot1	1.373	4.979	lvot1	0.930	3.456
	DW_{Orig} 0.354					
	DW_{Tran} 1.544					
	Adj-R^2 0.918					

TABLE 2.4 (e) Subsidized Borrowing Rates

Levels, LSDV

		Cochrane-Orcutt n 429			Panel-corrected SE (XTGLS) n 430		
	Criterion	Coefficient	t-stat	Criterion	Coefficient	z
ECON	lgro	-0.119	-4.693	lgro	-0.157	-4.787
	lval	0.165	1.140	lval	0.256	1.418
	lwag	0.012	0.060	lwag	-0.168	-0.783
	lspl	-0.025	-0.312	lspl	-0.029	-0.301
POL	llob	0.029	1.120	llob	0.025	0.682
	lama	-0.023	-0.966	lama	-0.037	-1.252
	ldan	-0.033	-0.402	ldan	0.194	2.295
	lvot	0.660	2.107	lvot	0.219	0.774
	DW_{Orig} 0.366					
	DW_{Tran} 1.490					
	Adj-R^2 0.630					

Differenced, LSDV

		Robust SE n 408			Panel-corrected SE (XTGLS) n 408		
	Criterion	Coefficient	t-stat	Criterion	Coefficient	z
ECON	dlgro	-0.078	-0.531	dlgro	-0.227	-1.558
	dlval	0.092	0.541	dlval	0.108	0.723
	dlwag	0.049	0.271	dlwag	0.229	1.075
	dlspl	-0.019	-0.284	dlspl	-0.018	-0.237
POL	dllob	0.029	2.405	dllob	0.019	0.702
	dlama	-0.007	-0.418	dlama	0.005	0.290
	dldan	-0.150	-0.776	dldan	-0.181	-1.668
	dlvot	0.545	1.044	dlvot	0.886	2.603
	Adj-R^2 0.180					

Lagged Levels, LSDV

		Cochrane-Orcutt n 417			Panel-corrected SE (XTGLS) n 418		
	Criterion	Coefficient	t-stat	Criterion	Coefficient	z
ECON	lgro1	-0.073	-3.294	lgro1	-0.088	-3.108
	lval1	0.266	2.094	lval1	0.330	2.116
	lwag1	-0.281	-1.546	lwag1	-0.288	-1.550
	lspl1	-0.054	-0.768	lspl1	-0.064	-0.804
POL	llob1	0.025	1.098	llob1	0.024	0.729
	lama1	-0.028	-1.347	lama1	-0.034	-1.309
	ldan1	0.212	2.980	ldan1	0.335	4.601
	lvot1	0.305	1.114	lvot1	-0.017	-0.066
	DW_{Orig} 0.302					
	DW_{Tran} 1.445					
	Adj-R^2 0.686					

TABLE 2.4 (f) Tariffs

Levels, LSDV

	Cochrane-Orcutt n 429			Panel-corrected SE (XTGLS) n 430		
	Criterion	Coefficient	t-stat	Criterion	Coefficient	z
ECON	lgro	-0.005	-0.452	lgro	-0.015	-0.969
	lval	-0.082	-1.212	lval	-0.023	-0.257
	lwag	-0.264	-2.692	lwag	-0.235	-2.158
	lspl	-0.088	-2.286	lspl	-0.107	-2.385
POL	llob	0.006	0.449	llob	-0.001	-0.109
	lama	0.017	1.508	lama	0.016	1.044
	ldan	0.107	2.770	ldan	0.315	7.313
	lvot	0.448	3.031	lvot	-0.007	-0.048

DW_{Orig} 0.338

DW_{Tran} 1.432

Adj-R^2 0.680

Differenced

	Cochrane-Orcutt n 407			Panel-corrected SE (XTGLS) n 408		
	Criterion	Coefficient	t-stat	Criterion	Coefficient	z
ECON	dlgro	-0.060	-0.874	dlgro	-0.042	-0.589
	dlval	-0.030	-0.463	dlval	-0.052	-0.739
	dlwag	-0.084	-0.835	dlwag	-0.180	-1.721
	dlspl	-0.041	-1.285	dlspl	-0.062	-1.899
POL	dllob	0.002	0.177	dllob	0.003	0.304
	dlama	0.016	1.799	dlama	0.016	1.703
	dldan	0.040	0.877	dldan	0.084	1.752
	dlvot	0.075	0.492	dlvot	0.203	1.315

DW_{Orig} 1.451

DW_{Tran} 2.090

Adj-R^2 0.005

Lagged Levels, LSDV

	Cochrane-Orcutt n 417			Panel-corrected SE (XTGLS) n 418		
	Criterion	Coefficient	t-stat	Criterion	Coefficient	z
ECON	lgro1	-0.024	-1.941	lgro1	-0.029	-1.880
	lval1	0.059	0.847	lval1	0.125	1.305
	lwag1	-0.395	-3.971	lwag1	-0.379	-3.400
	lspl1	-0.081	-2.087	lspl1	-0.117	-2.501
POL	llob1	0.004	0.348	llob1	-0.001	-0.053
	lama1	0.009	0.818	lama1	0.009	0.549
	ldan1	0.108	2.767	ldan1	0.297	6.839
	lvot1	0.250	1.656	lvot1	-0.230	-1.564

DW_{Orig} 0.346

DW_{Tran} 1.330

Adj-R^2 0.666

TABLE 2.4 (g) Quotas

Levels, LSDV

		Cochrane-Orcutt n 207			Panel-corrected SE (XTGLS) n 208	
	Criterion	Coefficient	*t-stat*	Criterion	Coefficient	*z*
ECON	lgro	0.051	0.515	lgro	0.107	0.896
	lval	0.142	1.693	lval	0.138	1.305
	lwag	0.266	-2.418	lwag	-0.364	-2.700
	lspl	0.057	1.120	lspl	0.091	1.440
POL	llob	0.030	-2.741	llob	-0.023	-1.882
	lama	0.008	-0.683	lama	-0.015	-1.060
	ldan	0.573	-3.971	ldan	-0.828	-5.098
	lvot	-0.454	-1.934	lvot	-0.121	-0.474
DW_{Orig} 0.290						
DW_{Tran} 0.674						
Adj-R^2 0.934						

Differenced, LSDV

		Robust SE n 192			Panel-corrected SE (XTGLS) n 192	
	Criterion	Coefficient	*t-stat*	Criterion	Coefficient	*z*
ECON	dlgro	-0.035	-0.405	dlgro	0.005	0.068
	dlval	0.142	1.660	dlval	0.104	1.841
	dlwag	-0.059	-0.639	dlwag	-0.130	-1.478
	dlspl	0.026	0.718	dlspl	-0.005	-0.146
POL	dllob	-0.015	-1.115	dllob	-0.022	-3.233
	dlama	-0.003	-0.340	dlama	-0.008	-1.230
	dldan	0.097	0.772	dldan	-0.094	-0.730
	dlvot	-0.164	-0.989	dlvot	-0.359	-2.008
Adj-R^2 0.615						

Lagged Levels, LSDV

		Cochrane-Orcutt n 207			Panel-corrected SE (XTGLS) n 208	
	Criterion	Coefficient	*t-stat*	Criterion	Coefficient	*z*
ECON	lgro1	0.067	0.669	lgro1	0.139	1.148
	lval1	0.017	0.196	lval1	-0.005	-0.042
	lwag1	-0.139	-1.213	lwag1	-0.290	-2.019
	lspl1	0.101	1.928	lspl1	0.116	1.760
POL	llob1	-0.002	-0.196	llob1	-0.002	-0.145
	lama1	0.015	1.204	lama1	0.012	0.767
	ldan1	-0.375	-2.530	ldan1	-0.716	-4.553
	lvot1	-0.386	-1.568	lvot1	-0.081	-0.315
DW_{Orig} 0.314						
DW_{Tran} 0.699						
Adj-R^2 0.930						

TABLE 2.4 (h) R&D Subsidies

Levels, LSDV

		Cochrane-Orcutt n 407			Panel-corrected SE (XTGLS) n 408	
	Criterion	Coefficient	t-stat	Criterion	Coefficient	z
ECON	lgro	0.010	0.093	lgro	-0.023	-0.217
	lval	0.396	0.715	lval	0.424	0.690
	lwag	-0.457	-0.744	lwag	-0.494	-0.743
	lspl	0.866	3.130	lspl	0.857	2.779
POL	llob	-0.076	-1.178	llob	-0.085	-1.034
	lama	-0.104	-0.970	lama	-0.134	-1.314
	ldan	-0.323	-1.396	ldan	-0.200	-0.835
	lvot	-1.930	-2.642	lvot	-1.823	-2.611
	DW_{Orig} 1.063					
	DW_{Tran} 2.184					
	Adj-R^2 0.394					

Differenced, LSDV

		Robust SE n 375			Panel-corrected SE (XTGLS) n 373	
	Criterion	Coefficient	t-stat	Criterion	Coefficient	z
ECON	dlgro	0.018	0.032	dlgro	-0.978	-1.687
	dlval	0.162	0.244	dlval	1.165	1.706
	dlwag	0.052	0.049	dlwag	0.133	0.148
	dlspl	0.017	0.035	dlspl	0.037	0.090
POL	dllob	-0.011	-0.114	dllob	-0.018	-0.133
	dlama	-0.118	-1.489	dlama	-0.088	-0.961
	dldan	-1.067	-2.467	dldan	-0.586	-1.500
	dlvot	-2.563	-1.879	dlvot	-2.468	-1.938
	Adj-R^2 0.257					

Lagged Levels, LSDV

		Cochrane-Orcutt n 396			Panel-corrected SE (XTGLS) n 397	
	Criterion	Coefficient	t-stat	Criterion	Coefficient	z
ECON	lgro1	-0.253	-2.790	lgro1	-0.210	-2.201
	lval1	0.405	0.698	lval1	0.536	0.901
	lwag1	-1.404	-2.268	lwag1	-1.336	-2.037
	lspl1	1.115	3.988	lspl1	1.030	3.326
POL	llob1	-0.010	-0.152	llob1	-0.010	-0.120
	lama1	0.157	1.466	lama1	0.155	1.499
	ldan1	0.356	1.569	ldan1	0.279	1.183
	lvot1	-1.596	-2.158	lvot1	-1.694	-2.416
	DW_{Orig} 0.981					
	DW_{Tran} 2.201					
	Adj-R^2 0.418					

CHAPTER 3

Political Economy of the
Most-Favored Sectors

FROM AN EXAMINATION of the reasons why some sectors were selected, the quantitative analysis now turns to establishing which sectors were
the most-favored ones in postwar Japan. Using the same aggregate dataset as
in the econometric analysis, in this chapter I track, rank, and correlate all the
variables of interest, namely TIPs and the criteria for selection. The evidence
presented in this chapter is not about what the Japanese government said it
was going to do (it could say one thing and do another) or about what we
think the Japanese state must have been doing because of Japan's industrial
success (hindsight is almost always perfect).

Instead, by analyzing and correlating all the trends in the data, this chapter does two things. First, based on the disbursement of higher and lower
levels of TIPs across the entire manufacturing range, it establishes which sectors were actually more favored by the Japanese state relative to all others.
Second, in keeping with the goal of the book overall, it also provides another
set of evidence on the economic or political criteria driving government
choices. By looking closely at the overall process of "selection" and "non-se-
lection" across all sectors at key intervals in the postwar era, this analysis offers enough variation to assess the validity of the two hypotheses with which
we began.[1] Before descending into the empirical trenches, however, a word
on the method: An overwhelming amount of data is analyzed very comprehensively in this chapter, and it might all seem very cryptic throughout. But
everything falls into place if we simply remember the goal of this structured
data analysis: find out who got what and why.[2]

The remainder of the chapter is divided into three sections. In the first
section, the goal is to establish which sectors were more favored by the
Japanese government relative to others between 1955 and 1990. It therefore
examines the overall movement of Japanese TIPs that were used as instru-

ments of selection across all industries, namely net subsidies, net transfers as a percent of output, taxes or tax relief, JDB loans, subsidized borrowing rates, tariffs, quotas, and R&D subsidies. The analysis focuses exclusively on the disbursement of these eight "hard" or tangible measures of TIPs to get a clearer sense of just how systematic the process of Japanese selection was both before and after the first oil shock in 1973. With the assumption that sectors that received higher levels of these hard TIPs relative to others were more favored by the government, it then proceeds to an ordinal ranking of the eight TIPs across the twelve sectors.[3] While a complicated task, scrutinizing the movement of the TIPs across industries and over time allows us subsequently to determine the most-favored sectors across the postwar era— that is, the sectors relatively and consistently the beneficiaries of higher levels of TIPs by the Japanese government.

In the second section, the aim is to establish the determinants of the most-favored sectors, using the hypothesized criteria for selection as discussed earlier. Focusing on characteristics such as their economic strength and political influence, each sector is examined relative to the others, again both before and after the 1973 oil shock. The economic importance of the sectors is assessed through levels of growth, value-added, wages, and spillover potential. Alternatively, the relative political power of the same sectors is measured through votes, channels for both formal and informal lobbying by industries, and estimated donations by each sector to the government. Finally, then, by ordinally ranking these characteristics in each set of criteria we are able to determine the most economically strategic and the most politically influential of all the sectors.

In the final section, the idea is to put together the evidence from the first and the second sections—the TIPs to and the characteristics of the twelve sectors, respectively—in order to determine why the most-favored sectors were the most favored. Doing this helps us to see which set of criteria, economic or political, explains the allocation of TIPs to the most-favored sectors more consistently than the other. It also helps to serve as a broad check on the actual validity of the econometric results presented earlier. The overall results from this structured data analysis mirror the complexity of Japanese industrial selections that was evident in the econometric analysis but at the same time also lend comparatively more support to the economic hypothesis.

Establishing the Most-Favored Sectors 1955–90

This section focuses on the record of Japanese industrial selections in the postwar era, specifically by examining the disbursement of TIPs across twelve industrial sectors. To reiterate, the industries include processed food

(FD), textiles (TX), paper and pulp (PP), chemicals (CH), petroleum and coal (PC), ceramics (CE), basic metals (BM), fabricated metals (FM), general machinery (MA), electrical machinery (EM), transport equipment (TE), and precision instruments (PI). In the first part of this section, the movement in each of the eight TIPs is examined separately, focusing largely on differences at the extreme poles and upper end of the data. In addition, the data are tracked both before and after the 1973 oil shock in order to determine whether this exogenous shock changed allocations substantially across the sectors. In the second part, the goal is to use these findings to establish a ranked distribution of the TIPs, which, in turn, allows us to determine the most-favored sectors in the postwar era.

WHO GOT WHAT?

Net Subsidies

Before the first oil shock, the processed food industry was the highest recipient of net subsidies, with a comfortable average margin of about ¥300–350 billion over all the other industries. The second-highest recipient of subsidies was the petroleum and coal sector, with a margin of about ¥150–250 billion over the remaining industries, which increased gradually but steadily. Overall, both the food and the petroleum and coal industries remained well above every other industrial sector in terms of subsidies allocations.

What about the remaining ten sectors? Although it is easier to speak of relatively higher amounts among these sectors, to keep things in perspective it should be remembered that all reported net subsidies were less than ¥30 billion until about 1959. However, we can see the beginning of favoritism toward the electrical machinery and transport equipment sectors. In 1955, both of these two sectors had a negligible advantage of about ¥3–5 billion, but by 1959 their advantageous position becomes much more visible, with an average of about ¥20 billion over the other sectors in terms of net subsidies. Between 1959 and 1965, the electrical machinery sector was clearly favored over the others. In 1965, the transport sector passed the electrical machinery sector to become the third-highest recipient of net subsidies and largely enjoyed this lead up to 1973. At the other end of the data, we find that ceramics, precision instruments, and paper and pulp were the relatively least favored of all the sectors.

After the oil shock, the processed food sector continued to dominate the picture in terms of total allocation of subsidies, followed by the petroleum and coal sector. Yet it is important to note that while both of these sectors continue to get the highest proportion of subsidies compared to the other sectors, their rate of increase in the subsidies is among the lowest across the period. The third-highest ranking sector is transport equipment, followed by the electrical machinery sector, which is also reminiscent of the previous period. Both of these sectors see slow but steady increases in net subsidies from about ¥270 billion in 1955 to about ¥1 trillion at the end of the period. Interestingly, the fastest increase in the rate of subsidy allocation is in the general machinery sector at around 700 percent, though the actual amount of net subsidies remains low. The same pattern is also true both for the chemicals and the ceramics sectors. All of the remaining five sectors received total net subsidies averaging less than or about ¥100–400 billion over the entire period.

Net Transfers as a Percent of Output

The evidence on the net transfers before the first oil shock tallies nicely with that on net subsidies, with both petroleum and coal and processed food dominating the picture; the only difference between net transfers and subsidies is that the ranking of these two sectors is reversed. Despite variations by year over the period, both the petroleum and coal and processed food industries retained an average lead of about 16 percent and 8 percent, respectively, over the remaining ten sectors. The next three highest recipients of net transfers are the electrical machinery, precision instruments, and transport equipment sectors, though their lead over the remaining seven sectors should not be exaggerated. At their peak, total net transfers to these three sectors did not exceed 4.5 percent of gross output, and until 1973 their average lead over the other sectors did not exceed 1 to 2 percent. At the lower end, net transfers to ceramics, chemicals, general machinery, fabricated metals, pulp and paper, textiles, and basic metals ranged between 0.5 and 1.5 percent of gross output. In 1975, these sectors exhibited an overall simultaneously faster rate of increase in total net transfers, though they only ended up with an average of around 2 percent.

In the post oil–shock period, once again both the petroleum and coal and processed food sectors dominate the scene. Net transfers were highest to the petroleum and coal sector and remained at an average of about 15 percent of gross output until the early 1980s, after which they increased to over 23 percent. The processed food industry is the next highest ranked sector, and although net transfers dropped sharply in 1974 from 10 percent to 3 percent, they picked up almost immediately the following year, continued to increase steadily until 1990, and stabilized around 10 to 12 percent.

What about the other sectors? There is a subtle difference between these sectors, though it should be remembered that net transfers as a whole to these sectors never exceeded 4 percent of gross output. Transport equipment, electrical machinery, and precision instruments are slightly elevated above the rest in terms of net transfers, which averaged about 3 percent. In the early 1980s, net transfers to the transport equipment sector became visibly distinct, only to merge back indistinguishably with the other sectors by 1989. Electrical machinery, too, is slightly elevated above the remaining sectors, as is the precision instruments sector, but once again they merged back with the other sectors in the early 1980s. Net transfers to the other seven sectors never exceeded more than 1 to 2 percent, and the only thing worth remarking is that net transfers to both the ceramics and the textiles sectors picked up in 1989 and showed an upward trend.

Taxes

The data on tax rates are uniform for some industries across the time period, and changes occurred across some industries at roughly the same rate.[4] Though the difference in the rates is not extreme—the difference in the tax rates between the highest and lowest is about 0.05 percent; between clusters of industries the tax rate differential is about 0.02 percent—there is nevertheless a definite hierarchy in which sectors were favored for selection, as evidenced by the payment of lower taxes across certain periods

The tax rates for 1960 are generally representative of the period before the first oil shock. During this period, the textiles sector had the lowest tax rate at an average of 0.32 percent and was therefore the most favored of all for most of the period. The second-lowest tax rate category at about 0.34 percent includes the chemicals, petroleum and coal, and ceramics sectors. As a whole, six sectors, including basic metals, fabricated metals, general machinery, electrical machinery, transport equipment, and precision instruments, had the second-highest tax rate at approximately 0.36 percent. Least favored of all were the processed food and pulp and paper sectors, with the highest tax rates at 0.37 percent. By 1963, however, the picture had changed substantially, with the same cluster of six industries receiving preferential treatment via lower tax rates, averaging relatively the lowest tax rate of around 0.335 percent. But this tax favoritism lasted only about four years, and all of them registered the second-highest tax rates by the early 1970s. And by the early 1970s, tax rates had equalized roughly across all the twelve sectors at around 0.34 percent.

In the post oil-shock period, the tax rates for 1977 are roughly representative of the tax structure between 1973 and 1976. The textiles sector is clearly the beneficiary of the lowest tax rates at about 0.3752 percent, followed by basic metals, fabricated metals, pulp and paper, and processed food. The highest tax rates are found in a cluster of four industries at 0.397 percent, namely general machinery, electrical machinery, transport equipment, and precision instruments. The next highest rates are in the chemicals, petroleum and coal, and ceramics sectors. With slight modifications, this pattern on relative taxes holds until 1990.

Japan Development Bank (JDB) Loans

The evidence on Japan Development Bank (JDB) loans shows a marked consistency as a measure of government allocation of funds. Until the early 1960s, the basic metals sector received the highest loans, averaging around ¥10 billion. In 1960, the chemicals sector clearly became the highest recipient of JDB loans and retained an average lead of about ¥20–25 billion over the other sectors until 1973. Textiles had started off as the third-highest recipient of JDB loans in 1955 at a total of ¥8 billion but lost that lead to the transport equipment and general machinery sectors less than four years later. In 1968, it regained its lead over the general machinery sector but was only the fifth-highest recipient by 1973. The remaining seven sectors—processed food, ceramics, precision instruments, petroleum and coal, fabricated metals, pulp and paper, and electrical machinery—are generally indistinguishable from each other in that they all remain in the range of about ¥2–10 billion for the period.

But in 1968, JDB loans to the petroleum and coal sectors shot up and kept increasing sharply from about ¥8 billion to over ¥90 billion in 1973. By 1971, JDB loans to this sector exceeded those to even the transport equipment sector. In 1973, petroleum and coal was the third-highest recipient of JDB loans, preceded only by the chemicals and basic metals sectors. In fact, after the oil shock there is no question that three sectors—petroleum and coal, basic metals, and chemicals—were distinctly advantaged in terms of JDB loan allocations. Basic metals was the highest recipient, followed in rough order by the petroleum and coal and chemicals sectors. Throughout the period, these three sectors together retained an average lead of about ¥200–250 billion over all the other sectors.

JDB loans to the remaining sectors also show a distinct pattern, though all of them individually received less than about ¥120 billion at any given year during this period. In 1955, the transport equipment sector was the fourth-highest ranked recipient of JDB loans, averaging about ¥50 billion. It retained this lead until 1980, when it was visibly overtaken by the ceramics sector, but it regained its lead in 1989. In 1983, however, it was overtaken by the electrical machinery sector, which ended the period as the fourth-highest recipient of JDB loans at around ¥150 billion. Within the remaining sectors, for much of the period processed food and pulp and paper are the next highest recipients of JDB loans, followed by the textiles sector, which had started off in 1955 right behind the transport equipment sector. Notably, precision instruments was consistently the lowest recipient of JDB loans.

Subsidized Borrowing Rates

The evidence on subsidized borrowing rates is somewhat different from that on the straightforward one on JDB loan allocations, at least in the era before the oil shock. The chemicals sectors had the most consistently highest subsidized borrowing rates across the period until 1969, that is, it relied most on government credit. In 1967, the petroleum and coal sector saw a very sharp rate of increase in its subsidized borrowing rates, which quickly surpassed those of the chemical sector. The basic metals sector, which had started off as the highest ranked in 1955, had a declining rate of subsidized borrowing, which picked up slowly in 1968. The general machinery sector lost its third-highest lead to the ceramics sector in 1966, and within the next two years the transport equipment joined ranks with the ceramics sector. The remaining sectors had very low rates of subsidized borrowing, often with electrical machinery as the lowest ranked of all throughout the period. Although there are variations in the time series for subsidized borrowing rates in various years, the pattern holds fairly well across the pre-oil-shock period.

After the 1973 oil shock, the evidence on the straightforward allocation of JDB loans suggests that the basic metals, chemicals, and petroleum and coal sectors were the highest recipients during 1973 to 1990, as they were during 1955 to 1973. The same continues to be true for subsidized borrowing rates during this period. In fact, the evidence on subsidized borrowing rates is clearer in some respects than that on JDB loans. The petroleum and coal sector consistently had the highest subsidized borrowing rates, which were substantially above all the other sectors. The next highest subsidized borrowing rates were in the basic metals and chemicals sectors, followed by the ceramics and then the pulp and paper sectors. Interestingly, transport equipment and electrical machinery had among the lowest rates of subsidized borrowing.

Tariffs

Based on the estimations, it is clear that tariff protection was consistently the highest in the transport equipment sector, followed by the textiles and processed food sectors until 1965. At their peak in 1963, these three sectors enjoyed effective rates of protection at 62 percent, 54 percent, and 48 percent, respectively. What about the remaining nine sectors before the 1973 oil shock? There is also a distinct pattern here. In the next tier, the precision instruments and chemicals sectors had the next highest rates at an average of about 25 percent until 1965. These two sectors were followed very closely by the electrical machinery and basic metals sectors in terms of effective rates of protection at about 21 percent. Surprisingly, average protection in both the ceramics and general machinery sectors is virtually indistinguishable across the period. Petroleum and coal and fabricated metals had comparatively low average protection that never exceeded more than 13 to 15 percent. Although tariff protection in the pulp and paper sector picked up from an average of 6.8 percent between 1955 and 1963 to an average of 14 percent between 1964 and 1973, it had the lowest relative rate of effective protection of all twelve sectors.

In an era where nontariff barriers came to dominate the conduct of trade policy, it is imprecise to measure "total" import protection afforded by tariff rates alone. Given this caveat, the evidence suggests that the processed food sector enjoyed the highest effective rates of protection by a substantial margin, which kept increasing across the period, followed by the basic metals and textiles sectors. The remaining sectors all have estimated rates of protection averaging less than 20 percent, and there is nothing striking about any one sector. Among these low-ranking sectors, general machinery and electrical machinery have some of the lowest rates of protection, with transport equipment least protected of all.

Quotas

For quota coverages, the earliest figures begin in 1965, and from then the coverages are found to be at the highest levels in the processed food sector, where prices were approximately an average of 45 to 50 percent of world prices. Leaving aside the food sector, which had an average 20 to 25 percent lead in quota coverages over the remaining eleven sectors, the next most-favored sectors are the petroleum and coal and transport equipment sectors, with coverage of about 20 percent. General machinery, electrical machinery, and chemicals were, respectively, the next most-protected sectors over the period, but only by a margin of about 5 to 8 percent over the remaining six sectors. The sectors that were consistently the least covered until 1973 include ceramics, textiles, basic metals, precision instruments, fabricated metals, and pulp and paper. Together, they had meager quota coverages ranging between 1 and 5 percent.

After the oil shock, again we find the highest quota coverage in the processed food sector, followed by the transport equipment sector. In the next tier, chemicals had the highest quota coverage, followed by the petroleum and coal sector. Both the general machinery and precision instruments sector also stand out from the remaining sectors. Notably, textiles had among the lowest quota coverages throughout.

R&D Subsidies

Until the late 1960s, the allocation patterns of R&D subsidies are virtually indistinguishable across the industries. Between 1966 and 1970, the electrical machinery, transport equipment, general machinery, and chemicals sectors were clearly favored over all the rest. The electrical machinery sector retained a lead of about ¥2–4 billion over all the other sectors and continued to enjoy a slow but steady increase in R&D subsidies until the end of the period. The next clearly favored sector is transport equipment, for which R&D subsidies peaked between 1969 and 1971 and then stood out commandingly over all other sectors at about ¥25 billion, leaving it as the highest-favored sector. General machinery, too, had a slow increase in R&D subsidies until 1971, immediately after which they shot up to about ¥12 billion. Finally, while the chemicals sector also enjoyed a lead over all the remaining eight sectors, for which allocations remain indistinct throughout the period, R&D subsidies to this sector do not show the dramatic increases as in the other more favored sectors.

After the oil shock, roughly the same sectors continued to receive the highest levels of R&D subsidies. Both transport equipment and electrical machinery retained a visible and commanding lead over all other sectors, with the former having an average lead of about ¥2–4 billion over even the latter. R&D subsidies to the transport equipment sector also had a more cyclical nature, whereas those to the electrical machinery sector were characterized by a slow upward trend until about the mid 1980s. From then on, the levels of the subsidies began to decline for both the sectors. The chemicals sector also enjoyed a lead of about ¥500 million over the other sectors for the better part of the 1980s. However, R&D subsidies to this sector remained much below both the transport equipment and electrical machinery sectors. The only other remarkable thing about the allocation of these subsidies is that the petroleum and coal and general machinery sectors had a slight advantage over the remaining sectors. As in the previous period, all of the other sectors are by and large indistinguishable from each other in terms of any such R&D subsidies allocations.

ORDINAL RANKING OF ALL TIPS

While it is useful to examine the overall record of TIPs across the twelve sectors, we still have to establish where the bulk of the resources were transferred. This can be done using an ordinally ranked distribution of all TIPs, which allows us to compare their movement across industries and over time in a consistent manner. The process of ranking involves two distinct steps: first, using predetermined procedures to establish the ordinal rankings; second, identifying the most-favored sectors in postwar Japan based on the extreme poles of the rankings.

Some Considerations in Ordinal Ranking

Before proceeding, we should be aware of some methodological concerns associated with ordinal rankings—concerns that also highlight the tremendous complexities in establishing industrial selection patterns in a straightforward way, let alone thinking about applying Japanese patterns elsewhere in a facile manner.

First, in examining the disbursement of TIPs in the previous section, it was immediately clear that they did not move consistently in one direction for any given sector. Sometimes, in fact, the TIPs seem to be working at cross-purposes even within a sector. For instance, while processed food may have been the most selected sector in terms of subsidies or import protection, it was also the sector with the highest tax rate or lowest tax relief during the same period.

Second, using eight different TIPs as measures for industrial selection might also be subject to the claim that some TIPs, such as tax relief, are more important than others and therefore deserve more weight in the analysis. This is a problematic position, for the simple reason that we have no way of justifying giving more weight to one TIP than another. In interviews with policy-makers, which form the basis for the qualitative evidence in the next chapter, what came across was the uncertainties regarding the efficacy of any one of the TIPs as an instrument of selection. In this analysis, therefore, all the TIPs are treated equally. Tax relief, for example, is considered to be no more or less important in any sense than net transfers or effective rates of protection.

Third, even a cursory look at the data across the industries makes it immediately clear that "selection" itself is hardly a dichotomous variable. All of the twelve sectors clearly have a ranking on each of the eight measures of TIPs. It is thus more sensible to think of selection as higher and lower levels of TIP disbursements on a continuum. But to establish the most-favored sector, we have to know what constitutes a "higher" and "lower" level of TIPs. There is no really good answer, and this eventually requires a judgment call on my part as explained in the next section. Similarly, while the trends are more or less uniform across the entire period, there are years in which the same sector has a higher or lower rank on the TIPs. How, then, does one decide which years to choose, given that some sectors are more favored in one year than another? To ensure impartiality, a decision was made beforehand to do the analysis at five-year intervals. It is worth pointing out that the observations across the TIPs in the years chosen are more or less consistent with the trends in the series across the time period under analysis.

Finally, although the ordinal rankings of the TIPs between 1 and 12 are valid for drawing inferences, it is important to know a serious limitation of the procedure. In the emphasis on relative positions, ordinal ranks discount large and small differences between the actual values of the data equally. For example, a difference between 100 and 101 is treated the same as a difference between 100 and 1,000 and so on. Fortunately, in the data at hand, there are substantial differences in the values between the sectors, with the information even more clear at the extreme poles of the entire rank, which is where this analysis concentrates.

Procedures for Ordinal Ranking

Despite these caveats, one advantage of using ordinal ranking is the systematic way it allows us to compare trends and patterns across industries and over time. This is key if we are to make generalizations about industrialization beyond Japan.

In establishing the ranking, the first step is to identify the position of all the eight TIPs for all the twelve industrial sectors in specific representative years spaced out over the entire postwar period. Here the representative years between 1955 and 1990 are taken at approximately five-year intervals, which in practice works out to the following years: 1955, 1960, 1966, 1972, 1973, 1978, 1984, and 1990. On average, the trends in these years also hold for the years in between. By examining both the time-series and cross-sectional trends in the data at roughly five-year intervals, the analysis makes very clear which sectors were more favored not just in a specific year but also across the entire period. In addition, this breakdown of postwar Japanese TIPs into specific time periods is important because it allows me, albeit imperfectly, to control indirectly for a host of other factors that may also affect the government selections, such as ideology, culture, domestic political cultures, macroeconomic conditions, foreign pressures, and so on across the same period. Looking at twelve different industries at very different intervals of time ensures that such factors vary, while allowing us to test the validity of the two central hypotheses at hand.

The evidence presented in Table 3.1 is based simply on ranking the TIPs to a sector in a given year, with 1 representing the most-favored status and 12 representing the least favored. To give an example: In 1955, a rank of 1 for net subsidies in the processed food sector signifies that processed food was the most favored of all sectors in the industrial economy for that TIP and for that time. In the same year, the fabricated metals sector was least favored by net subsidies, so it gets a rank of 12. In short, each TIP to a sector is assigned a value on a scale of 1 to 12 for each of the representative years. Only in the case of taxes or tax relief, where several sectors have a similar ranking, is the position of each sector determined by counting the sectors ahead of it.

Assessing the Ordinal Ranking

What can we make of the results? It is immediately obvious that nothing is systematic in any one of these years. While each sector has a definite rank relative to the others at any given point in time, there is nothing consistent about the ranking across all the TIPs for the same sector. A reasonable first conclusion is that there is no overarching grand strategy at work. Were this true, we would see, for one thing, all the major TIPs move in the same favorable direction for a selected sector and particularly for those that emerge as economically strategic.

TABLE 3.1

Ranked Distribution of TIPs to All Industrial Sectors by Interval Years, 1955–90

(a) 1955 Rankings

	Net Subsidies	Net Transfers	Tax Relief	JDB Loans	Subsidized Borrowing	Tariffs	Quotas[a]	R&D Subsidies[b]	Average[c]	Count[d]
Food (FD)	1	1	11	8	11	3	—	9	3.71 TE	57.14 TE
Textiles (TX)	6	11	1	3	4	2	—	7	3.86 CH	57.14 CH
Paper & Pulp (PP)	10	10	11	9	9	12	—	10	4.43 EM	57.14 PC
Chemicals (CH)	5	7	2	2	2	5	—	4	4.86 TX	57.14 TX
Petroleum & Coal (PC)	2	2	2	7	3	10	—	11	5.14 BM	42.86 BM
Ceramics (CE)	9	6	2	10	10	9	—	6	5.29 PC	42.86 EM
Basic Metals (BM)	7	12	5	1	1	7	—	3	6.29 FD	42.86 FD
Fabricated Metals (FM)	12	9	5	12	12	11	—	8	6.71 MA	28.57 PI
General Machinery (MA)	8	8	5	6	7	8	—	5	7.43 CE	14.29 CE
Electrical Machinery (EM)	3	3	5	5	8	6	—	1	7.57 PI	0.00 MA
Transport Equipment (TE)	4	5	5	4	5	1	—	2	9.86 FM	0.00 FM
Precision Instruments (PI)	11	4	5	11	6	4	—	12	10.14 PP	0.00 PP

In the ranked unweighted TIPs, 1 represents the highest rank (i.e., most favored sector) and 12 the lowest (i.e., least favored sector). Note that both net subsidies and net transfers are included in the rankings here but even when net subsidies are not included the final ranking remains the same. Designated years are roughly five years apart over the postwar period.

[a]Data not available for some years. When QTA data are not available, the total number of TIPs is counted as seven for the calculations.

[b]Data for sectoral R&D Subsidies is sometimes not given for unstated reasons of confidentiality, particularly for the paper & pulp and petroleum & coal industries. Any such sector is assigned the lowest rank.

[c]Unweighted average of ranks of TIPs by sector in ascending order (1 = most-favored sector).

[d]Total number of TIPs with rank 4 or lower as percentage of the total number of TIPs by sector in descending order (100% = most favored sector).

TABLE 3.1 (b) 1960 Rankings

	Net Subsidies	Net Transfers	Tax Relief	JDB Loans	Subsidized Borrowing	Tariffs	Quotas[a]	R&D Subsidies[b]	Average[c]	Count[d]
Food (FD)	1	2	11	7	10	3	—	11	3.57 CH	57.14 CH
Textiles (TX)	7	11	1	6	11	2	—	9	3.86 TE	57.14 TE
Paper & Pulp (PP)	11	9	11	5	6	12	—	12	5.57 MA	42.86 MA
Chemicals (CH)	5	7	2	1	1	5	—	4	5.57 PI	42.86 PI
Petroleum & Coal (PC)	2	1	2	12	7	10	—	8	5.71 BM	42.86 FD
Ceramics (CE)	9	6	2	9	9	9	—	7	5.86 EM	42.86 EM
Basic Metals (BM)	6	12	5	2	2	7	—	6	6.00 PC	42.86 PC
Fabricated Metals (FM)	12	8	5	11	8	11	—	10	6.43 FD	28.57 BM
General Machinery (MA)	8	10	5	3	3	8	—	2	6.71 TX	28.57 TX
Electrical Machinery (EM)	3	4	5	10	12	6	—	1	7.29 CE	14.29 CE
Transport Equipment (TE)	4	5	5	4	5	1	—	3	9.29 FM	0.00 FM
Precision Instruments (PI)	10	3	5	8	4	4	—	5	9.43 PP	0.00 PP

(c) 1966 Rankings

	Net Subsidies	Net Transfers	Tax Relief	JDB Loans	Subsidized Borrowing	Tariffs	Quotas[a]	R&D Subsidies[b]	Average[c]	Count[d]
Food (FD)	1	2	11	7	8	1	1	7	2.63 TE	87.50 TE
Textiles (TX)	8	11	7	4	9	3	8	9	4.63 CH	50.00 FD
Paper & Pulp (PP)	12	10	11	8	5	12	12	12	4.75 FD	50.00 MA
Chemicals (CH)	5	7	7	1	1	6	6	4	5.13 MA	50.00 EM
Petroleum & Coal (PC)	2	1	7	11	10	11	3	11	5.38 EM	37.50 CH
Ceramics (CE)	10	6	7	6	2	8	7	5	5.88 BM	37.50 PC
Basic Metals (BM)	6	12	1	3	6	4	9	6	6.38 CE	37.50 BM
Fabricated Metals (FM)	9	8	1	10	11	10	11	10	7.00 PC	25.00 PI
General Machinery (MA)	7	9	1	5	3	9	4	3	7.13 PI	25.00 TX
Electrical Machinery (EM)	4	4	1	9	12	7	5	1	7.38 TX	12.50 CE
Transport Equipment (TE)	3	5	1	2	4	2	2	2	8.75 FM	12.50 FM
Precision Instruments (PI)	11	3	1	12	7	5	10	8	10.25 PP	0.00 PP

TABLE 3.1 (d) 1972 Rankings

	Net Subsidies	Net Transfers	Tax Relief	JDB Loans	Subsidized Borrowing	Tariffs	Quotas[a]	R&D Subsidies[b]	Average[c]	Count[d]
Food (FD)	1	2	12	10	10	1	1	11	4.25 PC	75.00 PC
Textiles (TX)	9	11	3	5	6	2	9	10	4.38 TE	62.50 TE
Paper & Pulp (PP)	12	10	11	9	7	4	12	12	4.50 CH	50.00 CH
Chemicals (CH)	6	6	4	1	2	8	5	4	4.88 BM	50.00 BM
Petroleum & Coal (PC)	2	1	4	3	1	11	3	9	6.00 FD	50.00 FD
Ceramics (CE)	10	7	4	7	4	10	8	7	6.38 EM	37.50 EM
Basic Metals (BM)	5	12	1	2	3	3	7	6	6.38 MA	25.00 MA
Fabricated Metals (FM)	8	8	1	11	11	6	11	8	6.88 TX	25.00 TX
General Machinery (MA)	7	9	7	6	8	9	4	1	7.13 CE	25.00 CE
Electrical Machinery (EM)	4	3	7	8	9	12	6	2	8.00 FM	12.50 FM
Transport Equipment (TE)	3	4	7	4	5	7	2	3	8.38 PI	12.50 PP
Precision Instruments (PI)	11	5	7	12	12	5	10	5	9.63 PP	0.00 PI

(e) 1973 Rankings

	Net Subsidies	Net Transfers	Tax Relief	JDB Loans	Subsidized Borrowing	Tariffs	Quotas[a]	R&D Subsidies[b]	Average[c]	Count[d]
Food (FD)	1	2	10	9	9	1	1	10	3.88 TE	75.00 TE
Textiles (TX)	9	11	11	5	7	3	10	11	4.38 CH	62.50 PC
Paper & Pulp (PP)	12	10	12	10	6	4	12	7	4.50 PC	50.00 FD
Chemicals (CH)	7	6	5	1	3	5	4	4	5.38 FD	50.00 CH
Petroleum & Coal (PC)	2	1	5	3	1	9	3	12	5.88 EM	50.00 EM
Ceramics (CE)	10	7	5	6	4	8	9	6	5.88 BM	37.50 BM
Basic Metals (BM)	5	12	8	2	2	2	7	9	6.38 MA	25.00 MA
Fabricated Metals (FM)	8	8	8	11	8	6	11	5	6.88 CE	12.50 CE
General Machinery (MA)	6	9	1	7	10	10	5	3	8.00 PI	12.50 PI
Electrical Machinery (EM)	4	3	1	8	11	12	6	2	8.13 FM	12.50 TX
Transport Equipment (TE)	3	4	1	4	5	11	2	1	8.38 TX	12.50 PP
Precision Instruments (PI)	11	5	1	12	12	7	8	8	9.13 PP	0.00 FM

(f) 1978 Rankings

	Net Subsidies	Net Transfers	Tax Relief	JDB Loans	Subsidized Borrowing	Tariffs	Quotas[a]	R&D Subsidies[b]	Average[c]	Count[d]
Food (FD)	1	2	5	7	7	1	1	10	4.25 FD	62.50 PC
Textiles (TX)	8	8	3	6	9	3	8	9	4.38 BM	62.50 TE
Paper & Pulp (PP)	11	10	4	8	5	4	10	12	4.75 TE	50.00 FD
Chemicals (CH)	6	7	10	2	3	5	3	4	4.75 PC	50.00 BM
Petroleum & Coal (PC)	2	1	10	3	1	6	4	11	5.00 CH	50.00 CH
Ceramics (CE)	9	6	10	5	4	7	9	6	6.50 EM	25.00 EM
Basic Metals (BM)	5	12	1	1	2	2	7	5	6.75 TX	25.00 TX
Fabricated Metals (FM)	10	9	1	10	8	9	10	8	7.00 CE	25.00 PP
General Machinery (MA)	7	11	6	11	11	10	5	3	8.00 PP	12.50 CE
Electrical Machinery (EM)	4	3	6	9	10	8	10	2	8.00 MA	12.50 MA
Transport Equipment (TE)	3	4	6	4	6	12	2	1	8.13 FM	12.50 FM
Precision Instruments (PI)	12	5	6	12	12	11	6	7	8.88 PI	0.00 PI

(g) 1984 Rankings

	Net Subsidies	Net Transfers	Tax Relief	JDB Loans	Subsidized Borrowing	Tariffs	Quotas[a]	R&D Subsidies[b]	Average[c]	Count[d]
Food (FD)	1	2	3	7	7	1	1	9	3.38 PC	75.00 PC
Textiles (TX)	10	7	4	9	10	2	8	8	3.88 FD	62.50 FD
Paper & Pulp (PP)	11	10	12	8	5	6	9	12	4.38 CH	50.00 CH
Chemicals (CH)	7	8	5	2	3	5	2	3	4.50 BM	50.00 BM
Petroleum & Coal (PC)	2	1	5	3	1	4	4	7	5.50 TE	50.00 TE
Ceramics (CE)	8	6	5	4	4	7	9	6	5.88 EM	25.00 EM
Basic Metals (BM)	5	12	1	1	2	3	7	5	6.13 CE	25.00 CE
Fabricated Metals (FM)	9	9	1	10	9	9	9	10	7.25 TX	25.00 TX
General Machinery (MA)	6	11	8	11	12	10	6	4	8.25 FM	12.50 FM
Electrical Machinery (EM)	4	5	8	5	6	8	9	2	8.50 MA	12.50 MA
Transport Equipment (TE)	3	3	8	6	8	12	3	1	9.13 PP	12.50 PI
Precision Instruments (PI)	12	4	8	12	11	11	5	11	9.25 PI	0.00 PP

TABLE 3.1 (h) 1990 Rankings

	Net Subsidies	Net Transfers	Tax Relief	JDB Loans	Subsidized Borrowing	Tariffs	Quotas[a]	R&D Subsidies[b]	Average[c]	Count[d]
Food (FD)	1	2	1	8	8	1	1	7	3.13 PC	87.50 PC
Textiles (TX)	11	4	1	9	10	2	8	9	3.63 FD	62.50 FD
Paper & Pulp (PP)	10	6	5	6	4	6	9	12	4.38 CH	50.00 CH
Chemicals (CH)	7	7	6	2	3	5	2	3	4.75 BM	50.00 BM
Petroleum & Coal (PC)	2	1	6	3	1	4	4	4	6.50 TE	37.50 TE
Ceramics (CE)	9	3	6	7	6	7	9	6	6.50 EM	37.50 EM
Basic Metals (BM)	6	10	3	1	2	3	5	8	6.63 CE	37.50 TX
Fabricated Metals (FM)	8	5	3	11	9	9	9	11	6.75 TX	12.50 CE
General Machinery (MA)	5	9	9	10	11	10	6	5	7.25 PP	12.50 PP
Electrical Machinery (EM)	3	12	9	4	5	8	9	2	8.13 FM	12.50 FM
Transport Equipment (TE)	4	11	9	5	7	12	3	1	8.13 MA	0.00 MA
Precision Instruments (PI)	12	8	9	12	12	10	7	10	10.00 PI	0.00 PI

A few examples should make this point more clearly. In 1955, the textiles sector had the highest tax relief (or lowest taxes), the second-highest effective rate of protection (tariffs), the third-highest level of JDB loans, and the fourth-highest rates of subsidized borrowing. It was clearly a favored sector in terms of these measures. Yet it fared poorly in terms of net transfers as a percent of output and not particularly better in terms of net subsidies. Or take the chemicals sector. Again, it was the second-highest sector in terms of tax relief, JDB loans, and subsidized rates of borrowing. It was also roughly advantaged in terms of tariffs, net subsidies, and R&D subsidies. Yet it did not do particularly well in terms of net transfers as a percent of output. Finally, of all the sectors, the allocations to the transport equipment sector seem the most advantageous in terms of consistency. It was certainly the sector with the highest effective rate of protection and the second-highest level of R&D subsidies, and its rankings for the other TIPs, while not topmost, were at least consistently fourth or fifth.

An examination of each of the eight years shows that this inconsistency is also true of all the other key years, and it is no doubt a good representation of the movement of TIPs at any given point in time. These assessments lead to a general one: The real world of Japanese TIPs was hardly coherent. This adds a further realistic complication to the task of establishing which sectors were more favored than others, a task that is tackled next.

Identifying Selection

The ranked distributions allow us to see which sectors were more or less favored by a TIP in a given year. But now we have to go a step further and establish which sectors were consistently more favored across all the TIPs and across the entire postwar period. To make things simple, we have to establish who got selected and who did not by using ordinal ranks.

Although by stressing "selection" and "nonselection" I force continuous variables into a dichotomy, the more important issue concerns defining these very terms. I will begin by using averages and counts as shown in Table 3.1 with the general idea that sectors that were most favored would consistently have higher levels of TIPs. First, averages refer to the mean of the rankings for each sector in a year, where 1 is the highest rank and 12 the lowest. To see how these averages compare across all the sectors, they are ranked in descending order (that is, from the highest average rank across all the sectors to the lowest average rank across all the sectors). In sectors that were more favorably selected, the average across all the TIPs should be higher (that is, closer to 1) than in those that were not selected. This is shown in Table 3.1 under "Average" for the eight years.

Second, because averages can be thrown off if there is a very large or small rank, it is also useful simply to count the number of TIPs that are highly favorable to a sector, and by highly favorable is specifically meant a rank of 4 or lower in any TIP category, thereby placing it in the top third range of selection. In sectors that were targets of preferential selection, there should consistently be more categories of TIPs having a rank of 4 or lower than those that were not. Again, this is shown in Table 3.1 under "Count" across all eight years.

Next to the key issue: What exactly constitutes a favored sector? I distinguish favored sector from nonfavored sector in the following way. A favored sector is one that has an average rank of 5 or below and/or at least 55 to 60 percent of the eight TIPs in its favor as indicated by a rank of 4 or below. Any sector not meeting these requirements is designated not favored. These are both, in my view, fairly generous cutoff points.[5] Despite these and other complications, a certain hierarchy emerges clearly among the twelve sectors, and it holds fairly consistently across the postwar years. Finally, then, Table 3.2 separates the twelve manufacturing sectors into those that were favored and those that were not by the key interval years between 1955 and 1990.

TABLE 3.2

Industrial Selection by Key Interval Years

(a) Immediate Postwar Era

	1955	1960	1966	1972
Selected[a]	Transport Equipment	Transport Equipment	Transport Equipment*	Transport Equipment*
	Chemicals	Chemicals	Chemicals	Petroleum & Coal*
	Textiles		Processed Food	Chemicals
	Petroleum & Coal		General Machinery	Basic Metals
	Basic Metals		Electrical Machinery	
	Electrical Machinery			
Not Selected[b]	Processed Food	General Machinery	Basic Metals	Processed Foods
	Ceramics	Precision Instruments	Petroleum & Coal	Electrical Machinery
	General Machinery	Basic Metals	Ceramics	General Machinery
	Precision Instruments	Electrical Machinery	Precision Instruments	Textiles
	Fabricated Metals	Petroleum & Coal	Textiles	Ceramics
	Paper & Pulp	Processed Food	Fabricated Metals	Fabricated Metals
		Textiles	Paper & Pulp	Precision Instruments
		Ceramics		Paper & Pulp
		Fabricated Metals		
		Paper & Pulp		

Most-Favored Sectors in Postwar Japan

What can we make of the evidence on the most-favored sectors? It is worth reflecting on the results in Table 3.2 in some detail, for they offer immense insight into the processes of industrial selection even at this level of aggregation. First, it is clear that the immediate postwar years involved reconstruction and recovery in basic sectors such as coal, steel, and chemicals. This comes across clearly in the sectors selected up to and including 1955. Some of the most-favored sectors in the late 1960s—chemicals, general machinery, electrical machinery, and transport equipment—were clearly those designated by MITI in its heavy and chemical industrialization "visions" for the 1960s. In general, such visions showcased the direction in which the government believed the Japanese industrial structure should be headed.

Second, the evidence on the most-favored sectors is remarkably stable. From virtually the beginning of postwar TIPs, both the transport equipment—which includes automobiles, aircraft, and shipbuilding—and the

TABLE 3.2 (b) After the First Oil Shock

	1973	1978	1984	1990
Selected[a]	Transport Equipment*	Transport Equipment*	Petroleum & Coal*	Petroleum & Coal*
	Petroleum & Coal*	Petroleum & Coal*	Processed Food*	Processed Food*
	Chemicals	Chemicals	Chemicals	Chemicals
	Processed Food	Processed Food	Basic Metals	Basic Metals
		Basic Metals		
Not Selected[b]	Electrical Machinery	Electrical Machinery	Transport Equipment	Transport Equipment
	Basic Metals	Textiles	Electrical Machinery	Electrical Machinery
	General Machinery	Ceramics	Ceramics	Ceramics
	Ceramics	Paper & Pulp	Textiles	Textiles
	Precision Instruments	General Machinery	Fabricated Metals	Paper & Pulp
	Textiles	Fabricated Metals	General Machinery	Fabricated Metals
	Fabricated Metals	Precision Instruments	Precision Instruments	General Machinery
	Paper & Pulp		Paper & Pulp	Precision Instruments

[a]To be designated to the "Selected" category, a sector must satisfy preferably both of the following conditions. First, it must have an unweighted rank average of roughly 5 or below, indicating that it was among the most heavily favored by the government. Second, it must have at least 55–60 percent of the eight TIPs in its favor, again indicating top government favoritism.

[b]Any sector not meeting the conditions for "Selected" is automatically designated to the "Not Selected" category.

*Definite selection.

chemicals sectors were consistently among the most-favored sectors. In fact, chemicals holds this advantage in every one of the eight years analyzed and was favored long after even the transport equipment sector lost its advantageous status in the early 1980s.[6]

Third, by the early 1970s TIPs were not moving completely in line with MITI's stated vision of promoting a knowledge-intensive industrial base. Although transport equipment and chemicals were definitely favored, electrical machinery, one of the most economically strategic of all sectors, was only selected briefly in the late 1950s and then again in the late 1960s and was clearly not among the most-favored sectors throughout much of the postwar period.

At this point, it would be useful to discuss how and in what ways information from different research methodologies can be combined in making final assessments about results. As case studies in the next chapter make clear, computers and semiconductors, both classified under electrical machinery, were strongly and consistently favored by MITI with a host of creative TIPs like research consortia and procurement policies. But this should not be taken to constitute a significant difference in the results, depending on the level of industrial aggregation used. After all, there is no denying that, even at the level of aggregation in this chapter, electrical machinery was selected and promoted at key points in time. And if all we were concerned with were semiconductors, it is important to know that the sector as a whole was among the most favored in the late 1960s, just at the time when the world semiconductor market was dominated by American producers.

This point about weaving together information from different levels of industrial aggregation can be better made with reference to another sector. Transport equipment, with industries such as shipbuilding, airplanes, and automobiles, was one of the most consistently favored sectors in the postwar period. So if the favoritism shown to shipbuilding, airplanes, and automobiles can be picked up at the aggregate level of the transport equipment sector, why is it so difficult to see a similar pattern emerging for (say, semiconductors or computers within) the electrical machinery sector? The sensible answer is that while it was selected for support, the electrical machinery sector has largely been left to its own fate.

Let us get back to the 1970s, as there are other patterns that need attention as well. Fourth, then, by the late 1970s there was an understandable need for continuing to protect and promote the petroleum and coal sector, but what is the justification for allocating TIPs to the basic metals and processed food sectors? Again, the subsequent qualitative evidence suggests that MITI has had a long institutionalized relationship with the steel industry and that potentially TIPs are locked into the fortunes and travails of this basic materials sector, which is still considered key to industrial activities and has great political power. What about the other sectors? Why may they have been selected? There is the chemicals sector, which received attention as an economically strategic sector up until the 1970s. Within it, however, petrochemicals have been undergoing structural adjustments because of the 1973 oil shock and have attracted a lot of government TIPs. Processed food is possibly even more politically volatile, having as it does links with the agricultural sector, which has been the mainstay of LDP support for much of the postwar era.

Let me sum up. The actions of the Japanese government demonstrate only too clearly that the real world of industrial selection or of allocating TIPs is highly complex. But there is enough evidence to suggest that for a good part of the early postwar era, the rhetorical visions of the Japanese state stressing the importance of the high-technology frontier have been matched by its actions. Economic criteria have potentially played a role, with political pressures perhaps having an effect or creeping in over time. But this is just speculation. To draw more definite conclusions, we have to determine the actual reasons for these selections, and this leads to results that end up complementing the econometric evidence from the previous chapter.

The Criteria for Selection

A brief summary here is useful. As the previous section shows, there can be little dispute that the Japanese government has subsidized and protected industrial sectors across eight measures of TIPs. But some sectors—specifically, chemicals, transport equipment, processed food, petroleum and coal, and basic metals—were clearly favored over others for much of the postwar period. What factors, if any, did these sectors have in common that led to their selection? And were such factors absent in the sectors that were not selected?

To begin to answer these questions systematically, we first need to examine the economic and political characteristics of the sectors that may determine their selection as hypothesized earlier. This section is in two main parts. The first part examines only the economic criteria across all sectors and uses them to establish a ranking of the most economically strategic sectors. The second part then turns to examine the political characteristics across the same sectors and ends with a ranking of the most politically influential sectors.

ECONOMIC CHARACTERISTICS BY SECTORS

This section will first briefly discuss the time series trends in the economic criteria across all twelve sectors, pointing out the relative performance of the sectors both before and after the first oil shock in 1973. It will then turn to determining the most economically strategic sectors. Again, the main procedure relies on an ordinal ranking of the economic criteria, with the basic goal of identifying sectors with the highest levels of growth, wages, value-added, and spillover potential. The criteria are averaged in five-year sets, which are then rank-ordered from 1 as the most economically strategic sector to 12 as the least economically strategic. Each of these five-year sets is prior to those eight representative years in which the TIPs were ranked in the previous section. The results are set out in Table 3.3.

Main Sectoral Trends

For growth rates, until about 1960 little seems to distinguish the sectors from each other, as all of them remained well below ¥2 trillion in terms of production levels. Yet the processed food and textiles sectors stand above the rest, and by 1960 their lead is clear. Only in 1971 did the processed food sector clearly relinquish its lead to the transport equipment sector, which had the highest output levels at the end of the period at around ¥11.7 trillion. The textiles sector did not show any remarkable increases, and by the mid

TABLE 3.3

Most Economically Strategic Sectors by Time Periods, 1955–90

(a) 1955–59

	Growth	Value Added	Wages	Spillover Potential	Average[a]	Count[b]	Top Economic Sectors[c]
Food (FD)	11	3	7	8	7.25	25	Transport
Textiles (TX)	12	2	12	6	8	25	equipment
Paper & Pulp (PP)	8	10	5	11	8.5	0	Chemicals
Chemicals (CH)	10	1	4	1	4	75	Basic metals
Petroleum & Coal (PC)	5	12	2	10	7.25	25	
Ceramics (CE)	9	8	9	7	8.25	0	
Basic Metals (BM)	7	4	1	3	3.75	75	
Fabricated Metals (FM)	6	9	11	12	9.5	0	
General Machinery (MA)	3	5	6	5	4.75	25	
Electrical Machinery (EM)	1	7	8	2	4.5	50	
Transport Equipment (TE)	2	6	3	4	3.75	75	
Precision Instruments (PI)	4	11	10	9	8.5	25	

In the ranked unweighted economic criteria, 1 represents the highest rank (i.e., most economically strategic sector) and 12 the lowest (i.e., least economically strategic sector). Economic criteria are lagged for five-year averages prior to each of the representative years appearing in Table 3.3, e.g., 1955–59 for 1960, etc.

[a]Unweighted average of ranks of economic criteria by sector (1 = most economically strategic sector).

[b]Number of economic criteria with ranks less than or equal to 4 as percentage of the total number of economic criteria by sector (100% = most economically strategic sector).

[c]To be designated a top economically strategic sector, a sector must possess at least 75% of the economic criteria with a rank between 1 and 4 and/or a rank average of 4 or lower across the criteria. In addition, it must possess an unweighted rank between 1 and 4 for spillover potential.

*Definite economically strategic sector, i.e., one in which all four criteria have a rank of 4 or lower.

(b) 1961–65

	Growth	Value Added	Wages	Spillover Potential	Average[a]	Count[b]	Top Economic Sectors[c]
Food (FD)	4	4	5	6	4.75	50	Transport equipment
Textiles (TX)	10	6	12	7	8.75	0	Chemicals
Paper & Pulp (PP)	7	10	7	11	8.75	0	
Chemicals (CH)	8	1	4	1	3.5	75	
Petroleum & Coal (PC)	1	12	1	12	6.5	50	
Ceramics (CE)	6	9	8	8	7.75	0	
Basic Metals (BM)	12	7	2	4	6.25	50	
Fabricated Metals (FM)	5	8	10	10	8.25	0	
General Machinery (MA)	11	2	6	5	6	25	
Electrical Machinery (EM)	9	3	11	2	6.25	50	
Transport Equipment (TE)	2	5	3	3	3.25	75	
Precision Instruments (PI)	3	11	9	9	8	25	

(c) 1967–71

	Growth	Value Added	Wages	Spillover Potential	Average[a]	Count[b]	Top Economic Sectors[c]
Food (FD)	11	5	10	6	8	0	Transport equipment
Textiles (TX)	12	6	12	9	9.75	0	Chemicals
Paper & Pulp (PP)	9	10	6	12	9.25	0	General machinery
Chemicals (CH)	8	3	3	2	4	75	Electrical machinery
Petroleum & Coal (PC)	3	12	1	11	6.75	50	
Ceramics (CE)	7	9	8	8	8	0	
Basic Metals (BM)	10	7	2	5	6	25	
Fabricated Metals (FM)	4	8	7	10	7.25	25	
General Machinery (MA)	1	2	5	4	3	75	
Electrical Machinery (EM)	2	1	11	1	3.75	75	
Transport Equipment (TE)	6	4	4	3	4.25	75	
Precision Instruments (PI)	5	11	9	7	8	0	

TABLE 3.3 (d) 1973–77

	Growth	Value Added	Wages	Spillover Potential	Average[a]	Count[b]	Top Economic Sectors[c]
Food (FD)	2	4	11	6	5.75	50	Transport equipment
Textiles (TX)	12	8	12	10	10.5	0	Chemicals
Paper & Pulp (PP)	6	10	6	12	8.5	0	
Chemicals (CH)	4	5	3	2	3.5	75	
Petroleum & Coal (PC)	1	12	1	11	6.25	50	
Ceramics (CE)	7	9	8	7	7.75	0	
Basic Metals (BM)	8	6	2	5	5.25	25	
Fabricated Metals (FM)	11	7	7	9	8.5	0	
General Machinery (MA)	10	2	5	4	5.25	50	
Electrical Machinery (EM)	9	1	10	1	5.25	50	
Transport Equipment (TE)	5	3	4	3	3.75	75	
Precision Instruments (PI)	3	11	9	8	7.75	25	

(e) 1979–83

	Growth	Value Added	Wages	Spillover Potential	Average[a]	Count[b]	Top Economic Sectors[c]
Food (FD)	7	4	11	7	7.25	25	Transport equipment*
Textiles (TX)	11	9	12	10	10.5	0	Chemicals
Paper & Pulp (PP)	8	10	6	12	9	0	General machinery
Chemicals (CH)	5	5	3	2	3.75	50	Electrical machinery
Petroleum & Coal (PC)	2	12	1	11	6.5	50	
Ceramics (CE)	9	8	8	8	8.25	0	
Basic Metals (BM)	12	6	2	5	6.25	25	
Fabricated Metals (FM)	10	7	7	9	8.25	0	
General Machinery (MA)	4	2	5	4	3.75	75	
Electrical Machinery (EM)	1	1	9	1	3	75	
Transport Equipment (TE)	3	3	4	3	3.25	100	
Precision Instruments (PI)	6	11	10	6	8.25	0	

(f) 1985–89

	Growth	Value Added	Wages	Spillover Potential	Average[a]	Count[b]	Top Economic Sectors[c]
Food (FD)	9	5	11	8	8.25	0	Transport equipment*
Textiles (TX)	11	9	12	11	10.75	0	Chemicals
Paper & Pulp (PP)	6	10	6	12	8.5	0	General machinery
Chemicals (CH)	7	4	2	2	3.75	75	Electrical machinery
Petroleum & Coal (PC)	12	12	1	10	8.75	25	
Ceramics (CE)	5	8	7	7	6.75	0	
Basic Metals (BM)	10	7	3	5	6.25	25	
Fabricated Metals (FM)	1	6	8	9	6	25	
General Machinery (MA)	3	2	5	4	3.5	75	
Electrical Machinery (EM)	2	1	10	1	3.5	75	
Transport Equipment (TE)	4	3	4	3	3.5	100	
Precision Instruments (PI)	8	11	9	6	8.5	0	

1960s it was taken over by four other sectors, namely electrical machinery, general machinery, basic metals, and chemicals. Compared to the perform-ance of these sectors, the remaining ones are characterized by slow growth performance, with the precision instruments sector starting and finishing at the lowest levels of growth. After the oil shock and for the remainder of the period under analysis, three sectors came to dominate the industrial pic-ture—transport equipment, electrical machinery, and processed food—all of which started off with a production level at approximately ¥10 trillion in 1973. In less than a decade, the electrical machinery sector took over the processed food sector in 1980 and the transport equipment sector in 1982. By 1983 and until the end of the period, it had the highest production lev-els, and between 1979 and 1990 it had the highest growth levels. In terms of production levels, the transport equipment sector was second, followed by the general machinery sector in the late 1980s. Both of these sectors also ex-hibited among the highest growth levels. The chemicals and basic metals sectors do not show any remarkable increases either in the production or growth levels, but whereas the basic metals sector went into a decline in the early 1980s, the production levels in the chemicals sector show an upward trend. The petroleum and coal sector experienced increased production lev-els in the early 1980s but declined for the rest of the period. Textiles, ceramics, and pulp and paper had among the lowest production levels, with precision instruments at the bottom of the pack.

For value-added levels, once again little distinguishes the sectors from one another, as they all registered values of under ¥500 billion until the early 1960s. But the chemicals sector began with a slight lead over all the other sectors, which it held roughly until 1967. Thereafter, the highest value-added levels were in the electrical machinery sector, followed by general machinery. In the period between 1967 and 1973, both of these sectors, as well as the transport equipment sector, experienced a sharp increase in their value-added levels in the magnitude of about 350 percent. The textiles sector, which began with the second-highest value-added level, very quickly dropped its lead to these rising sectors. The ceramics, pulp and paper, and precision instruments industries had relatively the lowest recorded value-added levels, with petroleum and coal standing consistently at the very bottom of the pack. After 1973, it is obvious that electrical machinery, transport equipment, and general machinery had the highest value-added levels, with electrical machinery having a substantial lead of about ¥5–7 trillion over even the other high value-added sectors. The processed food sector is the next highest sector in terms of value-added and was only overtaken by the chemicals sector in the mid 1980s. The remaining sectors did not exhibit any significant or sudden increases in value-added levels.

For wage levels, although there are clearly sectors with higher and lower wage levels, there is nothing startlingly outstanding about any one sector in particular, with the exception of the textiles sector. The textiles sector consistently had the lowest cash earnings of all other sectors, which averaged roughly about ¥18,000 until 1965 and about ¥60,000 until 1973. Comparatively also, the electrical machinery sector had among the lowest wages throughout this period. The top two high-wage sectors include petroleum and coal and basic metals, with average cash earnings that were roughly equivalent at ¥45,000 in the early to mid 1960s and an average of ¥87,000 until 1973. The next two high-wage sectors include the transport equipment and chemicals sectors. The remaining six sectors all had roughly equivalent levels and increases in their respective cash earnings across the period. After the oil shock, the top two high-wage sectors were petroleum and coal and basic metals, with average wages of around ¥350,000 in the mid 1980s, followed closely throughout the period by the chemicals sector. The transport equipment and general machinery sectors were next, with wages at around ¥320,000 in the mid 1980s, followed closely by pulp and paper. Interestingly, wages in the electrical machinery sector are indistinguishable from those in ceramics and precision instruments. Throughout this period, textiles had the lowest wages, and those in the processed food sector were only slightly higher.

For estimating the spillover potential, the earliest systematic data begin with the R&D figures from 1959 onward. From virtually the beginning, two sectors stand out and continue to do so until the first oil shock. These two sectors, electrical machinery and chemicals, consistently had the highest potential for spillovers. Until 1967, both of these sectors averaged ¥60 billion in R&D expenditures, which was well above the average of ¥20 billion for the remaining sectors. These two sectors experienced a sharp increase in their R&D expenditures in the late 1960s right up to 1973, with an increase of 167 percent in the electrical machinery and 112 percent in the chemicals sector. Around 1964, the transport equipment sector also began to show a consistent promise of spillovers, and by the late 1960s R&D expenditures in that sector increased sharply by about 156 percent. During this time, the general machinery and basic metals sectors also picked up their R&D expenditures and ended with an average lead of about ¥20 billion over the remaining seven sectors. During this same time period, these seven sectors averaged about ¥18–20 billion in R&D expenditures. There is little doubt that the electrical machinery sector had the greatest potential to provide any spillover benefits after the oil shock. R&D expenditures in this sector were substantially above every other sector, beginning with about ¥400 billion in 1973 and ending with around ¥3.2 trillion in 1990. The next two highest R&D intensive sectors, chemicals and transport equipment, which had roughly similar levels, did not even come close to this level of expenditure. General machinery did not exhibit any startling amounts or increases in its R&D expenditures. The remaining sectors averaged about ¥100–400 billion across the entire period.

Establishing the Most Economically Strategic Sectors

The economic measures discussed in the preceding section speak to the theoretical criteria deemed important in both the general strategic trade policy literature and the specific Japan-related works discussed in Chapter 1. Assuming that the measured criteria—that is, growth, value-added levels, wage levels, and R&D expenditures—are reasonable proxies for the theoretical ones, they will now be used to establish a hierarchy from economically strategic to economically nonstrategic sectors among all the twelve sectors.

Specifically, this will be achieved by rank-ordering the averages of the four economic criteria under six subperiods between 1955 and 1990. In other words, the economic criteria are lagged with respect to the years for which the selection is made: 1955–59 for 1960, 1961–65 for 1966, 1967–71 for 1972, 1973–77 for 1978, 1979–83 for 1984, and 1985–89 for 1990. Depending on how favorably endowed they are with levels of the economic criteria, the sectors are then rank-ordered from the most (1) to the least (12) economically strategic. To give an example: For the period 1955–59, we find that textiles was the slowest-growing sector with a rank of 12, and, conversely, electrical machinery was the fastest-growing sector with a rank of 1.

In order to determine the most economically strategic sectors, we have to see which of the twelve sectors was characterized most consistently by higher levels of the criteria in each of the time periods. But how high is high, and how low is low? This question shows the necessity of establishing a cutoff point for what constitutes an economically strategic sector, and this requires a defensible judgment call. I determined that to be designated an economically strategic sector, a sector must possess at least 75 percent of the criteria with a rank of between 1 and 4 and/or an average of 4 or lower across the criteria. Most important, since the quintessential defining feature of a strategic sector is its potential for technological spillovers, in addition to the features above, any designated sector must also possess a rank between 1 and 4 in the spillover potential criterion.

Table 3.3 shows how this leads to a ranked determination of the most economically strategic sectors, that is, transport equipment, chemicals, general machinery, and electrical machinery. These sectors correspond fairly well to our general understanding of what the economically strategic sectors have been in postwar reality.

For the purposes of this study, however, more important is the issue of whether these economic criteria actually played a role in the selection decision. We already know from the evidence on the most-favored sectors that only two of the topmost economically strategic sectors, namely chemicals and transport equipment, were consistently favored over the postwar period. The other two in the cohort, electrical and general machinery, enjoyed a very brief burst of selection and support through TIPs early in the postwar years. But before making any definitive conclusions, it is vital to turn to the political characteristics of the same twelve industries in order to more convincingly establish the general conditions under which TIPs have been allocated by the Japanese state.

POLITICAL CHARACTERISTICS BY SECTORS

To show that economic criteria were consistently important, for example, is not the same as proving that political ones must not have been. To make any sort of a general case, political variables also have to be examined at least as systematically. I now turn to evaluating the importance of the political characteristics of the same twelve industries that may also potentially have influenced the disbursement of TIPs.

This section will first briefly discuss the relative trends in the political characteristics of the twelve industries, again with attention to trends both before and after the first oil shock. Second, the focus will be on establishing the most politically influential sectors. As before, this will be done by rank-ordering the averages of five-year sets of the political criteria prior to the representative years in which the TIPs are ranked. The results are set out in Table 3.4.

Main Sectoral Trends

For votes potential, I focus on employment levels. In 1955, the textiles sector had the highest number of people employed, followed by the processed food sector, and textiles continued its dominant lead until the early 1970s. At the same time that the processed food sector stabilized and barely showed any growth in terms of employment during the period, both electrical machinery and general machinery experienced rapidly increasing employment levels in the late 1960s. The result was that general machinery was soon overtaken by the electrical machinery sector, which ended up at the highest position just before the first oil shock. Throughout this period, the transport equipment sector shows slow but steady increases in its employment levels, followed by the fabricated metals sector. The remaining six sectors all show either very modest increases or decreases (chemicals), with petroleum and coal consistently at the bottom. After the oil shock, with the obvious exception of the electrical machinery sector, almost all the sectors within this period show either stable or declining rates in the number of people employed. Among these, the textiles sector saw the most rapid decreases in its employment levels. The processed food, general machinery, and transport equipment sectors began with stable levels of employment that picked up slightly in the late 1980s. The remaining sectors are clumped together and generally also show steady but slightly increasing levels of employment, as in the ceramics sector. The petroleum and coal sector had by far the lowest rates of employment, which seem not to change at all.

For formal and informal institutional features that can potentially influence the selection process, we have *dantai* and *amakudari*. For *dantai*, there is a distinct pattern in terms of which sectors had more of them between 1955 and 1973 and therefore afforded more opportunities for influencing the allocation of TIPs either directly or through politicians. Two sectors dominated the total number, that is, the food sector, which had an estimated total of about sixty *dantai* in operation, followed closely by the textiles sector with about fifty-five. The next most noticeable sectors in this respect are the chemicals and the transport equipment sectors, both of which have roughly an equal number of about forty *dantai*, followed by the general machinery and basic metals sectors. All of the remaining sectors, including electrical machinery, averaged about ten to twelve *dantai* each. In the period after the oil shock, five sectors stand out distinctly in terms of total number of new *dantai* across the period. As before, the top position was held by the processed food sector, with an estimated nineteen new *dantai*. It was fol-

TABLE 3.4

Most Politically Influential Sectors by Time Periods, 1955–90

(a) 1955–59

	Votes	*Dantai*	*Amakudari*	Lobbying Contribu- tions	Average[a]	Count[b]	Top Political Sectors[c]
Food (FD)	2	3	—	9	4.67	66	Processed food
Textiles (TX)	1	1	—	6	2.67	66	Textiles
Paper & Pulp (PP)	10	10	—	5	8.33	0	Transport equipment
Chemicals (CH)	5	2	—	3	3.33	66	
Petroleum & Coal (PC)	12	12	—	—	12	0	
Ceramics (CE)	8	7	—	7	7.33	0	
Basic Metals (BM)	7	4	—	1	4	33	
Fabricated Metals (FM)	9	10	—	10	9.67	0	
General Machinery (MA)	3	5	—	8	5.33	33	
Electrical Machinery (EM)	6	8	—	4	6	33	
Transport Equipment (TE)	4	5	—	2	3.67	66	
Precision Instruments (PI)	11	8	—	—	9.5	0	

In the ranked unweighted political criteria, 1 represents the highest rank (i.e., most politically influential sector) and 12 the lowest (i.e., least politically influential sector). Political criteria are lagged for five-year averages prior to each of the representative years appearing in Table 3.3, e.g., 1955–59 for 1960, etc.

[a]Unweighted average of ranks of political criteria by sector (1 = most politically influential sector).

[b]Number of political criteria with ranks less than or equal to 4 as percentage of the total number of political criteria by sector (100% = most politically influential sector). Between 1955 and 1959, no data are available for *amakudari*, and therefore total number of criteria is taken as 3. Accordingly, in this case 66% of the political criteria qualifies for political influence.

[c]To be designated a most politically influential sector, a sector must possess at least 75% of the political criteria with a rank between 1 and 4 and/or a rank average of 4 or lower across the criteria. In addition, it must possess an unweighted rank between 1 and 4 for votes.

(b) 1961–65

	Votes	*Dantai*	*Amakudari*	Lobbying Contributions	Average[a]	Count[b]	Top Political Sectors[c]
Food (FD)	2	2	3	9	4	75	Processed food
Textiles (TX)	1	1	12	7	5.25	50	Electrical machinery
Paper & Pulp (PP)	10	11	11	5	9.25	0	
Chemicals (CH)	7	3	1	2	3.25	75	
Petroleum & Coal (PC)	12	12	7	—	10.33	0	
Ceramics (CE)	9	7	9	6	7.75	0	
Basic Metals (BM)	8	5	8	1	5.5	25	
Fabricated Metals (FM)	6	9	6	10	7.75	0	
General Machinery (MA)	3	5	5	8	5.25	25	
Electrical Machinery (EM)	4	7	3	4	4.5	75	
Transport Equipment (TE)	5	4	2	3	3.5	75	
Precision Instruments (PI)	11	9	9	—	9.67	0	

(c) 1967–71

	Votes	*Dantai*	*Amakudari*	Lobbying Contributions	Average[a]	Count[b]	Top Political Sectors[c]
Food (FD)	3	2	3	8	4	75	Processed food
Textiles (TX)	1	1	12	9	5.75	50	Electrical machinery
Paper & Pulp (PP)	10	12	10	5	9.25	0	
Chemicals (CH)	9	4	1	3	4.25	75	
Petroleum & Coal (PC)	12	10	7	—	9.67	0	
Ceramics (CE)	7	8	8	6	7.25	0	
Basic Metals (BM)	8	6	6	2	5.5	25	
Fabricated Metals (FM)	6	8	11	10	8.75	0	
General Machinery (MA)	4	5	4	7	5	50	
Electrical Machinery (EM)	2	7	2	4	3.75	75	
Transport Equipment (TE)	5	3	5	1	3.5	50	
Precision Instruments (PI)	11	10	8	—	9.67	0	

TABLE 3.4 (d) 1973–77

	Votes	*Dantai*	*Amakudari*	Lobbying Contributions	Average[a]	Count[b]	Top Political Sectors[c]
Food (FD)	3	2	3	7	3.75	75	Processed food
Textiles (TX)	1	1	10	11	5.75	50	Electrical machinery
Paper & Pulp (PP)	10	10	12	6	9.5	0	
Chemicals (CH)	9	4	2	4	4.75	75	
Petroleum & Coal (PC)	12	11	6	1	7.5	25	
Ceramics (CE)	7	7	8	8	7.5	0	
Basic Metals (BM)	8	5	11	3	6.75	25	
Fabricated Metals (FM)	6	9	9	12	9	0	
General Machinery (MA)	4	6	4	9	5.75	50	
Electrical Machinery (EM)	2	8	1	5	4	50	
Transport Equipment (TE)	5	3	5	2	3.75	50	
Precision Instruments (PI)	11	11	7	10	9.75	0	

(e) 1979–83

	Votes	*Dantai*	*Amakudari*	Lobbying Contributions	Average[a]	Count[b]	Top Political Sectors[c]
Food (FD)	3	1	3	7	3.5	75	Processed food
Textiles (TX)	2	2	12	11	6.75	25	Electrical machinery
Paper & Pulp (PP)	10	9	11	6	9	0	
Chemicals (CH)	9	4	2	4	4.75	75	
Petroleum & Coal (PC)	12	12	6	1	7.75	25	
Ceramics (CE)	7	7	10	8	8	0	
Basic Metals (BM)	8	6	9	3	6.5	25	
Fabricated Metals (FM)	6	9	7	12	8.5	0	
General Machinery (MA)	4	5	4	10	5.75	50	
Electrical Machinery (EM)	1	8	1	5	3.75	50	
Transport Equipment (TE)	5	3	5	2	3.75	75	
Precision Instruments (PI)	11	11	8	8	9.5	0	

(f) 1985–89

	Votes	Dantai	Amakudari	Lobbying Contributions	Average[a]	Count[b]	Top Political Sectors[c]
Food (FD)	4	1	4	7	4	75	Processed food
Textiles (TX)	2	2	11	11	6.5	50	Electrical machinery
Paper & Pulp (PP)	10	9	12	6	9.25	0	
Chemicals (CH)	8	4	2	3	4.25	75	
Petroleum & Coal (PC)	12	12	9	1	8.5	25	
Ceramics (CE)	7	7	8	8	7.5	0	
Basic Metals (BM)	9	6	7	4	6.5	25	
Fabricated Metals (FM)	6	9	9	12	9	0	
General Machinery (MA)	3	5	3	10	5.25	50	
Electrical Machinery (EM)	1	8	1	5	3.75	50	
Transport Equipment (TE)	5	3	5	2	3.75	50	
Precision Instruments (PI)	11	11	6	9	9.25	0	

lowed closely by the general machinery sector with eighteen; ceramics and textiles, both with seventeen; and transport equipment with thirteen. Both paper and pulp and chemicals saw an addition of only eight new *dantai* each, and again the electrical machinery was among the lowest-ranking sectors. It is also useful to note the total figures for the sectoral *dantai* across the entire period between 1955 and 1990. Overall, both the processed food and textiles sectors had a significant lead of about thirty to forty *dantai* over all the remaining sectors, thereby suggesting a greater, though by no means necessarily effective, lobbying voice as a whole through electorally sensitive politicians. In order, the next highest ranking sectors include transport equipment, chemicals, and general machinery, which had between forty and fifty *dantai* each. Finally, the remaining sectors, which are considerably below all the rest, all had an average of about twenty *dantai*.

For another potentially informal channel of political influence, we also have *amakudari*. Between 1955 and 1973, the highest total number of *amakudari* positions took place in the chemicals sector with an estimated 95 government officials approved for retirement in this sector, and the sector as a whole retained a substantial lead of about 15–20 such positions over even the next highest tier of industries. Within this tier, the sectors with an average of about 60–70 *amakudari* positions during the period are, in order, electrical machinery, transport equipment, processed food, and general machinery. Among the remaining sectors, petroleum and coal as well as basic metals barely stand out above the others. Interestingly, the textiles sector had the lowest number of *amakudari* positions identified. In the period after the oil shock, the most-coveted sector was clearly electrical machinery, for which 250 officials were approved for work between 1973 and 1990. The chemicals sector received the second-highest number of government officials estimated at around 200 people. Tied for third, the general machinery and the processed food sectors received 150 officials each. Next, the transport equipment sector stands out with about 100 approvals, but only in comparison to the remaining sectors, which received an average of 40–50 officials during the period. Total figures for *amakudari* between 1955 and 1990 also confirm the lead enjoyed by the electrical machinery sector, followed fairly closely by the chemicals sector, in terms of approved positions. While comparatively neither the chemicals nor the electrical machinery sector had high numbers of *dantai*, they do rank significantly above the remaining sectors in terms of *amakudari*. Overall, the next most conspicuous sectors are processed food and general machinery with roughly 200 approved *amakudari* positions, followed by the transport equipment sector with about 175 such positions. The remaining sectors all had less than or equal to 100 government officials approved for descent.

For estimated lobbying contributions, we have the lobbying power function. The lobbying power function estimations suggest that between 1955 and 1973 four sectors potentially contributed the highest yen amounts for TIPs. Among these, the basic metals sector is estimated to have been able to contribute the highest yen amount for TIPs from 1955 to the early 1960s. While its contributions were subject to downturns, it nevertheless still ended as the second-highest ranked contributor in 1973. The next highest contributor at the beginning of the period in 1955 is the transport equipment sector, which slowly but steadily emerged as the top-contributing sector by the end of the period. From the mid 1950s, three other sectors were also conceivably top lobbying contenders for government TIPs: chemicals, electrical machinery, and precision instruments. The chemicals sector peaked over all other sectors during the mid 1960s and emerged as the third-highest potential contributor in 1973. Electrical machinery is also distinct from the remaining sectors over the entire period, earning itself the fourth-highest position in the early 1970s. Precision instruments contributions peaked in 1962, and while slightly above all the other remaining sectors, its estimated contributions are virtually indistinguishable from the remaining sectors, which tend to clump together. Finally, the last thing that stands out clearly is that the fabricated metals contributed the least over the period. After the oil shock, the lobbying power function shows a similar pattern to the previous period but with the result that the petroleum and coal industry springs out from virtually nowhere to dominate the entire post-1973 pattern. Given the oil price shock in 1973, this pattern is perhaps understandable. If the extraordinary estimations of the petroleum and coal sector are taken out, the remaining eleven sectors exhibit roughly the same relative ranking as before. The transport equipment sector both begins and ends the period with the highest possible potential and power in terms of lobbying for favorable TIPs, followed by the chemicals and basic metals sectors. The electrical machinery sector is estimated to have been the next most powerful sector. The remaining sectors all clump together, again reminiscent of the previous period.

Establishing the Most Politically Influential Sectors

Politically influential sectors should be able to muster up more votes, more formal and informal means of pressuring the government, and greater yen donations or contributions for politicians. As discussed in Chapter 1, any so characterized sectors should see a greater number of TIPs moving in their favor, especially in a representative democracy.

The next task is to determine the relative political power of each sector and then to rank-order them from the most to the least influential sectors. As before, I use the average of five-year sets between 1955 and 1990 in six subperiods, that is, 1955–59 for 1960, 1961–65 for 1966, 1967–71 for 1972, 1973–77 for 1978, 1979–83 for 1984, and 1985–89 for 1990. Depending on the levels of the political criteria, all sectors are then rank-ordered from the most (1) to the least (12) politically influential. To give an example: For the period 1955–59, we find that textiles was the top sector in terms of vote potential with a rank of 1, and petroleum and coal the lowest with a rank of 12.

Using these rankings, we then have to determine which of the twelve sectors ranked as the most influential on the basis of all of the political criteria for a given time period. Once again, it is important to note that this procedure requires a judgment call on my part. I determined that to be designated a politically influential sector, a sector must possess at least 75 percent of the criteria with a rank of between 1 and 4 and/or an average of 4 or lower across the criteria. In addition to these characteristics, any such sector must also possess a rank of between 1 and 4 on the votes criterion, which is considered to be the most politically influential of all criteria.

Table 3.4 shows how this leads to a ranked determination of the most politically influential sectors that holds almost consistently throughout the entire period between 1955 and 1990. Given the stringent conditions for relative political power and the weight assigned to the employment/votes criterion, only two sectors emerge as being the most powerful, namely processed food and electrical machinery.

Finally, we turn to the issue of whether the political criteria played a role in the selection decisions over time or, more specifically, whether they affected the allocation of TIPs. The analysis in the previous section showed that transport equipment, chemicals, petroleum and coal, processed food, and basic metals were by and large the most consistently favored sectors throughout the postwar period. Based on the evidence here, only one of these sectors, processed food, was the most politically influential sector during the same period. Given the setup here, despite the importance accorded to the logic of political motivations, it appears to have had little sway in the selection decisions.

Rather than continuing to make broad generalizations that treat the economic and political hypotheses separately, the following section examines their effect in combination across six different sub-periods between 1955 and 1990. Although both political and economic factors come into play in the disbursement of TIPs in reality, this eclecticism is unsatisfying because to make any sort of argument for the dilemma of selection that has a bearing on development strategies, we have to know whether one mattered more than another. The following section shows that by breaking down the analysis of the TIPs and the two sets of criteria, the evidence supports the economic hypothesis comparatively more than the political one.

TIPs, Criteria, and the Rival Hypotheses

The first section in this chapter established the most-favored sectors by examining and rank-ordering eight TIPs in eight specific years between 1955 and 1990. The second section established the most economically strategic and most politically powerful sectors by examining and rank-ordering sets of appropriate criteria. In this final section, I put these two pieces of evidence together in an effort to ascertain whether, in keeping with my key research agenda, Japanese TIPs were determined overall by economic or political criteria for much of the postwar period.

An important consideration at this point is that of simultaneous causality between the criteria for selection and the TIPs. This means that if TIPs to a sector—such as to transport equipment—affect its economic performance in some way—say, increase in growth—then, in turn, the growth potentially affects the favorable disbursement of TIPs to the sector in question. For this reason, in the discussion of the economic and political criteria earlier, a great deal of emphasis was placed on lagging the criteria with respect to the TIPs. As the sets of criteria are lagged—that is, the successive rank-ordered sets of criteria are all prior to the eight years for the rank-ordered TIPs—we are in a position to be able to ascertain whether the criteria for selection at time $t-1$ had any effect on the TIPs at time t.

In moving from a description to a more sustained explanation, the emphasis on the overall should be borne in mind because, as the previous sections as well as the earlier econometrics chapter made clear, the reality of industrial selection is complex and nuanced. But this statement is both trivial and obvious, and stating it does not mean that the task of deriving something general should be abandoned in favor of heralding the complex. Moreover, the mere presence of complexity does not mean the absence of a pattern and should, at the very least, not deter us from seeking out and explaining some phenomenon of interest.

The primary focus below, then, is on understanding the general pattern under which TIPs have been allocated by the Japanese state by examining six five-year intervals immediately prior to 1960, 1966, 1972, 1978, 1984, and 1990. Ideally, criteria (or at least some of them) present in sectors that were selected should be absent in the ones that were not. Even more ideally, irrefutable evidence for the economic hypothesis would mean that selected industries be economically strategic but not politically influential and, conversely, irrefutable evidence for the political hypothesis would mean that selected industries be politically influential but not economically strategic.

At a secondary level, the concern is also to see what the pattern above, in turn, generally suggests about who—the bureaucrats or the politicians—ultimately controlled the allocation of TIPs. By putting together the information on the most-favored sectors and the criteria-endowed sectors across the same period as in Table 3.5, I am finally in a position to be able to provide solid and systematic evidence for or against the two hypotheses, both period by period and also overall.

Relation of 1955–59 Criteria to 1960 Industrial Selections

In retrospect, 1959 marked the beginning of the high growth rate period that was to cast its golden shadow for well over a decade. According to a MITI vision, the 1960s were designated the era for the promotion of development of heavy and chemical industries, namely heavy machinery and petrochemicals. The evidence in 1960 suggests clearly that only transport equipment and chemicals were the most-favored sectors in terms of being the recipients of the highest levels of government TIPs. This confirms the findings in the qualitative evidence where these two sectors—more specifically, sub-sectors within them such as shipbuilding, automobiles, aircraft, and petrochemicals—received great attention from the MITI bureaucrats during the designated heavy and chemical industrialization drive throughout the 1950s and 1960s. There is little doubt that these sectors were selected on the basis of economic criteria, with a view to industrial restructuring and long-term economic welfare. Both of them were marked by some of the highest value-added levels and, more important, showed among

TABLE 3.5

Relation of Criteria to Industrial Selection by Key Time Periods, 1955–90

(a) Relation of 1955–59 Criteria to 1960 Selections

	Economically Strategic		Politically Influential	
	Yes	No	Yes	No
Selected	Transport Equipment Chemicals	—	Transport Equipment	Chemicals
Not Selected	Basic Metals	Processed Food Petroleum & Coal General Machinery Electrical Machinery Textiles Ceramics Fabricated Metals Precision Instruments Paper & Pulp	Processed Food Textiles	Basic Metals Petroleum & Coal General Machinery Electrical Machinery Ceramics Fabricated Metals Precision Instruments Paper & Pulp

(b) Relation of 1961–65 Criteria to 1966 Selections

	Economically Strategic		Politically Influential	
	Yes	No	Yes	No
Selected	Transport Equipment* Chemicals	Processed Food General Machinery Electrical Machinery	Processed Food Electrical Machinery	Transport Equipment* Chemicals General Machinery
Not Selected	—	Basic Metals Petroleum & Coal Textiles Ceramics Fabricated Metals Precision Instruments Paper & Pulp	—	Basic Metals Petroleum & Coal Textiles Ceramics Fabricated Metals Precision Instruments Paper & Pulp

*Definite selection.

(c) Relation of 1967–71 Criteria to 1972 Selections

	Economically Strategic		Politically Influential	
	Yes	No	Yes	No
Selected	Transport Equipment* Chemicals	Petroleum & Coal* Basic Metals	—	Transport Equipment* Chemicals Petroleum & Coal* Basic Metals
Not Selected	General Machinery Electrical Machinery	Processed Food Textiles Ceramics Fabricated Metals Precision Instruments Paper & Pulp	Processed Food Electrical Machinery	General Machinery Textiles Ceramics Fabricated Metals Precision Instruments Paper & Pulp

(d) Relation of 1973–77 Criteria to 1978 Selections

	Economically Strategic		Politically Influential	
	Yes	No	Yes	No
Selected	Transport Equipment* Chemicals	Processed Food Petroleum & Coal* Basic Metals	Processed Food	Transport Equipment* Chemicals Petroleum & Coal* Basic Metals
Not Selected	—	Electrical Machinery General Machinery Textiles Ceramics Fabricated Metals Precision Instruments Paper & Pulp	Electrical Machinery	General Machinery Textiles Ceramics Fabricated Metals Precision Instruments Paper & Pulp

TABLE 3.5 (e) Relation of 1979–83 Criteria to 1984 Selections

	Economically Strategic		Politically Influential	
	Yes	No	Yes	No
Selected	Chemicals	Processed Food* Petroleum & Coal* Basic Metals	Processed Food*	Chemicals Petroleum & Coal* Basic Metals
Not Selected	Transport Equipment General Machinery Electrical Machinery	Textiles Ceramics Fabricated Metals Precision Instruments Paper & Pulp	Electrical Machinery	Transport Equipment General Machinery Textiles Ceramics Fabricated Metals Precision Instruments Paper & Pulp

(f) Relation of 1985–89 Criteria to 1990 Selections

	Economically Strategic		Politically Influential	
	Yes	No	Yes	No
Selected	Chemicals	Processed Food* Petroleum & Coal* Basic Metals	Processed Food*	Chemicals Petroleum & Coal* Basic Metals
Not Selected	Transport Equipment General Machinery Electrical Machinery	Textiles Ceramics Fabricated Metals Precision Instruments Paper & Pulp	Electrical Machinery	Transport Equipment General Machinery Textiles Ceramics Fabricated Metals Precision Instruments Paper & Pulp

the greatest promises in terms of spillover potential for the benefit of the rest of the economy. Although basic metals is also among the most economically strategic of sectors, it lost its most-favored status during the 1960s in which the bulk of government TIPs continued to go to chemicals and heavy machinery.

Alternatively, transport equipment also exhibits political characteristics that could have been influential in the selection decisions. Yet this point is unconvincing, for if the logic of political motivations applied in the disbursement of TIPs in this period, it should have applied with even greater force in the case of two far more politically powerful sectors, namely textiles and processed food. Neither of these two sectors commanded the bulk of the TIPs, which continued to go to the sectors designated by the MITI bureaucrats as worthy of attention.[7]

Relation of 1961–65 Criteria to 1966 Industrial Selections

As in the previous period, in 1966 both transport equipment and chemicals continued their most-favored status, and their ranks were joined by processed food, general machinery, and electrical machinery. Very clearly, the bulk of the resources were still being concentrated by the bureaucrats precisely in accordance with their vision of a chemical and heavy industrialization drive.

In the early 1960s, processed food, electrical machinery, and general machinery were not economically strategic, yet they were key targets of selection. At first reading and, certainly in post hoc inference, it is all too easy to make the case that because intervention occurred and both the electrical and general machinery sectors became economically competitive worldwide, the TIPs to these sectors must not only have been motivated by economic criteria but must also have caused the marked success in these industries globally. While nothing can be said on the specific issue of causality between TIPs and eventual competitiveness, the evidence at the time that these decisions were being made definitively supports the viewpoint that strategic economic criteria played a major role in the selection decision. Of the five most-favored sectors, four—transport equipment, chemicals, general machinery, and electrical machinery—exhibited particularly the promise of great technological change as evidenced by the spillover criterion.

Two of the five sectors—processed food and electrical machinery—were also among the most politically influential sectors, though as before it is hard to make a pressing case for the political angle. First, processed food no doubt enjoyed a most-favored status simply because of its link with the agricultural sector, which has been the mainstay of LDP support for much of the postwar era and as such has enjoyed the same highly protected position as it does in other OECD countries. The processed food sector is actually under the jurisdiction of the Ministry of Agriculture, Forestry, and Fisheries (MAFFA).[8] Second, electrical machinery, which started out as being politically influential and remained so for much of the postwar period in terms of vote potential, has far more in common with other economically strategic sectors than it does with politically influential ones. For this reason, its brief selection in the 1960s is undoubtedly due to its economic characteristics as it fit the bureaucratic vision of the times.

Relation of 1967–71 Criteria to 1972 Industrial Selections

The 1970s were designated as the era of promoting the development of knowledge-intensive industries but were also labeled the transition period due most notably to the first oil shock in 1973. The selections in 1972 that are identical to those in 1973 suggest that while both transport equipment and chemicals continued their most-favored status, they are also joined by the basic metals and petroleum and coal sectors. None of these sectors was politically influential, and the latter two even less so than the former two. What, then, explains their selection?

As before, there is little doubt that transport equipment and chemicals were selected for their economic characteristics, and especially for their benefits for the rest of the economy. The stories of the other two sectors are more nuanced and also show that a quantitative analysis needs to be supplemented with some understanding of the historical and institutional legacies that are not readily apparent otherwise.

Basic metals, for instance, does not emerge influential in terms of the quantitative political variables identified in this study, though in interviews officials deem it one of the most politically powerful sectors in Japan. The same qualitative evidence also suggests that the steel industry is a proven historical favorite of MITI, and is still widely considered basic to national economic security. The quantitative variables used in this study do not pick up such historical and institutional angles as well as the case studies do. That knowledge, however, becomes useful in the interpretation here. In the early 1970s, the basic metals sector found a great number of TIPs moving in its favor just as the start of an impending downturn in the worldwide steel industry was taking shape. At that point, the interests of both the politicians and the bureaucrats converged for entirely different reasons, the former motivated by an electoral logic and the latter by the desire to support steel's designated status as a basic sector. Given its designated status in the industrial economy, there were other sound economic arguments for its continued support, some of which come across more convincingly in the qualitative analyses.

The petroleum and coal sector also found itself the object of vigorous TIPs in the early 1970s and retained this favored position both because of the shift from coal to oil as an energy source and the oil price shock in 1973. Given Japan's crucial dependence on oil as an advanced industrial economy and its continued lack of domestic raw energy sources, the support for this sector also was clearly motivated out of a basic need for economic self-preservation—a fact, once again, on which both politicians and bureaucrats could agree.

Finally, two of the most politically powerful sectors at the time—electrical machinery far more than processed food—were not selected for support. As in the previous era, both in terms of the selections made and not made, it is difficult, on the basis of quantitative evidence alone, to see the overwhelming logic of political motivations to the selection decisions overall.

Relation of 1973–77 Criteria to 1978 Industrial Selections

While the 1970s had been proclaimed the era of promoting knowledge-intensive industries, the actual disbursement of TIPs shows virtually no striking change in this direction. More important, the electrical machinery sector, which had been the subject of a great deal of attention—and particularly one of its subindustries, semiconductors, which is at the heart of a revolution in knowledge-intensive industries—did not at any time in the postwar era enjoy the overwhelming and unqualified support across the eight TIPs that it is widely assumed to have enjoyed. The one exception is in R&D subsidies, in which this sector was consistently the second-highest recipient after the transport equipment sector. In fact, the evidence suggests that apart from the brief burst of wholehearted support in the late 1960s, this sector as a whole was largely left to cope on its own, despite its tremendous spillover potential. Once again, the information from the case studies proves useful in the interpretation. Some of the key industries in this classification—such as computers and semiconductors—were the beneficiaries of quite a few creative TIPs, such as funded research and guaranteed markets from public institutions. In addition, the timing is important, for this sector as a whole was promoted briefly at a time when Japanese firms were just beginning to compete in key electronic industries with American ones.

As before, transport equipment and chemicals appear to have been selected overwhelmingly because of economically strategic characteristics in this setup. But the case studies again remind us that petrochemicals, which was an industry under MITI's jurisdiction, also ran into structural problems because of the first oil shock, and this generated enormous political pressures for relief.[9] As for the whole of chemicals, we are also reminded through the case studies that MITI shares jurisdiction with both MAFFA and the Ministry of Health and Welfare (MHW), and not all of the selection at this aggregate level can be attributed solely to MITI.

Also as before, basic metals and petroleum and coal continued to enjoy support, for the same reasons as described in the previous era. The only change was that processed food, again for reasons described earlier, returned as one of the most-favored sectors. It is the only one of the selected sectors that is politically powerful, and once again the argument for political motivations behind TIP disbursement remains weak, as the only other equally politically powerful sector, electrical machinery, did not enjoy any support at all. This potentially points more to the institutional differences between MAFFA and MITI, with the former more open to political influences. In comparison, political factors appear not to have had a consistent effect on the disbursement of MITI's TIPs overall.

Relation of 1979–83 Criteria to 1984 Industrial Selections

The 1980s were designated the era of building a more knowledge-intensive industrial structure through creativity, which referred, in addition to the emphasis on the previous decade's vision, to a further focus on the burgeoning field of information technology. Yet in actuality, little was different.

The disbursement of TIPs changed relatively little over the five-year interval. Virtually all the sectors that had been selected almost consistently over the previous three decades—chemicals, processed food, petroleum and coal, and basic metals—continued their most-favored status for the same economic reasons as before. The chemicals sector continued to be characterized by its potential widespread benefits to the rest of the economy, though once again MITI's jurisdiction over only one part of the whole industry as well as the political pressures from the petrochemicals industry should be kept in mind. Both processed food and petroleum and coal experienced a tremendous change toward even more favorable TIPs to themselves than in the previous period, and basic metals also continued to enjoy its advantageous TIPs.

The one major change was that transport equipment lost its most-favored status during this period, just at the time the Japanese automobile industry became the number one producer in the world. This provides evidence of TIP withdrawal, which MITI officials stress in the interest of international competitiveness. It is important to note that this withdrawal or deselection takes place in a sector characterized by some of the highest growth, value-added, wages, and spillover levels. Interestingly enough, this change also came at a time when the transport equipment sector as a whole could boast considerable political clout in influencing the allocation of TIPs to itself. As before, a similar disregard is shown for the political influence potentially exercised by the electrical machinery sector. All of this suggests that MITI did, in fact, make its decisions largely on the basis of an economic logic and remained fairly impervious overall to political influences, as claimed by its officials in the interviews.

Relation of 1985–89 Criteria to 1990 Industrial Selections

The selections in 1990 are identical to the one immediately before, and only a few essential points need be added. The cases studies show how the chemicals sector, and particularly petrochemicals as a highly energy intensive sector, ran into severe structural problems largely as a result of the two oil shocks. Yet it is worth noting that, at least on the basis of almost all the theoretical criteria, chemicals emerges as one of the most economically strategic sectors and as the last of the most-favored ones in its cohort. Basic metals and particularly processed food and petroleum and coal continued to enjoy vigorous government support. As a result, the conclusions about the economic and political hypotheses that applied to the previous era apply equally to this time period.

One final comment is necessary. If the case for the economic hypothesis is strong, it lies uneasily in face of the fact that only one of the four economically strategic sectors was consistently selected for support. This accords (as explained more fully later) with the MITI officials' emphasis on selecting and then deselecting sectors to ensure competitiveness, a pattern that fits the most economically strategic sectors particularly well. All of them—electrical machinery, general machinery, transport equipment, and chemicals—were selected and then, with the exception of chemicals, deselected in succession. Unlike the very massive and concentrated selection in earlier times, only one or two kinds of TIPs continued to be slanted in their favor. R&D subsidies continued unabated to the top four economically strategic sectors well into the 1990s and well above those to all the remaining sectors in the manufacturing range. In addition, research consortia also continued to be organized by the government in these sectors.

Alternatively, the political hypothesis that both votes and campaign contributions, or even informal channels of influence, had a tremendous impact on the allocation of TIPs to particular sectors can once again be rejected. Only processed food had the kind of political influence that was potentially influential in the disbursement of TIPs. However, electrical machinery, under MITI's jurisdiction, was equally politically influential, and at no time did it enjoy the kind of advantageous TIPs that processed food, under MAFFA's control, did.

Summing Up the Evidence on the Structured Data Analysis

What does this second round of empirical evidence suggest about the logic of industrial selection in postwar Japan? There is comparatively more evidence in favor of the economic hypothesis, which points to the role of economic criteria as the main determining factor in MITI's industrial selections. Conversely, the same evidence discounts the importance of the alternative hypothesis that stresses the relative political power of different industries as the major explanation for the allocation of TIPs. Not only is there greater weight to the economic hypothesis for more than four decades, there is also the important fact that MITI consistently selected the same sectors across the postwar period, namely chemicals, basic metals, petroleum and coal, and transport equipment. The stability in terms of these industrial selections is stunning given the enormous changes in the global and domestic political economy. And this is a point of no small consequence.

In the mid 1970s, it was clear that Japan had entered a new era. International and domestic changes had begun in the 1960s, but their effects did not materialize until the 1970s. In 1960, the government announced the Plan for Trade and Foreign Exchange Liberalization, which helped to free imports from the old system of licenses and foreign exchange quotas and which also meant the bureaucracy lost a great deal of tangible leverage in order to intervene in the private sector. Pressures for trade liberalization increased also as Japan joined several international institutions, the General Agreement on Tariffs and Trade (GATT) in 1955 and both the International Monetary Fund (IMF) and the OECD in 1964. Further, the Tokyo Round had begun earlier in 1973 in the midst of the first oil shock, a deep worldwide recession, and rising protectionism. One of the principal outcomes of the six and a half years of negotiations under this round of the GATT was the reduction of tariffs on manufactured goods. Throughout much of the early 1970s, the importance of tariffs and quotas diminished as tangible instruments of TIPs, and, astonishingly, Japan ended up with lower average tariff levels than both the United States and the European Union (EU) in the early 1980s.[10] From the point of view of industrial selections, MITI ended up with both a limited set of policy tools at its disposal and a manufacturing base that was becoming weaker in some traditional sectors and dynamic in those hailed as the wave of the future.

There were also other notable differences and significant problems. After the "Nixon shock" in 1971, the world monetary regime moved from a fixed, dollar-gold monetary regime to a managed, flexible-rate monetary regime by 1973. Between 1973 and 1974, the price of oil quadrupled. Domestically, due to a mismanagement of domestic monetary policy, the inflation rate increased to 30 percent, and nominal wages increased by 50 percent. The unemployment rate doubled, and for the first time Japan faced negative real-growth rates.[11] As the qualitative evidence makes clear as well, because of the yen appreciation and oil price hikes, many (heavy) industries that were highly dependent on imported oil and/or exports began to face severe structural problems. These problems became even more disruptive due to a steep yen appreciation between 1977 and 1978, the second oil shock in 1979–80, and the Plaza Agreement in 1985. The late 1970s also witnessed the beginning of the relative economic decline of the United States, which had serious repercussions for industrial selection in Japan. Against these burgeoning problems in the international economy, Japan became a particular focus of attention in the United States. Americans criticized the seemingly chronic Japanese trade surplus, the industrial structure in Japan, the intransigence of the Japanese bureaucracy, and particularly Japanese TIPs in high-technology industries. All of these factors, the argument went, and especially the role of MITI, created an "unfair" playing field for Japan's advanced industrial competitors, both in the United States and the EU.[12]

Despite the changes in the 1970s and 1980s, the trends in industrial selection remained stable. The fact that there were obvious and visible changes in both the international environment and the industrial structure somehow appeared to have no effect on the relative disbursement of TIPs, especially to chemicals, basic metals, petroleum and coal, and to some extent transport equipment. What accounts for this astonishing stability in industrial selections, and how does it fit in with the rest of the postwar selections? As the structured data analysis here shows, the evidence at successive slices in time favors the economic hypothesis over the political one. But it also reveals a subtle pattern in the method of selection and deselection—a central but little understood feature of Japan's industrial policy.

By 1955, transport equipment, chemicals, textiles, and electrical machinery had all also been definitively selected. Textiles is the one sector that almost immediately lost its most-favored status, although it ranked consistently high in terms of tariff protection and, as discussed in the next chapter, continued to inspire very specific and ostentatious legislation led by the politicians. Despite its topmost political power in terms of sheer votes, it never regained its favored status for the rest of the postwar period. It largely found itself out of favor by the mid 1960s, and its deselection went almost hand in hand with its demise. A strong case can be made that, despite the political pressures, as soon as the comparative advantage in textiles began to shift elsewhere, so did the actual TIPs to this sector. The only politically influential sector that was consistently selected from the late 1970s onward was processed food, and it was characterized by the highest levels of votes as well as organized *dantai*. But processed food is under the jurisdiction of MAFFA, not MITI, and is also the sole domestic market for agriculture that is as protected and shielded in Japan as in other OECD countries.

Transport equipment, chemicals, general machinery, and electrical machinery have been the quintessential economically strategic sectors, characterized almost consistently from the immediate postwar period onward by the highest growth rates, highest value-added levels, and the greatest potential for technological change that stood to spill over into the rest of the economy. If any sectors deserved to be selected purely for economic reasons, these were the ones. Were they selected by the Japanese state, specifically MITI? The answer is a resounding yes.

Their selection began as early as the mid 1950s, well in advance of the MITI vision for the 1960s that emphasized the promotion of the development of heavy and chemical industries. In 1955, three of the four sectors—transport equipment, chemicals, and electrical machinery—were among the most-favored sectors. Relative to the other sectors, they were commended almost equally by their economic characteristics. Although the transport equipment sector was also politically influential at the time of the selections, it had far more in common with the other strategic sectors, electrical machinery and chemicals, than with the only other politically influential one selected at the time, textiles. But even as it became clear that both the general and electrical machinery sectors would go on to change the industrial face of Japan, they were deselected fairly fast and left largely to their own fates. Transport equipment similarly lost its most-favored status by the early 1980s in terms of tangible selection. Its cohort, chemicals, was the last of the most-favored sectors, with jurisdictional rivalries, structural adjustment concerns, and economic considerations such as knowledge-intensity leading to a continued emphasis on selection.[13]

To sum up, the evidence on the industrial selections favors the economic hypothesis and tallies nicely with the version of events that the MITI officials give in the next chapter. But while MITI may well have had the upper hand in allocating TIPs, particularly up until the 1980s, it chose not to deploy them as heavily as it could have. Here is what the evidence shows: If no politically powerful sector was ever able to capture the allocation of TIPs, it is also equally true that no economically strategic sector could boast the same for long. Both of these assertions hold across the postwar period, and, with the sole exception of petroleum and coal and basic metals, TIPs did not get locked for good into any one sector. In other words, there is a fairly stable selection and deselection pattern.

Some suggest that even with the demise of hard or tangible TIPs, selection continues to favor the strategic sectors. In fact, MITI officials do not deny that acquisition of key technology niches is of keen concern for the very survival of the Japanese industrial structure. Irrespective of any friction that it may spark with the outside world, a host of creative TIPs still continue to go to designated industries like semiconductors, aircraft, and now space. But even in these industries, as a newly reorganized Agency for Industrial Science and Technology (AIST) maintains, the concern is with providing timed TIPs, selecting then deselecting, in order to ensure competitiveness in international markets. This single point cannot be stressed enough where industrial strategies are concerned, and it takes on added importance considering the speed and volatility of technological changes.

In the aggregate, then, the evidence suggests that MITI supported winners. But more important, having given them a gentle push down the learning curve, it also knew when to start letting them grow up on their own.
Whatever else it may or may not be credited with doing well, this broad pattern of selections and deselections across all the industries and much of the
postwar period is commendable at an aggregate level. As I will argue in the
end, this emphasis on deselection needs to be an integral part of our thinking on industrial strategies at a general theoretical level.

But before coming to any definite conclusions about the uncovered patterns, we need to assess how and in what ways the quantitative evidence tallies with the realities of policy choices across industries and over time. To do
this, we turn next to the historical and more detailed information in case
studies.

CHAPTER 4

Criteria and Perceptions in
Historical Perspective

IN CHAPTERS 4 and 5, the focus will be on using case studies that allow us to assess historical and perceptual concerns in Japanese industrial selections over the same postwar period as in the quantitative analyses. In both
chapters, I take a close look at the actual economic and political considerations that affect government choices across industries and over time. Examining the flow of decisions in one industry allows us to assess the validity of
the hypothesized criteria for selection in the real world, and specifically at
MITI, which has had jurisdiction over almost all the industries under examination here. By then comparing the criteria or factors in one industry with
the rest, I seek to establish whether there has been a general logic behind industrial selections in Japan.

What is the merit of this approach? Although even case studies and interviews cannot ultimately do justice to the richness of reality, they are a
necessary step in showing what happened and, perhaps more important,
what was thought or perceived, with some degree of historical accuracy.
Even if disdained by the quantitatively minded, these research techniques are
the only way to find out the actual motivations behind policy-makers' decisions to favor industries. This solid descriptive analysis is, in any event, better than a bad explanation or facile efforts at causal inference.[1] By forcing us
also to contend with details and complexity in the real world, this method
brings its own kind of rigor to the inference process and, in doing so, warns
against superficial generalizations. In fact, having examined the particular
gives us more credence in interpreting the general. The emphasis on industry cases and interviews does not mean that this approach is any the less systematic, however. By keeping a clear focus on the dependent and independent variables across very different cases, we can get clear results that facilitate
the chain of inference in this book.[2]

The remainder of this chapter consists of three major parts. The first part briefly sets out the research strategy, discussing the industry cases as well as the sources used to gather information on the criteria for selection. The second part examines each of the ten cases in more detail, focusing on assessing the rival hypotheses. The final part sums up the evidence. It shows how the complexities evident in interpreting the earlier quantitative approaches resonate in the results from this method as well. But here also we find evidence that comparatively favors the economic hypothesis over the political one and especially points to the criteria of spillovers and linkages as having a very important influence on initial selection processes.

Research Strategy

CASES

To shed light on the logic of industrial selection in Japan using qualitative approaches, I use two sets of case-study results in the final empirical chapters. First, in this chapter, I focus on analyzing ten industry cases that have been widely studied by Japan scholars, though never with a direct emphasis on the criteria for selection. The sectors, which fall under the broader industry categories at the two-digit SITC level used in the quantitative analyses, are coal, steel, textiles, petrochemicals, shipbuilding, automobiles, machine tools, computers, semiconductors, and aircraft.[3] Why these industries? Taken together they represent a sample of industries with very different characteristics that do not remain constant even within the same industry over time. Taken in succession, these industries also represent macro-shifts in the Japanese industrial structure from the immediate postwar era to the present. By examining these different cases over time, we can determine both general and specific factors motivating the government TIPs in a historical setting.

Second, in the next chapter, I bring the issue of industrial selection up to date in Japan by providing a more detailed case study of the commercial space launch industry. Launch vehicle capabilities are crucial for placing military, civilian, and commercial payloads in orbit and as such constitute one of the stated pillars of Japan's space program. As a whole the $50 billion launch industry represents one of the major, cutting-edge strategic sectors of the twenty-first century. The dominant players in this global industry are the United States and the European Union, with China, Russia, and India emerging as contenders or collaborators with the big two. Japan also has made serious efforts to break into the global competition. Despite many tangible failures and setbacks, as well as the increasingly pivotal role of the private rather than the public sector, this industry continues to attract attention from the Japanese government. As before, the key issue will be to determine what criteria, beliefs, and perceptions are driving the favoritism, irrespective of success or failures in terms of outcomes. Surprisingly, despite the basic importance of this industry, there are virtually no case studies on the subject, and certainly none that assesses the industry in the context of theoretically informed works.

With the exception of the space launch industry, all the other industries have been closely scrutinized by Japan scholars and have become the basis for many generalizations about the Japanese political economy at large. As a result there is an enormous wealth of details on Japanese TIPs in each industry case, including creative intervention measures that defy quantification. Fortunately, this simplifies my task here in that I do not have to go searching for primary evidence on TIPs but can use the existing evidence in the present research agenda.

FILLING A LACUNA

Unfortunately, however, the existing works do not do a systematic job of telling us why the Japanese state disburses TIPs the way it does—that is, the logic behind industrial selection. To put it simply, we can extract the TIPs deemed important easily enough but not really the criteria by which they moved. That is the lacuna I seek to fill here. My goal, to be clear at the outset, is not to replicate the many excellent studies that focus on the politics and policy of TIPs in the industry cases below but merely to add the dimension of the criteria for selection to each one of them. In the conclusion to the book, I will turn to highlighting the informational, organizational, and ideological context within which TIPs have been carried out, but here I focus strictly on the narrow agenda of assessing the rival hypotheses.

It is important to know at the outset that official documents tend to be sketchy on the specific criteria, if forthcoming at all. To give a typical recent example: Alluding to the importance of spillovers and linkages as criteria, a MITI white paper, "National Strategies for Industrial Technology," in 2000 stresses government support in priority or strategic sectors that seem likely to have a "wave effect" in many industrial technology fields.[4] Looking back at the early postwar period, some claim that the thinking moved from general economic concerns in the early postwar years to more specific (though hardly consistent) criteria like high-income elasticity of demand and/or high productivity later on.[5] In fact, MITI documents state that the ministry did use the criteria of rising productivity and income elasticity in industrial policy at a broad level.[6] Although such criteria were to find their way into other official MITI documents, such as the "visions" announced by the Industrial Structure Council that pointed toward desirable movements in the industrial structure for Japan, they appear to justify the TIPs only in retrospect.[7] Others also lent their voice to this skepticism, pointing out that any such criteria also happened to satisfy other industries that were not similarly favored.[8] Rather than dispute the merits of these criteria, I turn to establishing an evidentiary base for the criteria used by the Japanese government, and this chapter represents a first broad cut at identifying and systematizing the criteria using qualitative approaches.

Keeping in mind the economic criteria and political factors suggested in Chapter 1, my goal is to see whether all the theorizing had anything to do with the reality of selection decisions. To my knowledge, there has not been a systematic attempt at finding out whether any criteria have mattered in the Japanese selection decisions or, for that matter, anywhere else. And since my concern is not the welfare implications of the criteria but rather their relevance in the selection decisions, I judged that it would be most useful to turn to those who are actually involved in the selection processes.

INTERVIEWS

My key research strategy was to interview as random a sample of officials as feasible in order to ascertain the validity of the hypothesized criteria, as well as to determine other factors that drive the process. Between 1997 and 2002, I conducted more than a hundred interviews with individuals in MITI and supplemented those with interviews of individuals in the Japan Development Bank (JDB), Ministry of Transport (MOT, for shipbuilding), Science and Technology Agency (STA, in the Prime Minister's Office), Economic Planning Agency (EPA), and the Ministry of Education (MOE). To ensure consistency and quality, I also sought to supplement the MITI interviews with interviews of those at major industry associations that interact with the government, as well as utilizing official or secondary sources whenever possible. Almost all the interviews were conducted in Japanese and lasted an hour on average. The interviews were structured so that the same questions and criteria were presented for discussion with each individual, and the officials expanded the analysis's horizon by adding details germane to their experience. All personal interviews are cited directly in the analysis below, identifying the interview number, the agency, and the year of the interview.

At MITI, where the bulk of the interviews were carried out, I concentrated on interviewing officials in the three major bureaus responsible for overseeing TIPs and programs in specific industries. These were the Basic Industries Bureau (under which are found divisions on the steel and petrochemicals industries), Machinery and Information Industries Bureau (dealing with machine tools, automobiles, computers, semiconductors, and aerospace), and the Consumer Goods Industries Bureau (for textiles). To get a more general picture of the processes, I also interviewed officials in the Agency of Natural Resources and Energy (for coal), Agency for Industrial

Science and Technology (AIST, for the high-technology industries), Environmental Protection and Industrial Location Bureau, Industrial Policy Division, and Budget and Accounts Division. One reason for talking to officials in both the vertical bureaus (those that deal directly with industries) and the horizontal bureaus (those that deal with functional issues) was to get a more solid picture of the specific and general factors motivating the TIPs. Cross-checking each with the others helps in assessing the validity of the criteria thought to be important.

Additionally, I was fortunate enough to be able to interview officials who ranked from vice ministers and executive directors down to deputy directors, across all bureaus. This allowed me not only to get a good range of opinions but also ones that reflected (potentially) generational differences among the officials. In doing so, I learned a great deal about institutionalized features, both formal and informal, that affect the industrial selection process and thus the government choices made. The process is often contentious, messy, and hardly as consistent as the theory in Chapter 1 would lead us to believe. I should also mention that the quality of the interviews, and thereby the information gleaned, varied considerably.

Once the interviews had been conducted, the research strategy turned to examining each industry case in isolation, starting from those that were of concern in the immediate postwar era. In each case there were two basic steps. The first was to examine briefly the record of initial selection, meaning generally the allocation of favorable TIPs. This was done in order to show the extent to which sectors were selected. The second, on which I concentrate here, was to extract the criteria deemed influential in the selection process, principally by relying on the primary interviews and then supplementing that information from government materials and secondary sources. One point deserves attention and came up in the interviews. Since the officials often discussed the evolution of thinking about an industry in historical terms, they were careful to point out that they were basically making educated (and experienced) guesses as to what happened before their time. Ideally, I would have liked to interview decision-makers from the early postwar era as well, but since that was impossible I relied on the officials' judgment with respect to the criteria for selection in earlier times, making sure to supplement it with other primary and secondary sources whenever possible.

By criteria is meant not just the economic factors but also the political concerns and pressures that are brought to bear in the policy-making process. Much to my surprise, the stories about political pressures and constraints were at least as forthcoming as the economic ones by bureaucrats who could have chosen to denigrate such factors and stress their power or autonomy from politicians. Because of the forthrightness with which bureaucrats discussed a range of formal and informal pressures, whether from politicians or others, I did not interview any politicians for this project. I should add, however, that stories about the politics of selection were largely confirmed through interviews at the industry associations that interact with both bureaucrats and politicians. This allowed for a more nuanced understanding of policy bargaining and consensus building between bureaucrats, politicians, and industries than allowed for in the theoretical frameworks. In addition, I learned to appreciate the role that sheer perceptions play in the industrial selection process, irrespective of whether the sectors get favorable TIPs. This was particularly true of the criteria of spillovers and linkages among industries that were—and still are, as the interviews make clear—widely considered, both at the government and industry level, to be pivotal in nurturing Japan's technological survival. The remainder of this chapter, as well as the next one, focuses on highlighting the logic of industrial selection across the eleven cases and takes us from the immediate postwar period to the dawn of the twenty-first century.

The Industry Cases

In this section, I trace the relevance of the political and economic criteria across ten well-known industries in postwar Japan. To reiterate briefly, my goal is to determine why government officials selected each of these industries for support across the postwar period, not to judge whether the TIPs were causing successes or failures in the industries themselves. For each industry, I weave together a historical survey, focusing largely on extracting the criteria for selection that were consistently dominant in the relevant interviews as well as in other primary and secondary sources.[9] The results are summarized in Table 4.1 at the end of this chapter.

COAL

In the immediate postwar era, coal was intensely favored under the priority production system that is judged to have laid the foundation for the high-growth period.[10] Under this system, there was an intensive distribution of TIPs to coal and other specified priority industries, regardless of the consequences for civilian consumption or inflation. In practice, this meant concentrating diverse and creative TIPs such as materials rationing, reconstruction financing, price controls, price support subsidies, and import allocations, which constituted an invisible subsidy under the multiple exchange rate system then in existence.[11] By some accounts, the Japanese bureaucracy was able to exercise the greatest authority and influence over TIPs during the occupation itself.[12]

Why did the government favor coal? In part the situation demanded it. A defeated Japan found itself cut off from critical coal fields in Manchuria, Korea, and North China that it had amassed in its quest for a continental empire. There was no disagreement either among the postwar American occupation forces in charge of administering reforms in Japan—headed by the Supreme Commander of Allied Powers (SCAP)—and the remaining Japanese officials and intellectuals that coal was strategic because of the extensiveness of its uses. Between roughly 1946 and 1949, no one questioned the importance of economic recovery itself and thereby reindustrialization, for both of which coal was considered key. Shortages in coal would choke recovery and progress in other equally crucial sectors that were the backbone of the Japanese economy, like steel production, rail transportation, and the chemical fertilizer industry (itself essential to the food industry).[13] The extensiveness of the uses of coal was undeniable and fits well into themes about input linkages across sectors.

Economically, the country was grinding to a near standstill, plain for all to see. In the autumn of 1946, attempts to decrease inflation only served to accelerate it further, with the disastrous result that production dropped precipitously across several sectors. In addition, the potential of political unrest from maltreated foreign workers and miners in the coal industry also led to grave concerns. Foreign workers fled from Japan in the hundreds of thousands after the war, further crippling production and, by extension, economic recovery.[14] In a country that could not afford to buy foreign energy supplies immediately after the war, coal production understandably became a symbol of the country's revival, as it was the only source of domestic fuel for both private use and industrial consumption such as electric power, gas, railways, and steel. So widespread was this perception of the critical nature of coal that even the public patriotically rallied behind the coal effort.[15] One official summed it all up: It was easy to support coal because there was a consensus, both domestically and internationally, that basic Japanese industries should be revived in order for Japan to go forward.[16]

Looking back at that era, another official said that there were never formal a priori criteria for the coal and energy industries. Japan was and continues to be poorly endowed in the way of domestic energy resources, and national economic security demands a focus on their provision. Coal therefore found itself the intense object of government TIPs because it was the chief energy fuel in Japan and was critical to immediate industrial production.[17] In fact, the emphasis on garnering energy fuels for an advanced economy like Japan is still a key concern.[18]

But although this concern with national energy security may well have been there in the early postwar period, it was certainly not the only reason for the industry's continued selection. By 1950, coal production had roughly doubled and would hit a postwar high of 55.5 million tons in 1960, bringing it up to wartime highs. Coal's revered status as the chief energy source did not last long, however. In the late 1950s, it began to face competition from cheap Middle East oil, and Japanese industries began the inexorable shift toward oil as an alternative energy source.[19] Already between 1950 and 1953, the share of oil in the total primary energy supply had shot up from about 5 to 18 percent. The recession of 1953–54 confirmed the impending structural decline of coal, which was also largely due to the tremendous cost advantage of using oil.[20] In 1961, when oil imports were fully liberalized, the production of coal stood at 55.4 million tons, but by 1994 this figure had dropped to 6.7 million tons.[21] As a result, imported oil comprised roughly 75 percent of primary energy supplies, with well over 50 percent of that going into industrial use alone. Today coal comprises a mere 16.4 percent of the primary energy supply of Japan, with more than 90 percent of the coal demand met through imports chiefly from Australia, Canada, and the United States.[22] As the structural shift to oil became clear, one official suggested ruefully that MITI realized it had "overdone" the emphasis on the priority production system—a process that was to make structural adjustment much harder from the 1970s onward.[23] Nobody had foreseen that things were going to change swiftly, and not for the better as far as the coal mining industry went.

Inevitably, as oil replaced coal as the chief source of industrial energy generation, the coal mining industry went into a severe and speedy decline, with a handful of coal mines still in existence in 1970 and only two operational in 1997. This made coal the hotbed of political attention from very early on in areas such as Kyushu, Hokkaido, and Ibaraki Prefectures.[24] The regional concentration of the industry is what brought the politicians swiftly into the game, with the closure of a coal mine often meaning the demise of an entire town.[25] Concentration meant visibility as well, and the plight of the coal miners, whether for political or structural adjustment reasons, could not really be ignored at the national level. Unlike bureaucrats at MITI, politicians had always strongly opposed the closing of any mine, even though they could never stop the private-sector participants from shutting down a mine. In large part, the politicians had to make noise because the coal lobby held enormous influence among the conservative parties. Even today, with only two mines in existence in the whole of Japan, there continues to be a Special Committee on Coal Policy in the Diet with about twenty-five members, roughly half of them from the LDP.[26] There is also a special budget for coal policy that has been financed out of an oil tax since the late 1960s and is used for compensation and adjustment.[27]

The political noise was brought to bear on the bureaucrats. But there was a common denominator to both the politicians' and bureaucrats' concerns, namely the socially explosive problem of labor dislocation. From roughly 500,000 mine workers in the early 1950s, the number fell to roughly half as much by the early 1960s. By 1975 there were 20,000 miners, and this number decreased to 7,000 as of 1991. It was the number of employed and unionized miners that ensured government attention. There were clearly different motivations for that combined attention on employment—politicians because of electoral concerns and bureaucrats because of the effect on the long-term industrial structure. Politicians did not normally oppose the restructuring or closure so long as "retirement payments" were guaranteed for the displaced workers. These payments came from the exiting firm as well as substantial amounts, sometimes as high as 50 to 70 percent of the total, from MITI. Additionally, MITI and the exiting company have had to ensure that there are future employment opportunities for such workers, either in nearby areas or elsewhere. Even MITI officials sympathized with the workers' plight, drawing a distinction between national and regional interests. Although price inefficiency from the viewpoint of the industrial macroeconomy demanded that a mine be shut down, the lack of other means of subsistence at the regional level ensures that the mine continued operation with a great deal of backing from the government. For this reason, a balance was sought, and both politicians and bureaucrats agreed to a "soft landing" in terms of jobs, retirement payments, and regional solutions. All the ministries offered special programs to encourage regional development after closure. In July 1962, for example, bureaucrats from both MITI and the Ministry of Construction joined forces in the Coal Mine Area Rehabilitation Corporation, which played a leading role in helping to attract at least a few reluctant industrial enterprises to the devastated coal mining regions. But it was essentially the government that continued to support and favor the industry.

The goal was eventually to phase out, or deselect, the industry, but political and social pressures at the regional level played a great part in retarding that goal. Even as MITI tried to force industries like electricity or steel to buy coal at certain set prices because of political pressures, it also attempted to rationalize the industry given its inevitable decline.[28] Although several MITI plans to this effect were rejected by the industry, MITI did push the Coal Mining Rationalization Law through the Diet as early as 1955, which served as the legal basis for supporting programs of scrapping and modernizing the existing mines. From then on its Coal Industry Rationalization Council began the trying task of scrapping and modernizing existing mines in an effort to make Japanese coal competitive on world markets. But by the early 1960s, the council acknowledged that the shift from coal to oil represented an irreversible structural trend, though probably for political reasons it optimistically projected the production of 50 million tons of coal.

The necessity of deselection was apparent also to the politicians, who clearly understood the nature of the structural decline. In fact, some politicians appeared to be committing political suicide as far as public stances went. In 1954, Prime Minister Yoshida Shigeru ordered MITI to bring coal prices down for end users such as steel and other heavy industries that had been protesting against high coal prices since 1949—which was exactly opposite to what the coal industry wanted and was lobbying to keep.[29] In 1962, Prime Minister Ikeda Hayato publicly agreed with the idea of gradually phasing the coal industry out of existence.[30] In 1980, the government dropped production targets even further, but domestic Japanese coal was so expensive that industries like steel refused outright to buy it. Sectoral subsidies to coal also did not move for long to the dictates of the electoral logic because, expressed as a percentage of total subsidies disbursed by the government, they went down swiftly from a high of 14.3 percent in 1969 to 4.5 percent in 1974.[31] In 1991, the Coal Mining Council issued a report on the future of coal policy that set out the fundamental direction for Japan's future coal policy. The report made it clear that the 1990s would be the final stages of structural adjustment of the coal mining industry in Japan and urged the remaining market players to diversify into other businesses.[32] No longer would TIPs be prolonged to this sector, whose domestic existence was clearly over.

There is also a clear difference in the criteria for selection immediately after the war and later in the era marked by the intensifying rivalry with oil. Initially, there is little doubt that coal was selected because its recovery was essential to the entire postwar effort at economic reconstruction. Both its extensiveness of uses at the time and its status as the chief energy fuel in Japan led to its designation in the production priority system. Although there is evidence that favors the economic hypothesis, the case for a bureaucracy engaged in strategic industrial plotting would be somewhat exaggerated. This is largely because the initial choice to support this sector was less a matter of strategy and more one of economic necessity that made itself clear to all—bureaucrats, politicians, and SCAP.

Subsequently, the structural nature of the decline made it clear that the industry would not be able to compete in world markets and that Japanese industry could get along without coal being produced domestically. Nor was there much point in trying to keep firms in the industry, when they clearly wanted to get out of the coal business altogether. Moreover, once companies made the decisions to do so, neither politicians nor the bureaucrats could stop their exit, with the result that politicians could not afford to pin their electoral fortunes on this industry as a whole. All this created an expectation for deselection, but for reasons of regional stability as well as political concerns, the process has dragged on for decades. By 2002, the goal was to phase out the industry completely in Japan.[33]

STEEL

Given the symbiotic relationship between coal and steel in which the production of the latter relied heavily on the former, it is not surprising that they were both deemed critical to the entire recovery effort under the guidelines of the priority production system. Despite concerns voiced by both the Bank of Japan (BOJ) and the Ministry of Finance (MOF) about the financial viability of favoring a sector that went against Japan's existing comparative advantage, MITI strenuously promoted the steel industry with several kinds of TIPs. With specific legislation in place by the early 1950s, the TIPs came in various guises. Under the priority production policy, the Reconstruction Finance Bank (RFB) supplied over 80 percent of the total loans to the steel industry, and most city banks followed the later lead of the JDB in providing support to the sector. In addition, about 70 percent of the total funds requested from the World Bank were earmarked for the steel sector.[34] Two direct government subsidies were also granted outright, a raw-materials subsidy and a price subsidy for pig iron and steel products, both of which ensured the industry's survival.[35] Most well known of all, perhaps, was the administrative guidance exercised by the Steel Subcommittee of the Committee on Industrial Funds. The subcommittee developed three rationalization investment plans that allowed MITI to try to coordinate activities in the sector over time.[36] The impending downturn in the global steel industry in the 1970s led to further concerted government efforts in the domestic industry, often in the form of administrative guidance and cartels.[37] What remains indisputable over the decades is that MITI had a very strong interest in the fortunes of the steel industry. The question is why it has been so insistent on favoring the steel industry.

Officials today claim that they followed the same reasoning in the case of the steel industry as they did for the coal industry in the immediate postwar era. The steel industry was selected in the priority production system because it formed the infrastructure for the whole economy. Without it, other Japanese industries would be stymied, especially if left dependent on the caprices of the world economy. Here was an industry whose stable domestic supply could spur the development of other domestic industries. There was a very high domestic demand for its output, and given that the steel industry did not have to start from scratch, it had the potential to satisfy such demand quicker than it could without the government's help.[38]

To this day, steel inspires its own brand of national economic security concerns, given its significance to Japan's industrial activities far more than any other metal. For the more senior officials, who have had a longer history of dealing with the industry and feel as if they have grown up with it, intervention in steel is still thought of in terms of *kokkanari*—the idea that steel is the nation.[39] From this perspective, while criteria like value-added and growth rates may be used in planning, most important is the emphasis on the industry's extensiveness of uses. From the start, it was not so much the sector itself as what it meant for end users like automobiles, construction, and household goods.[40] Estimates suggest that of the total domestic production in the late 1990s, the automobile industry commanded 17 percent, industrial and electrical machinery 5 percent, shipbuilding 3 percent, and construction about 7 percent.[41] Remarkably, economic security is also a concern that end users of steel in Japan cite as being important for supporting the steel industry domestically, even though they can import much cheaper steel from developing countries.[42]

The reasons behind the rationalization efforts are linked to MITI's concern with the industry's competitiveness, and the interviews on this point tend to reflect the goals rather than the determinants of the TIPs, though it is difficult to disentangle them in retrospect.[43] All three of the major rationalization plans stemmed from the concern that demand was high and competition intense. Japanese industries had to bring down the price of their steel to remain viable in world markets. Therefore, the key motivating idea behind government support was that a smaller number of companies would promote economies of scale that would decrease cost, increase quality, and make steel cheap and abundantly available for both domestic and international markets.[44] This reasoning was behind the effort to merge Yawata and Fuji into Nippon Steel, which was, as a matter of fact, to emerge as the world's biggest producer of crude steel by a significant margin in 1975. For many, the Yawata–Fuji merger was seen as revealing a historical "soft spot" that MITI held for the steel industry.[45]

To some extent, the criteria MITI deemed important in selecting and supporting the industry were no doubt magnified also by the immense influence and lobbying power that the steel industry commands. The steel industry has traditionally been close to the LDP, through both personal and institutionalized networks. It has also enjoyed closer access to the LDP through Keidanren, many of whose past presidents have come from the steel industry. The Japan Iron and Steel Federation (JISF), which acts as the industry's spokesperson with the government and the rest of the world, is one of the three industries that is physically located within the Keidanren building in Otemachi—a fact that many officials believe is a serious indication of the industry's political power because it ensures even closer access to the LDP. Moreover, they point out that voting concerns and campaign contributions are also considered very important by politicians with regards to this industry and greatly increase pressure on bureaucrats to intervene favorably. Part of the industry's influence also comes from holding a lot of economic power within a region, as in the case of coal, which again contributes to its political influence all the way up to the prime ministership.[46]

But also as in coal, there is room for cooperation among the politicians and bureaucrats, although it stems from two very different motivations. Because of its closeness to the politicians, the steel industry is a serious contender for favorable TIPs. And TIPs, as well as a host of creative administrative measures, have been forthcoming. But to suggest that politicians have forced bureaucrats in the steel case is off the mark because, in fact, bureaucrats also prefer to favor the industry for the economic reasons stated above. About the only things that have restrained the government TIPs are the external pressures from Japan's trading partners and budgetary constraints.

From the early 1980s onward, in light of the trade friction with the United States and the competition from newly emerging countries, many began to think that the declining domestic steel industry would go the way of coal and textiles. By 1995, the Japanese steel industry was also suffering from stagnant domestic demand as end users cut back their production and exports declined with the rise of the yen. But MITI bureaucrats even today side with those who see future growth potential in the industry worldwide.[47] Additionally, they see the steel industry as sitting on the verge of technological breakthroughs that will redefine other domestic industries. The potential for linkage externalities is not only considered a key criterion but thought to become even more important in the industry in the future, since it will continue to pull along other industries as well.[48]

According to officials, although deselection in terms of formal tangible TIPs has taken place, MITI has certainly not withdrawn its attention from the industry from a research point of view and intends to keep pushing the major steel players on this front.[49] Whereas the industry looks to producing next-generation technologies to achieve sweeping cost reductions, MITI looks largely to the shape of the industry's future potential. It initiated an urban steel study group, led by the steel industry, which is concerned with the feasibility of developing new steel applications for urban building materials. More recently, it launched a supermetal development project to study critical structure-controlled metallic materials. On a parallel track, the STA started an R&D program to study structural materials that can be used in future technologies.[50] Within the Iron and Steel Institute of Japan (ISIJ), a Technology Study Committee, coordinated by MITI, is involved in assessing the technological ability of foreign steel industries, as "megacompetition" is seen to be lurking around the corner. The committee is also involved in assessing or proposing any structural technological transformations in the industry by 2020. To encourage large-scale joint research, MITI is also constantly involved in a Four Member Information Exchange Meeting, with other leading steel-related Japanese institutions, to examine industry-wide themes that can be turned into practical joint research.[51]

What changed in the 1990s was the emphasis on technological breakthroughs that could redefine industrial activities. In this case, too, the hypothesized criteria for selection, such as growth rates, linkage externalities, and even the potential for further employment, are all pertinent, and this comes across very clearly in the interviews. But what comes across even more clearly is that the attention toward the future of steel is still there, whether the industry itself wants it or not, simply because steel will long remain a basic materials sector that affects the health of a great many other Japanese industrial activities.[52]

Overall, the broad patterns with respect to the criteria for selection can be summarized as follows. In the immediate postwar era, the emphasis was on the potential for growth rates and, increasingly, on the industry's extensiveness of uses. This is an emphasis that has not changed drastically over the years. Additionally, the concern with regional employment and votes adds its own dimension of political and social pressures. The historical relationship of the steel industry to the government, and particularly its close relationship both to the politicians through Keidanren and to the bureaucrats in the industry-specific divisions at MITI, has ensured that it enjoys a double advantage. Whereas politicians can dress up their electoral concerns with high-minded economic reasons, the bureaucrats can use the political pressures to buttress their already strong support of the industry for exactly such economic reasons.

TEXTILES

After the war, Japan's comparative advantage lay in labor-intensive industries like textiles that also held out the potential for earning foreign exchange. But in direct contrast to positions held by the BOJ and SCAP, which urged concentration on light established sectors such as textiles, MITI favored heavy industry instead.[53] But despite its reluctance, MITI has devoted a great deal of attention to this sector. MITI's most concerted efforts in the sector began in the early 1950s when it attempted to promote the shift toward synthetic fibers by establishing large-scale modern plants. TIPs took the form of JDB loans for machines and equipment, special training facilities to educate production workers in the new techniques, subsidized acquisition of raw materials and, most important, the transfer of technology from American (as well as some European) firms that were kept out of the domestic market. Textiles has consistently enjoyed the highest estimated effective rates of protection of any manufacturing sector, beginning with a high of about 54 percent in the mid 1960s and ending with still a considerable lead at 38 percent in the early 1980s. In addition to high levels of subsidies, both JDB loans and special depreciation allowances were tailored to rationalize and modernize the existing plant and equipment investments in the 1970s and 1980s.[54] Other policies, such as MITI-sanctioned cartels, were set in place to eliminate "excessive competition" in the industry well into the 1960s and 1970s.[55] As competition intensified, there was also a great deal of specific legislation designed ostensibly to draw attention to the government's efforts at alleviating the hardships in the sector.[56] Both the 1978 and 1983 laws on stabilization and structural adjustment were partially designed with textiles in mind.

On the surface, the reasoning behind MITI's support was the importance of growth rates in the immediate postwar era, especially as they related to the potential for export earnings.[57] In fact, growth rates and value-added were the key criteria in almost all the various categories of textile industries that emerged as leading-edge ones in their time. This was true, for example, of silk before the war and of cotton in the 1950s.[58] Over the course of the years, an internal MITI document points to six criteria that have traditionally been important in the decision-making process concerning the textiles industry as a whole. These include the number of factories, the number of employees, growth rates in production levels, value-added levels, and the levels of exports and imports expressed in yen amounts.[59] Of these, most officials state that over time the most important have been growth rates and employment levels because they directly affect the country's economic and social stability, especially in the aftermath of the war.

But as in the immediate postwar era, so today MITI's reluctance toward this sector remains. It is particularly dominant in the horizontal bureaus at MITI, which deal with more functional broad-ranging issues in the economy. While there is an acknowledgment of the importance of economic criteria in the newer niches in the textiles sector, there is a more pessimistic view of the remainder of the industry as far as its future in Japan is concerned. Some suggest outright that it is better to let this kind of low value-added and labor-intensive industry go to developing countries and so free up resources in Japan that can be more productively used elsewhere.[60] Others add that, in general, the textiles industry has negligible backward and forward linkages and that it does not have much of a positive influence on other industries in any event.[61] Increasingly, however, even in the vertical bureaus that deal more directly with specific industries, there is an emphasis on phasing out, or at least more forcibly deselecting, parts of the textile industry.[62] What explains this reluctance and, despite it, the support to textiles?

The initial reluctance stemmed from the fact that this was not a crucial industry that could pull along labor and capital in other sectors of the economy. But the real fear behind the reluctance was the increasing perception of the industry as a "declining" or "backward" one, and this perception turned into concrete reality over time.[63] Although Japan was the world's largest exporter of cotton products between 1951 and 1969, the textiles sector as a whole was hard hit as East and Southeast Asian countries began to overtake the domestic industries in the mid 1960s with production and exports of synthetic yarns and textiles. While overall textile imports stood at 5.8 percent of total internal demand in 1971, they shot up to 16.2 percent in 1973. Furthermore, with the rapid appreciation of the yen in the 1970s as well as higher wage costs, Japanese firms found it hard to compete with imports even in the domestic market, which was fast becoming stagnant.[64] Japan's protection of textiles through various TIPs was to lead it into severe disputes with the United States in the 1950s and 1960s.[65] In fact, such external pressures forced MITI to intervene even further in the industry and introduce distortions such as cartels that have proved hard to dislodge and compensations that have skewed incentives for smaller producers.[66] This combination of events meant that, in general, things went from bad to worse for the Japanese textiles industry as a whole, with all the traditional sectors showing increasing import penetration levels well into the mid 1990s.

Despite the overall declining image of the textiles sector, with growth rates, value-added levels, and employment figures dropping steadily over the years, some officials with jurisdiction over this industry defend MITI's support in rosy terms. They claim that the presently somber picture of textiles coexists with bright "new frontiers" in the industry. This refers, for example, to synthetic fibers in which East Asia is catching up and carbon fibers in whose development Japan leads the world. In fact, the sector as a whole caught the attention of MITI bureaucrats only with the advent of synthetic fibers. These in particular were promoted vigorously not only because they represented upscale technology but also because they could have a widespread impact on creating new products in the industry. The same is also now held to be true for high performance superfibers, which can potentially be used in numerous consumer and industrial applications, such as advanced machinery found in the aerospace industry. Carbon fibers, more specifically, may well be used in rockets, space suits, and airplanes. Such niches, still in the making, are said to need outright government encouragement. In small measures, MITI encouragement is forthcoming because of these niches' high value-added and high-technology potential, as well as the fact that the market for them will grow.[67] No less important is the idea that such niches can also pull the Japanese textiles industry forward in the face of intense existing competition from the developing countries.[68] Despite these newer optimistic claims, the fact remains that the decline of the textiles industry has been artificially retarded overall because of government support. And this has been done largely out of both political pressures and social concerns.

By 1970, the textiles industry employed over 1.7 million people and produced 750,000 tons of natural fibers and 1.29 million tons of synthetic fibers. Even as late as the 1980s, the textiles sector had over 150,000 establishments engaged in both upstream and downstream industries, an additional 200,000 wholesalers and retailers, an estimated 1.29 million workers directly engaged in production and processing, and a further 1.13 million workers in its distribution network.[69] The sector as a whole could not be ignored politically—and it was not, as the evidence on the legal flurry for the allocation of TIPs demonstrates only too well.

The organizational structure of the industry has contributed directly to its influence on national policy-making to this day. Most of the firms in the industry tend to be small and medium-sized enterprises (SMEs). Since such business owners have consistently provided an average of about 25 percent of the total support to the LDP between 1955 and 1980, there is every reason to expect that politicians would have a keen interest in the legislation within this sector.[70] The SMEs also enjoy direct institutionalized access to the bureaucracy through one of the external agencies of MITI, the Small and Medium Enterprise Agency. In fact, officials say that both the SMEs and the industry associations bypass politicians altogether and directly attempt to influence the responsible MITI division for more favorable TIPs—and that this kind of lobbying is common to all industries under MITI's jurisdiction.[71]

Industry associations can also be very useful to politicians, who are interested in advancing their political fortunes through vote-division strategies, especially in the old single non-transferable vote (SNTV) multimember electoral districts. Legislative TIPs can be used to sanction the formation of, for example, spinning and weaving cartels based on the existing industry associations, and these cartels would later actually prove very hard to dislodge for political reasons.[72] Ostensibly, such cartels were sanctioned in order to promote growth and exports in the industry. But in fact they can also provide a useful basis to a political party for splitting support to their multiple candidates in the same district, as the candidates could turn around and dispense pork in the form of loans and subsidies to their specific constituents.[73]

By far the most important reason for this industry's political influence lies in its location. It is geographically concentrated into what are called *sanchi*, literally meaning production areas, which also contributes greatly to the industry's political influence. Because an area is involved almost entirely in the production of one kind of textile, people in the area vote in a block for those politicians whom they think will benefit the region. The block vote may be as much as 30 percent of the potential votes in the area, which makes it very sizable and of major import to the politicians. This has a direct effect on the policy-making process, because bureaucrats cannot ignore political demands.[74] In fact, the bureaucrats do not ignore them anyway, since the *sanchi* may be the only source of regional employment. This regional concern also continues to motivate TIPs, even though the number of employees engaged in production has fallen further from about 1.2 million workers in the early 1990s to about 882,000 as of 1995.[75] Given the falling numbers in employ-

ment levels, rapid labor dislocation and resulting social instability remain, as
they do in the coal industry, as much a source of keen concern to the bureaucrats as to the politicians. Once again, therefore, both of these sets of actors have an incentive to cooperate, though they operate out of very different motivations.[76]

SHIPBUILDING

Shipbuilding was designated a priority reconstruction sector after the
war, but it was the Shipbuilding Bureau of the MOT, not MITI, that acquired jurisdiction over the sector. MOT's TIPs to the industry have been
no less active, however. Since the end of the war, the shipbuilding sector as a
whole has been disproportionately reliant on government TIPs, which have
decreased in intensity over time.[77] Given that there was no effective domestic demand for ships after the war, one of MOT's first actions was to institute a Planned Shipbuilding Program in May 1947, through which a government shipping corporation supplied funds for purchasing ships from the
domestic producers and then leasing them on to shipping companies. Together the shipping corporation and the RFB provided well over 70 percent
of the funds for purchasing ships, with the remaining amount supplied by
other government institutions and private banks.[78] When the RFB stopped
making loans in 1949 (following the Dodge mission to control inflation), the
JDB picked up the slack. Between 1950 and 1970, as much as 30 percent of
the JDB's total loans went to shipbuilding, making it one of the prime beneficiaries. During the same time, roughly 54 percent of the total loans sanctioned by the Export-Import Bank of Japan went to shipbuilding, particularly to boost the export drive.[79] In comparison to all other manufacturing
countries, the industry also enjoyed the highest special depreciation ratios as
well as the highest annual reduction in its interest burden. Additionally, it
was protected with high tariff rates that remained in effect until 1975.[80]

After the first oil shock, the MOT stepped in to intervene, but this time
in an industry characterized by excess capacity, excess labor, and increased
foreign competition from developing country producers. The 1978 stabilization law was used to designate shipbuilding as a structurally depressed industry, and the industry firms filed a joint application for relief at the
MOT.[81] The MOT then instituted recession cartels lasting well into the
early 1980s.[82] But essentially the industry firms bore the major costs of adjustment, particularly in the form of operation curtailment and capacity reduction, which were highly contested among the individual firms. The
MOT also instituted demand-pull measures such as low-interest loans for
ships purchased by Japanese shipping companies and special purchase of
ships by the Japanese government for the self-defense forces.[83] Once again,
what kind of factors determined support to this sector over time? Although

this is a good case to see what kinds of factors affected selection in a different ministry, access to officials in the MOT proved to be unsatisfactory, and my analysis had to rely on MITI and secondary sources as well.

Humiliated on the world stage as a military power and brought to its knees in the war, Japan favored the shipbuilding industry because of its potential symbolism for the nation's industrial might and its "news value" both domestically and internationally at the time.[84] Sheer geopolitics also played an important role in motivating the government to support both shipbuilding and shipping.[85] After all, Japan is an island country that is highly dependent on seaborne trade—imports of raw materials and exports of goods—for its economic survival.

Most important at the time, perhaps, was the idea that shipbuilding was the first modern industry in Japan, and its growth would also help propel the development of other fledgling industries such as steel, machinery equipment, and shipping. Like many others at the time, this industry, too, was favored early in the postwar years primarily because of its backward and forward linkages to the rest of the industrial sector.[86] In addition, the expectation was that technological improvements within this industry would spill over into new sectors like automobiles and aircraft.[87] Other key criteria right after the war were the potential for high growth rates in the industry and the potential for foreign exchange earnings.[88]

The Japanese shipbuilding industry specialized in the construction of both tankers and supertankers responsible for carrying crude oil around the world, and it was primarily an export industry at a crucial time in the country's economic development.[89] An average of over 60 percent of its production was marked for export well into the 1980s, making it a valuable source of foreign exchange earnings right after the war. The first postwar ship export order for two Norwegian whalers was received in 1948, with export booms recorded in 1955, 1963, and 1965.[90] By 1965, the shipbuilding industry had captured 50 percent of the world market, but this rosy picture did not last long in the wake of the first oil shock in 1973 and the increased competition from other newly industrializing countries. In the early 1970s, orders declined precipitously, with the result that Japanese ship production fell from 16 million tons in 1976 to 5 million tons in 1979.[91] These events led the MOT to issue many administrative guidance recommendations, such as the famous one limiting the industry to forty major shipbuilding companies and setting upper limits on operating hours for 1977 and 1978.[92]

But structural adjustments were not the only reasons for government support. As late as 1980, the shipbuilding sector had approximately 1,500 shipbuilding companies, 1,600 related companies, and 4,000 subcontractors. Total employment rates in the sector overall stood at about 361,000 people, including those in shipbuilding, subcontracting, and related industries. By

1986, the total employment had fallen to 145,000 and then stabilized at an average of around 125,000 workers for the next decade. Subcontractors, typically SMEs, nearly halved from 90,000 in 1995 to 41,000 in 1986 and then fell further to 32,000 by 1995. Given the rapid and unwelcome changes, the SMEs in this industry were to exercise their political power as well, with the result that a great deal of favorable legislation was enacted.[93] Additionally, in the face of the economic crisis, the industry associations exerted political pressures and made demands that have been important in the policy-making process.

More important than the employment and SME pressures, however, was the political power of the dominant firms in the industry. About 85 percent of the industry production has been concentrated in a handful of major firms, including Mitsubishi Heavy Industries, Kawasaki Heavy Industries, Ishikawajima-Harima Heavy Industries, Hitachi Zosen, Mitsui Engineering and Shipbuilding, Sumitomo Heavy Industries, and Sasebo Heavy Industries. Although its policies pertained to the entire industry, the MOT was accused of concentrating its attention on these bigger shipbuilding companies after the war.[94] The companies that dominate the industry are also very close to the LDP and have traditionally held a lot of influence with the politicians.[95]

There were some well-publicized cases in which politicians had the upper hand, given the visibility of the political pressures in the shipyards. Sasebo Heavy Industry had been deemed too inefficient to be worthy of government financial aid when its major shareholders (Nippon Steel and Nippon Kokai) and its major bank (Daiichi Kangyo) refused to extend or guarantee further loans. The MOT, MOF, and BOJ followed the lead of the private financial markets in this matter. But Sasebo was the largest employer in Sasebo City (6,600 workers out of a total of 100,000 people), and political pressures were brought to bear upon the Diet. The upshot of all this was that Prime Minister Fukuda himself ordered the resolution of the issue, and the BOJ ended up by urging private creditors to resume loans to Sasebo Heavy Industries.[96]

Whatever the political agenda, however, in reality the sector was never bailed out on a grand scale by the MOT bureaucrats, who consistently placed the direct burden of adjustment on the depressed industry members themselves.[97] By the late 1980s, as the concern with efficiency and downsizing continued, more than forty-four medium-sized companies exited the industry altogether, reducing the shipbuilding capacity by 40 percent. The closure of the Hakodate Dockyards in January 1990 led to bitter accusations that the government only pretended to help and was not doing much for the plight of those affected outright in the industry. Even the highly politicized Sasebo Heavy Industries bailout had a loan structure that encouraged efficiency, and later Sasebo was to merge with Kuroshima Shipbuilding Company in an effort to become more competitive. The remaining companies consolidated into eight big groups and made concerted efforts to bounce back on their own.[98]

To sum up, the shipbuilding industry was favored in the immediate postwar era because of its promise of high growth rates, the consequent potential of foreign exchange, and the fact that it provided backward and forward linkages to a range of other industries. During the glorious export boom years until the late 1960s, the industry did not get much government attention but lobbied for exactly that once it started to decline after the first oil shock. The political power of the SMEs and the big firms in the industry combined to keep political focus on the plight of the workers, who were visibly affected by the decline. Despite the publicized cases in which political pressures seemed dominant, however, there appeared to be far more legislative efforts than actual TIPs to alleviate the decline. In fact, over the course of twenty years it was the industry firms themselves that bore the direct burden of the adjustment efforts by diversifying, restructuring, or simply exiting. The only reason the industry was not allowed to phase out altogether was that, as in the immediate postwar era, national economic security demanded that a country dependent on seaborne trade should have the means to be able to rely on itself.

PETROCHEMICALS

While not the prime focus for support immediately after World War II, except for chemical fertilizers, the chemicals, and especially petrochemicals, industry received lavish attention from MITI in the designated period of the heavy and chemical industrialization drive during the 1950s and 1960s. In 1951, MITI published a report expressing the urgency of establishing a petrochemicals sector. By 1955, MITI had designated petrochemicals as an infant industry and made assurances that it would ensure the provision of sufficient and cheap raw materials for the development of high polymer petrochemicals. In 1962, the Petroleum Industry Law was enacted, which made the construction of refining facilities contingent upon government permission. The law specifically gave priority to the establishment of refineries to supply feedstock to petrochemicals and power companies.[99]

Although MITI's earlier attempts to have more a of say in the industry were unsuccessful, it was eventually able to set up several consultative groups in the mid 1960s, which allowed it to interact with the industry.[100] The existence of the 1949 Foreign Exchange and Foreign Trade Control Law as well as the 1950 Foreign Capital Law made industry realize that these consultative bodies were not entirely toothless. Industrial developments and ventures in petrochemicals required the importation of foreign technology, which in turn required government licenses under a wide variety of situations.[101] Foreign exchange allocations, as well as tax incentives, were used to acquire technology both from the United States and European countries, which was key to the set up of the whole industry.[102] While synthetic fibers, fertilizers, and petrochemicals were the first target of support with a host of specific legislation, more tangible TIPs for promotion included preferential loans from the JDB and other government banks, accelerated depreciation, and reductions in corporate income taxes. From 1955 onward, petrochemicals were the object of sustained government TIPs, as evidenced in the Petrochemical Industry Plan.[103] All did not proceed smoothly, however. Despite the desire of MITI to concentrate the industry into a small number of firms achieving high returns to scale, the four originally approved complexes—Mitsui Petrochemical, Mitsubishi Petrochemical, Sumitomo Petrochemical, and Japan Petrochemical—dating from the mid 1950s were joined by numerous other firms by the early 1970s. Administrative guidance was used to direct investment in the private sector so as to eliminate possible "excessive competition."[104]

On the whole, petrochemicals did very well until the oil shock hit in 1973. The reason was simple. Petrochemicals are essentially chemicals made from petroleum, such as plastic, synthetic rubber, textiles, surface active agents, and paint, and their production relies heavily on naphtha, which is imported primarily from the Middle East.[105] The second oil shock in 1979 did even more damage. MITI therefore spent considerable effort to clean up the mess of excess capacity and sluggish sales through adjustment policies.[1066] Coupled with extralegal administrative guidance, MITI officially used legal cartel policies to assist the petrochemicals sector. In addition to domestic restructuring, MITI also encouraged the industry firms to look for cheaper raw materials and new markets. To this end, it lured the firms abroad with financial, tax, and insurance assistance through Japan's foreign-aid program.[107] The fact that the petrochemicals industry ran into severe structural problems a decade or so down the line is irrelevant to the issue of why it was so favored initially. Once again, the question is why.

The intensive support of petrochemicals, and especially plastics, was motivated largely out of the basic nature of the industry, which has implications for and linkages to almost every other industry. Nor could such products simply be imported, with the government openly taking the position that domestic production should replace imports in this basic industry.[108] Some officials suggest that national economic security concerns demanded that they be domestically produced.[109] Others point out more specifically that the sector generated outputs that were extensively used throughout the economy—chemicals produced fertilizers crucial to agriculture; petrochemicals produced inputs for a very wide range of industrial activities. Although potential growth rates, value-added, and profits were important in the initial favoritism as well, the fact of petrochemicals being so basic to such a diverse range of economic activities took precedence over other considerations.[110]

Importantly, there was also the catch-up element, with the concern that generally Japanese chemicals-related industries were technologically back-ward compared to their counterparts in the United States and Europe. As in many other industries in the early postwar years, this had a great psycholog-ical effect on efforts to favor this sector. The position of the petrochemicals industry in the advanced Western countries at the time and the fact that it was seen to be basic to their industrial economies were two of the most im-portant reasons behind MITI's active interest in this industry.[111] In fact, some suggest bluntly that there were no clear criteria for selection and that the bureaucrats selected and favored those industries for promotion that the general public felt psychologically, and both politicians and bureaucrats agreed tacitly, Japan should have as an expression of its industrial might, such as chemicals and later petrochemicals.[112]

The immediate motivations for the intervention changed drastically once the first oil shock hit the industry—immediate because the fundamental view of the "basicness" of the industry did not change in the meantime. And there is little doubt that political pressures played a role or even that they continue to do so especially in petrochemicals. As one official pointed out, the petrochemicals industry association maintains very close contacts with MITI, but it has also relied actively on politicians to make its case. In part, the political power of the industry stems from the fact that its firms are well-known giants that have become even larger with a spate of mergers in the 1990s—Mitsubishi Chemical merged with Mitsubishi Petrochemical in 1994, and Mitsui Toatsu Chemical merged with Mitsui Petrochemicals in-dustries more recently.[113] These firms, along with Asahi and Sumitomo, in-dividually hold a great deal of political power and are close to politics and politicians, both directly and especially through their dominant presence at Keidanren. One evident measure is found in the fact that before the LDP broke up, there was a Petrochemicals Committee in the Diet that sought fa-vorable legislation on the industry's behalf. The industry's influence has in-creased also with its close association with the domestic petroleum industry, which is by many accounts one of the most politically powerful industries in Japan. Like steel and electricity, the petroleum industry association is physi-cally represented in the Keidanren building, which is considered a hallmark of great political influence.[114]

In fact, it is not just these firms but the entire industry, with roughly ten dominant firms, that is considered politically powerful. Unlike the larger chemical industry association, the petrochemicals industry association is a more active pressure group than most, with sizable campaign contributions to match. More than other industry associations, it constantly agitates against taxes that burden its member firms' operating costs. Additionally, politicians have brought these constituents' demands to bear on the bureaucrats at both MITI and MOF, even more so as the industry went into structural depression. But specific demands by politicians are restricted to general favors like taxes or decreases in regulation that affect all the firms equally.[115] Here again, there are incentives for cooperation between the politicians and MITI bureaucrats, with the latter having little choice but to help the industry toward better times since they were largely responsible for helping create the industry in the first place.

Unlike the textiles sector, industry mergers, in-house R&D efforts, and favorable taxes have allowed the chemicals industry to shake off its structurally depressed image on the whole. It is now regarded as a basic high-technology industry, with the highest value-added levels in all of the manufacturing industries.[116] Like the textiles sector, however, there are also specific niches in the petrochemicals industry, as well as the chemicals industry more generally, that are considered very important. But there is a difference, because these emerging developments are seen to have meaning not just for the industry but rather for the whole economy. The niches, namely biotechnology, biochemicals, and new materials, are supposed to bring fundamental and profound benefits to the Japanese industrial economy at large. Biotechnology, in particular, has long been singled out as being of critical importance in terms of its widespread benefits, though the emphasis is much more on basic R&D than outright TIPs. In fact, one official suggested that what continues to draw MITI's attention to the sector is its knowledge-intensity, as shown by a very high number of researchers who may become the source of widespread benefits. No less important, the official went on to point out, is the expected growth in this niche, with the size of the market estimated to go from about $10 billion today to about $100 billion by the first quarter of the twenty-first century.[117] The broad industrial trends, in short, force the government to look beyond petrochemicals.

Favoring the new trends in the industry is hard for two reasons. First, with the exception of R&D support, formal TIPs are severely limited. Just as there is a general conclusion that MITI needs to promote R&D and commercialization of these new fields, there is also the recognition that petrochemicals is a mature industry that will eventually be more appropriate for manufacturing efforts in developing countries rather than in an advanced industrial economy like Japan.[118] But this is more easily recognized than implemented as a conscious policy choice, given that petrochemicals still constitutes about 30.5 percent of the total output in the chemicals field as a whole. More important, the petrochemical firms are politically very powerful, having a reach all the way up to the highest levels of government. For the time being, politicians have taken no interest in pinning their electoral fortunes on these emerging fields, given their stake in the old one. But it is entirely possible that both the continued decline and competition in petrochemicals from the East Asian countries could change the climate of opinion against this sector as a whole, as it has in textiles.

Second, along with MITI, there are also many other government players in the field who jealously guard their respective jurisdictions. MITI, for example, wants jurisdiction over the basic chemical goods sector as a whole. As of July 1997, there had been institutional changes in response to new trends in the industry, with the basic chemical division and chemical products division merging into one at MITI and more concerted resources devoted to the Biochemical Industry Division. But MITI is not the only one with an interest in the sector.[119] The Ministry of Health and Welfare wants to keep jurisdiction over pharmaceuticals, and the Ministry of Agriculture, Forestry and Fisheries is not going to give up its jurisdictional claim over the new high-technology fertilizers for livestock and agriculture. Because the emerging technology has many faces and the potential to cross over into many diverse fields, jurisdictional battles make favoring even key R&D efforts quite difficult.

Whatever the difficulties in reality about favoring the new niches, there is no disagreement as to why they should be so favored. And remarkably this agreement exists despite the fact that there is little by way of substantial information or data about actual prospects. In creating new knowledge that will support emerging new industries, the biotechnology and bioscience fields are somehow seen to possess the ability to transform the chemical industry at a fundamental level in the near future. As is true in so many other industries, one of the most important reasons is also that Japan is still backward in a key industry in which the United States, Germany, and Britain are so advanced. The biofields, it is widely believed, represent the next most important industries after computers, which have so radically altered the world. There is absolutely no question about their potential for high growth rates, high value-added, and high spillover potential, which we cannot begin to understand. For these reasons and for the fact that the balance of economic power may one day depend on this industry, the official opinion is that Japan, too, must indigenize this industry no matter what the cost.

AUTOMOBILES

Although SCAP gave formal permission for the production of trucks only and the manufacture of cars remained limited until 1949, MITI had already instituted a Basic Automotive Industry Policy in 1948.[120] This was followed by several well-known policies that showed MITI's determination to favor and support this sector. In 1955, it came up with blueprints for a "people's car" that was rejected by industry as infeasible. In 1962, it tried to rationalize the industry through a Draft Law for the promotion of the automobile industry. The idea was to concentrate the roughly ten-firm industry into three groups, each specializing in a certain type of car. The industry would then preferably be led by two firms—Nissan and Toyota—but smaller and newer firms such as Honda resisted this idea, and the largest and most distinguished *keiretsu*, Mitsubishi, was definitely displeased at being left out of industry leadership.[121]

Using the 1956 Temporary Special Measures Law on Promoting the Machinery Industries, MITI began by supporting the automotive parts industry, not the final-assembly industry. Initially valid for five years, this law was renewed twice and provided the legal framework for MITI's actions in the auto parts industry between 1956 and 1971.[122] In 1956, an Auto Parts Committee was formed to provide a channel of communication between government and business. The actual auto parts reforms between 1956 and 1966 were concerned with achieving economies of scale by modernizing the existing plant facilities and by reducing the number of producers in forty-five of ninety-five parts categories through mergers. The JDB and the Small Business Finance Corporation (SBFC) provided over $50 million in low-interest, long-term loans during the ten-year program for revitalizing the auto parts sector.[123]

For the major players in the auto sector, TIPs to the sector—which included protective tariffs, quotas, and other nontariff barriers such as import restrictions via the allocation of foreign exchange—were designed to discourage direct foreign investment.[124] There were also favorable tax rates and special depreciation allowances, with the sector recording among the highest proportions of special depreciation to total depreciation, peaking at about 42 percent in 1960.[125] As a whole, the auto industry was also one of the prime beneficiaries of the JDB, which offered 32 percent of its total loans to the sector between 1961 and 1965 and an additional 54 percent of its total loans during 1966 to 1974. With the onset of trade and capital liberalization, the JDB also provided funds for the spate of mergers in the late 1960s.[126] Additionally, export promotion policies were put in place to boost the sector's efforts, with the result that the share of automobile exports went from about 0.3 percent of total exports in 1955 to about 20 percent by 1980.

There is little doubt that this industry was heavily favored and supported by MITI well into the early 1980s, despite severe divisions in the government at large in the immediate postwar era. On the one hand, the BOJ and MOT generally maintained that automobile imports be allowed freely. Their argument that the country's limited resources would be better served by concentrating on industries in which Japan had comparative advantage (such as textiles) and which did not face such devastating foreign competition was very legitimate at the time. Additionally, since auto parts constituted a significant proportion of the total automobile production and since their import consumed immense amounts of scarce foreign exchange, it also made sense to concentrate on other sectors. Yet MITI disagreed, seeking active support of the industry. The question of who would prevail, however, became moot with the outbreak of the Korean War in 1950, and MITI won the debate by historical default because of the special procurement boom. History records, however, that MITI began urging the indigenization of this sector long before the Korean War windfall.[127] And again the question is why—what made this industry stand out for favoritism?

The immediate motivation, as with so many other industries at the time, was the potential for high growth rates and the acquisition of foreign exchange earnings.[128] But more important from the long-term perspective was the thinking that the auto industry was of vital importance to the future of Japan's industrial status. The most important reason for selection was the potential for backward and forward linkages between the automobile sector and other sectors in the economy, such as steel, chemicals, tires, and machinery.[129] There was very clearly an expectation that the size and scope of this particular industry would both pull along and benefit other supplier and user industries. Its high-technology status was considered to be key in the transmission of knowledge benefits that would affect operations in all Japanese sectors. Both of these motivations continued to guide policy even after the industry was fully revived and competitive by the late 1970s. In fact, looking back at that era, one official pointed out that the idea of technological spillovers became indistinguishable from that of linkages in this one heavy industry.[130]

The "reason within reasons" from the perspective of the government was that this was the quintessential strategic industry, given to oligopolistic competition and huge economies of scale that could deter potential rivals.[131] The government, official opinion suggests, therefore had to play a role to make sure that Japanese firms were not deterred, given the advanced nature of the American industry at the time. As in many other heavy industries, in this industry government TIPs were motivated overall by a desire to catch up fast with the advanced industrial countries, especially with the United States.[132] What was true of this industry in its infant stage still continues to be true today as far as some officials are concerned, with the exception that now it is generally seen as a kind of basic industry that pulls along a great many other domestic ones. It is also seen to hold out the possibility of further advances in key niches like auto environmental technology and electrical cars. Here again, the focus is on preserving the linkages and updating the entire industrial structure with these kinds of knowledge and linkage spillovers. And here again, MITI may play a role, though far more modest than before because of the decrease in its actual powers and the increase in the industry's competitiveness.[133]

With the increase in the automotive industry's economic strength has also come a corresponding increase in its political power. It ranks as the second-largest industrial sector in the Japanese economy (after electrical machinery and equipment), representing nearly 13.4 percent of the value of the total manufacturing output in Japan today. Within the machinery industries alone, it commands a substantial share of 30 percent of the total.[134] Given the thirteen dominant firms in the industry, among them Toyota, Nissan, Mazda, Honda, and Mitsubishi, there is very little question that this has been a politically powerful sector from the point of view of campaign contributions to politicians, which has gone on to affect the industry's support.[135] Additionally, there has been a great incentive for politicians to exploit the fact of huge amounts of concentrated workers and firms under the old SNTV multi-member district system. One in ten workers in Japan is said to be engaged either directly or indirectly in the automotive industry. The industry firms are themselves geographically concentrated in specific prefectures, such as Aichi and Shizuoka, and in the surrounding Tokyo area. In fact, some officials point out that employee voting was actively encouraged by both the labor unions and managers in a firm.

The industry also lobbies directly at the Automobiles Division at MITI, in addition to exerting influence on individual politicians and bureaucrats.[136] The political influence of the thirteen major Japanese producers of cars, trucks, buses, and motorcycles is further enhanced by their collective lobbying efforts through membership in the Japan Automobiles Manufacturer Association (JAMA). Like most other industry associations, the JAMA has lobbied actively for tax reductions relating to the purchase and ownership of vehicles and specifically the discrepancy between auto taxes and the taxes applied to most goods and services.[137] The smaller auto parts firms also actively lobby through one of the external agencies of MITI, the Small and Medium Enterprise Agency, which is set up specifically to deal with their demands and which generates a lot of political pressures for the bureaucrats.[138] Given its potential for voting power and campaign contributions, politicians pay a lot of attention to this industry, which in turn generates pressure on the bureaucrats.[139] But pressure to do what? MITI bureaucrats are only too happy to favor this industry as it is, and this again points to preferences matching between these two sets of actors.

There is a possibility that the auto industry is now a mature industry that will experience a decline, generating even greater political pressures for support and favoritism when it does so.[140] But all of this is irrelevant to the fact of its initial favoritism, as well as the continued interest in its well-being for the benefit of the Japanese industrial economy. Well into the early 1970s, it was favored because of the potential importance of its linkages and knowl-edge spillovers to the rest of the industrial activities in the economy. Much of that remains true even today, with officials suggesting this sector's linkages across the spectrum of industrial activities. If electrical cars ever begin to take the place of more conventional cars, these are exactly the kinds of criteria that will continue to garner support for what will no doubt remain a key in-dustry.

MACHINE TOOLS

In 1955, the machine tools sector had both large firms that dominated the production of finished goods and numerous small and medium-sized firms that engaged in the production of a wide range of materials and compo-nents.[141] The industry was devastated by SCAP's decision to confiscate up to 50 percent of the machine tools industry capacity for reparation payments, which was later redistributed to Japanese manufacturers in the wake of the Korean War. These economic hardships, among others, were instrumental in getting the machine tool firms to form a *gyōkai*, industry association, which would then represent the many interests in the industry to the government and also signal appropriate policies.[142] Only in the late 1950s did MITI turn to supporting this sector, and it continued to do so despite the huge number of firms and their evident reluctance to have their freedom of operation cur-tailed by government interference.

The industry was designated for attention specifically in the 1956 Ma-chine Industry Law, which was used to try and rationalize the industry, and later the more general 1957 Electronics Industry Law.[143] These laws formed the legal basis for the provision of low-interest loans (6.5 percent annually) through the JDB that were directed at upgrading equipment and technology in the sector. By the late 1950s, the JDB was providing upward of 33 percent of the total industry financing. Though preferential loan treatment contin-ued, the total loans to the machinery sector did not exceed about ¥10.6 bil-lion in over five years. By many accounts, a definite import substitution strategy was at work because of various TIPs, such as MITI subsidies for re-search and production of experimental machine tools, systematic study of foreign machine tools in government-sponsored research facilities, release and sharing of government-developed technology, and subsidies for the pur-chase of domestic products in order to counterbalance highly favorable for-eign credit terms for purchase of foreign machinery.[144]

Although MITI allowed the importation of foreign machine tools, the concern with the continued poor quality of domestic production as well as the lack of foreign exchange meant that such importation was monitored and approved strictly on a case-by-case basis. In fact, only machine tools that could not be substituted for in Japan or that were essential to large-scale industrial activities could be imported throughout the 1950s and 1960s. Given the size and number of firms, MITI's key goal was rationalization, in coordination with the industry association, the Japan Machine Tool Builder's Association (JMTBA), which also formed in 1957. By 1960, an Agreement on the Concentration of Production was drawn up, which was not only full of contradictions but also lacked any sort of enforceability. Firms continued to enter the industry against MITI's wishes and to engage freely in the production of goods most suited to their operations.

In the wake of trade liberalization in 1961 and the capital liberalization movement in 1966, MITI revised the 1956 law so as to continue supporting the industry. JDB low-interest loans were later supplemented with those from the SBFC, drawing attention again to the continued importance of SMEs in the industry. In 1968, the Basic Machine Tool Industry Promotion Plan focused on the necessity of expanding exports to alleviate anticipated balance of payment problems with capital liberalization. There was again a failed effort through JMTBA to establish an agreement, which focused on the addition of new product lines and the entry of new firms into the sector. By the time that the 1956 law expired in 1971 and the Electrical Machinery Law was passed in the same year, MITI had retreated from attempting to restructure, specifically cartelize, the industry. Although trade friction with the United States, as in the 1982 Houdaille case and the 1987 Toshiba-Konsberg affair, caused suspicions about MITI's continued support of the sector, in reality MITI was restricted mostly to supervisory injunctions.[145] Whatever the truth of these perceptions, the fact of the matter is that while machine tools was selected and promoted actively by MITI, the very number of firms in the industry was a barrier to tight business-government relations. But this did not stop MITI from continuing to legislate and try to support this sector, which brings us to the question why.

In the late 1950s, selection was prompted by the prospects for growth rates and, more important, by the realization that this industry was critical even to the basic industries that would come in its wake. The key thinking at the time was that the machine tool technology was fundamental to everything else and also to the acquisition and assimilation of higher levels of technology. In retrospect, officials believe that this industry's selection at the time was motivated by its extensiveness of uses and its linkages to the rest of the industrial economy. And this became clearer only as the huge requirements of machinery in industrial development became obvious in the late 1950s.[146] Certainly these criteria take precedence over those that are now thought to be important, such as high-income elasticity of demand or high productivity because, as officials point out, these sound a little too complicated to be convincing in the budgeting process.

Practically, the most important reason for this industry's selection can be attributed to the home firms' weak competitive and backward position compared to those in the United States and European countries.[147] In many instances, the numerous Japanese firms were so small that they were widely regarded as being a bottleneck to the development of the overall industry, because they showed no promise of being able to achieve economies of scale or productivity that would make them competitive in the global market. Yet the firms were able to succeed on their own merits. Today, the Japanese industry stands as the leading global producer of numerically controlled machine tools, which form about 80 percent of the total machine tools produced. Overall, Japan accounts for 27 percent of the total global production, making it the world leader in production for fifteen years since 1982.[148] But the comparative positioning of countries is still important. In fact, some officials maintain that having the world's largest market shares or cheap prices is no cause for celebration as Germany and Switzerland are still far ahead of Japan in terms of quality, and other competitors in East Asia are close behind.[149]

So while officially there are no or few TIPs, this does not mean there is any the less interest in the fate of this industry. In fact, officials believe that there is a "natural current" of industry that is moving inexorably forward, from basic machine tools to electrical machinery and now onto mechanatronics and information machinery industries. Again, the same criteria as above continue to be relevant even today in the decision-making process. There is still a strong belief that this industry's products are the building blocks that affect industrial performance throughout the economy. As in the immediate postwar era, the thinking today is also that if Japan does not have the ability to produce the high-technology version of basic machine tools, it will not be able to produce other things as well or as much as its competitors. The most favored niches in the industry are those that promise the greatest technological advancements and benefits, such as mechanatronics and robotics.

Once again, the thinking is that this is a basic industry with immense potential for linkage externalities, and it is hardly of import that this is an industry whose output is earmarked almost entirely for intermediate consumption by such industries as automobiles, computers, household electrical goods, or even office equipment. TIPs have been motivated by the principle that internal economies of scale in the production of even intermediate goods like machine tools can still become external economies to the industries that are buying those goods.[150] No less important is the growth potential in this industry, with the observation, for example, that American producers can only fill 50 percent of their own internal market.

Despite the importance of the economic side of things, there is also a substantive political case for favoritism. This industry is characterized by as close to perfect competition as possible, with hundreds of firms that are family or privately owned, so political influence is not a mere matter of industrial concentration.[151] Rather, geographical concentration is a source of political clout, particularly in prefectures like Aichi with sixteen firms and Shizuoka with eleven firms.[152] Aichi Prefecture, which has almost all of the industry's dominant firms, is one of the industry's regions that has held a great deal of influence with the politicians under the old electoral system.[153] Regional influence has not, however, translated into political power at the national level, particularly at Keidanren, the presidency of which almost always goes to the head of one of Japan's largest firms. Although the industry can claim to have had a vice president at this institution, no Keidanren president has ever come from this industry, which some officials believe is further testimony to its political weakness.[154]

The market structure combined with the old SNTV multimember electoral system potentially also structured the political incentives for politicians to favor this industry. Why were there so many repeated attempts at cartelization, when each was bound to prove as futile as the countless previous ones? One reasonable concern is the effectiveness of an industry-wide cartel with hundreds of members. The same concern applies even when cartels are organized around product categories that are dominated by small firms. The attempt makes some sense from the viewpoint of the electoral logic, because the organization and coordination of such cartels would require a trade or industry association. These, in turn, could be an effective means for splitting the vote in multimember SNTV districts.

But this reasoning has to be considered in the context of the way that lobbying is actually carried out by the industry. The firms, either collectively or individually, do not make demands upon the government for favorable TIPs through the politicians or the Diet at large. This is true across the board for all industries. The JMTBA, which has about a hundred industry firms as members, represents the overall industry concerns directly at MITI, specifically at the Industrial Machinery Division under the Machinery and Information Industries Bureau. In fact, the executive director of JMTBA is almost always an ex-MITI official and primarily plays an intermediary role between the industry firms and MITI, bypassing the politicians altogether.[155] Individually, when they need to, the bigger firms take their demands directly to the same MITI division as well. The smaller firms do the same by going directly to MITI's external Small and Medium Enterprise Agency, which has been put in place to deal with the concerns of just such firms. In fact, SMEs are important not just to politicians but also to MITI for reasons of social and economic stability—a factor that again hints at a potential venue for cooperation among these two sets of actors.

What also casts doubt on this reasoning is that cartelization did not represent the only type of intervention in the industry, and concentrating on it alone gives an incomplete picture. Most important of all, both rationalization and cartelization attempts subsided by 1971, whereas the electoral logic surely did not. There were also numerous other TIPs, ranging from strategic manipulation of foreign exchange and import controls to export promotion policies, that do not lend themselves as easily to the political explanation. In sum, although the machine tools industry is a very difficult case for MITI's selection altogether, there is no question that it was favored until the early 1980s. And the reasoning behind those selections shows that while political pressures potentially explain some policies, the larger picture suggests that economic concerns had a relatively greater role to play.

COMPUTERS

The first computer was exported to Japan in 1954, and it did not take too long for MITI to appreciate and publicize the importance of this industry.[156] In 1955, MITI issued a report that stressed the critical importance of computers to the future economy, and the industry then moved ahead and launched computers for domestic consumption.[157] The 1957 Electronics Industry Law was crucial for forming the legal basis of support for the computer industry and was used by MITI to coordinate business–government activities through the industry association, the Japan Electronics Industry Development Association (JEIDA).

Government TIPs came in four specific forms: financial loans, procurement policies, protectionism, and cooperative R&D projects. There were substantial problems in coordinating all the government actors, with actors like the finance ministry opposed to indigenizing this industry and Nippon Telegraph and Telephone (NTT) colliding head on with MITI on certain procurement issues.[158] In all, though, there was little disagreement over the desirability of the TIPs. Financial assistance was provided through several institutions. The JDB, and even more so NTT, disbursed both direct and indirect forms of financing, ranging from specific promotional loans for online systems and data processing to loans for large-scale research projects.[159] Additional monies were provided through the Fiscal Investment and Loan Program (FILP), based on pooled postal-savings and national pension accounts, at key points in time. JDB funds were also used to set up the Japan Electronic Computer Corporation (JECC) in August 1961. The JECC essentially financed domestic computer purchases. Although the government increasingly discouraged reliance on the company, as late as the period between 1970 and 1981 roughly 30 percent of all domestic machines sold or rented continued to go through JECC.

The most important TIPs came in the form of import restriction and selective allocation of foreign exchange for the import of new technology. By several accounts, the deliberate delaying of the trade and capital liberalization allowed the computer industry a highly beneficial reprieve that had a net positive effect on its ability to compete internationally. Since 1955, there had been a tariff level of 15 percent on computers, and it was only to drop slightly to 13.5 percent in 1972. By the early 1970s, however, Japan was under considerable American pressure to liberalize. Although MITI made announcements concerning liberalization in the early 1970s, many foreign manufacturers continued to complain that significant impediments to both capital and trade liberalization remained because of preferential links between Japanese computer manufacturers, their affiliated *keiretsu*, and public-sector agencies.[160] Imports of computers fell from 80 percent in 1959 to 20 percent in 1968, and by another measure purchases of foreign computers also dropped from 93 percent to 42.6 percent during the same period.[161]

Despite foreign pressures and the relatively backward status of Japanese computers, MITI continued its emphasis on the indigenization of computer manufacturing, as was evidenced in new legislation and new consortia and projects attuned to potential changes in the industry's overall makeup. In 1970, the Information-Technology Promotion Law was enacted to encourage the development of software in conjunction with the original emphasis on hardware.[162] To ensure the legal basis for its role, MITI combined the 1956 Machine Industry Law and the 1957 Electronics Industry Law into the 1971 Temporary Measures Law for the Promotion of Specified Electronics and Machinery Industries. One of the purposes of this law was specifically to direct financing toward integrated circuit manufacturers, and well over 20 percent of the funds allocated under this law actually went to the electronics sector as a whole. The 1971 law was superseded by the 1978 Law on Temporary Measures for the Promotion of Specified Machinery and Information Industries, which was tailored to direct attention toward the increasing integration of the machinery, electronics, and information-processing industries.[163] This particular piece of legislation was in keeping with MITI's proclaimed vision for the 1980s that stressed the creative knowledge-intensification of the industrial structure as a whole. Even today, regardless of how well Japanese computers have done commercially, the interest in computers and related products is far from over. Again, the question is why was there this favored status at all?

The answer, as one official pointed out, does not depend on any profound quantitative or statistical analysis but simply on observations of the advanced American industry. Growth rates were certainly important, as was the concern with high value-added. But the decisive factor was the potential for technological spillovers or linkage externalities and the widespread perception that computer technology would underwrite the next generation of industries. The idea, considered practical at the time, was to make this industry the center of favoritism and then let others grow up around it.[164] The same reasoning held at NTT and in the government at large. Diet leaders and other politicians also proclaimed the strategic importance of the computer technology as a whole for the information age, and they exhorted NTT, MITI, and industry to work together in the national economic interest as the tug and pull between the government agencies started in earnest.[165]

Almost every official confirms this basic view. Some say that the motivating factor for TIPs across a range of industries in those early years, including computers, was explicitly to catch up with the more advanced industrial nations of the time. Consequently, the most important reason for why the computer industry was so favored in Japan was the fact that the industry was so advanced in the United States. But what was it specifically about the industry that drove the intense favoritism initially? IBM was the model for what Japan wanted to achieve, and the perceived wide-ranging impact of its technology was the most decisive specific criteria in garnering support for TIPs across the entire government.[166] Some also add that while computers were thought to be a basic technology, with high value-added and few raw materials or energy requirements, the criteria for selection were themselves established by studying IBM and gauging its potential for growth, demand, and linkage effects on other industries, especially telecommunications.[167] That MITI was playing an intense game of technological catch-up with IBM became clear early on. In 1960, MITI singled out IBM for attention in Japan because it held the basic patents for computer technology that were deemed necessary for domestic manufacture.[168] IBM was allowed to produce locally in Japan in return for cross-licensing those patents to the then thirteen computer manufacturers in Japan.[169] Consortia, too, such as FONTAC and the Fifth-Generation Project, have been ubiquitous in this industry as in no other, with MITI assuming half to all of the costs of collaborative ventures, which were designed explicitly to catch up with and surpass IBM's lead in the sector.[170]

There does not appear to have been any hesitation with respect to indigenizing the industry at all, irrespective of outcomes in terms of success or failure. From the start, officials suggest that there was always an emphasis on having a "homemade" computer to serve domestic users so that Japan did not have to depend on any other country for what was then, as now, perceived as a basic technology.[171] And this remains true even today, when it is clear that despite the heavy favoritism shown to computers, they have not achieved the international competitiveness that their core technology, semiconductors, did.[172] Still, it is worth noting that while Japan missed the PC boom, it did develop an internationally competitive computer mainframe industry. In comparative terms, however, the Japanese computer industry held less than 10 percent of the world computer market share in the late

1980s. Like almost every other business analyst in the world until the late 1980s, MITI and Japanese firms also became sidetracked by IBM's vision of the reign of mainframes.[173]

Even as the disappointing commercial results in the computer hardware industry were coming in, there was a profound shift in overall thinking about the "appropriate" industrial structure in Japan. The thinking shifted from an emphasis on the *jyucōchōdai* (profound-deep-long-large) to *keihaku-tanshō* (light-thin-short-small)—that is, a shift from, say, steel, shipbuilding, and petrochemicals to biotechnology, computers, and software.[174] In keeping with this shift, it was the software side of the equation that took on great importance for MITI. Like computers in their heyday, software is now considered to be yet another flow in the "natural current of industry."[175] Software is seen to lie at the heart of the information society that will deeply affect all aspects of Japanese industry, economy, and society at large. Again there is a palpable danger of being backward in information technology, which can affect the competitive performance of domestic industry firms at a fundamental level. And this time around Microsoft is the advanced model with which Japan has to catch up.[176]

But it is not so easy to pick this industry out for favoritism. For one thing, given Microsoft's head start in operating systems, there is not much chance for Japan to be commercially successful. For another, there is not much of an industry to pick up, as software developers tend to work independently and are hardly organized in "megafirms." Most important of all, it is an issue of creativity, as far as developing next-generation software goes, with one or two individuals potentially capable of changing whole ways of doing things. This was evident in the TRON (The Realtime Operating-system Nucleus) saga, where literally one individual embarked singlemindedly on the goal of creating a computerized society.[177] So the best that can be done is to boost interest in the software industry through tax incentives or through encouraging venture capital, as traditional channels of finance through banks tend to be big-business oriented and very risk averse. This focus on entrepreneurs means, in turn, stressing financial liberalization.[178] Just as nobody could have predicted the reversal of the American industry's fortune in semiconductors, Japan's venture into software remains an open-ended issue. One official suggested that what is clear is that the software industry is going to grow explosively, and domestic firms may well increase their market share if, according to a few officials, some Japanese genius like Bill Gates comes along.[179]

What about the potential role of political pressures in determining favoritism, first in computers and now software? It is noteworthy that NTT had close relationships with several firms—Fujitsu, Hitachi, NEC, and, to a lesser extent, Oki—that enjoyed a privileged supplier status with NTT and that were also prime beneficiaries of government support both in the production of telecommunication and later computer equipment. Although this link between NTT and its traditional Japanese suppliers began to weaken after April 1985, when NTT was privatized, many officials suggest that this political connection had a key effect on the heavy initial favoritism shown to the sector.

Compared to steel, oil, or utilities, the electronics sector as a whole is, however, politically very weak. This is even more true for software. The industry association, JEIDA, does lobby actively on behalf of the firms directly at MITI and also at a more general level through Keidanren. But because the major firms are internationally competitive and because they are fierce competitors with each other, they tend not to engage in collective lobbying. Still, these firms have a great deal of political clout that is not immediately apparent from their lobbying activities or voting potential and that has played a role in their favoritism. Over the years, they have acquired a good many "faces," in the words of one official, that boosts their relative political power. NEC, Fujitsu, Hitachi, and Oki are considered part of the NTT family. NTT has been a monopoly for most of its existence and wields a great deal of power within the government, a fact that has not changed much since its privatization. Similarly, Hitachi, Toshiba, and Mitsubishi have very close ties to electricity/power plant utility companies like TEPCO (Tokyo Electric Power Company). TEPCO is one of the ten members of the Federation of Electrical Power Companies, which has its offices in the Keidanren building and is, by all accounts, a very influential force in domestic politics. In the event that the firms do not make requests directly to MITI or find their demands rejected, these affiliations ensure that their concerns are also brought to bear on the bureaucrats by the politicians. And this can have an effect on garnering actual support from the government for some firms rather than others.[180]

But by an large both industry and government officials maintain that in the high-technology industries, there is a distinct emphasis on keeping the selection process neutral by shielding it from political pressures and friction. More important, as in computers or information technology early on, so today politicians exhibit little interest at the start-up of any project or industry, since the possibility of votes or campaign contributions tends not to materialize until much later in the game if at all.[181] While there is an undeniable hard truth to the political angle, it is difficult to see its dominant relevance in the computer industry, particularly in the early moves to support the industry.

Computers were among the first industries to be identified as knowledge-intensive in the 1970s, an identification that continued well into the 1980s. In the space of about twenty years, numerous large- and small-scale projects, whose goals emphasized exactly this point, would be sponsored by

MITI. Their agendas demonstrated that it was not just the telecommunications sector that stood to benefit but also consumer electronics and heavy electrical machinery that would be transformed by this key technology. The emphasis was on linkages as well as technological externalities, which is why MITI went to extreme lengths to keep out foreign competition, first IBM and then Cray, even as foreign pressure increased for Japanese politicians to do otherwise. The ambition to indigenize the computer industry stemmed, as officials make clear, from MITI's belief that this industry stood at the heart of a technology that would have widespread benefits for Japan's industrial structure as a whole.

SEMICONDUCTORS

If the Japanese computer industry, both in terms of hardware and software, has never quite acquired international status, the same cannot be said of the Japanese industry's reputation in semiconductors, which truly were and are at the heart of the entire postwar revolution in the global electronics industry.[182] As with computers, MITI was slow to realize the potential for this key technology. The infamous story is that in 1953 it rejected an unknown firm's request to purchase transistor technology from abroad, and that firm went on to become the Sony Corporation, which revolutionized the application of transistor technology in compact electrical goods.[183] The transistor invention that MITI rejected subsequently developed in stages into the semiconductor technology of today.[184] As in other industries, it was the fact of Japanese firms responding to American-led developments in the field that were to shake MITI into action in the late 1950s.

The legal basis for MITI's actions was, once again, provided by the 1957 Electronics Industry Law, followed by the 1971 Temporary Measures for Electronics and Machinery Industries Law, and finally the 1978 Temporary Measures for Machinery and Information Industries Law. Throughout the 1970s, the Japanese semiconductor industry as a whole enjoyed the benefit of delaying tactics pursued by MITI with respect to capital liberalization, which almost always lagged behind trade liberalization.[185] In the 1960s, Japanese tariff rates for integrated circuits (ICs) were at around 15 percent, and while they dropped to 12 percent in 1972, these effective rates remained higher than American ones until the 1980s.[186] But if figures alone were not enough to reveal some of MITI's efforts to foster an indigenous sector, the discriminatory treatment accorded to Texas Instruments (TI), which then dominated about 30 percent of the world market, left no doubt that the industry was being nurtured in Japan with serious intent, even if MITI's resources were limited.[187]

There were additional TIPs. The semiconductor industry, specifically the IC technology, has had some direct government financing, though on a very modest scale. The JDB disbursed loans at preferential interest rates (1 percent below prime rate), but throughout the 1970s the total sums were negligible (only $30 million in 1980), with some suggesting that their more important function was to serve as a "signal" to private lenders.[188] Similarly, direct support from MITI for high-tech R&D was also paltry.[189] One important thing the government did provide directly was a secure domestic market through preferential procurement practices. The role played by the U.S. military and space agency procurements in the development of the American semiconductor industry was also matched in Japan through nonmilitary sources. The JECC and especially NTT (which refused to buy even any foreign or domestic computer system containing foreign semiconductors) are widely considered to have played a pivotal role in indigenizing and diffusing the technology domestically.

The lack of direct government finance was more than made up for by indirect government support as well. This indirect support from NTT and MITI came primarily in the form of funding for large-scale projects that were concerned with advancing the state of semiconductor technology. IBM was once again the scourge that would whip the Japanese government into action, this time with respect to memory semiconductors. In 1973, after it transpired that IBM was intending to use VLSI memories, both NTT and MITI ventured into VLSI projects from the mid 1970s onward, with NTT emphasizing applications in telecommunication equipment and MITI in computers. MITI funded about 40 percent of the cost of its VLSI project between 1976 and 1980.[190] MITI's Electrotechnical Laboratory (ETL) worked in conjunction with Fujitsu, NEC, Hitachi, Toshiba, and Mitsubishi Electric, with the express aim of developing a 256K-bit semiconductor device.[191] The VLSI project—which was among the last to be organized directly by MITI with domestic firms—is often cited as having been crucial to Japan's leapfrogging in the industry.[192] This is because it advanced the state of semiconductor technology generally and Japanese capabilities in process technology, such as silicon crystal growth and processing, more particularly.[193] It was widely deemed to have brought Japanese firms up to the same technological level as American firms in producing state-of-the-art memory devices.[194]

The Japanese government's use of the many TIPs, both direct and indirect, with which it attempted to favor the semiconductor industry is indisputable. The further fact that TIPs continued regardless of international trade friction, especially with the United States, is a testimony to the seriousness with which the industry was supported. In fact, tax incentives and national projects are still important TIPs according to some officials.[195] For example, the Association of Super Electronics Technology (ASET) project, which had an original time span of five years between 1995 and 2000, allowed the major firms to research the "next-next" generation of semiconductor technology.[196] So why was and is the semiconductor industry so favored?

As with computers, it was the backward position of the Japanese semiconductor industry vis-à-vis the American one at the time that was the overall impetus behind MITI's actions. In 1965, the world semiconductor market was dominated by five American semiconductor producers. In 1978, American companies still held 56 percent of the world market and Japanese companies a mere 28 percent. As many officials pointed out, looking at the advanced American industry was crucial in convincing the government that supporting this high value-added and high-technology industry could similarly raise Japan's economic welfare in the future.[197] Given the importance of what came to be seen as a basic technology, MITI also did not want to see Japan dependent on America or any other country for it.[198]

Despite the statements now made by the officials, however, the most important thing to note is that the industry was not favored initially by MITI and took root in Japan largely because of private efforts. Even as late as 1979, MITI's favoritism was focused on IBM's "future systems" in computers, and especially on its 360 series. As several officials pointed out, semiconductors were never the first or foremost target. MITI began to support the semiconductor market not for its own sake but rather for its potential to further the fortunes of the computer industry, which was MITI's main target. As the Japanese firms moved to acquire and produce the IC technology, MITI realized that the technology was of a basic nature and could have a wide impact on the rest of the industrial economy. From the 1970s onward, the semiconductor technology got selected with greater intensity because of the potential for growth rates and especially technological spillovers and linkage externalities in the domestic industrial economy. Practically put, the selection was spurred on by the reasoning that semiconductors would be used in a range of existing industrial activities.[199]

Other observers also suggest that MITI selected semiconductors basically as a means of furthering the potential of the computer industry, just as NTT was to make moves to do the same for the telecommunications sector.[200] Roughly the same firms that had acquired both competence and experience in producing telecommunication equipment and later computers—NEC, Fujitsu, Toshiba, Hitachi, Mitsubishi, and Matsushita—were to turn their attention to the American-led developments in semiconductor devices beginning in the late 1950s.[201] They were to acquire further knowledge and competence in the manufacture of semiconductor devices by assimilating the rapid technological advancements being made in the American industry—the integrated circuit in 1959, the microprocessor after 1971, and VLSI in the late 1970s.[202] The Japanese industry first began in the 1960s and concentrated almost entirely on replacing transistors with simple semiconductor devices in consumer electronics. By the mid 1970s, however, the industry had moved toward the acquisition of advanced IC capability that would serve the demands of the domestic telecommunication and computer industries and would also definitively place it in the thick of international competition.[203] As is well known, what the Japanese industry was able to achieve in the international marketplace, both in terms of speed and scale, left its rivals incredulous in the 1980s.[204]

Given the economic power that these firms came to have, it is also reasonable to expect that they have held a great deal of political influence that affected their favoritism. By many accounts, the industry firms have contributed sizably to politicians' campaigns, hold a great deal of voting potential, and wield influence at the highest level of government.[205] The Electronics Industry Association (EIAJ) alone, which has 570 industry firms as its members, receives estimated donations of about $2 billion per year from its members. The EIAJ, as well as the larger firms, goes directly with specific requests to MITI's Machinery and Information Industries Bureau and its Industrial Electronics Division. EIAJ officials add that these bureaus and especially divisions at MITI are the real "windows" to the government in Japan.[206]

The extreme competitiveness between the industry firms waters down individual demands and forces the firms to lobby for very general TIPs that affect all members equally, such as taxes or deregulation. In terms of political lobbying and campaign contributions, the EIAJ coordinates its efforts with Keidanren. At Keidanren, however, any industry-specific demands become even more diluted because there the industry firms are pitted against other completely different industries such as steel, automobiles, and finance. With the changes in the political system, Keidanren now also tends to turn to MITI more directly, rather than to the politicians, in terms of lobbying on behalf of all industries. Additionally, some MITI officials suggest that because the industry tends to be internationally oriented, the major industry firms tend to have little to do with domestic politics altogether.[207]

There is little doubt that the industry agitates politically or even that it has political clout. But on the whole, as EIAJ officials remark in a frustrated manner, the industry appears to have had difficulty in becoming politically influential for both structural and institutional reasons, compared especially to steel or utilities. And the major TIPs chosen as selection instruments by MITI and also by NTT—specifically, the pro-Japanese procurement policies and the VLSI project—do not lend themselves easily to political explanations. Instead, they reflect the intense concern of the Japanese government with diffusing the new technology throughout the economy and moving forward in the industrial game. And that interest is by no means over. Even today, the semiconductor industry is seen as one with tremendous potential for further knowledge and linkage spillovers.[208]

AIRCRAFT

Despite SCAP's ban on all aircraft production after the war, it was the Americans who initially helped revive the industry with their special procurements during the Korean War.[209] When the Americans left Japan, MITI maneuvered deftly on the grounds of national defense and gained complete jurisdiction over both the military and civil aircraft sectors in July 1952, leaving the transport ministry out in the cold. In the very same month, MITI, which like the Japan Defense Agency (JDA) sought to encourage domestic aircraft production, established the legal basis for the allocation of government TIPs to this sector by ensuring the passage of the Aircraft Industry Manufacturing Law through the Diet. This brought the same prewar players back into the business.[210]

Initial progress in the sector began with the military side, as the JDA insisted on having its equipment and ordnance, including aircraft, produced domestically. But this progress was also boosted once again, in no small measure, by the Americans. The 1954 Mutual Defense Assistance Agreement between the United States and Japan allowed the Japanese to produce American military aircraft for use by the Japanese Self-Defense Forces. Both direct production as well as coproduction and licensing agreements with the United States over the subsequent years helped advance the technical state of the field among Japanese aircraft firms.[211]

Well into the early 1980s the JDA accounted for nearly 90 percent of the Japanese industry sales, which was generally characteristic of both the previous and the next decade.[212] While important, this military demand alone was deemed severely inadequate for expanding aircraft demand, both because of the 1 percent of GDP ceiling on total military expenditures and also the informal ban on military-related exports. From the start it was understood that the real growth in aircraft would come from a competitive civilian aircraft industry, and in retrospect it is clear that indigenous military production, at least from MITI's point of view, was merely a means to establish a technological base in Japan for that end.

The 1954 Aircraft Industry Development Law allowed MITI to focus exactly on that end. It empowered MITI not only to approve any entrants into the industry but also to allocate subsidies, tax breaks, depreciation benefits, and low-interest loans from the BOJ and the JDB as it saw fit. Between 1953 and 1959, the law was also used to provide indirect subsidies to the industry-created consortium called the Japan Jet Engine Company (JJEC), whose goal was the development of an indigenous jet engine.[213] In 1958, the Second Aircraft Industry Development Law was passed, whose consequences would long be cited as one of MITI's worst failures. The law allowed for the creation of Nihon Aircraft Manufacturing Company (NAMCO) in June 1959, an industry-based national policy company in which the government took a 50 percent equity share and guaranteed full subsidization of development costs.[214] Essentially, the 1958 law authorized funding for the indigenous development of the YS-11, which emerged as the first Japanese-produced twin-engine passenger jet in 1962. But with a small domestic market, strong competition from the Europeans in the American commuter market, poor sales, and incompetent marketing and product support networks, the YS-11 was never to achieve commercial success and was abandoned in 1973.[215]

Both the domestic financial failure of the YS-11 and the international dominance of American commercial jets by that time did little to curb MITI's efforts in developing a national aircraft sector. This time around, however, due largely to the extremely competitive realities of global trade in the industry, MITI encouraged coproduction through joint projects with foreign partners by sponsoring the creation of the Japan Commercial Transport Development Corporation (JCTDC) in 1973.[216] It then used the JCTDC to disburse *hojokin*, which were direct loans from the ministry that were to be paid back only if a designated project was successful.[217] This spurred on the aircraft firms. In 1984, for example, with the approval of the Japan Aircraft Development Corporation (JADC), Japanese firms acquired 25 percent of the work share in a project with Boeing for developing the 7J7 (which was later abandoned by Boeing in 1987).[218] In addition, they were engaged in the joint production of a new technology fan-jet engine with Rolls Royce and moved into the jet engine business on a full-scale basis. In 1986, the 1958 Aircraft Industry Promotion Law was revised for the third time to reflect the government's continued interest in the coproduction of aircraft and aeroengines, and NAMCO was transformed into the International Aircraft Development Fund (IADF), whose task would be to promote collaboration efforts with foreign firms.[219]

By all accounts, the global commercial aircraft industry is a textbook "strategic sector" case as understood in the new international economics. It has huge economies of scale that serve as an effective deterrent to potential entrants who face far higher fixed costs than do incumbent firms. This means that, realistically, the global commercial aircraft industry can only support one or two profitable producers at a time.[220] But even the severe competitive friction between America's Boeing and EU's Airbus, which have divided up world production between them, is not seen as an effective enough deterrent.[221] Whether it was the JDA intent on producing jet fighters or MITI bent on building commercial aircraft, the long-cherished goal of the Japanese government to develop an indigenous aircraft industry became fully apparent to the outside world only during the FS-X (Fighter Support-Experimental) controversy with the United States in the late 1980s.[222] What also became clear was that this government favoritism continued despite the sector's meager economic achievements in the postwar period.[223] Why this unmitigated support?

The most important reason for favoritism is the most obvious. Military demand has sustained the industry for the better part of its postwar history, and this defense angle sets it apart from all other industries. Even today well over 70 percent of the industry's production is earmarked for defense products, with the remainder in commercial aircraft parts.[224] In fact, the emphasis on defense, according to the pervasive official view, is the main reason why the "market mechanism" does not apply to this industry, nor should it be allowed to. And it is also why all countries in the world, including Japan, scramble to appropriate this sector regardless of whether it is economically efficient to do so.[225]

But national security is not the only reason cited for its selection. From the beginning, it has been thought economically strategic in much the way theorists have in mind. In the 1970s, MITI's vision pointed to the importance of knowledge-creating industries for the economy, such as aircraft. In the 1980s, MITI's vision again pointed to the aircraft industry as a typical knowledge-intensive, high value-added, spillovers-generating sector that deserved government assistance. In the early 1990s, there was continued emphasis on technological and linkage spillovers, along with national security, as key aspects of this industry.[226] In fact, even today, no limits are seen to this industry's linkage externalities, which go on to influence newer industries like composite materials, supercomputers, and advanced materials.

Even when alliances and joint projects were encouraged—such as the development and production program for the 767/777 passenger jets, the joint development of the F-2 support fighter with Lockheed-Martin, and the international development and production of the V2500 engine—the motivation for doing so was to indigenize niches in an overall sector that exhibited high value-added and potential for spillovers.[227] Today the possibility of indigenizing the sector—producing and marketing a full-fledged commercial plane—is thought to be remote for reasons of steep costs and risks. But while this may be the general thrust of opinion in the industry, it is not so at MITI, a fact that is a source of great friction in the interactions between MITI and industry, according to one official source. At MITI, the current emphasis on producing high value-added products like cockpits, engines, and total systems is considered somewhat of a compromise, given both industry reluctance as well as the limited availability of TIPs. In any event, the debate over whether Japanese firms should stick to subcontracting versus concentrating on producing a full-fledged plane is far from over.[228] In fact, the upper echelons of MITI—consisting of those who can actually recall domestic aircraft production before the war—still want to see this industry take root in Japan once again, despite opposition from domestic firms and the realities of international competition.[229] The continued and increased demand from airlines for new aircraft and Boeing's delivery delays in providing them in the past are also keen incentives for anyone with ambition to enter the market.[230]

In the meantime, what about the role of political pressures in terms of favoritism? Because of the defense angle, the role both of political pressures and politicians tends to matter less to the logic of favoritism.[231] And even if politicians exerted pressure, it could hardly be said that they were forcing bureaucrats to favor the industry since the bureaucrats wished to do precisely that. Nor does the total employment level of about 40,000 workers, which may be of interest to politicians, sway government TIPs. In fact, the defense angle ensures that this industry's firms are privileged like no others in Japan. But this is not to deny the tremendous lobbying power within this industry, including as it does Japanese industry giants like Kawasaki, Mitsubishi, Fuji, and Ishikwajima-Harima, which sit at the apex of the Japanese aerospace industry. Their combined lobbying platform gives them additional power in the form of the Society of Japanese Aerospace Companies (SJAC), whose 170 members include the bulk of the firms engaged in the production of aircraft, fuselages, engines, and space vehicles and related equipment.[232]

The SJAC, however, does not concentrate its lobbying power on politicians but rather directly on the officials at STA and MITI. Because of the tremendous problems of aggregating the member firms' specific requests, the lobbying demands tend to be more general in nature. That is, the SJAC lobbies for general TIPs that affect all its members equally, such as seeking to lower taxes or deregulation, rather than specific ones for specific companies.[233] Through Keidanren, the big firms do look to the politicians to play a role. But this role is restricted more to large-scale political support that affects the firms' competitive positions worldwide. For example, the idea is that politicians should help secure markets abroad in the way that President Jacques Chirac did in China for French firms. Or, as another example, the politicians should concentrate on giving political backing to mergers among existing companies, such as the Boeing-McDonnell one supported more recently in the United States.[234]

Political backing is also being sought by both the industry and the firms for what is perceived as the logical metamorphosis of the existing industry into another one, namely space. At present, no Japanese firm is fully dedicated to the business of aerospace, which now comprises a mere 10 to 20 percent of overall business even in the big companies. The scale of space activities is even smaller. But once space activities did begin in Japan in earnest from the 1970s onward, reaching international levels of technology and operational potential in the 1990s, the government began to take a keen interest in the future of this sector. The shift toward space activities gives us an "in-the-making" opportunity to find out why the Japanese government favors what is widely considered a potential winner industry in the future. That will be the task of the next chapter.

Summing Up the Evidence on the Industry Cases

To briefly reiterate, the goal of this analysis was to establish why TIPs were disbursed, not whether they were effective or appropriate. What did we learn? The ten cases analyzed above leave us with a good sense of the criteria and other historical factors that motivated the policy choices to favor these industries. They are also useful for establishing the perceptions and situational factors that affect policy choices. Table 4.1 sets out the main findings from each of the cases analyzed, so only a brief discussion is necessary here.

According to the officials, MITI has generally selected industries on the basis of high growth rates and value-added levels and especially the potential for technological spillovers and linkage externalities. If only one criterion had to be pinpointed, it would be the wide-ranging benefits, or importantly, perceptions about such benefits, from an industry, specifically its ability to pull along pools of labor and capital in other industries.

Setting aside the reconstruction period, shipbuilding, petrochemicals, machine tools, automobiles, and especially aircraft were all heavily selected for support in the 1950s and 1960s with this rationale in mind. Automobiles, semiconductors, and aircraft continued to be favored for exactly this reason, with the superiority of the American industries serving as models throughout the 1970s and 1980s. Officials maintain, and the earlier quantitative evidence backs them up, that each of these industries has now been formally deselected, with MITI's role relegated to one of supervisory injunctions and a focus on private-sector R&D activities.

Deselection or withdrawl of TIPs, though politically difficult, was especially urged in industries like textiles and coal, both of which were widely perceived to fail demonstrably on the key criterion of spillovers or linkage externalities. And here is where the officials admit without hesitation to the electoral reasoning, discussing pressures from politicians that impinge on the policy choices across industries. While votes and campaign contributions are certainly mentioned and are considered very important, the most influential political factor is the one least amenable to quantitative analysis, namely lobbying pressures via institutionalized channels of access. Moreover, rather than stress whether bureaucrats or politicians ultimately reign supreme in terms of policy choices, the bureaucrats speak of the extensive and ongoing

TABLE 4.1

Major Criteria for Selection Cited across Industries and over Time

Industry	Economic Criteria	Political Criteria	Rival Hypotheses
Coal	Critical to economic recovery in postwar era; chief energy fuel; basis for advanced industrial economy; basis for regional economic subsistence; theoretical criteria of growth and extensiveness of uses cited	National energy security; general national economic security concerns; intense vulnerability of Japan in raw materials; political and social pressures with demise of domestic coal industry; theoretical criteria of votes and lobbying pressures cited	Economic hypothesis especially supported in immediate postwar era with emphasis on extensiveness of uses; political hypothesis gained credence subsequently; formal deselection delayed due to both political pressures and socio-regional concerns as industry declined
Steel	Critical to economic recovery; basis for advanced industry economy; rationalization concerns; theoretical criteria of value-added and especially spillover potential, and extensiveness of uses cited	National economic security concerns; regional concentration; theoretical criteria of votes, and especially lobbying pressures via institutionalized channels of political access cited	Economic hypothesis supported with emphasis on spillovers and extensiveness of uses; relevance of political hypothesis acknowledged widely; formal deselection instituted but intent of favoritism continues
Textiles	Potential for foreign exchange; in emerging niches theoretical criteria of growth and value-added cited	Regional industrial concentration leading to political influence; lobbying pressures directly through politicians; theoretical criteria of votes; and especially lobbying pressures via institutionalized channels of political access cited	Economic hypothesis not supported in immediate postwar era but used as cover to justify acquiescence to political pressures; formal deselection desired but delayed due to political pressures
Shipbuilding	Model of other advanced industrial economies; potential for foreign exchange; theoretical criteria of growth, value-added, and spillover potential cited	Geopolitics of island nation; dependency on seaborne trade; lobbying pressures directly through politicians in wake of oil shock; theoretical criteria of votes; and especially lobbying pressures via institutionalized channels of political access cited	Economic hypothesis supported in immediate postwar era; political hypothesis gained support in wake of oil crisis; formal deselection instituted as industry firms bore main burden of adjustment
Petrochemicals	Model of other advanced industrial economies; theoretical criteria of growth, value-added, spillover potential and extensiveness of uses cited	Political pressures in wake of oil crisis; theoretical criteria of votes, campaign contributions, and especially lobbying pressures via institutionalized channels of political access cited	Economic hypothesis supported in early postwar period; political hypothesis gained support in wake of oil crisis; formal deselection difficult because of dispersed jurisdiction over industry

Industry	Economic Criteria	Political Criteria	Rival Hypotheses
Automobiles	Model of other advanced industrial economies; theoretical criteria of growth, value-added, spillover potential, and linkage externalities cited	Theoretical criteria of votes, campaign contributions, and especially lobbying pressures via institutionalized channels of political access cited	Economic hypothesis supported strongly in early postwar period to present, with linkage externalities still considered vital; economic reasoning still relevant even as political hypothesis acknowledged; formal deselection instituted but intent of favoritism continues
Machine Tools	Model of other advanced industrial economies; theoretical criteria of growth, spillover potential, and linkage externalities cited	Regional industrial concentration leading to political influence; theoretical criteria of lobbying pressures via institutionalized channels of political access cited	Economic hypothesis supported in early postwar period; political hypothesis shows relevance throughout; formal deselection forced to take place due to number and actions of maverick firms in sector
Computers	Model of other advanced industrial firms (IBM, Microsoft); theoretical criteria of growth and especially spillover potential and linkage externalities cited	Patronage of key firms; political influence of firms via many circuitous channels; theoretical criteria of lobbying via institutionalized channels of political access cited	Economic hypothesis supported in early postwar period with spillovers still considered vital; political hypothesis retains credence; formal deselection instituted but intent of favoritism continues
Semiconductors	Model of other advanced industrial economies; theoretical criteria of growth, value-added, spillover potential, and linkage externalities cited	Patronage of key firms; theoretical criteria of votes, campaign contributions, and lobbying via institutionalized channels of political access cited	Economic hypothesis supported in postwar period with linkage externalities still considered vital; political hypothesis retains credence; formal deselection instituted but intent of favoritism continues
Aircraft	Model of other advanced industrial economies, as well as Japan's own past; theoretical criteria of growth, value-added, and especially spillover potential and linkage externalities cited	Patronage of key firms; theoretical criteria of campaign contributions and lobbying via institutionalized channels of political access cited	Economic hypothesis supported strongly in early postwar period to present, with linkage externalities still considered vital; political hypothesis not well supported; formal deselection instituted but intent of favoritism continues

compromises and bargains among all actors. They are also frank in admitting that good old-fashioned political pressures can sway both the selection and deselection process contrary to bureaucratic preferences. But equally important is the idea that bureaucrats and politicians sometimes have the same preferences in terms of support, say in declining industries or even rising ones, even though they may operate out of very different motivations—a fact that makes the unilateral arrow of influence in principal-agent models appear far too simplistic.

Overall, then, the qualitative evidence here complements the quantitative evidence established earlier and gives us a clearer sense of the factors that have actually mattered in the policy-making process. Remarkably, together the two show us that there is not much difference between the MITI officials' rhetoric and their actual actions over the postwar period. Here, too, as the interviews and case histories make clear, the economic reasoning has a comparative edge in the face of political factors and pressures that are ever present in a representative democracy. And despite pressures and problems, it also holds in the next chapter, as we move to the analysis of a single sector, the commercial space launch services, that is considered vitally strategic for national economic security by most observers of broad industrial trends.

CHAPTER 5

The Commercial Space Launch Industry

IN THIS CHAPTER, I turn to a detailed investigation of the criteria for selection in one of the least-known Japanese sectors, namely the commercial space launch industry. Space launch vehicles, whether expendable or reusable (or both), are designed to carry payloads into space. Vehicles like rockets, for example, can transport payloads, such as military or commercial satellites, into low (LEO), medium (MEO), or geostationary (GEO) Earth orbits.

Given the paucity of information on space politics in Japan, this chapter provides an extensive background on the historical and competitive realities within which the Japanese government has attempted to select the industry for support.[1] Despite severe setbacks, the Japanese government's interest in indigenizing the commercial launch vehicles industry is still ongoing, and there are no indications that this interest will abate anytime soon. For this reason, an examination of this industry offers a particularly important window into the politics, economics, and perceptions behind industrial selection in Japan today—factors that may potentially serve as benchmarks for Japan's actions in both this sector and other high-technology industries in the future.

This case study is divided into three parts. The first part establishes the contours of the global industry that Japan has been attempting to break into. It is extremely important to understand the context of global competition, in large part because it figures so prominently in the interviews with respect to Japan's ability to catch up with and survive among the older established players. The second part lays out the realities of Japan's space policy, identifying the principal actors in the industry. It also provides an overview of the main stages of Japan's rocket generations and how these have fared in terms of breaking into the global commercial launch vehicles market. The third part focuses on the government TIPs to this industry. In keeping with the main goal of this work, it then ends by highlighting the criteria and perceptions that are driving government TIPs to this sector. Like the previous chapter, this one also relies principally on government documents and especially on interviews with officials involved in Japan's space policy-making. The evidence suggests that the principal criteria in this case are spillovers and linkages at the broadest level. In addition, while officially the emphasis is on market commercialization of Japan's launch vehicles, interviews suggest clearly that national security concerns are a prime reason for government favoritism to this industry.

The Global Context[2]

Until the mid-1980s, launch service providers, led by the United States, focused on government payloads rather than on commercial ones. This changed slowly over time, and by the mid 1990s, although governments were still key players, the ratio had begun to shift in favor of commercial payloads due largely to the boom in the global telecommunications market.[3] The trend toward commercialization was fueled by upswings in satellite buying from places like Asia. Hughes, for example, took twenty-five satellite orders in 1995, twenty-two of which were from commercial customers and only three from the U.S. National Aeronautics and Space Administration (NASA).[4] Similarly, the high-profile $3.4 billion Iridium system led by Motorola contributed mightily to the trend toward commercialization. The future of the Iridium system, in fact, generated a great deal of excitement about the prospects for big LEO mobile satellite systems that were due to go into effect near the end of the 1990s. Other big LEO ventures included Loral-led Globalstar, TRW-led Odyssey, and Inmarsat-led ICO Global Communications. In all of these, four competing ventures alone represented about $12 billion worth of investments.[5] Thus it is not a surprise to find that major private companies like Hughes, the world's leading commercial satellite maker at that point, began to push large amounts of funding into the development of satellites.[6]

Governments also did the same. In the United States, military planners in the Pentagon sought to take advantage of technologies developed and launched by the private sector. Meanwhile European Space Agency (ESA) officials, perceiving themselves to be in an unbelievably intense race with the United States, also became actively involved in supporting new telecommunication technologies by private companies.[7] For all these reasons, in the early 1990s one estimate concluded that while revenues generated by the launch industry were only one-tenth of the satellite industry, the projected growth in the demand for satellites would swiftly bring new players into the launch vehicles game.[8] Despite concerns about oversupply later down the line, the widespread perception was that commercial launch vehicle services would be spurred by the seemingly limitless demand for sophisticated telecommunication satellites in GEO and LEO orbits, as well as for other related equipment.[9]

By the end of the 1990s, however, the picture was a little more somber, with important consequences for the entry of new players in the launch vehicles game. The basic demand for more and more commercial satellites at varied orbits that were seen as driving the demand for launch vehicles took something of a hit.[10] For one thing, it was unrealistic to assume that the kind of past commercial demand in the relatively new satellite market would continue on an explosive upward trend forever, for the simple reason of market saturation, where the sizable portion of the demand for new satellites for both established and newcomer operators had already been established. Even if such systems needed replenishment, this would not be happening until the mid to the late 2000s.

For another thing, there was and is the "Iridium flu."[11] Iridium's spectacular bankruptcy in 1999 led to widespread negative perceptions about the commercial satellite industry as a whole in business and financial circles, and consequently there were many questions about the desirability of producing new satellite systems altogether.[12] In the United States, forecasts put out by the Federal Aviation Administration's Office of the Associate Administration for Space Transportation (AST) and the Commercial Space Transportation Advisory Committee (COMSTAC) showed a similar downward revision of the numbers. In 1999, AST/COMSTAC projections were that an average of 51 commercial space launches would occur annually through 2010. But the estimates in 2000 showed nearly a 20 percent reduction, with the present forecast that an average of only 41.4 commercial space launches will occur annually through 2010 in large part because of failures like Iridium.[13]

Whatever the accuracy of the predictions, it is a safe bet that the existing and more established launch service players will automatically receive a substantial portion of the market. In 1999, seventy-eight orbital launches were carried out, thirty-six of which were commercially designated payloads that generated about $2.2 billion in revenues.[14] United States and European launch service providers dominated the market, launching thirty-four of the total thirty-six commercial payloads.[15] Who exactly are these established players, and what does their dominance suggest about the viability of potential new entrants?

DOMINANT GLOBAL COMPETITORS

Arianespace

The key leader in one field of commercial launch services is Europe's Arianespace, which has 50 percent of the market for payloads bound for geostationary transfer orbits (GTOs).[16] Created in March 1980, Arianespace consists of forty-one aerospace and engineering firms from twelve European countries, fifty-three corporate shareholders, eleven banks, and the ESA.[17] The largest single shareholder is France with about 57 percent of the total shares, followed by Germany with about 18 percent and Italy with 7 percent. Arianespace entered the new century in an extremely strong competitive position, with twelve consecutive successful launches in 2000 alone.[18] Its reputation for cost-effectiveness, speed, and reliability has already made it an indisputable leader in the field, with many of its customers being repeat ones.

Until 1999, Arianespace's Ariane 4 was considered the most reliable launch vehicle in the world, with only eight failures in 117 launches since 1988. With this record, this launch workhorse won the confidence of most satellite and other payload producers, and American private firms have even commissioned more than half of its launches.[19] But given the increasing weight of payloads, especially satellites, the long-running Ariane 4 rocket is gradually being phased out over the next several years in favor of the new generation heavy-lift Ariane 5. After a shaky debut in 1996 and subsequent test flights in 1997 and 1998, the Ariane 5 became fully operational at the end of 1999 and completed its first full year of commercial service in 2000 with five successful commercial flights.[20] Overall, with its record of successful launches and continued demand from both previous and new customers, Arianespace is poised to take a commanding lead in the commercial launch services market.[21]

Lockheed Martin

Arianespace's main competitors are basically from the United States, with Lockheed Martin and Boeing at the top of the list. Lockheed Martin is one of the world's largest space and defense companies and has a long tradition of being active in the government launch business.[22] Since the mid 1980s, the company has worked closely with the U.S. Air Force and later NASA to develop and launch vehicles for military and government payloads. In this sphere, its series have included the Titan, Athena, and Atlas rockets. The Titan series is not available for commercial purposes. The Athena series, while operational, has had relatively little commercial demand. As discussed below, it is the Atlas series that has moved definitively forward in the commercial launch arena, with a heavy-lift Atlas V currently in development.[23]

Overall, Lockheed Martin approached the commercial launch market in two distinct ways, one through a long-term and costly partnership with NASA and the other through multinational ventures with other companies. On the government side, NASA began to put forward the idea of the Reusable Launch Vehicle (RLV) Technology Program in the mid 1990s in an effort to remain competitive in the commercial launch business. Using a partnership with the U.S. Air Force and private industry, the goal was to develop experimental flight vehicles—X-33 and X-34—that could potentially provide revolutionary and cheap access to space.[24] In 1996, NASA awarded Lockheed Martin about $900 million to build the half-scale prototype X-33 as the fundamental technology driving next-generation reusable launch systems that incorporated single-stage-to-orbit (SSTO) characteristics. The company put an estimated $200 million of its own money into the prototype, while also planning to funnel as much as $5 billion into the private development of the actual full-scale VentureStar.[25]

While the X-33 was to have first flown in March 1999, its estimated date of flight was later changed to 2003.[26] Lockheed Martin and its team of subcontractors were unable to complete the X-33 satisfactorily under the $912 million NASA commitment that ended in December 2000. The program was then stretched out to March 2001 with an additional $68 million from NASA in order to keep the X-33 team involved in the project.[27] But in March 2001, NASA terminated the X-33 and X-34 projects in the face of mounting criticisms, budget limitations, and project uncertainties.[28] In its place, NASA focused attention on the Space Launch Initiative (SLI), which would support entrepreneurial space launch companies like Kistler and Kelly Aerospace and eventually lead to a Fiscal 2005 decision on full-scale development of a reusable launch vehicle.[29]

Since the primary purpose of the X-33 joint project was to give a solid sense of how a full-scale prototype would perform under actual circumstances, the real payoff would have been in the VentureStar, which was, ideally, intended to replace the government-owned Space Shuttle. A VentureStar fleet, built entirely by Lockheed Martin, would have become essential not just for the commercial satellite market but also for NASA, which was interested in using it for ferrying crews and supplies to the International Space Station. The SLI initiative differs from VentureStar in that it focuses primarily on getting humans and cargo into orbit for NASA rather than simply launching payloads for NASA.[30] NASA began to announce contracts for this "second-generation" reusable launch vehicle effort by the middle of May 2001.[31] The VentureStar effort is not yet over, as Lockheed Martin has turned to the U.S. Air Force to seek funding for its stalled X-33 program. The selling point, supported by some and questioned by others, is that the service needs a reusable spaceplane or space-maneuvering vehicle for military purposes. Contingent on whether the Pentagon actually makes a decision to fund the project at the cost of several hundred million dollars for at least two years, the VentureStar may well become a reality.[32] There is little doubt that the VentureStar remains a huge technology leap and, if successful, will revolutionize cheap access to space in the long term and secure Lockheed Martin's place among the dominant players in the global industry.

In the more medium term, however, Lockheed Martin has also attempted to enter the commercial launch services market more directly through joint ventures and mergers. In 1993, Lockheed Martin established the Lockheed Khrunichev Energia International joint venture in order to market the Russian Proton launch vehicle exclusively. In 1995, it then merged this joint venture with Martin Marietta, which had purchased the General Dynamics Space Systems Division and its Commercial Launch Services subsidiary responsible for marketing the Atlas launch vehicles.

International Launch Services (ILS), a joint-venture stock company, was the direct result of the Lockheed and Martin Marietta merger announced on 10 June 1995. With the formal original organizational structure of these two entities intact, ILS continues to operate as the main contracting entity for Proton and Atlas launches.[33] In July 1999, ILS also received the exclusive right to market the Angara class of launch vehicles, currently in development almost entirely domestically by Khrunichev of Russia and capable of handling payloads ranging from small to medium-sized LEO satellites to medium-sized and heavy LEO or GTO spacecrafts.[34] In 2000, ILS became a serious and established player in the competitive commercial launch market with six Proton and eight Atlas launches of almost perfect operational reliability, two dedicated launch sites in Florida and Kazhakstan capable of simultaneous and independent launches, over $1 billion worth of contracts for launches altogether, and a backlog of about $3 billion representing launch contracts for forty launches.

Boeing

The other serious player on the United States side is the Boeing Company. With the merger of Boeing and McDonnell-Douglas in August 1997—a move that shunted aside the seismic importance even of the merger between Lockheed Martin and Martin Marietta—Boeing became the single largest aerospace company in the world.[35] Like Lockheed Martin, Boeing has had long-standing experience with space transportation systems, including NASA's Space Shuttle, the world's first reusable space launch system, since the early 1980s. Here Boeing, in a joint venture established with Lockheed Martin in the form of United Space Alliance (USA) since 1996, has been the primary contractor for NASA's Space Shuttle programs.[36]

On its own, Boeing's main series has included the historic Delta rockets, the mainstay of NASA's and the U.S. Air Force's missions and payloads into space. Although the production of Delta rockets halted in 1981 due to the advent of the Space Shuttle, the Delta launch vehicles were resurrected in 1986 with the announcement that the Shuttle would not be carrying commercial payloads. Although the Delta II series that emerged afterward was used primarily for U.S. Air Force payloads, the Delta III series was driven primarily by a desire on Boeing's part to enter the lucrative commercial launch market for GTO payloads that were too heavy for the original series.[37]

But Delta III has had a shaky debut, and its future is not entirely certain. In 1998, the inaugural Delta III rocket exploded after it took off, destroying the satellite it was carrying. The second mission in 1999 also ended up with an engine failure, and the payload ended up in useless orbit.[38] Finally, in August 2000, to prove the rocket's safety, reliability, and long-term viability in the commercial launch market, Boeing decided to absorb the $85 million cost of flying the Delta III since it could not secure a customer. Fortunately, the third mission was successful with a simulated payload, and Boeing now has eighteen Delta IIIs worth about $1.5 billion on order, but there are few payloads assigned to those slots. Even with the successful mission, the estimated projection is now about four to six commercial missions starting in about 2002.[39]

The success of the third Delta III mission is also crucial for the reason that it is the transition vehicle for the ongoing development of the Delta IV Evolved Expendable Launch Vehicle (EELV) for medium-sized to heavy payloads.[40] Once the Delta IV becomes operational in the commercial arena, Boeing will phase out the Delta III. What is important, above all, is Boeing's commitment to the commercial launch business, with the top executive at Boeing pointedly stating that space projects, rather than commercial aircraft, represent the greatest opportunity for near-term growth at Boeing.[41] On this front, Boeing more recently made another aggressive move designed to cash in on the potentially lucrative commercial satellite industry to complement the launch side of its operations.

In January 2000, Boeing announced the acquisition of the space and communications businesses of Hughes Electronics Corporation, the world's largest satellite maker, for $3.75 billion in cash—a move some analysts dubbed a match made in heaven despite Hughes's problems.[42] According to Boeing, this acquisition, cleared by U.S. and European regulators in October 2000, is expected to boost its annual space and communication revenues by more than a third for a total of about $10 billion and allow it to gain a leading position in the global space and communication market that is itself expected to grow from its current annual figure of $40 billion to $120 billion by 2010.

Like Lockheed Martin, Boeing also remains committed to a presence in the commercial launch business indirectly through a multinational joint venture enterprise established in April 1995. The group is Sea Launch, with Boeing owning 40 percent, Russia's RSC-Energia owning 25 percent, Anglo-Norwegian Kvaerner Group of Oslo owning 20 percent, and Ukraine's SDO Yuzhnoye / PO Yuzhmash owning 15 percent.[43] Each partner is responsible for different operational contributions, and Boeing provides overall analytical and physical systems integration and missions operation. Since all launch sites in the United States are owned and controlled by the government, private launch providers face uncertain costs and unlimited liabilities, as well as the possibility of commercial launches being preempted by government ones.[44] In order to mitigate some of these concerns, the truly novel idea behind Sea Launch is the use of a modified oil rig in the Pacific Ocean, approximately 2,200 kilometers southeast of Hawaii, for commercial launches.[45] By launching from the equator, rockets can use Earth's rotation to provide additional boost, and payloads have shorter distances to travel to their orbital locations, use less fuel, and cost less.[46]

The Zenit 3SL rocket, manufactured by Ukraine in tandem with Russia, was designed exclusively for Sea Launch operations for delivering large payloads to GTO. After payload processing and launch vehicle integration in the home port in Long Beach, California, the Zenit 3SL is then loaded onto a converted oil-drilling platform that sails to the equator, where the rocket is positioned, fueled, and launched. The company now boasts a fifty-day turnaround between launches from its floating platform, with the possibility of even using the command ship to fetch a second rocket and payload, leaving the platform at sea. The inaugural flight for Sea Launch, with a demonstration payload on the Zenit, took place successfully in March 1999. This was also followed successfully with the launch of a real satellite in October 1999. With a two-for-two record, Sea Launch looked poised to butt heads with the established players in the commercial arena. But then disaster struck in the form of a prelaunch sequence glitch in March 2000, and the Zenit failed to deliver the satellite for a crucial customer into space.[47] But despite this failure and strong criticisms by competitors about Sea Launch's lapses in production, overall market confidence in the Sea Launch venture remained strong, and with justification.

Sea Launch rebounded quickly, establishing its presence with two faultless back-to-back launches. In fact, the fourth mission was crucial not just for restoring confidence in the viability of heavy-lift launches by Sea Launch as a multinational venture but also for securing additional customers, since many of them required a minimum of three successful launches before trusting a new booster like the Zenit 3SL.[48] In July 2000, Sea Launch successfully placed a satellite into GTO, and in October 2000 it launched the world's heaviest commercial communications satellite for a telecommunication company based in the United Arab Emirates, with the additional promise of the next satellite in line for the same company.[49] Thus far, all three of the successfully launched satellites have been built by Boeing Satellite Systems or its predecessor, Hughes Space and Communications—confirming Sea Launch's, and especially Boeing's, intention of moving forward in an integrated and aggressive fashion in both the satellite and launch business. With a success rate of 80 percent, a launch backlog of about seventeen payloads, and an operational capability for processing and launching at least eight launches annually, it is safe to say that Sea Launch is going to be one of the premier launch suppliers for the heavy-lift launch capabilities.[50] In June 2001, Sea Launch also began to seek U.S. government launch contracts such as through NASA, though at this stage it seeks to stay away from competing for military payloads.[51]

Overall, there can be no question that Arianespace, Lockheed Martin, and Boeing remain the dominant players in the commercial launch arena. And in this arena, launch costs are crucial since they can serve as potential deterrents to hopeful entrants.[52] Everything depends on the payload weight and orbit required and thus the launch vehicle itself. For Arianespace, launch costs run $65–$125 million for the Ariane 4 and about $150–$180 million for the Ariane 5. For Lockheed Martin and ILS, the Proton launches cost $90–$112 million, and the Atlas launches run $75–$170 million. For Boeing and Sea Launch, the Zenit launches are estimated to cost about $35–$95 million.

There is an additional factor complicating the cost structure and the viability of new entrants. Since dual-manifesting is now feasible with launch vehicles able to take off with two satellites at one go, it is estimated that roughly half of the forecasted satellites will be launched simultaneously, especially with the heavy-lift launchers. The size of the market, perhaps more now than ever before, matters for any new entrants into the commercial launch vehicles game. At present there are forty to forty-five launch vehicle programs that are or plan to be operational in the near future. The New Ariane, Delta, and Atlas boosters, as well as the Proton and Zenit, are already well ahead in the game, especially as the commercial satellites continue to become heavier.[53] But given the existing dominant players who will no doubt automatically receive a substantial portion of the market no matter which way it is headed, it is difficult to see how all these newer entrants will remain viable as commercial ventures.[54]

China and India

The competitive realities discussed above have not stopped many other nations from wanting to enter the commercial launch arena. In fact, Japan is not unique in its desire to break into the space league of the dominant players. Despite severe setbacks for two years that almost made its Long March launch vehicles virtually uninsurable until 1996, the state-owned China Great Wall Industry Corporation, for example, continues onward with upgrading its booster for both light and heavy launches.[55] With the simultaneous deployment of three satellites to LEO orbits by the Polar Satellite Launch Vehicle (PSLV) in May 1999, the Indian government also heralded its own arrival into a specific niche of the commercial launch market.[56] Like China, it, too, has been aggressively upgrading the PSLV for both LEO and GTO capacity.[57] In April 2001, India successfully launched its most advanced rocket, the Geosynchronous Satellite Launch Vehicle (GSLV-D1), capable of deploying heavy payloads into space.[58] Even if operational capability is not fully viable for all launches, both China and India are able to secure manifests simply because of global launch backlogs and, more important, the cost factor that many analysts deem key to long-term survival and success in the industry. Again, depending on the weight and orbit required, China's Long March launches can cost as little as $20 million for LEO and $75 million for GTO-bound payloads. The estimates for India's present and upgraded boosters range from $15 million to $45 million.[59]

Thus, despite justified concerns about the slowdown in the commercial launch arena, the costs as well as the uncertainties, the question is still not whether governments are interested in favoring the launch vehicles sector.[60] They clearly are. With the increased impetus given to reusable launch vehicles, governments in the United States, Europe, and Japan are all moving toward greater roles in the process of forging ahead. In fact, there is a widespread sense that these projects cannot be driven by the market but may very well have to be driven by governments.[61] The harder question is why governments continue to persist in their favoritism. To answer, the next two sections assess the realities of launch vehicle development, as well as the government thinking and support, which have been crucial to the indigenization of the Japanese space industry.

Realities of Space Policy in Japan

The commercial launch vehicles sector has formed one of the two main pillars of the Japanese space program, the other being satellites.[62] From a commercial point of view, space industry activities are dominated by space vehicles—launch vehicles, space shuttles, and satellites—followed by ground facilities, software development, and data processing and analysis.[63] But it is still small compared to other industries, and all of these segments combined to produce a turnover of about $3.7 billion, exports of about $240 million, and employees at an estimated 11,000 figure well into the close of the 1990s.[64]

The financial picture aside, there is also a historical and institutional trajectory of development in this industry that deserves careful attention. This section first sets out the main public and private players involved in Japan's space program. It then focuses on the main rocket generations in Japan, from the Lambda series that launched Japan's first satellite in space to the ongoing development of the next generation H-IIA.

From the beginning, Japan's rocket R&D was subject to the intrusion of not one but rather several major government institutions.[65] The actual launch vehicles research began principally at the University of Tokyo in the mid 1950s, with a small group of intensely committed engineers and scientists. From there, it eventually led to the establishment of the Institute of Space and Aeronautical Science in 1964 at the University of Tokyo, which functioned as a university-based research institute, and which was responsible for more systematic efforts at rocket development. In 1981, this institute was reorganized and taken over by what was then the Ministry of Education (MOE), and it is presently known as the Institute of Space and Astronautical Sciences (ISAS). Because of the amalgamations instituted under the Japanese administrative reforms, the Ministry of Education became the Ministry of Education, Culture, Sports, Science, and Technology (MEXT) effective 6 January 2001.[66] Continuing with its emphasis on core R&D, even today ISAS remains the main interuniversity locus of activities and research in both space sciences and technology under the newly reconstituted MEXT.

The Space Activities Commission (SAC), established in 1968, is an independent senior advisory body under the Prime Minister's Office and has been responsible for formulating the fundamental policies of Japan's space program. It has also been responsible for interacting with the Science and Technology Agency (STA), the other main player in the space program. Until recently, STA was under the jurisdiction of the Prime Minister's Office, with the status of a ministry whose head had the status of a minister of state for science and technology. Again, however, because of the administrative mergers in January 2001, MEXT's minister is serving concurrently as the minister of science and technology as well as of education, and STA is now subsumed under MEXT. Both the National Aerospace Laboratory (NAL) and the National Space Development Agency (NASDA) were until recently under STA's jurisdiction and are similarly now part of MEXT. With respect to launch vehicles, the focus in the early stages was on the development of small-scale, solid-fuel rockets that could launch scientific satellites, the first of which was launched in 1970. It was the general emphasis on getting into space as a whole that led to the creation of NASDA on 1 October 1969. NASDA was able to rely on the technology transfer provisions in the 1969 United States–Japan Space Technology Agreement to produce rockets specifically for launch application satellites.

One of the major criticisms of the Japanese space program until recently was its split jurisdiction, specifically between NASDA and ISAS, as well as the relations of the government agencies with the private sector.[67] Typically, at the head of Japan's space program as a whole, NASDA has conducted both engineering and hardware development and is still the primary agency responsible for developing the next-generation H-IIA launcher series. ISAS has concentrated on basic scientific space research and still takes the lead in all science and planetary programs. Although they have teamed up and done R&D together with respect to launch vehicles, culminating in the ongoing J rocket series, there were issues of jurisdictional rivalries between the two agencies.

NASDA has also been the bigger of the two agencies in terms of personnel and budgets. As of 2000, NASDA had a staff of about 1,000, whereas ISAS had about 300 employees. Similarly, NASDA's overall budget of about $1.7 billion dollars was far greater than ISAS's average of about $200 million.[68] Some international perspective is necessary here in terms of budgets, however. In the United States, NASA spends an average of about $13 billion a year for its space projects. In comparison, Japan's combined official budget for its space program totaled around $2 billion, which leaves very little room for operational and developmental mistakes. As it is, a succession of failures in both satellites and launch vehicles has led to widespread domestic criticisms of the Japanese space program, its jurisdictional splits, and its ineffectiveness in establishing Japan's credibility as a player in the global commercial space arena. While consolidated under MEXT and waving the cooperation flag, ISAS and NASDA have not really merged in any real sense, with their various fields of competence still intact.[69]

Other far less pivotal government players also have ambitions in the space sector. The Ministry of Posts and Telecommunications—now transformed into the Ministry of Public Management, Home Affairs, Posts and Telecommunications—has had an interest in space activities related to radio waves, and it oversees other interested players like the Communications Research Laboratory (CRL), Nippon Telegraph and Telephone (NTT), Kokusai Denshin Denwa (KDD), and the Japan Broadcasting Corporation (NHK). The Ministry of Transport—now known as the Ministry of Land, Infrastructure, and Transport—has long been investigating the establishment of a multipurpose satellite system that would essentially cover the telecommunication needs of the ministry as a whole.

At the beginning of July 1997, two separate divisions at MITI, aircraft and space, both under the Machinery and Information Industries Bureau, formally merged into the Aircraft, Ordnance, and Space Division. This division continues to exist under the ministry's new designation as the Ministry of Economy, Trade, and Industry (METI). While no formal reason was given for this merger, the idea continues to be that this focus on aerospace as a whole was the same as that found in the United States and the EU, and moreover allowed for a bigger emphasis on space activities.[70] But in terms of the talent, resources, and budget, METI has been neither the most important nor the biggest player that is helping to shape this sector's prospects. As the ministerial space budgets show, the newly constituted MEXT is the dominant government player, with a space development budget of ¥200 billion as compared to ¥10 billion for METI.[71]

METI's main activities in the field are focused on the promotion of industrial utilization of space, with a specific emphasis on remote sensing and uses of microgravity.[72] Even under its newly minted description, METI, the ministry retains its interest in the space sector largely through its connections to the main firms involved in the space business, specifically those comprising the Rocket System Corporation (RSC).

No discussion of the central players in the Japanese commercial space enterprises would be complete without reference to the private firms with a vested stake in the business. RSC, a Tokyo-based consortium funded by over seventy Japanese companies, was established in 1990.[73] Formed out of the long-running efforts of Mitsubishi, it was modeled after Arianespace, the European launch service provider, specifically to offer commercial launch services using the H-II and J-I family of launch vehicles.[74] Some of the main participating firms include Mitsubishi Heavy Industries, Ishikawajima-Harima Heavy Industries, Kawasaki Heavy Industries, NEC, Mitsubishi Corporation, and Nissan Motors, which sold its entire aerospace and defense unit for about $374 million to Ishikawajima-Harima in February 2000.[75] In a 2001 global survey, Mitsubishi, NEC, and Ishikawajima-Harima ranked among the top fifty space revenue–generating firms, and both are heavyweights in the Japanese space development arena.[76] While their space-related revenues are considerably lower than either Lockheed Martin's or Boeing's, which ranked at the top, in terms of total sales Mitsubishi and NEC rank among the top global players. Mitsubishi is the main leader in the group, and although its leadership has been resented by some of the other heavyweights, it has thus far been successful in keeping RSC focused on the potential for launch service profitability in the future, even when the prospects for such profits have appeared murky to the other members of the consortium. It has also been the systems integrator for all of the main rocket series in Japan discussed below, with Ishikawajima-Harima and Nissan largely as the key subcontractors.

MAIN ROCKET GENERATIONS

With respect to launch vehicles, Japan's rocket effort began in the 1920s, reached very modest success based on German rocket designs during World War II projects under Mitsubishi, and were stymied because of the SCAP ban on the production of aircraft and rockets in the postwar era.[77] It was not until after the Korean War and the American exit from Japan that rocket production began to take shape. A private individual—"Dr. Rocket"—

rather than the government eventually paved the way for rocket development. Under the almost single-handed determination of Hideo Itokawa, best described as the Japanese Robert Goddard, Japan's independent launch ambitions began with the Pencil rocket, designed and launched twenty-nine times by Itokawa and his associates. In 1955, public demonstrations of the Pencil were given in Tokyo, though the scientific community was not always convinced of their utility. From there, Japan's rocket series have moved in stages, showing a country clearly in quest of an indigenous and independent launch service capability (see the timeline in the appendix to this chapter).[78]

After the Pencil, the next rockets were the Lambda and Mu series, whose development by Nissan Motor Company in conjunction with the Institute of Space and Aeronautical Sciences at the University of Tokyo, the predecessor of the present-day ISAS, became key to launching satellites independent of foreigners.[79] In February 1970, Japan became the fourth nation in the world to put a satellite, albeit a test one, into space using the upgraded Lambda series. By August 1972, Japan had successfully placed three scientific satellites in orbit. Although the Mu series culminated in the present sixth-generation M-V that can launch astronomy satellites and planetary missions for the Japanese government, Japan also moved solidly in the direction of more powerful rockets that could be used in the commercial arena.[80]

By the mid 1970s, Mitsubishi had begun development of the N-1 series based on the use of licensed American technology rather than indigenous technology. The N-I series not only carried the first engineering test satellite for the budding telecommunication field but also allowed Japan to be only the third country in the world to reach GEO orbit in 1977. In all, N-1 placed seven satellites in orbit between 1975 and 1982 that were concerned with testing telecommunication technologies. While Japan also continued to use the American Delta launcher for actual telecommunication satellites, it began to think about upgrading to the N-II series, which could handle heavier payloads and would reduce reliance on foreign launches. Again Mitsubishi was key to the enterprise, and again it developed the N-II based on licensed American technology. In all, between 1981 and 1987 the N-II launcher placed eight test, communication, and weather satellites into orbit.

Japan's ultimate ambition was the creation of an operational and competitive rocket. None of the fifteen N or nine H-1 missions was ever lost through launch failures, which boosted Japanese confidence that Japan could break into the competitive commercial launch market.[81] The H-1 series represented a leap in indigenous technological advancement, since it meant using cryogenic propellants and an inertial guidance system made in Japan.[82] Since about 84 percent of the H-1 was made with equipment designed and built in Japan, it was a vital step in establishing independent launch capability in a country trying to catch up with the more established vehicles in both the United States and Europe.[83] In 1986, on its initial launch, the H-1 successfully took three payloads into orbit, thereby establishing its ability to handle heavier missions. Between 1987 and 1992, the H-1 took an additional eight satellites successfully into orbit.

In the same month that the H-1 was making its debut as a launch vehicle, NASDA also sanctioned the development of the H-II. The H-II was constructed with the twin goals of technological autonomy and commercial service entry.[84] It succeeded in terms of the first goal. From start to finish the H-II was designed, developed, and launched by the Japanese using the lessons learned during the earlier rocket series. It was capable of handling primary missions for intermediate GTO- and LEO-bound payloads. Although the H-II had a troubled development history, many observers believed that its first flight in February 1994 laid all qualms about its launching viability to rest.

Trouble began with its very next flight in August, which started off with ignition problems and was eventually a partial failure, since it did not deliver its payload, the *Kiku 6* satellite, into GEO orbit.[85] Between 1995 and 1998, however, the H-II managed to dispel those doubts by successfully placing four more payloads into space. In fact, the H-II was hailed as one of the most advanced rocket systems in the world in terms of its integration of modern materials, electronics, computers, and propulsion.[86] But its costs at around $165–$170 million per launch were prohibitive for commercial purposes, and the H-II remained captive to Japanese government payloads.[87] More important in terms of reliability assessments, the H-II had consecutive failures that tarnished it fatally. In February 1998, it had a partial failure when it was unable to deliver its payload to the correct orbit.[88] Its death knell came with an outright launch failure in November 1999, when both the rocket and the payload had to be destroyed minutes into the flight because the rocket began to veer off course.[89]

The H-II failure at the end of 1999 had wide-ranging repercussions, the most important of which was that it cast the indigenous development of a launch vehicle in a very poor technical and commercial light.[90] Japanese officials cited it as the "most painful experience" in domestic launch vehicle development.[91] By the end of 1999, NASDA had to scrap the H-II program altogether and canceled the subsequent flight of an almost fully developed H-II (Number 7), last in its series, which was to have launched experimental and communications satellites.[92]

The aftereffects of the failures also reverberated in the future course and development of the J-1 launch vehicles. Designed as a combination of both the H-II and M-3SII rockets, the J-1 series vehicles were to carry small LEO payloads with estimated commercial launch prices running $30–$45 million. The J-1's only flight, in February 1996, can best be termed a partial success, since the launch was perfect but the payload, the prototype HYFLEX shuttle, sank after it splashed down and could not be recovered.[93] From a jurisdictional perspective, this was a blow, since the J-1 was designed and developed using the expertise of both ISAS and NASDA—a move that was surely partially designed to showcase the potential of interagency cooperation for Japan's space program as a whole. In the follow-up, an SAC task force labeled the J-1 rocket "slightly inferior" both in terms of quality and cost since its price averaged more than twice the global average.[94] Although research for the J-1 Upgrade Launch Vehicle started in November 2000, an evaluation report of the Subcommittee for Space Transportation suggested postponing any actual development plans of the small rocket program while still encouraging ongoing research.[95]

In the place of both the H-II and the J-1, the production focus of the Japanese launch ambitions has henceforth been on the H-IIA launch vehicle family, with at least five distinct versions.[96] The SAC has advocated the H-IIA as Japan's prime launcher, which makes it unlikely that the government will support the development of another launcher. In 2002, Ishikwajima-Harima Heavy Industries, one of the major players in RSC, was greatly irked to find that the government would not provide pecuniary support for the development of the Galaxy Express (GX) rocket it was championing. The official government reason was that the lack of technical information about the first stage had dire implications for the safety of the GX. But perhaps the more important reason was that the GX rocket would have technically broken the Japanese space policy of indigenous development, as NASDA aimed to combine technologies with Lockheed Martin.[97]

Thus, overall, despite official reprimands, H-II failures, H-IIA production delays, high costs, falling budgets, and fleeing business opportunities, Japanese space-related government agencies have not lessened their commitment to entering the commercial launch service arena. What role has the government played in this process? More important, from the point of view of this book, why has it been involved at all?

TIPs and the Criteria for Selection

With the background on both the international and domestic realities of launch vehicle competition in place, this section identifies Japanese government support to the industry as evidence of its seriousness in indigenizing the sector. In keeping with the main theme of the book, it then assesses the criteria for selection, both economic and political, that are potentially driving the Japanese government's continued interest in this industry.

GOVERNMENT TIPS

In terms of actual government support shown to the space industry sector, official TIPs are quite modest. As the discussion below makes clear, the TIPs and tactics by the government fit the broad pattern of selection-deselection in this case quite well. If anything, the emphasis has been on deselection from the start, and the burden is on the private sector to succeed in the increasingly tough global competition described earlier.

Unlike the past, there is no push to have a specific space industry law because, according to most officials, trade partners like the United States may take this as yet another sign of specific industry targeting. The legal basis for action is therefore provided under the Basic Law on Science and Technology enacted in November 1995, which stresses the general importance of promoting any related industries.[98] In 1996, this law was used to formulate a Science and Technology Basic Plan. Its goal is to transform Japan from an adjunct nation dependent on others into a truly autonomous country able to contribute to technology competition.[99]

From the budget of the space program as a whole to the direct involvement and support of the government, it cannot be asserted that massive TIPs are being used to transfer resources to this sector. Although there is developmental funding provided through NASDA, officials claim that direct subsidies are also not considered an option because of the limited budget and U.S. pressures for a level playing field. In addition, legal constraints on government subsidies under the World Trade Organization (WTO) further force cost discipline. Nor are R&D subsidies considered the overarching option, with the basic technology already in place and with potentially little meaning again for the cost angle.[100]

To some extent this is true. Total budget allocations for space development as a percentage of GDP hit a postwar high of 0.05 percent in the mid 1970s and have since then fluctuated between 0.03 and 0.04 percent of GDP.[101] Budget increases have also been characteristically low, with the MOF granting nominal increases of about 2 percent per year more recently and a mere 5 to 7 percent in the past. Institutionally, the resources have been concentrated at NASDA to pursue more effective development.

But specific figures do make it clear that the government has borne close to the full costs of the development of the major launch vehicles, with the developed technologies then being transferred to companies in the process of privatization. In fact, the development of launchers is considered the government's responsibility.[102] Estimates provided directly by MEXT state that the earlier N-I and N-II cost the government ¥94 billion and ¥130 billion, respectively. More recently, the government paid out a total of ¥212 billion for the H-II and ¥105 billion for the H-IIA for development and flight-test costs.[103]

The critical element of support concerns procurement of Japanese launch vehicle services. With the relatively more successful H-IIA operation since 2001, the overall concern is with establishing its reliability in both domestic and global markets. Here launch costs are critical. For payload capabilities of ten tons, present estimates suggest that the H-IIA launch costs may be a little over ¥10 billion and need to be brought down to under ¥9 billion in order to be competitive in the international launch services market.[104] To that long-term end, the Japanese government has guaranteed another eight missions until 2006 for the H-IIA because the dominant view is that it will take at least another four years before Japan will become competitive globally.[105] This time frame can be crucial for the very survival of Japan's rocket program because the U.S. Air Force–subsidized EELV, a commercial rocket that will eventually replace the existing U.S. Delta III, Atlas, and Titan boosters, was set to become operational in 2002. This is happening at the time that the H-IIA is finally making its debut. In a head-to-head competition, delays of even a year or two, which are entirely possible given the H-IIA's history, could have severe competitive implications for securing satellite launch customers.[106] These fast-paced realities mean, as industry participants acknowledge, that Japanese government procurement alone is not enough to guarantee long-term survival in the international launch vehicle market.

This is where the Japanese private sector comes in. The impetus for the formation of the RSC was partly to ensure successful commercialization of the H-II launchers though a deliberate and concerted effort to reduce costs. But historically that is not the only reason suggested for its formation. On 15 June 1990, a United States–Japan Agreement on the Policies and Procedures for the Procurement of Non-R&D Satellites was concluded between the two governments, bringing to an end a "Super 301" investigation by the U.S. trade representative. On the Japanese side, many of the key firms involved in the space business, and especially the production of the H-II launcher series, such as Mitsubishi, believed that the agreement represented a total concession by the Japanese government to American trade pressures.[107] From the point of view of players in the Japanese industry, the dire implication was that the H-II would get fewer satellite launches since interested parties would go for cheaper launches from abroad in competitive procurement situations. The emphasis on commercialization also galvanized the firms to seek support from both NASDA and METI in the form of securing foreign procurements in order to fill the slots on the H-IIA's schedule.

The RSC, composed as it is of Japan's heavyweight aerospace firms, can well be thought of as a functional parallel to a government-sponsored procurement agency, much like the Japan Electronic Computer Company (JECC) discussed in the previous chapter.[108] The RSC's main procurement activities, however, go beyond government or national contracts to foreign ones in order to establish a foothold in the global launch services market. Thus far there has been limited success. In 1996, buoyed by the then successes of the H-II, Hughes Space and Communications signed an estimated $1 billion deal with RSC, with ten launches commissioned on the H-IIA beginning in 2000.[109] This historic deal was crucial to establishing the credibility of RSC as a viable entrant in the global competition. A unit of Loral Space and Communications, Space Systems/Loral, had also signed on for an additional ten flights on the H-II, again contributing to establishing the Japanese as significant players in the commercial launch arena.

But as the H-II was struck by the back-to-back failures described earlier, procurement trouble hit home with a vengeance. Much to the consternation of RSC, Hughes, now part of Boeing, canceled the ten firm launch orders in May 2000, citing the unreliability of the Japanese launch vehicles.[110] Space systems/Loral, the other major RSC client, has not canceled its contract but has requested and received its prepaid portion.[111] According to industry personnel, the most important thing the government can do to support the industry, and especially the commercial viability of the H-IIA, is to ensure procurement not just from foreign but also from domestic sources.[112]

While both the STA and NASDA have been involved on the R&D side, METI is characteristically concerned with the business potential and welfare impact of the space industry. This, according to its officials, is its main concern through RSC. For a variety of reasons, unlike other industries in the past, the space industry cannot just be picked up for promotion through all kinds of tangible TIPs. From the early 1980s, the idea has been to sell the potential of space-related businesses (such as in the no-gravity field) to the firms in terms of how it would affect their profits and sales.[113] Reportedly, firms have been reluctant to move in, given the untested fields as well as their backward status that has, as in so many other previous industries, galvanized government support. Within the present division at METI, therefore, there continues to be innovative thinking about the kinds of institutional and infrastructure support that would encourage firms to move into this sector more wholeheartedly. With respect to launch vehicles specifically, the goal is to make RSC more competitive in world markets vis-à-vis rivals in the United States, Europe, Russia, China, and India.

The key idea from a commercial point of view is "cost-consciousness," that is, making sure that products such as rockets or satellites have comparatively lower costs while still maintaining excellent quality. In addition, the idea is to shorten the time of a product's delivery date. Both of these aims are consistent with the emphasis on deselection, rather than selection, made perhaps even more relevant by virtue of the hawkishness with which the United States, and to a certain extent Europe, monitors Japanese developments in this sector.[114] To this end, allowing the importation of cheaper parts and giving tax breaks are under immediate consideration, because these would be the fastest ways to encourage the domestic firms—though none of this can be guaranteed in the ongoing flux of administrative and budgetary changes in Japan today.

On the whole, the private sector, whether or not through RSC, is having to deal directly with the vagaries of foreign competition. Government agencies, whether ISAS, NASDA, MEXT, or METI, both in their old and newly transformed states, continue to emphasize the importance of thinking in explicitly commercial terms, discouraging direct government support or pointing to its limited nature particularly in comparison to that found in the United States and Europe. It is not that the industries do not want the support. They certainly do. But they do not necessarily get it if their demands stand in the way of indigenous launch-development capability, as the case of the GX rocket championed by Ishikawjima-Harima showed earlier. The emphasis given to indigenization comes across in the efforts made in some of the earliest postwar rocket series to the present development of the H-IIA, which now stands at the heart of Japan's entire commercial launch ambitions. Despite the established dominance of Western players and the limited nature of official government TIPs, Japanese actors have not backed off from the development of a competitive space launch vehicle. Why? What is so important about this particular industry that it must be indigenized?

CRITERIA FOR SELECTION

No matter what their differences or jurisdictional battles, the official reasons for focusing on the space industry sector are the same across the board in the government agencies, whether in actual documents or in interviews. SAC, which has been formulating the fundamental policies on Japan's space activities since 1978, sets the tone for the entire enterprise on civilian use of future space activities. Pointing to the fact that space technology is a highly sophisticated generic technology that integrates various fields of science, SAC's vision is that the space industry will not only lead to new technologies but may well give rise to entire new industries in materials, computers, robotics, electronics, communications, and information processing.[115] In 2002, SAC put out the latest national space plan, citing once again the importance of expanding the knowledge capital base.[116]

The STA points to the importance of space development for providing solutions to global environmental problems, increasing communication in the society at large, and potentially creating new technologies and industries in materials and electronics.[117] From the perspective of the whole Japanese economy, the criteria of growth and spillovers in this technology- and knowledge-intensive industry are driving concerns about its place in the Japanese economy.[118] NASDA, too, points to the immeasurable impact of the industry on other fields, both in the past and the future.[119] Along the same lines, METI also considers space to be a high-growth and high value-added sector, with great potential for technological spillovers that will affect the future industrial destiny of Japan.[120] Recently, it pointed exclusively to aerospace as an industry that will allow Japan to retain its manufacturing advantage through the creation of "third-ware" industries built on a fusion of existing hardware and software capabilities.[121] In short, the widespread perception in the Japanese space-related governmental institutions is that this leading industry of the twenty-first century will spur transformations in existing technologies, underwrite the future of the information society, and expand the frontiers of humankind.[122] On behalf of the industry firms, the SJAC points to the potential profits to be made in an industry that promises to spill over into many different activities in the future.[123]

It is difficult to appreciate the importance attached by Japanese official to positive technological spillovers, and the role these play in industrial advancement, without reference to the perceptions and beliefs of Japanese government officials. Most point to the idea that the space industry as a whole draws upon existing linked industries and technologies and thus has the spillover potential to take Japan's manufacturing base to the next level.[124] Others state that the reason why the Japanese government is so interested in Japan's launch capability is because space technology stimulates other fields.

But there is increasingly another reason for the interest, and it is not just coming from the bureaucrats but also from several powerful members of the Diet, where there is a newborn committee related to space affairs.[125] Every single interviewee confirmed that launch vehicles are crucial for Japan's national security. They can potentially be used not only to launch information gathering satellites (IGS), a nonmilitary expression for reconnaissance satellites, but are also potentially equivalent with ICBMs. This is an aspect of Japan's launch vehicle policy that is becoming increasingly easier to discuss openly, although, as many observers have noted, the Japanese public and private actors involved in technology matters consciously choose to avoid association with defense production.[126] However, it is a public fact that since May 1993, when North Korea test-launched a Nodong-1 missile that landed in the Sea of Japan, Japanese defense and space-related agencies have considered launching spy satellites.

These domestic debates came to a head in August 1998, when North Korea launched a multistage Taepodong-1 missile whose nose cone flew over Honshu and landed in the Pacific Ocean. In direct response to this North Korean threat, there was a flurry of domestic political rhetoric and activity over the necessity of launching spy satellites. Even strict adherents of Japan's defense-only security policy concurred with the necessity of better intelligence and information in order to safeguard Japan's territorial integrity.

Whereas it had considered buying them from the United States, by early April 1999 Japan had formally announced that it would be developing and launching four spy satellites by 2002, and subsequently 2003, on its own.[127] More important but less obscure from the high-profile public debates was the basic necessity of how Japan would get those satellites into orbit. This is exactly where space launch vehicles become crucial in the defense arena. As it turns out, if all goes well, the four reconnaissance satellites will be launched using the H-IIA—making Japan far more independent in terms of its intelligence-gathering capabilities and thereby also strengthening its defense resources at a basic level.

While the national defense capabilities argument can be used by the government space-related institutions to galvanize more support for the domestic industry from the politicians, it is also one that can be used effectively by private-sector firms to garner more direct developmental funds from the government. This can done either individually by heavyweight firms like Mitsubishi through NASDA, or in the impressively combined lobbying power of either the SJAC or RSC through politicians or other government agencies.[128] The focus of such efforts, given the emphasis on commercialization as well as the vigilance of Japan's trade partners in this particular sector, means government support for securing procurement whether at home or abroad in the active manner of Arianespace.

Although criticisms of the space program as a whole abound in Japan these days, the launch vehicle sector, both for reasons of technological externalities and defense, is shielded from the influence and interest of politicians.[129] While there is some electoral impact because the sector comprises the concentrated firepower of Japan's heavyweight aerospace firms, it is hard to make the argument for unilateral influence from politicians to bureaucrats if the firms want more favorable policies. For one thing, the firms, whether individually or through their combined platforms, are more likely to approach the government space agencies directly, often bypassing politicians altogether. After all, the government space agencies are far more interested in the fate of the launch vehicles sector and what it ultimately means for Japan's long-term economic and security policy. What made the job of industry influence problematic was also the bifurcated nature of Japan's space agencies, which limited effective cooperation and support for the industry. The recent amalgamation of organization at MEXT may have important implications for the overall political backing and sanctioning of further developments in this sector. For another, politicians are surely not immune to defense-related arguments in this sector.

Moreover, given the succession of failures in the Japanese space program, the real challenge is to worry less about political pressures and more about how to keep the private firms even interested in the potential profitability of the space sector in general and the launch vehicles business in particular. As it is, the aerospace business in total comprises a mere 10 to 20 percent of the total business even in the big firms, with space-specific activities even lower. There can be little question, however, that in a very general sense both the politicians and the public do ultimately have national pride in Japan's space program as much as the bureaucratic agencies do. Despite all manner of problems, there continues to be a strong consensus in both the public and private spheres that Japan's goal should be the development of an indigenous launch vehicle, with the present hopes pinned largely on the H-IIA.

Future Trajectories

Given these realities—the limited nature of government support, the skittishness of business firms, joint collaboration with foreign players, the recent setbacks, but still the very real consensus on indigenization—it would be helpful to end by discussing where Japan's space launch vehicles program is headed. First, it is important to remember that setbacks and disasters are not unique to Japan. Some of the presently dominant global players have also been similarly plagued. Boeing's Delta III, for example, has had a rocky and uncertain ride until very recently. To prove its worth the third time around to potential customers, Boeing had to swallow the cost of sending the rocket up. Japan's H-IIA program may well have to go the same route, since it has already lost potential customers and desperately needs to attract them back in order to remain viable in the commercial launch arena at the global level. A few successive launches by the H-IIA, with the Japanese government absorbing the cost of one or two, could very well bring Japan back definitively into the commercial game since costs as well as technical reliability matter in the long run.

   Second, short-term agreements, partnerships, and joint ventures may be key to Japan's ultimate quest for indigenization. Again, the Delta III, one of the largest and most powerful privately funded launch vehicles ever developed, is equipped with hardware from contractors like Mitsubishi.[130] This kind of know-how is crucial for Japan's launch vehicles ambitions as a whole because Mitsubishi has played the pivotal role of system integrator for all the major rocket series in Japan, including the H series. But the focus on expendable boosters is not the only way to go. Arianespace now has an agreement with NASDA to expand the commonality of technical components between the Ariane 5 and the H-IIA. Since, according to this agreement, the H-IIA will be equipped with satellite mounts compatible with the Ariane 5, Arianespace clients who run into launch troubles or failures will have the option of an emergency back-up service through the Japanese. This will allow Arianespace, and to some extent the Japanese as well, to compete directly with established competitors like Boeing and Lockheed Martin in the United States.[131] On 31 January 2000, NASDA also signed an interim agreement with Centre National d'Etude Spatiales (CNES), the French space agency, in order to develop cooperation in the field of reusable launch vehicles. The goal is to pool services and exchange equipment and resources with a view to designing spaceplanes that constitute an important step toward developing technologies for the next generation of reusable launch vehicles.[132] These technologies may well end up butting heads directly with similar efforts in the United States, such as the possibility of continued public-private cooperation in the X-33 and X-34 projects and the new directions under NASA's SLI that focus on reusable launch vehicles.

To conclude, given the flux in the present administrative, political, and business spheres, whether the Japanese space agencies can actually support the launch vehicles industry or space sector as a whole as much as they would like is unclear. But what is clear is the logic that motivates them: technological linkages and externalities, as well as the very real defense and military implications. Even when political pressures exist for more favorable government support, however, the emphasis on government deselection forces Japanese firms to deal with the vagaries of economic competition from the start.

The buzzword is "commercialization," where the focus continues to be on assuring the ability of Japanese industry to rise on its own merits and compete in the global space launch arena.[133] In this respect, Japan is not unlike Europe, which has long sought to surpass the U.S. space industry. Perhaps the commercialization of the Japanese industry has a long way to go to catch up with the more established competitors in Europe and the United States, and perhaps it will get there only in fits and starts at the global level. The point is not that the Japanese are less than successful in the global launch vehicles industry at the moment. The point is that they remain in the game for the widespread benefits, perceived and tangible, that are then conferred upon the whole Japanese industrial base and that affect Japan's national security in the long run. In fact, Japan has not lost its emphasis on technology policy in the wake of a decade-long recession. If anything, the recession has only served to show all relevant domestic participants the necessity of Japan moving onward and upward in the high-tech chain, space ventures included.

This thinking in Japan's space-related institutions will no doubt also receive an added impetus from the recent emphasis on the importance of outer space in strategic and military planning in the United States.[134] In addition, political realities in northeast Asia, especially with respect to China and North Korea, have already forced Japan to seek a more militarized role in space, as the continuing saga of the four projected reconnaissance satellites shows. Nor does Japan want to play a humiliating "catch-up" in launch vehicles, or in space in general, with as-yet technologically backward countries like China or even India, both of which have made important strides in establishing independent and commercially viable launch vehicle capability.

All these reasons suggest that Japan's competitors should not be too hasty in writing off either public or private Japanese efforts. Since they stand to be direct participants in the global launch markets, Japanese corporations, through the RSC, are certainly cost conscious, as this remains key to competitiveness in the global commercial launch market. But despite tangible setbacks, they also remain interested and, through subcontracts and alliances, active in the development of an indigenous launch vehicle capability. What they would no doubt like to see, apart from direct financial aid for R&D, are government efforts to secure launch procurements either at home or abroad as an effective means of support in a highly competitive commercial market.[135]

Perhaps more important, the historically rooted emphasis on technology as the basis for Japan's economic and political survival means that the Japanese government continues to seek an indigenous launch vehicle capability.[136] Although there is a strong emphasis on commercialization, factors such as economic uncertainties, market turbulence and unpredictability, and issues of cost competitiveness do not necessarily thwart this ultimate objective. It is by no means clear that Japan will become a viable player in the global commercial launch vehicle industry. But what is clear is that, for the reasons discussed here, the Japanese government will make every effort to ensure that space launch vehicles are indigenized.

Appendix:
Timeline for the Japanese Space Program and Launch Vehicles

The pre-1990 section is compiled almost entirely from the websites of NASDA (www.nasda.go.jp), ISAS (www.isas.ac.jp), STA (www.sta.go.jp), and Jonathan McDowell's Launch Log (hea-www.harvard.edu/~jcm/space/log/launchlog.txt). The 1990s section uses RSC's website, (www.rocketsystem.co.jp), in addition to the aforementioned sources. Details that RSC chooses to omit are included. These are compiled from various print and electronic (spaceviews.com) news sources, and other official websites. Information has been checked against the Japanese space activities based on internal STA documents. Future mission schedules are taken from NASDA's website and indicated by FY.

1953   Dec   Hideo Itokawa and others form the Avionics and Supersonic Aerodynamics Group (AVSA) geared toward rocket development.

1954   Feb   AVSA, University of Tokyo, and Fuji Seimitsu Company
                (now Nissan) receive government funds to help develop
                Japan's first experimental rocket, Pencil.

1955   Apr   Institute of Industrial Science, University of Tokyo, con-
                ducts satisfactory experiments to launch the 23-cm-long
                Pencil rocket. Based on these tests, a 300-mm-long Pen-
                cil, a two-stage Pencil, and a tailfinless Pencil are tested in
                a lab attached to the University of Tokyo in Chiba City.
                Following Pencil, the 120-cm BABY Series is developed,
                consisting of the BABY-S, BABY-T, and BABY-R.

1962   Kagoshima Space center established and opened as full-
                scale launch site.

1964   Institute of Space and Aeronautical Science, University of
                Tokyo (the predecessor of present-day ISAS) established
                upon the recommendation of the Science Council of
                Japan. This institute develops many sounding rockets:
                S-210, S-310, S-520, K-9M, and L-3H (L-series).

1965   Jan   L (Lambda) Series L-3-2 has a successful flight beyond
                1000-km altitude.

1966   July   L-3H-2 clears 1,800-km summit altitude.

1968   Space Activities Commission (SAC) established.

1969   Oct   National Space Development Agency (NASDA) estab-
                lished. NASDA headquarters in Tanegashima, with
                branches in Kodaira and Mitaka and tracking stations in
                Katsuura and Okinawa.

1970   Feb   Japan's first satellite, OHSUMI, launched by the L-4S
                rocket.

1971   Feb   M-4S rocket's first launch, based on the success of L-4S.
                Tansei, a technological test satellite, is put into orbit. This
                marks the beginning of the M (Mu) Series rockets.

        Sept   Japan's first full-fledged scientific satellite, Shinsei,
                launched on an M-4S.

1972   June   Tsukuba Space Center established.

        Aug   Another M-4S launches Denpa, a full-fledged scientific
                satellite.

1974   Feb   M-3C rocket No. 1 launches Tansei 2.

1975   Feb   M-3C rocket No. 2 launches Taiyo.

        Sept   N-I Series launch No. 1, carrying Kiku-1 Engineering
                Test Satellite—developed by the transfer of technologies
                used for the U.S. Delta-Thor rockets.

1976	Feb	N-I rocket No. 2 launches Ume (Ionosphere sounding satellite).
	Sept	Development of N-II launch vehicle starts.
1977	Feb	M-3H (3rd-generation Mu with greater payload capability) rocket No. 1 launches Tansei 3.
	Feb	N-I rocket No. 3 launches Kiku-2 (Japan's first geostationary satellite).
	July	Delta 2914 (U.S.) launches Geostationary Meteorological Satellite (GMS) Himawari.
	Dec	Delta 2914 (U.S.) launches Communications Satellite (CS) Sakura.
1978	Feb	M-3H rocket No. 2 launches Kyokko.
	Feb	N-I rocket No. 4 launches Ume-2.
	Apr	Delta 2914 (U.S.) launches Broadcasting Satellite (BS) Yuri.
	Sept	M-3H rocket No. 3 launches Jiliken.
1979	Feb	N-I rocket No. 5 launches Experimental Communications Satellite (ECS) Ayame.
	Feb	M-3C rocket No. 3 launches Hakucho.
1980	Feb	N-I rocket No. 6 launches Ayame-2.
	Feb	M-3S (4th-generation Mu with improved launch accuracy) rocket No. 1 launches Tansei 4.
1981		Institute of Space and Aeronautical Science, University of Tokyo, reorganized to become the Institute of Space and Astronautical Science (ISAS), under direct control of the Ministry of Education.
	Feb	N-II Series No. 1 launches Kiku-3.
	Feb	M-3S rocket No. 2 launches Hinotori.
	Feb	Development of H-I launch vehicle starts.
	Aug	N-II rocket No. 2 launches Himawari-2.
1982	Sept	N-I rocket No. 7 launches Kiku-4. Completion of N-I launch vehicle operations (7 satellites launched).
	Sept	H-I launching facility built at Tanegashima.
1983	Feb	N-II rocket No. 3 launches Sakura-2a.
	Feb	M-3S rocket No. 3 launches Tenma.
	Aug	N-II rocket No. 4 launches Sakura-2b.
1984	Jan	N-II rocket No. 5 launches Yuri-2a.
	Feb	M-3S rocket No. 4 launches Ohzora.
	Aug	N-II rocket No. 6 launches Himawari-3.
1985	Jan	First M-3S-II rocket, still under development, successfully

		launches the Sagikake probe to Halley's Comet, a success for ISAS.
	Aug	Another M-3S-II rocket launches Suisei, which, along with Sagikake, succeeded in observing Halley's comet as part of the "Halley Armada" of spacecraft from the U.S., the USSR, Europe, and Japan.
	Sept	H-II launching facility construction begins at Tanegashima.
1986	Feb	N-II rocket No. 7 launches Yuri-2b.
	Aug	Development of H-II launch vehicle starts.
	Aug	H-I Series No. 1 launches Experimental Geodetic Satellite (EGS) Ajisai, Japan Amateur Satellite (JAS-1) Fuji, Magnetic Bearing Flywheel Experimental System (MABES).
1987	Feb	M-3S-II rocket launches Ginga, the X-ray astronomy satellite. Ginga later reentered the atmosphere.
	Feb	N-II rocket No. 8 launches Marine Observation Satellite (MOS-1) Momo. Completion of N-II launch vehicle operations (8 satellites launched).
	Aug	H-I rocket No. 2 launches Kiku-5.
1988	Feb	H-I rocket No. 3 launches Sakura-3a.
	Sept	H-I rocket No. 4 launches Sakura-3b.
	Sept	TR-I Series: TR-I-1 rocket launched—technical data acquisition for H-II development.
1989	Jan	TR-I-2 rocket launched—serves as basis for technical data acquisition for H-II development.
	Feb	M-3S-II rocket launches Akebono, a scientific satellite for observation of the northern lights.
	Aug	TR-I-3 rocket launched—technical data acquisition for H-II development.
	Sept	H-I rocket No. 5 launches Himawari-4.
1990	Jan	M-3S-II rocket launches Hiten, to conduct lunar swingbys. Hiten later ends up falling onto the moon.
	Feb	H-I rocket No. 6 launches Momo-1b, JAS-1b Fuji-2, Deployable Boom and Umbrella Test (DEBUT) Orizuru.
	July	Rocket Systems Corporation (RSC) established.
	Aug	H-I rocket No. 7 launches Yuri-3a.
1991	Aug	H-I rocket No. 8 launches Yuri-3b.
	Aug	M-3S-II rocket launches Yohkoh for solar observation.
	Sept	TR-IA Series: TR-IA-1—microgravity experiments.

1992	Feb	H-I rocket No. 9 launches Japan Earth Resources Satellite (JERS-1) Fuyo. Completion of H-I launch vehicle series (9 satellites launched).
1993	Feb	M-3S-II rocket launches ASCA, an X-ray astronomy satellite.
	Apr	Development of J-1 rocket starts.
	Sept	TR-IA-3—microgravity experiments.
1994	Feb	H-II Series rocket No. 1 launches Orbital Reentry Experiment (ORBEX) Ryusei and Vehicle Evaluation Payload (VEP) Myojo.
	Aug	H-II rocket No. 2 launches Kiku-6. Failure to inject satellite into orbit.
1995	Jan	M-3S-II's final act, the launch of the EXPRESS satellite, ends in failure.
	Mar	H-II rocket No. 3 launches Space Flyer Unit (SFU) and Himawari-5.
	Aug	TR-IA-4—microgravity experiments.
1996	Feb	J-I Series rocket No. 1 launches Hypersonic Flight Experiment (HYFLEX).
	Mar	H-II Launch Vehicle No. 7 and TR-IA Rocket No. 6.
	Apr	SAC 12-member task force deems J-1 rocket to be "slightly inferior."[a]
	May	NASDA announces its intention to scrap the J-1 launch rocket.
	Aug	H-II rocket No. 4 launches Advanced Earth Observing Satellite (ADEOS) Midori and JAS-2 Fuji-3.
	Sept	TR-IA-5—microgravity experiments.
1997	Feb	M-V Series makes its debut as the first M-V launches HALCA, the world's first space VLBI satellite.
	Sept	TR-IA-6—microgravity experiments.
	Nov	H-II launch vehicle No. 6 launches ETS-VII Orihime Hikoboshi and Tropical Rainfall Measuring Mission (TRMM).
1998	Feb	H-II rocket No. 5 launches COMETS Satellite—fails to put satellite into high enough orbit.[b]

[a]*Asahi Evening News*, 26 April 1998.

[b]The H-II rocket, then Japan's largest and most up-to-date launch vehicle, failed on 21 February 1998 due to premature shutdown forty-four seconds into the second-stage second burn. The H-II was carrying COMETS (Communication and Broadcasting Experimental Satellite), renamed Kakehashi satellite. Despite this failure to deliver the payload on target, however, all six H-II flights to date reached orbit, indicating that the Japanese could overcome technical launch difficulties.

	Mar	RSC—Order awarded for the Test Vehicle No. 1 of the H-IIA Launch Vehicle.
	July	M-V rocket No. 2 launches Nozomi, Japan's first Mars explorer.
	Nov	TR-IA-7 Experimental Space Rocket successfully launched from Tanegashima.[c]
1999	Nov	H-II Launch Vehicle No. 8 fails.[d]
	Dec	SAC decides to scrap H-II program in favor of developing H-IIA launch vehicle, based on H-II's failure in November.[e] Start of H-II Orbiting Plane Experimental (HOPE-X) to be passed over and project to be reconsidered anew.[f]
2000	Jan	NASDA and the Japan Marine Science and Technology Center (JAMSTEC) publicize the retrieval of H-II No. 8's lost engine.[g]
	Feb	M-V rocket No. 3 launches ASTRO E—failure. NASDA concludes a 20-year agreement with the Republic of Kiribati concerning the use of Christmas Island for constructing a landing site for HOPE-X, with the agreement to be reviewed at 7, 12, and 16 years.[h]
	June	H-IIA first-stage captive test successful.
	Sept	ISAS reschedules the M-V and ASTRO-E projects for FY2004 and FY2005, respectively, after the failure in February 2000.
2001	July	ISAS successfully performs limited tests on the Reusable Rocket Vehicle (RVT).
	Aug	NASDA launches H-IIA-F1 for a successful flight demonstration test with VEP-2 (H-IIA Vehicle Evaluation Payload #2) at Tanegashima.

[c] STA Today, December 1999.

[d] STA Today, January 2000; Financial Times, 18 November 1999. The launch of H-II No. 8 from the Tanegashima site ended in failure on 15 November 1999. This constituted the second major failure to hit the Japanese launch vehicle program in a little under two years. The H-II rocket was supposed to put a weather and air traffic control satellite in orbit, but the rocket failed four minutes into flight due allegedly to liquid hydrogen fuel leaks from cracked pipes leading to first-stage engine failure.

[e] Yomiuri Shinbun, 5 December 1999. NASDA announced that it would call off the production of the No. 7 H-II rocket. This was the first time in the history of the Japanese launch vehicle program that the domestic production of a major rocket was called off. NASDA also postponed the launch of the No. 1 H-IIA rocket in order to review the overall space program.

[f] STA Today, January 2000.

[g] STA Today, February 2000.

[h] STA Today, April 2000.

2002	Feb	ISAS attempts to put the Demonstrator of Atmospheric Reentry System with Hyper Velocity (DASH) into orbit as a piggyback payload on H-IIA-F2, developed by NASDA. The mission ends in partial failure.
	June	Government initially set to invest over ¥30 billion for Galaxy Express commercial launch vehicle to be developed by Ishikawajima-Harima. Later backtracks due to SAC official reasons of lack of information concerning safety.
FY2002	Sept	Projected Launch H-IIA with DRTS-W (Data Relay Test Satellite) and USERS (Unmanned Space Experiment Recovery System).
FY2002		H-IIA with ADEOS-II (Advanced Earth Observing Satellite II), Micro-Lab Sat, EOSS (Whale Ecology Observation Satellite System), and Fed Sat (Federation Satellite).
FY2002		H-IIA with information-gathering satellite.
FY2003		H-IIA with MTSAT-1R (Multi-Functional Transport Satellite-1 Replacement) and Third Ignition Experiment of H-IIA Upper Stage Engine.
FY2003		H-IIA with information-gathering satellite.
FY2004		H-IIA with ALOS (Advanced Land Observing Satellite)
FY2004		H-IIA with ETS-VIII (Engineering Test Satellite-VIII).
FY2005		H-IIA Augmented Test Flight (Flight Demonstration Test).
FY2005		H-IIA with SELENE (Selenological and Engineering Explorer).
FY2005		H-IIA Augmented with HTV (H-II Transfer Vehicle) Technology Demonstrator.
FY2005		H-IIA with Ultra-High-Data-Rate Internet Test Satellite (tentative name).

CHAPTER 6

TIPs from Postwar Japan

THIS STUDY HAS so far concentrated on providing a careful and systematic answer to the simple question of how governments choose industries to favor, specifically by looking at the postwar Japanese case. The plan of this final chapter is to discuss both the findings and their implications in three parts. The first part briefly sets out the argument over the criteria for selection, emphasizing why Japan is an ideal place to look for patterns. The second part summarizes the evidence from Chapters 2–5, which use both quantitative and qualitative evidence to answer the question at hand. The third part draws conclusions from the evidence and discusses its implications for the rival theories with which we began and also the prospects for industrial strategies in general.

The Criteria for Industrial Selection

When governments choose industries to favor, what criteria or factors affect their decisions to do so? The first step in attempting to answer this question is to understand that it has always been an implicit part of the debates over governments and industrialization. In Chapter 1, I explored these rival debates in the international political economy literature, with the goal of drawing out testable hypotheses for government selection. Because they have radically different assumptions about the motivations behind government choices, the rival theories naturally suggest two very different answers about governments' criteria for industrial selection.

One set of theories, typified most recently by the strategic trade policy literature, suggests that governments choose industries for economic reasons, such as high value-added, high growth, and, most important of all, the high potential for spillovers. In this view, governments choose such industries because they are concerned with the long-term national welfare that affects their relative economic standing in the international system. This, however, is only one view about the determinants of government choice. Another equally influential set of theories, coming from the standard endogenous policy literature, suggests that governments are motivated mostly by political factors. In other words, it is far more realistic to assume that governments are motivated by the electoral interests of the politicians who presumably run the government rather than anything as grandiose as the national economic interest. These electoral motivations ensure that a government favors industries where votes, campaign contributions, or lobbying pressures are important. In this setup, then, the idea is that governments should not select industries because the process of selection always becomes clouded for political reasons.

The curious thing about the criteria for selection, whether of the economic or political type as I have just described at a broad level, is not that they do not make sense at a theoretical level in the debates. As shown in Chapter 1, they clearly do. Both the rival economic and political criteria have a straightforward positive relationship with government decisions to select industries in theory. They both predict contradictory but very definite outcomes across industries and over time that are fully justified by their respective assumptions. The problem is simply that we have little empirical investigation of these ideas, or more specifically the criteria, side by side in a real-world case.

Keeping the general logic of the economic and political criteria for selection in mind, then, we have to ask whether such criteria actually matter to real government choices, as theory suggests. The question then is where do we look for an answer? This is where Japan comes in. Here, too, as Chapter 1 shows, the key works on Japanese political economy have the same underlying economic or political logic as the more theoretical works. Here again, scholars are divided over the motivations and criteria by which the Japanese government has chosen industries to favor. And here specifically, there is now a bitter debate about who actually governs Japanese economic policy-making in general and, by extension, the industrial selection process—bureaucrats or politicians, who are assumed to have very different agendas and motivations.

But why Japan at all? Without an understanding of the larger world political economy, it is difficult to appreciate the centrality of Japan to the debates over TIPs. The combination of several factors brought the debate over the Japanese government's selections to the forefront of theoretical and policy agendas from the early 1980s onward. I will now touch upon these very briefly, before summarizing the evidence on industrial selections from postwar Japan.

WHY JAPAN?

The most important factor in focusing attention on the Japanese case in the early 1980s was the theoretical advances made in international trade theory, which had a profound effect on the real-world policy debates. From the early 1980s onward, a specific branch of this literature, known better as the strategic trade policy literature, really opened the theoretical door to arguments for government intervention.[1] It ended up demonstrating, in a nutshell, that it was to the net economic benefit of the entire nation if a government favored strategic sectors. The specific idea was that credible government intervention would allow home firms to dominate the global industry over and above their rivals. That is, if a firm established its presence in such strategic (broadly synonymous with high-technology) industries first, its country was the one most likely to benefit. More important, if such a firm could show its rivals that its government was credibly committed to the firm's success, it was more than just set to compete; indeed, it was guaranteed that such a firm would dominate the market. Crudely put, the idea was that governments could distort markets and increase national economic welfare. What this was taken to mean, more popularly, was that mercantilism was finally rigorous and fully mainstream in a way it had never been before, simply because contemporary economists had now made the argument formal.

But these ideas and theories would probably not have become so popular had it not been for a genuine concern about the relative position of the United States in the world economy. This leads to another crucial factor. It is certainly remarkable that these theories became popular at a time in the 1980s when many notable Americans began to voice their intense concern about the economic decline of the United States, with what was then called the "diminished giant syndrome."[2] In fact, many American industries, such as semiconductors, commercial aircraft, telecommunication equipment, and machine tools, which had historically been committed to unconditional free trade, began to voice their concern about unfair competition in the international marketplace. In the view of these industries, the unfairness of the situation was more often than not driven by foreign governments' support of their home industries.[3]

Which brings us to Japan. When Americans talked about foreign governments or an unfair playing field, they usually had Japan in mind. Indeed, the reason why industrial policy seemed so attractive was because often the same people who were concerned with the economic decline of the United States and with the competitiveness of American industries were also anxious about what then seemed like the unshakable might of Japanese industries. Using one or two Japanese industries to bolster their arguments, especially semiconductors or automobiles, they pointed out that the Japanese government favored strategic industries through visible and invisible means, and that, furthermore, this kind of intense favoritism made Japanese firms more competitive in the global arena, often at the expense of their American rivals.[4] Here, too, strategic trade theory once again allowed many people to justify their interpretation of what they believed had been going on in Japan all along.[5]

To some extent, this kind of justification continues because the debates over Japanese TIPs are by no means over. There is still a great deal of interest in the long-running debate over the success of the Japanese government in choosing strategic sectors of the economy. Even today, the idea is that it gives firms preferential TIPs in order to foster their international competitiveness. Nobody now seriously questions the idea that the Japanese government is involved deeply in the workings of the economy, though many still quarrel over who directs that involvement, bureaucrats or politicians, each of whom operates out of very different motivations, as the debates make clear. Even today the Japanese government subsidizes sectors and protects them with tariffs and nontariff barriers and many other creative measures. But some sectors are clearly favored over others.

But which sectors exactly, and why? This is where the rival theories in the international political economy literature help us to get a handle on the problem of interest. Extracting hypotheses from these theories, as discussed in more detail in Chapter 1, we can set up the problem very simply in a neutral fashion: Have Japanese government choices been determined more by the economic or political criteria that rival theories suggest are important? Despite the fundamental relevance of this question to debates about governments and industrialization, there was disappointingly little by way of systematic empirical evidence. Even in the celebrated Japanese case, it was never clear that the government had actually selected industries based on an economic logic across the entire manufacturing range and over most of the postwar period, although many assumed that it had. Emboldened by the ideas in the new trade theories, for example, some asserted louder than before that Japanese choices had been determined by the strategic economic nature of key industries. Because of this assumption rather than any comprehensive empirical basis, scholarly and practical attention shifted unsurprisingly to the institutional features that could have made a difference in Japan's case.

But the fundamental question continued to stand: How actually did the Japanese government choose industries to favor on the whole? This issue is intensely empirical and decidedly practical. If there were some systematic economic criteria for selection across the postwar era and across the entire industrial economy, they might tell us a great deal about the veritable heart of the Japanese development model, with implications for the theories and industrial strategies in general. If not, then the very idea of a Japanese development model is foolish. Which is it, then? And how would we know for sure?

The Evidence

The only way to be sure about the operations of the Japanese developmental model is to examine the evidence across the entire industrial economy and across the entire postwar period in Japan. How can this be done practically? This is a problem especially since we are concerned both with doing justice to Japanese institutional peculiarities and also extracting generalizations that go beyond Japan. Because hypotheses are almost always easier stated than tested, the best way to assess them in the real world is to shift gears from a more aggregate to a very detailed analysis. Using different levels of industrial aggregation, I used three separate research methodologies to tackle the question—econometrics, structured data analysis, and case studies. As discussed below, each of these complements the others in successive steps by adding a slightly different dimension to the basic analysis.

ECONOMETRICS

The econometric analysis in Chapter 2 sets the stage for the entire investigation that follows because in one fell swoop it gives us a swift and commanding overview of the validity of the criteria. By allowing us to assess the impact of each criterion while controlling for all the other criteria in a way that is simply not possible with the other two approaches, it identifies the actual and relative weight of the criteria in the Japanese government's choices to favor industries.

The analysis relies on not one but several equally valid estimation techniques, using a dataset on TIPs as well as the economic and political criteria across all industries and over time at the two-digit SITC level. By then comparing results across the techniques, the goal is to see which criteria actually held their effects more consistently across the eight TIPs.[6] Sets of multiple regression analyses results are presented for the pooled time-series cross-sectional data on the eight TIPs, that is, across the twelve sectors and between 1955 and 1990. There are two sets of levels models based on the natural log of the variables, one with robust standard errors and the other with panel-corrected standard errors (PCSEs). There are also two differenced models based on the first differences of the natural log of the variables, once again with robust standard errors and PCSEs. Additionally, because there is a concern with endogeneity, another set of regression (in levels) is presented in which the industry attributes are lagged by one year.[7]

What did we learn? In general, controlling for the political criteria, this analysis supported the economic hypothesis for five out of eight tangible TIPs, which included net subsidies, net transfers, tax rates, quotas, and R&D subsidies. At the broadest level, we may say that the logic of economic motivations has had the upper hand in the Japanese government choices to favor industries across the postwar period. High value-added, high wages, and high potential for spillovers emerge as the most significant criteria for selection across almost all these TIPs. But this was hardly a one-sided story, and the political hypothesis emerged as important in its own right in several instances. Japan Development Bank (JDB) loans, subsidized borrowing rates, and tariffs were all sensitive to votes and campaign contributions, as the relevant theory suggests. The amazing part of the story overall, however, is that the economic logic continued to hold sway despite the presence of full-scale political pressures—something that we do not expect theoretically in a representative democracy.

STRUCTURED DATA ANALYSIS

Continuing at the same level of industrial aggregation, the structured data analysis in Chapter 3 also lends support to the econometric findings. More important, it gives us the first clue about deselection, the idea that government TIPs were withdrawn fairly consistently as well. In this analysis, the goal was to ordinally rank and correlate both the TIPs and the criteria for selection in order to determine both the most-favored sectors in postwar Japan and the reason for their favored status. In 1997, I was fortunate to discover that in assessing which industries to select among several high-technology alternatives, MITI, and specifically the Agency for Industrial Science and Technology (AIST), relied on a method of ordinal ranking of several criteria exactly like the structured data analysis here.[8]

What were the most-favored sectors? There is clearly a pattern to MITI's favoritism, and it can be broken down into two distinct periods—the pre- and post-1973 oil-shock worlds.[9] Moving from the early postwar era in which textiles, chemicals, transport equipment, and basic metals were all heavily favored, the emphasis shifted to general machinery and electrical machinery until the late 1960s. The key elements of the evidence suggest that from the mid 1950s to the late 1960s, sectors like transport equipment, chemicals, general machinery, and electrical machinery were favored intensely over the others. As in the econometric analysis, we also find that the potential for high value-added and spillovers was important in MITI's choice to favor these industries over others for roughly a decade beginning in the late 1950s. Among all the economic criteria, the criterion of spillovers is generally what distinguishes the selection of the most-favored sectors from the rest of the sectors.

Alternatively, it is hard to see the systematic relevance of political pressures, say in terms of votes and campaign contributions and lobbying efforts carried out by industry associations, particularly during this period. What is startling about the evidence is that these sectors were very much in line with MITI visions, which basically outline government thinking on where the industrial structure should be headed at a broad level. As I learned from interviews with government officials as well, until the 1970s the focus was on laying the groundwork—setting the base—for future industrialization by acquiring advanced technologies within these sectors and making sure that they worked together in an integrated manner for the benefit of the economy. In most cases, the specific motivation was not to rely on any one country for technologies that could be key to Japan's industrial economy in the future. In sum, the evidence on the most-favored sectors before the first oil shock in 1973 does not negate the presence of political pressures—the government officials do not deny it; the data analysis here certainly does not—but it does suggest that MITI managed to favor sectors based on their economic merit and long-term impact on national welfare.

But this kind of intensely focused favoritism did not last long. By the very early 1970s, this pattern began to unravel in the era after the oil shock. From about then on, a pattern was established for the most-favored sectors that was to remain almost unshakable until the mid-1990s. In 1973, transport equipment, chemicals, petroleum and coal, and basic metals became consistently the most-favored sectors for the remainder of the decade and at least half of the next. By the mid 1980s, transport equipment lost its most-favored status, leaving only chemicals, petroleum and coal, and basic metals as the most-favored sectors for the 1990s. How well do our hypothesized sets of criteria explain this later pattern of selection, as we move farther away from the immediate postwar era? Should we conclude that political pressures, and not economic considerations, came to play an increasingly decisive role in the Japanese government's choice to favor some industries over others? This is what we expect increasingly over time in a representative democracy.

The short answer, in my judgment, is no. In large part, the case for the economic hypothesis is made stronger by the evident weakness and inconsistency of the alternative political explanation. A few examples should make this point clearly. Textiles, about whose political power we hear so much in Japan, was the beneficiary of a great deal of ostentatious legislation but in actuality was favored only through tariff protection, and it was hardly ever the recipient of tremendous government support. Electrical machinery, which was to become one of the most politically powerful sectors by any measure of the quantitative criteria in postwar Japan, enjoyed only a brief most-favored status. Transport equipment, which is widely touted as being all politically powerful, lost its most-favored status by the early 1980s. Petroleum and coal and basic metals, which while nowhere near being the most politically powerful sectors according to the quantitative criteria but having tremendous political influence, are also considered basic intermediate industries vital to the functioning of an advanced industrial economy.[10]

So, in sum, even in the aftermath of the external economic shocks in the early 1970s, the evidence on the most-favored sectors suggests that while economic considerations matter far less in choosing industries to favor, political realities do not really seem to gain a great advantage in their stead. And here, concretely for the first time at the aggregate quantitative level, we get some evidence of the deselection process at work. MITI's TIPs have, in the aggregate, been withdrawn both from industries that were politically powerful and from those, interestingly enough, that were economically strategic. For example, as the above discussion clarifies, politically powerful sectors under MITI's jurisdiction, such as textiles, have not been consistently the most-favored ones over time. But similarly, economically strategic sectors, such as electrical machinery, have not benefited from the same intensity of TIPs for long. In short, foreshadowing a key issue that I will discuss in the next section, both such cases saw selection, which does not make MITI very different from its counterparts elsewhere, and deselection, which was MITI's forte.

CASE STUDIES

Because of the concern with patterns and generalization across all industries and over time, thus far the evidence I have presented concentrates on "hard" or tangible measures and remains at a high level of industrial aggregation. But just as critics of qualitative approaches are less likely to be convinced by anecdotal evidence alone, critics of strict quantitative approaches are also likely to remain skeptical of analyses devoid of historical and institutional considerations. Chapters 4 and 5, therefore, turned to a more detailed level of industrial aggregation, namely case studies as a final cut at investigating the selection process in postwar Japan.

The sample of industries, each of which falls under one of the more macrocategories at the two–digit SITC level in the quantitative analyses, included coal, steel, textiles, shipbuilding, chemicals, automobiles, machine tools, computers, and semiconductors. In addition, I examined the commercial space launch vehicles industry more closely because it has not been analyzed elsewhere before. Why these industries? The idea was to get as much cross-sectional variation and time-series progression in industry types as possible. By examining older industries along with newer ones across most of the postwar period, the goal was to establish the validity of the hypothesized criteria in actual cases of policy-making.

With the exception of the commercial space launch vehicles industry, a wealth of evidence exists on how and which industries were selected for support. But since there is virtually no direct evidence on the criteria for selection in existing works, I interviewed more than a hundred government and private-sector officials with jurisdiction over the relevant industries, as well as those with broader responsibilities, to find out what actually mattered in such selection decisions. The various space-related agencies aside, the bulk of the interviews were carried out in both the vertical and horizontal bureaus of MITI, whose authority extends over almost all the manufacturing range in the economy. Cross-checking criteria in the interviews, as well as supplementing them with interviews with individuals in agencies outside MITI and in industry associations, along with any materials found in existing official and secondary works, gives us fairly convincing evidence as to why different industries were favored across time.

The interviewing and literature-combing process had several effects. It allowed me to gain superb insights into the selection and, to a lesser extent, deselection process in Japan, which I was able to draw upon in judging the more aggregate quantitative evidence in retrospect. It was also a very useful way to find out whether the theoretical criteria actually had any bearing on real-world decisions and whether deselection was really institutionalized as a policy choice. Finally, the most important effect was that the tenor and intensity of the interviews left me with a deep understanding of why Japan is often considered the most "technologist of countries," both at the governmental and industry level.[11] Almost without exception, the heart of this technologist paradigm is about concepts—spillovers, linkage externalities, the idea that all good things advance together.

But what exactly did we learn? What did officials have to say overall with respect to the economic and political logic? How exactly did their beliefs, perceptions, and experiences shed light on the central question in this book? Fortunately, the interviews validate the importance of some of the hypothesized criteria for selection in Japan's case. Among the economic criteria, the officials repeatedly emphasized the significance of high value-added and the potential for externalities, especially linkages. Among the political ones, they stressed the weight of the electoral logic, pointing to votes, lobbying power, campaign contributions, and influence peddling behind the scenes that is not amenable to quantitative analyses. But MITI officials still claim that, in general, industrial selections in postwar Japan have been shielded from politics and politicians, especially until the 1980s. Even today, they appear less concerned with political pressures from within Japan than with calls for transparency from outside Japan. Overall, these claims are made credible by the fact that much of the quantitative evidence backs them up.

But the real virtue of the interviews and case studies is that they to go beyond the neat theoretical frameworks and allow us to uncover subtleties and nuances about the industrial selection process that are not captured in the hypotheses or the quantitative features alone. And they make clear the sheer importance of perceptions and intangibles in the industrial selection process, particularly as they relate to technology acquisition. To give a few examples: One widespread perception concerns how the Japanese industrial base can move forward in the future. Here the focus is on the criterion of high value-added, which rather than any precise economic meaning, appears to be imbued with some kind of technological mystique. Officials reason that, just to survive, the Japanese industrial base must move onward and upward technologically in the face of intense competition from the next tier of rapidly industrializing countries—and that it can only do so with a focus on ever higher value-added industries. It is in this context that officials speak about the necessity of deselection, letting industries go their natural way, especially in the volatile high-technology sectors in which both the speed and direction of change are unpredictable. The idea is that only by eventually withstanding international competition can such industries serve the national economic interest.

A perhaps even more widely institutionalized perception stresses the importance of moving Japan forward in an integrated manner, drawing upon the resources and talents of existing industries to create new futuristic ones—as evident in the ongoing struggle to establish a foothold in the commercial space launch sector. In this view, externalities—both in the sense of knowledge spilling over from one industry to benefit a range of others and also in the sense of an industry pulling along labor and capital in others—are critical. Almost every official brings up the importance of the *potential* of this criterion, adding that it is not precise measurements but rather perceptions about its efficacy that always sway public decisions in the end. The goal, in any event, is to create the possibility of further technological advancement by selecting industries characterized by high value-added and especially the high potential for spillover benefits. For many, the ambition is to see Japan as *the* technology R&D center—a supra Silicon Valley of sorts—for the advanced technology of the world, which would bring widespread benefits to the whole of the Japanese economy.

Importantly, talks about the presence of these economic criteria are also interwoven with concerns about labor and social unrest, as well as electoral maneuvering and pressures on the part of the politicians. Few dispute that the selection process can very often be determined by the political influence of an industry, especially in the more traditional or declining industries such as coal, steel, textiles, and even shipbuilding. Nobody denies that these factors have made a difference to prolonging some TIPs to these industries, but the problem is that the preferences of politicians and bureaucrats often match in sectors in which there may be larger social problems down the line.

With this in mind, it is difficult to speak of the unilateral influence of politicians on bureaucrats. As we saw in Chapter 1, this point is a controversial one in Japan studies, with observers characterizing either the bureaucrats or politicians as principal and agent of one or the other. But bureaucrats, though hardly omnipotent, are not merely passive agents of their political principals. The most troubling thing that the evidence suggests is that we may be drawing a line of battle when there is not such stark conflict.[12] To assume the principal-agent framework is to assume that the preferences of the politicians and bureaucrats are generally always at odds with each other. But in many practical cases, as, for example, employment concerns in declining industries, no one wants to see a bad situation also get socially explosive. Whatever the individual motivations of politicians and bureaucrats, the general preferences about how to deal with such issues and problems tend to be the same at least in the short term. The point is that rather than a unilateral arrow of influence going from the politicians to the bureaucrats, the real relationship is one of interactive accommodation, bargaining, and compromises and is also far more cooperative than allowed for by the theoretical caricature of the relationship.[13] None of this is meant to imply that this multifaceted cooperative process is smooth, only that it exists and needs to be investigated further.[14]

Industries can also directly attempt to pressure the bureaucracy. In fact, on the bureaucratic side of the equation, extensive efforts are made by both the industry and the bureaus with jurisdiction over the aforesaid industry simply to get to know each other. This access allows the officials to get up-to-date information about the relevant market or industry under their jurisdiction and therefore constitutes a major input into their own policy decisions, which are made with the fate of the whole industry in mind. The flip side, however, is that this kind of interactive approach allows for all manner of lobbying and carries with it a high risk of corruption, as is widely recognized.[15] As some officials discussed, there have been quite a few internal disciplinary actions taken against some MITI officials that are not issues for public consumption. One major means of avoiding prolonged MITI-industry contact is the personnel rotation system, which posts officials for an average of two years to any one position in the ministry before moving them elsewhere.[16] The important point is that the institutional access—the window to the private sector—is not dependent on any one person but has a life of its own.

In closing, many officials suggest also that the economics of choosing industries is becoming sophisticated both in order to counter public criticisms of wasteful industrial favoritism and to convince the conservative Ministry of Finance (MOF) during budget season. This is especially true for the space launch vehicles program as a whole, which has been buffeted by a string of successive failures in recent years. Others also suggest that policy decisions to support industries now are based more on practical issues, like market share, basic R&D research levels, the structure of the competition, and the whole issue of international competitiveness. Across the board, MITI (now METI) and space agency officials leave little doubt that they take the position of their domestic industries seriously even today, speaking always of how and where Japan stands in comparison to foreign countries, especially the United States, by industry and especially by technology. Officials also point out that perceptions about the relative backward position of Japan in a key technological industry, as in commercial space launch or nanotechnology or genomics, is the most important factor that very often galvanizes support across the government for a sector. Overall, it is very important to know that the industrial selection process, especially via creative new means, is far from over from the point of view of Japan's technological advancement.

Let me sum up this section on the evidence. From a macroeconometric approach down to a single case study, it is clear that even a simple question becomes complicated very fast in the real world. The layers of research methods used here helped tremendously in clarifying the answer from different angles. Going back and forth between the different methods not only makes us aware of the complexities in approximating the "truth" but also cautions us against extreme depictions of the Japanese industrial selection process. Each method—the econometrics, structured data analysis, and case studies—contributed uniquely to the support or rejection of the central hypotheses. Together, these three methods show that the economic logic has held sway in the Japanese government's decisions to favor industries up until the early 1980s and that it has not abated with respect to the high-technology industries.

The importance of the economic criteria, as well as a range of perceptions and ideas, is brought home with accuracy by almost all officials. Remarkably, the actual government choices made show that there has not been much difference between their rhetoric and actions over much of the postwar period. Even more remarkably, economic criteria have been central to the selection process in a representative democracy, where political pressures from politicians and industry groups have been consistently present. Overall, what we observe in Japan is that even though the micropolitical processes did take place as theory suggests—and as the interviews and case studies confirm—they did not greatly affect macro-outcomes across industries or over time in a consistent manner. By and large, as the evidence on the most-favored sectors makes clear, Japanese TIPs moved to broad economic concerns for most of the postwar period. In short, institutions intervened, made a difference to policy choices, and eventually refracted the outcomes from

204 TIPs from Postwar Japan

what we would expect to see in representative democracies. This evidence, standing contrary to the predictions of the mainstream political economy models, has some important implications not just for the theories with which we began but also for the debates on industrial strategies in general.

The Implications

I began with a simple question of how governments choose industries to favor, and the Japanese case offers up a clear answer. But having so far carefully presented what this work does, both in terms of the argument and the evidence, it is also worthwhile pointing out here what this work does not do. It does not begin by arguing in favor of or against state-led industrialization. It does not attribute causality between TIPs and outcomes in any industry; it does not, therefore, say that Japanese industries succeeded because of the Japanese government's interventions. It does not, in short, begin by purporting to explain the dazzling empiricism that is Japan's industrial success.

My ambitions, in fact, are much more modest in scope. All I do is assess the record on industrial selections in postwar Japan, as evidenced by the relative disbursement of government TIPs. In examining this record, I ask whether Japanese TIPs were moved more by economic considerations or political factors across the full range of industries in the economy over the postwar period. My specific project is crystal clear about its goal and mindful of its abilities to reach it. At each step, I show how context remains a complicated beast, and, despite this, how patterns can still be extracted with respect to Japanese industrial selections. In the end, I am able to say with some certitude that the Japanese government selected industries on the basis of an economic logic and that, contrary to what we would expect in a representative democracy especially over time, political pressures did not definitively sway government choices across the board.

This is an incredibly unexpected result, especially from the perspective of most mainstream economists and political economists who see politics, and their deductive models of political behavior, prevailing irrespective of cross-national differences in history and institutions and who are also not likely to be convinced by case studies evidence alone, which is often the main methodological tool of Japan specialists. Few, of course, are so naive as to believe that industrial selections in a representative democracy can move to economic dictates alone. In fact, the evidence, which comes to us both from the MITI bureaucrats themselves as well as from the quantitative analyses, confirms the importance of the electoral reasoning. The point is rather that the evidence on the political determinants of Japanese industrial selections is hardly as dominant across industries or over time as mainstream theory leads us to believe.[17] Based on the evidence from the Japanese case, I would like to suggest at least two things to take away from this work that bear upon our thinking on industrial strategies.

INSTITUTIONS AND INDUSTRIAL SELECTION

First, despite the recent derision about the prescience of the Japanese government, it is important to know that governments can play a positive role in the industrialization process. The reason why many observers, and especially economists, have feared endorsement of TIPs is because of the very real possibility that they will be captured or corrupted by political interests and that this has terrible consequences for the industrial economy in general. But what the Japanese case suggests is the importance of both formal and informal institutions that can play a powerful role in affecting or constraining policy choices and eventual outcomes.[18] This work provides indirect evidence about the importance of such institutional features stressed in many studies on Japan's political economy. The features that stand out can be divided into three categories: informational, organizational, and ideological.

In the informational category, there is a distinct emphasis on acquiring and analyzing information pertaining to specific industries and their niches. Information is the basis for making any kind of industrial selection decisions, and my interviews made it clear just how important this feature is in the day-to-day operations of MITI. There is no question that within MITI, the work of specific *genkyoku* or *genka*—divisions—with excellent information-gathering capabilities, based on significant interactions with the private sector, helps minimize the risk of poor choices. So important is the emphasis on gathering information and keeping abreast of changes in the industries that MITI officials speak of their role in the vertical bureaus as industry analysts, much like those in the private sector, who are responsible for monitoring trends and developments in a particular industry.

In fact, with the addition of *shingikai* (advisory bodies), which allow for specialists' input, as well as other more informal but regularized contacts with the private sector, MITI has deliberately cultivated informational arrangements that help it to reduce, not eliminate, the risk of making gross mistakes.[19] The emphasis on information is all the more important considering that most political economists deem governments, compared to the private sector, incapable of coming up with detailed information to form the basis for sound industrial selection decisions.[20] Because the government does not have the information, the argument goes, it is more likely to make poor choices in comparison to private-sector participants.[21] Since the acquisition of information is basic and since this institutional feature is a strong candidate for replication elsewhere, it would be helpful to study further how and in what ways it is transmitted between actors and with what potential consequences.[22]

Information, however, operates in an organizational setting that can potentially affect its utility for making choices. In the organizational category, several features stand out in the public and private sphere, as well as in the manner of their interaction, that suggest that information works in a Japanese environment historically geared toward insulation, but not complete autonomy, from political pressures. There is, for example, the formal decision-making structure at MITI that helps to lay an emphasis on the general rather than the specific interests in the industrial economy. The specific demands of the vertical bureaus that deal directly with industries are diffused as they move upward to the horizontal bureaus responsible for the well-being of the entire industrial economy. Moreover, peak business organizations, such as Keidanren, have officially given money to politicians or parties for aggregate but not specific concerns, again diffusing sector-specific interests for bureaucratic policy-making.[23]

Another important organization and historical feature is MITI's relative autonomy from politicians' demands and influence. Politicians in general are not able to make upper-level personnel appointments, to control promotions or postbureaucratic job opportunities, to bypass strict civil-service laws against dismissal of bureaucrats, or even to monitor policy details consistently due to few staff and little policy expertise.[24] A final feature that deserves attention is the fact that labor is organized along corporate lines and has traditionally been excluded from the national policy-making process. This again points to some space for policy-makers to take controversial actions that would otherwise not be possible, as in attempting to deselect declining industries. For its exclusion, labor has been compensated through policies of equitable distribution and wage hikes linked to productivity.[25]

Finally, in the ideological category, there was for a good part of the postwar period the keen developmental consensus spurred on by concerns over Japan's relative economic standing in the world.[26] The shared ideology of playing catch-up that was held by all major actors, namely bureaucrats, politicians, and industries, is historically considered an instrumental factor behind Japan's industrialization efforts.[27] While much of this consensus has lessened—after all, Japan has essentially caught up—it may well be that the present economic malaise could bring it back with a vengeance and give a much-needed boost to the course of the industrial economy once again.

More important, the ideological consensus or set of beliefs concerning the vital importance of technology to Japan has not disappeared in either the public or private sphere.[28] If anything, it has become even more important, especially given the constantly changing nature, speed, and direction of technology movements.[29] Close examination of specific sectors, such as commercial space launch vehicles, also shows that this developmental consensus is not quite as moribund as some now believe it to be. It was impossible dur-

ing most interviews to miss the palpable concern with technology acquisition and indigenization, with official after official pointing to high technology as the mainstay of Japan's national economic security in the long run.

These informational, organizational, and ideological features potentially
created space for bureaucrats to formulate and carry out policy contra to political pressures in a representative democracy. Although we do not know
quite how, the mediation of political influences and pressures through these
kinds of institutional features may well have attenuated their impact on policy choices and eventual outcomes. But which institutional features and why
remain unclear at this point. While they stress the importance of such features, Japan specialists have yet to tell us which of them matter more than
others in the industrial policy-making processes or even to give us a clearer
sense of their relative weight in economic policy-making in general. Now
that we have taken a step in establishing a more comprehensive footing for
the Japanese government choices—which before was more of an assertion
than a proven fact across the entire postwar Japanese economy—it would be
useful to examine these institutional features and the conditions under
which they could make a difference in selection, as well as deselection, outcomes.

POLITICS OF DESELECTION

The second thing to take away from this work concerns the emphasis on
the other, mostly ignored, side of the equation in debates over industrial
strategies—deselection rather than mere selection. As is well understood, the
main problem with TIPs is the difficulty of ending them, of ensuring some
sort of effective "sunset" provision from the start.[30] Although some MITI officials have stressed its importance, deselection is not mentioned outright in
the literature, but it is crucial for advancing our understanding of industrial
strategies.[31] By deselection I mean the reduction of wholesale TIPs to a sector or in some cases the withdrawal of TIPs altogether. This idea of deselection is a genuine concern of Japanese government officials and has become
of even greater concern more recently, especially as it is perceived that the
industrial game has shifted irreversibly to high-technology industries worldwide.[32]

Historically, some officials speak about planned protectionism in the
Japanese case, where the ideal government policy was explicitly to grant protection for a specified period, say a period of ten years, or to state the target
of production to be achieved in a specified number of years. After that, the
goal was to gradually phase out all protections, since only then could industries compete domestically and internationally.[33] Clarity on the principle of
deselection, in other words, would have a direct impact on industry expectations regarding government support and would also thereby make indus-

try participants more prudent about their own decisions regarding the adop-
tion of strategies and technologies that would eventually operate in a competitive environment.

While not perfect in the least, we do see a kind of selection–deselection
pattern as we look across the evidence, especially in sectors in which there
was no contested jurisdiction with MITI.[34] At the aggregate level, MITI
withdrew TIPs from politically powerful or economically strategic industries, and sometimes even from both. The key motivating factor behind deselection, as I learned at MITI, is to safeguard national economic security in
the long run precisely by exposing favored firms to the pressure of international competition. By committing itself credibly to a small role, either
through modest levels of TIPs or now even formal preset time limits, the
government agencies have tried to make sure that no expectations of dependence are created among the favored firms.[35] This, for instance, comes
across very clearly in the ongoing emphasis on "commercialization" of space
launch vehicles in order for the industry to indigenize successfully.

In part, this limiting role is now even more credible than during the early
postwar years because, by all official accounts, MITI is much weaker, has
fewer tangible policy tools, faces a lot more unavoidable pressure from politicians, presides over internationally oriented industries, and simply cannot
command (administratively or otherwise) as effectively as before.[36] It is also
credible because, as the evidence shows, even when MITI was fully armed it
played a fairly restrained role toward favoring industries, maybe in part because of fierce competition between Japanese corporations themselves.[37]

We can, of course, fully expect deselection to be harder for two reasons:
It must overcome not just policy inertia but also entrenchment of existing
political coalitions that benefit from the policies. Moving analytically well
beyond the research agenda here, I would even speculate that the reason why
deselection may causally lead to sound industrial performance is because the
credible commitment by the government to deselect changes industry expectations about relying on government support. Governments, in short,
need to worry less about favoring winners and more about withdrawing
TIPs from them lest the favored sectors are made into or turn out to be dis-
asters.From a practical perspective, we should worry less about replicating
path-dependent institutions and more about how governments can preset
support for specific industries for certain time periods. The best solution
might well be that the agency allocating the TIPs is dissolved after a set time
or, in the extreme, the means of pecuniary support are put in the hands of
foreign agencies so that no long-term expectations of dependence are created in the recipient industries.

What these findings mean for the pursuit of industrial selection elsewhere
is that a great deal more attention needs to be paid to this deselection pattern and the institutional foundations that made it possible in Japan's case,

such as the ones discussed earlier, before running out to claim that strategic industries should be favored or winners picked elsewhere. Besides, there are at least two other problems that should give any such advocacy serious pause for concern.

HOW DO WE KNOW WHAT WINNERS ARE?

The major problem with respect to industrial selection is that it is hard to know in advance what a winner is, and, as some MITI officials rightly stress, the exercise of choice among equally reasonable industry alternatives is very much a policy gamble in the end. It is worthwhile adding that this truism also applies to market participants. It was one thing when Japan was truly playing catch-up with advanced "models" before it, but a different and far more murky matter altogether when it is all caught up. This is especially true because of the volatile nature of high-technology industries but more fundamentally because there is a deficiency in our knowledge about the makeup of economically strategic sectors that holds both temporally and spatially.

The point here is that if there is some state of nature to economically strategic sectors that holds irrespective of whether they are targeted, it would be worth finding out empirically just what that is.[38] If there is no such discernable difference, we need to know that too. The criteria used in this study, such as value-added or spillover potential, are a first cut at distinguishing some sectors from their lesser cohorts, but by no means do they constitute an agreed-upon empirical basis for identifying strategic sectors. Here the Japanese case does well to remind us that perceptions, rather than any empirical facts about the validity of criteria such as spillovers or linkage externalities confer upon them a legitimacy that is hard to shake. For example, the Japanese steel industry, despite its relative decline, is still widely perceived as being highly strategic in the economy.

But are there, in fact, empirically identifiable and temporally robust criteria that exist in strategic sectors? And are these criteria not present in other sectors? Or is it just a question of degrees of their presence across sectors? In which case, how do we determine cutoff points to categorize all sectors?[39] Although nobody knows the answers to such questions, these are ultimately the kinds of practical issues on which the case for government selection will stand or fall. Given this uncertainty, it is not surprising that perceptions about what criteria or factors are important, as in the Japanese case, take on added importance in matters of policy choices, as they no doubt do everywhere.

DID INDUSTRIAL SELECTIONS MAKE A DIFFERENCE?

There is also a second reason for being cautious about using the evidence here to advocate a strategy of favoring some industries for support over others. One of the most reasonable questions about this entire project is a counterfactual one, and it goes to the heart of what is most of interest in the larger industrial policy debate. Had there been no industrial selection, would the Japanese industrial mix still look as it does today? That is, by one measure, would machinery and equipment, which comprised about 12 percent of the share of exports in 1955, still comprise 76 percent of the share of exports in 1994? Or to take another example, would textiles, which comprised about 37 percent of export shares in 1955, still comprise a mere 2 percent of export shares in 1994? If the answer here is yes, then the whole process of selection or deselection is superfluous because presumably TIPs make little or no difference to industrial outcomes.

Although I studiously avoided this issue for the sake of analytical clarity, it would be disingenuous to try and circumvent this core issue in the industrial policy debate entirely. To put it simply, this work made a careful distinction between showing the criteria by which industries were chosen at different points in time and subsequent outcomes in these industries at later points in time. And I stuck to the former research agenda. That is, at no point did I pretend to be claiming that TIPs were causing industrial successes or failures, whether measured by an industry's percentage increases or decreases in its export share, manufacturing output share, global market share, and so on over time. But since the "success" of TIPs in advancing industrial growth is of main interest to many observers, it is worth pointing out that all the major Japanese industries under MITI's exclusive jurisdiction that became internationally competitive were subjected to the selection-deselection pattern.

To expand a bit: As the quantitative evidence on the most-favored sectors shows, electrical machinery and general machinery, both of which went on to change the industrial face of Japan, were selected for support through massive TIPs in the late 1950s and later deselected by the mid 1960s. Transport equipment was similarly selected for support throughout the early postwar period and deselected in the early 1980s, just as the Japanese automobile industry first overtook the American one. The chemicals industry, which is under the split jurisdiction of the agricultural and health ministries, has been selected for massive support throughout the postwar period. Overall it is still, as chagrined MITI officials point out, the least globally competitive of all the strategic industries. They blame the prolonged selection as the major cause, again suggesting that had deselection taken place, especially in the petrochemicals industry in the aftermath of the oil shocks, it might well today have been enjoying the same fate as the others in its cohort. Recently, the focus on deselection has become even more important, stemming from a belief that the technological game has speeded up to such an extent that TIPs may not be able to keep up. The AIST's projects now, for example, stress definite five-year time limits for a national research project, in large part because there is great danger in supporting technological ventures that stretch interminably with no end or profitability in sight. The method and timing of TIPs are, in short, now designed explicitly to ensure that no expectations of dependence are created by the government in the favored industries or firms, whether they are going up or down.

But economists who have assessed the positive effects of industrial selection in the case of even imperfect industries maintain that there is little or no economic gain to be had from TIPs.[40] What this suggests more broadly is that the industrial structure would have turned out pretty much the same regardless of whether TIPs were used to select industries, even in the case of Japan. In other words, electrical machinery and transport equipment would still have risen, textiles and coal would still have declined. I believe this is generally true, but it remains a difficult counterfactual to prove or dismiss. Looking at the remarkable speed of Japan's industrial transformation, I am also inclined to believe that the crucial difference TIPs make may not be one of economic gain but rather one of gain in time. What does this mean?

The simple point is that what happened in Japan would have happened much slower (in rising industries) and much faster (in declining industries) had most-favored selection not taken place, but it would still have happened according to market dictates.[41] How much time are we talking about? At a casual level, a lot of time in a rising industry like semiconductors, with my guess that the VLSI project, among other TIPs, made Japanese semiconductor companies competitive by a good five or six years earlier than they would have been in the natural course of events.[42] The logic falls on the other side of the curve as well. Coal, which would have been finished off as a domestic industry in Japan in the 1970s, has had its existence stretched along for an extra twenty to thirty years. The more traditional Japanese textiles and apparel industry has declined rapidly out of existence between the 1970s and 1990s because massive and concentrated TIPs were not put in place to slow the downward trend.

TIPs, in short, act like a spring or cushion in time—that is, a spring on the way up and a cushion on the way down—but do not necessarily fundamentally transform the natural course of the market. These kinds of temporal "gains" and "losses" for sovereign governments are about the only kinds of counterfactual statements that make sense to me as far as the effect of TIPs goes, whether in Japan or elsewhere.

Thinking Ahead

Regardless of the difficulty of establishing winners or counterfactual scenarios, one thing remains true. When governments are backward and unwilling to wait for "natural" market outcomes that they perceive will leave their countries even further behind in the great industrial game, the temptation toward industrial selection sets in strongly in an effort to catch up with the advanced models. This is as true in Japan as it has been true historically everywhere.

Japan, sadly, has been dismissed in the popular imagination—perhaps a good thing if serious analyses can at last be carried out without fanfare. It is now fashionable to condemn the Japanese government, to look at the economic quagmire in Japan and conclude more easily than ever before that the government there could not possibly ever have done anything right.[43] But just as it is now fiercely under attack, there was also a time not too long ago when the Japanese developmental state seemed invincible. Quite apart from the fact that it is foolish to attribute contradictory outcomes to the same government—a government commendable yesterday because of growth, deplorable today because of a recession—casual observers forget that Japanese manufacturing industries are still formidable competitors across a range of industrial goods in the international arena. Even in sectors such as space launch vehicles, where indigenization has been a problem, the final verdict is still out on whether Japan will be able to break into the global industry and establish itself as a serious player.

Moreover, three things are worth remembering with a view to the future. First, just as America rebounded economically despite the pervasive predictions of doom and gloom a mere decade ago, it is simply a matter of time before there will be a reversal of fortune in Japan as well.[44] Although even a rebounded Japan will probably never again replicate its historic high-growth rates, such a reversal is likely to draw attention once again to Japan's policies regarding development, especially its industrial and high-tech development.

Second, the fact that Japan is now in a financial quagmire is irrelevant to how it actually achieved a stunning industrial catch-up with the Western world and secured its place among the great industrial powers of our day.[45] To go from literally ashes to being the world's second-largest economy is not a mere academic curiosity that can be swept under the media rug just because things do not look as glamorous as before.[46] What happened in Japan is real, and whatever patterns or strategies the Japanese government followed, especially in the early postwar period, are still of great relevance to backward industrializers.[47] MITI definitely played a role in industrial selection—a role that was made as important by what it did as what it did not do. As this work suggests, deselection, more than selection, may perhaps be key to advancing our understanding of a government's role in industrial development.[48]

Finally, those who believe that the interest of the Japanese government in the industrial and technological future of Japan has either diminished or disappeared would be sadly mistaken.[49] Despite its sobering and often frustrating competitive realities, the space launch vehicles case is a good reminder of this.[50] More important, even if a government agency like MITI has reached a stage where its existence could be questioned and where its past becomes more relevant elsewhere than to its own future, the simple fact is that industrial evolution itself has not reached some final plateau and never really will.

We stand today on the threshold of some of the greatest technological changes of all times in space, medicine, and quantum mechanics.[51] To think that governments in general, and the Japanese one in particular, do not care about these changes or are going to sit idly by and let markets go their merry way is to ignore the essence of perceptual connections between wealth and power that many political scientists think vital to the conduct of government policy. In fact, now that Japan is a great industrial power, it has to learn the greater game of "move-up" in the global technological competition.[52] Whatever its strategies at the public or private level, the Japanese government continues to take as much of a keen interest in the nature, direction, and speed of technology trends as any of the other industrial powers of our day. What are the winners of the future? How do we identify them? What can a government do to embed them in its national economy? These questions remain worthy of serious exploration. They also do well to remind us that the industrial game is not over, developmentalism is not dead.

Notes

Chapter 1

1. Krugman, ed., 1986, 12–15; Helpman and Krugman 1989, 5–9; Spencer and Brander 1983, Brander and Spencer 1985; Milner and Yoffie 1989. A real source of confusion lies in the word "strategic" and the many different ways it is used. Some political scientists have used "strategic" to mean a form of specific reciprocity or conditional most-favored status. Economists have used it in two other ways, only the second of which is of interest to this work. First, it is used in the context of international competition, with a focus on home actors making "strategic" moves to deter potential foreign rivals. Second, the term "strategic" is also used to indicate a tradable goods sector whose special characteristics, as discussed in the chapter, make it particularly appropriate for government TIPs. In this study, the word "strategic" is used only in this final sense of strategic sectors.

2. The research here has tried to incorporate some of the key propositions from this theory in examining the disbursement of Japanese TIPs across a range of industries. Some strong caveats apply, however. First, the sample of industries chosen for analysis (the entire manufacturing sector at the two-digit level) is a far cry from the sample of oligopolistic industries that form the backbone of the theoretical works. Second, the focus on relying on a wide range of TIPs is also far removed from the tidy focus on export subsidies and import protection found in these works. Third, the idea of dynamic scale economies that are wholly external to firms—and which are considered key in terms of identifying strategic sectors even if their very existence is disputed—cannot simply be captured by a focus on sectoral R&D expenditures alone.

3. Spencer and Brander 1983; Brander and Spencer 1985, esp. 84; Krugman 1990, 185–86, 190–92. The furor over the so-called strategic trade policy literature can be traced back to Brander and Spencer, whose work cast a permanent shadow over the traditional theory of trade under perfect competition. They did not just make the theoretical argument that export subsidies could be used to "profit-shift" from foreign to domestic firms in profit-earning imperfectly competitive industries. Indeed, they also strongly suggested that the very act of doing so was economically advantageous from the point of view of the whole nation. Similarly, in arguing that the practice of trade differed greatly from the accepted theory, Krugman's work was instru-

mental in demonstrating theoretically that import protection was a means of export promotion in oligopolistic industries. He also suggested that home government protection could give a home firm greater economies of scale in comparison to foreign firms and that therefore decreasing costs would confer a great advantage to home firms in expanding their market shares. Given their conclusions, both the Brander-Spencer "profit-shifting" model and the Krugman "import protection as export promotion" idea understandably found resonance in the age-old debate over mercantilist TIPs.

4. Krugman 1983, 123–55; Krugman in Krugman 1986, 14–17; Spencer 1986. The works by Krugman contain the most lucid overall discussions on the criteria for identifying strategic sectors and also the problems associated with measuring and using the criteria themselves.

5. Lawrence and Schultze 1990, 13–18. The new trade theories have very specific ideas about why certain kinds of rents may continue to persist in imperfectly competitive situations, which is also why it makes theoretical sense for home governments to try and appropriate them for the economic benefit of the nation through targeted TIPs. On surplus profits (rents), the idea is that high fixed costs or steep learning curves in highly specialized industries might deter the entry of new rivals, thereby allowing the existing firms(s) to earn surplus profits for quite some time. Here first-mover home government TIPs may deter foreign competition even more severely and fully allow profits to be shifted to home producers. On surplus or premium wages (rents), the idea is that wages are higher than elsewhere, usually in capital-intensive sectors, simply because firms find it extremely costly to have disruptions and are therefore willing to pay higher amounts to workers to induce them to maintain productivity at a higher level. If a government wanted to raise national productivity levels and real wages, it could target the expansion of output in such high-wage sectors.

6. Dixit and Grossman 1986.

7. Tyson 1990, 153–60. Apart from the standard arguments for why some industries may be of strategic significance (rents, linkage externalities, technological externalities), Tyson also highlights the concern that externalities may not be a pure public good that is international in scope. In fact, one of her key points is that technological externalities and knowledge oftentimes arise as a consequence of the production process itself and are therefore inherently local and path dependent in nature. Since they tend to accumulate and persist in a particular time and place, their presence or absence today may well determine the technological capabilities of and opportunities open to a nation in the future.

8. Krugman 1993, 363; Helpman and Krugman 1989, 8.

9. The formal models explicitly point to the role of export subsidies, R&D subsidies, or import protection as the major policies to which governments have to commit credibly. However, there is no reason why the same logic cannot also be extended to other TIPs as well since the basic idea is to push strategic industries down the learning curve as quickly as possible before the competitors move in. Nontariff (NTB) protection or favorable tax rates may, for example, also help toward this general end, as can a number of other TIPs.

10. Krugman 1995, 7, 15–29.

11. Krueger 1993, 54–59.

12. Borrus, Tyson, and Zysman 1986, 92.

13. Itoh et al., 1991, 40–42, 81–82, suggest also the importance of market failures as an argument for infant industry protection, especially in the context of a small country. In addition, they argue that infant industries with dynamic economies of scale and Marshallian externalities can potentially flourish if provided protection and that in such cases industrial policy can have far-reaching effects on industrial structures, as it potentially did in the Japanese case. This kind of protection is especially valid in follower countries that seek to catch up with leader nations.

14. Johnson 1982, 312, 318. Johnson, the original architect of this coinage and position, did not overstate MITI's strategic orientations or its ability to impose its preferences in the face of business resistance. Indeed, one of the key points his work illustrates is that cooperation between government and business is difficult to achieve and maintain and that business may well like government assistance but does not necessarily like government orders.

15. Johnson 1995, 102.

16. Pempel 1978, 736.

17. Zysman 1983, 234–51.

18. Prestowitz 1989, 248–85.

19. Dosi, Tyson, and Zysman 1989, 3–48.

20. Samuels 1987, 6, 9, 260–62.

21. Samuels 1994, 33–78, 337.

22. Okimoto 1989, 144–45.

23. Johnson 1982, 323. Johnson's careful tracing of the structural economic and institutional conditions under which MITI rose and came to exercise power leads him to conclude that other countries are better off designing their development strategies from "local materials."

24. Ibid., 28, 199, 206 (emphasis mine).

25. Okimoto 1989, 64–66, 79. Okimoto states that an industry designated a winner must contain research of a precommercial nature so that the participating firms do not gain a decisive advantage over the excluded firms, have an indispensable need for government assistance to start the venture and see it through, and also have a realistic time frame for the completion of the proposed project. Government support provided the "critical missing ingredient" for, among other things, launching projects of high capital costs, risks, and fundamental technological importance.

26. Zysman 1983, 238–40, points out that in the postwar era, Japan's comparative cost advantage lay in labor-intensive industries that were more appropriate to an economy with a scarcity of raw materials and capital. Yet MITI went contrary to its then comparative cost advantage in choosing so-called strategic industries. Zysman also clarifies some of the key criteria with which MITI selected industries. In his words, these were industries that "(1) were likely to expand with increase in income; (2) offered the possibilities of economies of scale from concentrated investment; (3) would drag the rest of the economy along in their wake; and (4) could become export industries" (240).

27. Dosi, Tyson, and Zysman 1989, 4, 13. The authors are also aware of the theoretical criteria of increasing returns under imperfect competition, or externalities. They point out that even with highly sophisticated tools, it is very difficult to measure them empirically.

28. Prestowitz 1989, 248–85, 508, gives another answer as well, which he thinks is a "good start" as criteria, namely "the industry should be crucial, it should be able to draw up its own research agenda, and it should contribute half the cost" (508).

29. Okuno-Fujiwara 1991, 278.

30. Samuels 1994, 14–32, 34, 49, 73, 244–46, 339. Samuels argues that MITI used a powerful metaphor to suggest why, for example, aerospace was a strategic industry. This metaphor—"the industry as the trunk of a tree with roots in key basic technologies and fruits in every variety of industrial and consumer product line" (245)— is a powerful example of how the Japanese see linkages or extensiveness of uses as the crucial characteristic of strategic sectors. In a similar focus on the impact of learning by doing on improving cost conditions, Itoh et al. 1991, 40–41, suggest that dynamic economies of scale or economies of time constitute the "minimum necessary condition" for government TIPs. This may potentially have been a consideration in the Japanese case.

31. Krugman 1993, 362. Krugman realizes there is a tension between advancing the newfangled view of the world economy that refutes the position that free trade is the best policy and advocating at the same time traditional views about the desirability of free trade policy. His defense for free trade policy is quintessentially pragmatic in a political sense: True, it may not be the best policy, but attempting to deviate from it in a rather too sophisticated way may well end up doing more harm than good, both for the economic welfare nationally and the implications for optimum tariff warfare globally. In other words, practically, no TIPs is the best tip Krugman has to offer.

32. Bates 1981, 2.

33. Krueger 1974, 293–94. Krueger's startling estimations of the use of economic resources to obtain politically created rents suggested losses of resources in equilibrium totaling up to 15 percent of GNP—losses that represented windfall profits to exactly those special interests that competed to obtain them. Although there is only evidence from two countries, India and Turkey, Krueger's estimations are meant to show that rents are quantitatively important and that the phenomenon no doubt extends to any case where there are means available for competing for the import licenses or other government TIPs.

34. Bhagwati 1980, 1982.

35. Bhagwati 1988, 50.

36. Anderson and Baldwin 1981, 1–30; Magee, Brock, and Young 1989.

37. Grossman and Helpman 1994, 833–36.

38. Stigler 1971, 3–6.

39. Peltzman 1976, 211–40; Hillman 1989, 25–37.

40. Hillman 1982, 1180–87.

41. The seemingly effortless interaction between politicians and voters is not without problems, however. For one thing, there is the significant problem of shirk-

ing. For instance, because of the secret ballot, voters may not deliver the votes they promise to a candidate unless they also pre-commit to campaign funds. Similarly, incumbents may shirk from implementing the same TIPs as promised in their campaign platforms unless they are to receive the funds after the TIPs are implemented or the shadow of future interactions prevents them from shirking.

42. Magee, Brock, and Young 1989, 47–51; Hillman and Ursprung 1988, 729–45.

43. Grossman and Helpman 1994, 834.

44. Magee, Brock, and Young 1989, 219.

45. Green and Shapiro 1994, 13–32; North 1990, 17–26.

46. Buchanan and Tollison 1984, 13, 19–21; Moe 1984, 1987. One point of relevance here is that if the bureaucracy is the ultimate arbiter of TIPs, then it makes more sense from the point of view of the rational lobbying groups to make political investments through other resources in entrenched bureaucrats rather than in what are often transient politicians. Extending the logic of political motivations further, surely bureaucrats also cannot be presumed any the less innocent of self-interest, as they may rationally grant/implement favorable TIPs to specific industries in exchange for economic rewards (e.g., *amakudari* in Japan) in the future from the same industry.

47. Weingast and Moran 1983; McCubbins, Noll, and Weingast 1987, 1989; Moe 1987.

48. Moe 1984, 765, suggests that because theoretical development is far from over, it still makes sense to try and first understand the full dimensions of the optimization problem before attempting to concentrate on specific constraints that vary with substantive context.

49. Muramatsu and Krauss 1984, 128; 1987, 516–54, 537–43.

50. Uriu 1996, 22–35.

51. Woo-Cumings 1999, 25–26.

52. Ramseyer and Rosenbluth 1993.

53. Johnson and Keehn 1994a, 14–22; Tullock 1994, 99; Ramseyer 1994, 99–101; Clemons 1994, 101–2; Johnson and Keehn 1994b, 102–4; Gownder and Pekkanen 1996, 363–84.

54. Baerwald 1986; Curtis 1971, 1988.

55. Johnson 1982, 1989.

56. The following discussion draws on Ramseyer and Rosenbluth 1995, 6–15, 120–41.

57. Johnson and Keehn 1994a, 14–22; 1994b, 102–4.

58. The overall analysis in this work is between 1950 and 1990, a time period that corresponds roughly to the undisputed tenure of the LDP in office from 1955 to 1993.

59. McCubbins and Rosenbluth 1995, 35–55; McCubbins and Noble 1995, 81–115.

60. See generally Patrick and Rosovksy 1976.

61. Saxonhouse n.d., 35.

62. Weinstein 1993, 1–25. Weinstein takes a hard look at the much-touted role of *gyosei shido* (administrative guidance), under which industries are said to follow the guidance of the Japanese government in raising prices or limiting production

through cartels. With few exceptions, his conclusion is that industries did not change their behavior and that government policy to coordinate industries, much less pick winners, was ineffectual.

63. Beason and Weinstein 1996.

64. Calder 1988, 1990.

65. Calder 1993, 4, 21, 269. Where the Japanese state has failed by and large, the reverse and explicit logic of Calder's argument is that market finance has been able to identify and support the promising sectors at remarkably early junctures in their respective product life-cycles.

66. Magee, Brock, and Young 1989, xvi. Because any such resulting policy is endogenous, it cannot be controlled by any of the actors involved. That is, since the policy reflects a "delicate political equilibrium that balances all of society's conflicting interests," it is naive to assume that it can change from this equilibrium in the short to medium term.

67. I want to be absolutely clear on one point. In this study, I am not attempting to test strategic trade policy theory, whatever that means in the popular imagination. The focus on the theoretical works is simply an attempt to show the broader theoretical background that is echoed in the key works on the Japanese political economy. Only the hypotheses derived from the Japanese works are being tested directly in this work. Insofar as the proxies for the theoretical variables are sound, the testing leads to some implications for the theoretical propositions that are discussed in the concluding chapter but neither affirms nor negates them irrefutably.

Chapter 2

1. Effective January 2001, MITI changed to METI (Ministry of Economy, Trade, and Industry), but the organizational focus on Japanese industry and technology remains. Given the historical period under consideration, I will refer mostly to MITI.

2. King, Keohane, Verba 1994, 110.

3. Goldberger 1991, 173, 346. Causality may well be needed to support interest in the parameters of a regression but not necessarily their actual estimation. In other words, causality is more a matter of the theory in economics and politics than of anything in statistics. Only if a theory is used carefully to specify the structure of a model can we be reasonably certain that the actual estimations of parameters from that model will help shed light on the hypothesized causality of the independent variables.

4. In part this is because we do not always know the true structure of serial correlation, which is particularly problematic in time-dominant series, as in this analysis, or the exact patterns of heteroscedasticity, which may be present in the stochastic portion of the world. Whenever confronted with these problems, we can only make educated guesses as to the exact nature of the problem (by statistical theory and by evidence from the data themselves) and either refine the model or transform the variables so as to obtain as consistent and efficient estimations of the parameters as possible.

5. Data on subsidies, taxes, JDB loans, tariffs, and quotas were graciously provided

by David Weinstein, and both the explanations and sources of these TIPs as found in the joint work by Beason and Weinstein 1996 are given directly in Table 2.1. I supplemented the authors' data on TIPs with the inclusion of R&D subsidies. With the exception of spillover potential, which was approximated through sectoral R&D expenditures also generously provided by David Weinstein, I extended the database by including additional economic and political variables on the industries at the same level of industrial aggregation and across the same time period as described in Table 2.2. For additional descriptive details on the data that are left out for reasons of space, see Pekkanen 1996.

6. I follow here Beason and Weinstein 1996 in which the authors also examine the TIPs individually.

7. Johnson 1982, 242–74; Upham 1987, 166–204.

8. Johnson 1982, 265.

9. Some concerns with this proxy should be noted. One is that R&D expenditures may not be spent on activities that promote learning and knowledge that potentially spill over to benefit other industries but may instead simply be plowed back into the industry of origin. Another is that they do not completely capture also the importance of linkages as set out in Chapter 1.

10. For one official statement of political funds for each of the major parties, see Jichisho (Ministry of Home Affairs), *Seiji Shikin Shushu Hokokusho* (Report on political funds contributions) (Tokyo: Jichisho).

11. Magee, Brock, and Young 1989, 10–11, 95–97. In using this specification, I should note some issues that have a bearing on its validity. First, in Japan, the postwar manufacturing sector is noted for having a "dual structure" that has both huge corporations and numerous small to medium-sized ones. In 1994, an estimated 99.1 percent of companies in the manufacturing sector were small to medium-sized corporations capitalized at roughly the same level, employing fewer than 300 employees, which together comprised 71.7 percent of the total manufacturing industry employees and produced roughly 51.9 percent of the total value (*Tsusansho* [MITI]: *Kogyo Tokei Chosa/Kogyo Tokei Hyo* [Census of Manufactures], Tokyo: MITI). Given that all of these industries are formidably well organized at the aggregate level, it is also important to look to institutional links as done subsequently through *dantai*. Second, the function assumes that all industries in a given sector have the same interest in the same TIP, but this is quite unlikely as, to give a very simple example, export-oriented firms may have little in common with domestic-oriented ones. Third, it is not clear that, just because a firm has higher sales or higher concentration or both, it will, in fact, attempt to lobby the government. In part, this would depend on how well the sector was doing economically and under what kind of general macroeconomic conditions.

12. Since the focus is on the political characteristics of the industries, national-level channels of influence such as those offered by *shingikai* (consultative government-business bodies formed at the behest of relevant ministries to aid in the policy-making process) and Keidanren (Japan Federation of Economic Organizations), which has traditionally been used to centralize political contributions to the government, have not been considered.

13. *Dantai* is used as a measure of sectoral influence because their numbers could potentially indicate the desires of politicians to use them as a basis for vote splitting in multimember districts and thereby garner personalistic votes. Thus apart from directly lobbying the bureaucracy, *dantai* could also exert influence via politicians. No attempt is made to establish the process or the means by which any such *dantai* actually influence the allocation of TIPs. Rather, the emphasis is on the hypothesis that the higher the presence of such *dantai* in a given sector, the more political leverage the sector is able to generate in having TIPs allocated in its favor, especially under the old electoral system.

14. This argument, for example, is made by Ramseyer and Rosenbluth, 1995, 141, especially in their discussion of cotton politics.

15. Uriu 1996, 25–26.

16. Not included in the analysis are the publishing and printing, lumber and wood, plastic, rubber, leather, and ordnance industries.

17. Berk et al. 1979, 389; Sayrs 1989, 7.

18. Hicks 1994, 170–73.

19. Beck and Katz 1995, 636.

20. It is worth pointing out that all these caveats about possibly varying ρ, heteroscedasticity, and contemporaneous correlations in TSCS data apply with equal force to qualitative work, except that there the problems are usually ignored, as are even single ρ's and cross-sectional variances.

21. O'Connell 1994, 227–30. This section relies heavily on O'Connell's lucid discussion of the problems and solutions in TSCS multiple regression analyses.

22. In the levels model, one-unit lagged values of the dependent variable are generally included in the models to lessen the serial correlation.

23. In a differenced model, the coefficient on the levels lag is not necessarily the only one to be persistent in time. Changes in the dependent variable may also have time-serial properties independent of the level convergence rate, and a lagged difference needs to be used to pick up this effect. For this reason, although they are not shown in the results, both the log of the lag (of the dependent variable) and the log of the differenced lag (again of the dependent variable) are included in all the differenced models.

24. Greene 1993, 428. Although the Durbin-Watson Statistic is reported frequently in time-series data, it is inappropriate in time-series models with lagged dependent variables (as in this case) because it is usually biased toward a finding of no autocorrelation.

25. Since we are dealing with lagged variables, the sample throughout is restricted to (1) greater than 1955 for the log-log levels models, and (2) greater than 1956 for the differenced log models. Similar adjustments are made to the sample for the robust regression estimates.

26. Sayrs 1989, 52–57. Endogenity brings forth the issue of reverse causality in that changes in the criteria for selection may themselves result from the TIP itself rather than simply the other way around as I have posited here. Although the key solution to managing violations of orthogonality in the linear model is two-stage estimation using an instrument for the troublesome variables, that step is not pursued

here. This is not only because such instruments are often highly correlated with the independent variables but also because the error structures in pooled TSCS data tend to be so complex that the two-stage estimation is not considered the best solution to endogeneity.

27. Ostrom 1990, 58–59. A few points should be made with respect to the lag. First, and most important, it is difficult to know the exact amount of time with which the criteria affect the TIP in question, and the theory examined here, from which the variables are derived, does not shed any light on the issue. Second, lagged values of the independent variables tend to be highly correlated with each other, making it very difficult to assess the impact of any of the independent variables on the TIPs. Third, having a lot of lags decreases the degrees of freedom, to say nothing of destroying any attempts at parsimony. Fourth, for every lagged variable, an observation has to be dropped from the entire data set. For these reasons, we have to be fairly cautious about interpreting the estimations as the ultimate truth.

28. Interview No. 102, Deputy Director, Project Planning Department, JDB, Tokyo 1997.

Chapter 3

1. This technique does not mean that the data are dichotomous but rather that the emphasis is on investigating the extreme poles of the data.

2. For a full-blown analysis of the data in this chapter, see Pekkanen 1996. For sources and descriptions of the data variables, see the tables on dependent and independent variables in Chapter 2.

3. It is very important to know that an ordinal ranking is only a number (1st to 12th in this project) occupied by an item in an ordered sequence, and it gives the same weight to a huge difference between those items as to a negligible difference among them. Such a ranking, therefore, does not utilize all the information that is actually present within the data, meaning specifically that it discards vital information contained in the distances between the actual values of the variables. For this reason, the differences at the extreme poles of the data are more reliable as the basis for inference here. In addition, ordinal correlations lack the certainty of statistical estimates, as there are no standard errors to validate the results. Fortunately, the econometric analysis in the previous chapter allowed me to deal with these concerns and also thereby allowed me some leeway to examine the data using different techniques.

4. As a check, to see if the same sectors that paid lower taxes were also the sectors with the highest levels of tax relief, I subtracted the sectoral tax ratio calculated earlier for each of the twelve industries from the overall effective tax rate for each year. The overall tax rate is calculated as the sum of all the taxes paid by all twelve industries divided by the sum of profits made by all twelve industries. Since each sector's tax relief is a deviation from the calculated mean, which is the overall effective tax rate, positive numbers mean lower than average taxes, and negative numbers mean higher than average taxes. In fact, the sectoral evidence for tax relief corresponds exactly to that on tax rates. Textiles and processed food were most advantaged by tax relief, and the electrical, metal, and transport sectors had virtually little relief, especially

after the oil shock. Although both the tax rate and tax relief measures are perfectly inverse to each other, that is, the highest-paying tax rate sector has, by definition, the lowest-ranking tax relief, I use the measures for tax relief for the ordinal ranking.

5. Despite my lenient interpretation of the evidence, there are still some instances that require a judgment call on my part. For example, this happens when a sector ranks high in average but not in count, as in, say, the basic metals sector in 1972. In such cases, I base my decision on an overall trend of support to the sector during the period.

6. An important point to note is that this analysis does not allow me to distinguish between TIPs for strategic economic reasons—as in the beginning of the favoritism shown to the chemicals sector—and those disbursed for political reasons—as in the continued favoritism shown to the chemicals sector—which the previous chapter made clearer. The only way to be certain on this issue is to rely also on qualitative evidence as in the next two chapters and use that information to supplement the quantitative inference here.

7. Throughout, it should also be noted that sectors that were not economically strategic or politically powerful were never selected. This tells us one of two things. First, if we believe that the economic and political characteristics explain the major portion of the disbursement of TIPs, we should be glad to see that sectors exhibiting neither were not selected. Second, however, this should also make us think whether the crisp focus on the economics versus the politics is all there is to the explanation of TIPs.

8. For the highly protected agricultural products to have a viable domestic market, it is inevitable that the processed food sector has also had to be one of the most severely shielded from foreign competition and one of the most heavily subsidized. In short, processed food rides as much, if not more, on the tails of political favoritism shown the agricultural sector than on its own political influence in terms of votes and *dantai*.

9. There is a key problem in this analysis that deserves to be mentioned. It has been easier simply to rely on the assumption that all sectors are growing and are ordinally ranked from the fastest to the slowest grower. In this case, there is no declining industry per se, and the conclusions are drawn based on how a particular sector is doing relative to all the rest but not really by how much or in which direction. Therefore one of the insurmountable difficulties in this analysis is that it is not possible to distinguish between selection based on strategic economic criteria (picking winners) and that based on structural adjustment assistance (liquidating declining sectors). Both of these are attempts at landscaping the industrial face of the nation, but both stem from very different specifications. One of the ways to get around this problem is to be aware of the specific case histories of each sector at a finer level of industrial aggregation, as in Chapters 4 and 5, and then to incorporate this knowledge in drawing inferences in the end.

10. Spero 1990, 91–97; Komiya and Itoh 1988, 193; Saxonhouse 1986, 9.

11. Okuno-Fujiwara 1991, 280–81.

12. Tyson and Zysman 1983, 15–59; Krugman in Krugman 1991, 1–8; Porges in Krugman 1991, 305–27.

13. The chemicals sector as a whole is under split jurisdiction, with both MITI and the Ministry of Health and Welfare claiming regulatory powers. Despite the structural adjustment problems that beset the energy-intensive petrochemicals industry in the wake of the oil shocks, all government agencies continue to cite the high R&D expenditures as being indicative of knowledge-intensity and therefore consider chemicals to be an economically strategic sector.

Chapter 4

1. King, Keohane, and Verba 1994, 38, 43, 45.

2. In isolation, these results would not be adequate for broader inference. This is because the analysis below uses the method of similarity such that the rival hypotheses are put to the test only in cases where TIPs are disbursed. In addition, as described at the beginning of the econometric analysis in Chapter 2, the industries occupy a very modest place in the standard industrial classification of the entire manufacturing range in Japan. One straightforward reason therefore for proceeding with the analysis below is that the aggregate and quantitative results serve as a powerful frame of reference for subsequent analyses. Since the earlier quantitative results demonstrated the importance of the economic hypothesis, I can afford to focus on it more closely and scrutinize its features as they played out vis-à-vis the political one in specific cases where industrial selections did take place.

3. This gives us an even picture across the entire manufacturing range just as in the quantitative analyses. For example, coal falls under the petroleum and coal category, steel under basic metals, machine tools under general machinery, computers and semiconductors under electrical machinery, and autos, shipbuilding, and aircraft under transport equipment.

4. MITI 2000b.

5. Komiya 1988, 6–9.

6. Quoted in Murakami 1996, 191.

7. Lincoln 1984, 16.

8. Suzumura and Okuno-Fujiwara 1987, 65–67.

9. Here I rely primarily on secondary sources for the background on the industry cases, especially the TIPs. For a broad overview of the statistics on the general macroeconomic situation, industrial conditions, and particularly tangible and legislative TIPs in this chapter, the essays in Komiya et al. 1988 are used extensively. More specific data are based on or calculated from those provided in that work. In addition, heavy use is made of the historical backgrounds, details, and quantitative evidence provided in the major works on Japanese political economy, such as Johnson 1982; Samuels 1987, 1994; Vogel 1985; Calder 1993; Okimoto 1989; Okimoto et al. 1984; Tsuru 1993; Ramseyer and Rosenbluth 1993, 1995; Friedman 1988; Anchordoguy 1989; Tilton 1996; Borrus et al. 1983; Prestowitz 1989; Fransman 1995.

10. Ohta et al. 1993, 11–16; Gao 1994; Hein 1994.

11. Kosai 1988, 32.

12. Johnson 1982, 173–76.

13. Department of State 1946, 14.

14. Vogel 1985, 98; Department of State 1946, 8–9. Foreign workers referred largely to Koreans and also to female Taiwanese, Chinese, and Caucasian prisoners of war.

15. Vogel 1985, 99. In fact, the "battle for coal production" was of such intense concern to everyone that billboards in front of Tokyo Station recorded monthly coal production.

16. Interview No. 5, Policy Planning Office, Minister's Secretariat, MITI, Tokyo, 1997.

17. Woronoff 1992, 98. In the early 1950s, there were 864 mines in operation employing 450,000 workers and producing about 50 million tons of coal. This production was able to cover three-quarters of Japan's energy requirements at the time.

18. Interview No. 16, Coal Department, Agency of Natural Resources and Energy, MITI, Tokyo, 1997.

19. The fact that coal was no longer price competitive relative to oil was not the only reason for its demise. Coal also became undesirable because of labor disputes, accidents, and exhaustion of the most efficient mines. In addition, because of its high sulfur content, it was considered an environmental hazard.

20. Samuels 1987, 106, 108.

21. MITI 1997a, 1; 1997b, 38.

22. MITI 1997a, 1, 3

23. Interview No. 27, Coal Department, Agency of Natural Resources and Energy, MITI, Tokyo, 1997.

24. MITI 1997a, 6; Department of State 1946, 3. Sixty-four percent of Japanese coal production came from the Kyushu mines, 21 percent from Hokkaido, and less than 15 percent from Honshu.

25. Interview No. 59, Coal Department, Agency of Natural Resources and Energy, MITI, Tokyo, 1997. This official was involved intimately in the closure of the Mitsui coal mine in Miike (Fukuoka), which was completed in March 1997, and I have relied heavily on his testimony here for the kinds of political pressures brought to bear on the allocation of TIPs to the coal sector.

26. Japan Government 1997, 213.

27. The interviewee pointed out that as the transition to oil became clear, it was decided that the oil industry should be taxed to bear the burden for the structural decline in the coal industry. How could this go through, especially given the strong opposition from oil? Given that the coal mine closures were a huge social problem in the 1960s and 1970s, there was really no discussion of the appropriateness of the oil tax. Moreover, in those days MITI was also exceptionally powerful and could get its way.

28. Interview No. 27, Coal Department, Agency of Natural Resources and Energy, MITI, Tokyo, 1997.

29. Samuels 1987, 106.

30. Vogel 1985, 104–5; Woronoff 1992, 198–99; Johnson 1978, 127–31.

31. Ogura and Yoshino 1988, 123.

32. MITI 1997a, 1. This report set the tone for government TIPs that were to move to two broad dictates, namely the continued emphasis on structural adjustment

issues (regional development, employment, environment issues, etc.) and Japan's overall energy policy.

33. Interview No. 27, Coal Department, Agency of Natural Resources and Energy, MITI, Tokyo, 1997.

34. Calder 1993, 112, 190

35. Kawahito 1972, 11, 12.

36. See Samuels 1994, 72–77; Yamawaki 1988, 282–92; Magaziner and Hout 1980, 55–67; and Kaplan 1972, 146–48, for a discussion of the First (1951–55), Second (1956–60), and Third (1961–65) Rationalization Plans.

37. The practices of administrative guidance and cartels reached their peak in the 1960s and were severely criticized both internationally and domestically in the aftermath of the 1973 oil shock.

38. Interview No. 17, Iron and Steel Administration Division, Basic Industries Bureau, MITI, Tokyo, 1997.

39. Interview No. 35, General Coordination Division, Minister's Secretariat, MITI, Tokyo, 1997.

40. Interview No. 24, Iron and Steel Administration Division, Basic Industries Bureau, MITI, Tokyo, 1997.

41. ISIJ 1996–97, 1.

42. Tilton 1996, 182–83.

43. As Yamamoto and Murakami 1980, 139, and Kawahito 1972, 53, suggest, the steel industry is often cited as one of MITI's success stories.

44. Interview No. 35, General Coordination Division, Minister's Secretariat, MITI, Tokyo, 1997.

45. Johnson 1982, 87, also points out that there is an old institutionalized relationship between MITI (and all its predecessors) and big steel and that this fact was not lost on the public. In fact, the press not only routinely pointed out that Yawata officials had an extraordinary influence on the government but also derisively nicknamed MITI the "Tokyo Office of the Yawata Steel Company."

46. Interview No. 17, Iron and Steel Administration Division, Basic Industries Bureau, MITI, Tokyo, 1997. Other interviewees also confirmed this basic political picture in the steel case.

47. ISIJ 1996–97, 1. There is a basis for expecting steady worldwide growth. The International Iron and Steel Institute (IISI) estimated that the 1995 world consumption stood at 655 million tons, up 55 percent from 1970. For the year 2000, the projection was 717 million tons and about 800–900 million tons by 2010.

48. Interview No. 24, Iron and Steel Administration Division, Basic Industries Bureau, MITI, Tokyo, 1997.

49. Interview No. 34, Machine Parts and Tooling Industries Division, Machinery and Information Industries Bureau, MITI, Tokyo, 1997.

50. JISF 1997, 3.

51. ISIJ 1996–97, 10.

52. Interview No. 5, General Coordination Division, Minister's Secretariat, MITI, Tokyo, 1997.

53. Calder 1993, 81.

54. Yamazawa 1988, 404.

55. Interview No. 3, International Trade Division, Consumer Goods Bureau, MITI, Tokyo, 1997. Johnson 1982, 224–25, shows that the intense effort to rationalize the industry—that is, the production levels of textiles goods—went back to the 1950s. In fact, MITI's first major case of "administrative guidance" is to be found in the textiles industry.

56. Ramseyer and Rosenbluth 1993, 121.

57. Interview No. 9, Industrial Statistics Division, Research and Statistics Department, MITI, Tokyo, 1997.

58. Interview No. 3, International Trade Division, Consumer Goods Bureau, MITI, Tokyo, 1997.

59. MITI 1997c, 3.

60. Interview No. 11, General Coordination Division, Minister's Secretariat, MITI, Tokyo, 1997.

61. Interview No. 2, Minister's Office, Minister's Secretariat, MITI, Tokyo, 1997.

62. Interview No. 64, General Affairs Division, Consumer Goods Industries Bureau, MITI, Tokyo, 1997.

63. Interview No. 3, International Trade Division, Consumer Goods Bureau, MITI, Tokyo, 1997.

64. Dore 1986, 205–6. The pace of decline in this industry was apparent very early on, with few thinking it would ever be irreversible given the severe competition from developing countries. Between 1955 and 1975, the share of the textiles sector's output to the total manufacturing output declined from 17 percent to 7.7 percent, and its share of sectoral exports to total exports declined from 37 percent to 12.5 percent.

65. Pelzman 1984, 112–27.

66. Interview No. 4, Commercial Policy Division, Industrial Policy Bureau, MITI, Tokyo, 1997.

67. Interview No. 41, Textiles and Apparel Products Division, Consumer Goods Industries Bureau, MITI, Tokyo, 1997.

68. Interview No. 42, Textiles and Apparel Products Division, Consumer Goods Industries Bureau, MITI, Tokyo, 1997.

69. Yamazawa 1988, 395–96.

70. Ramseyer and Rosenbluth 1993, 40.

71. Interview No. 3, International Trade Division, Consumer Goods Bureau, MITI, Tokyo, 1997.

72. Interview No. 3, International Trade Division, Consumer Goods Bureau MITI, Tokyo, 1997.

73. Ramseyer and Rosenbluth 1995, 137, 135–59.

74. Interview No. 42, Textiles and Apparel Products Division, Consumer Goods Industries Bureau, MITI, Tokyo, 1997.

75. MITI 1997c, 3.

76. Interview No. 11, General Coordination Division, Minister's Secretariat, MITI, Tokyo, 1997.

77. Yonezawa 1988, 428–29. To provide a legal basis for TIPs to this sector, the MOT enacted thirty-two separate pieces of legislation.

78. Vogel 1985, 35.

79. Ibid., 41. The Export Bank of Japan (founded in 1950) gave 38 percent of its total loans to assist the export of ships in 1951. Renamed the Export-Import Bank of Japan in 1952, it initially gave 63 percent and afterward roughly 40 percent on average until the early 1970s.

80. Ogura and Yoshino 1988, 131, 137–38, 142; Yonezawa 1988, 428.

81. By all accounts, the shipbuilding industry was an active participant in its own adjustment, which no doubt accounts for the relatively swift and efficient adjustments made in the industry as a whole.

82. Peck, Levin, and Goto 1987. Under the first cartel, shipbuilding firms were limited to 39 percent of their previous peak output, and under the second cartel this figure increased to 51 percent.

83. Ibid.

84. Komiya 1988, 8.

85. Woronoff 1992, 106. The fate of the Japanese shipping lines was linked to the shipbuilding industry from the start, and both were under the jurisdiction of the MOT. To ensure a captive market for the fledgling shipbuilding industry, Japanese shipping lines, for instance, were required to purchase Japanese ships under the Planned Shipbuilding Program.

86. Interview No. 36, Shipbuilding Division, MOT, Tokyo, 1997.

87. Vogel 1985, 57.

88. Interview No. 36, Shipbuilding Division, MOT, Tokyo, 1997.

89. Yamamoto and Murakami 1980, 164.

90. MOT 1995/96, 26.

91. Vogel 1985, 53.

92. MOT 1995/96, 27.

93. Yonezawa 1988, 429. In addition to receiving some of the relief provided by the 1978 law, the industry firms themselves also took advantage of various other permanent and temporary legislative provisions.

94. Vogel 1985, 32; Yamamoto and Murakami 1980, 163–64.

95. Interview No. 36, Shipbuilding Division, MOT, Tokyo, 1997.

96. Young 1991, 152–53.

97. Peck, Levin, and Goto 1987.

98. Young 1991, 147. The industry shed well over 50,000 workers, and by 1985 the sector had adjusted well enough to regain a 45 percent share in world output. Because of the rapid adjustments made by the firms, even critics of the stabilization and adjustment laws were silenced.

99. PAJ 1996, 47.

100. Tsuruta 1988, 69–70, 83–84, points out that a special industries law, which would have given MITI a great deal of regulatory powers vis-à-vis industry, was rejected by the Diet three times on the grounds that it violated the Antimonopoly Law. In addition, it alarmed the designated industries and also "finance" capital. The LDP had a keen interest in keeping its big business constituency—that is, both industry and finance—placated, and so it, too, was against the passage of the law.

101. Johnson 1982, 194–95, 217. The 1949 law required that all foreign exchange

earned by enterprises be sold to a foreign exchange bank within ten days of acquisition, thereby allowing the government to concentrate foreign exchange, which was
then used to control imports or attempt to banish them as in the case of import-
competing finished goods. The 1950 law, which was concerned explicitly with sep-
arating the acquisition of foreign technology (which was crucial) from foreign ownership (which was to be rejected in the quest for technological indigenization),
further gave the government the power to discriminate against foreign enterprises,
whose operations in Japan were severely curtailed with the requirement of licenses
and permissions issued by the Foreign Investment Committee (established under the
1950 Law) and later the Enterprise Bureau. Although pressure for liberalization began in the early 1960s, both of these laws remained in effect until 1979, after which
the 1949 law was revised and the 1950 law was abolished.

102. Interview No. 46, Commercial Policy Division, Industrial Policy Bureau,
MITI, Tokyo, 1997.

103. This analysis does not cover pharmaceuticals, that is, the production of drugs
and medicines, which are an extremely important subindustry in the chemicals sector. This industry has been regulated by the Ministry of Health and Welfare.

104. Tsuruta 1988, 69–75.

105. Tilton 1996, 124–26. In 1991, plastic accounted for about 61 percent of the
market, followed by synthetic rubber with 12 percent, textiles with 11 percent, surface active agents with 3 percent, and paint also with 3 percent.

106. Peck, Levin, and Goto 1987. The 1978 law established the procedures by
which a government agency could designate an industry "structurally depressed."
The law also empowered any such agency with planning capacity reductions in the
designated industry. The 1978 law was intended to have expired in 1983, but its
timetable for capacity reduction was, at least officially, upset by the second oil shock
in 1979. For this reason, the 1983 law was put in place for the period 1983–88. Basically, the restructuring continued for the same originally designated fourteen industries, plus an additional eleven, almost all of which were highly energy intensive.
While the two laws are generally the same, there are two key differences. The 1983
law has a broader range of financial support measures and more specific provisions
for business tie-ups or mergers.

107. Tilton 1996, 131–39. Projects were set up by Mitsui and Company in Iran,
Sumitomo Corporation in Singapore, and Mitsubishi in Saudi Arabia.

108. Tilton 1996, 127.

109. Interview No. 46, Commercial Policy Division, Industrial Policy Bureau,
MITI, Tokyo, 1997.

110. Interview No. 39, Chemicals Products Division, Basic Industries Bureau,
MITI, Tokyo, 1997.

111. Interview No. 55, Basic Chemicals Division, Basic Industries Bureau, MITI,
Tokyo, 1997.

112. Komiya 1988, 7.

113. Interview No. 88, First International Economics Affairs Division, Coordination Bureau, EPA, Tokyo, 1997.

114. Interview No. 46, Commercial Policy Division, Industrial Policy Bureau,
MITI, Tokyo, 1997.

115. Interview No. 88, First International Economics Affairs Division, Coordination Bureau, EPA, Tokyo, 1997.

116. MITI 1997d.

117. Interview No. 63, Basic Chemicals Division, Basic Industries Bureau, MITI, Tokyo, 1997.

118. Interview No. 55, Basic Chemicals Division, Basic Industries Bureau, MITI, Tokyo, 1997.

119. Interview No. 50, Biochemical Industry Division, Basic Industries Bureau, MITI, Tokyo, 1997. The remaining discussion draws upon this official's interview.

120. Some of the basic information and data in this case come from Mutoh 1988.

121. Woronoff 1992, 144; Johnson 1982, 286–89. There were some modest successes in these MITI-led mergers, as, for example, in the cases of Prince with Nissan, later Nissan with Fuji, and Toyota with Hino and Daihatsu. But because American firms could not invest in domestic Japanese production or firms at the time, it was only in the late 1970s, when barriers began to be lifted, that they could seize partnerships with some of the less-favored Japanese corporations—contrary to MITI's desires. Examples of foreign-domestic partnerships include Chrysler with Mitsubishi, Ford with Mazda, and General Motors with Isuzu and Suzuki.

122. Magaziner and Hout 1980, 70–73.

123. Kaplan 1972, 116–18.

124. Cusumano 1985, 23–26; Tsuru 1993, 113; Mutoh 1988, 312–17. Quotas on trucks were lifted in 1960 and on passenger cars in 1965. The sector enjoyed among the highest levels of effective rates of protection, with around 40 percent on passenger cars, 50 percent on luxury passenger vehicles, and 20 percent on small cars. In addition, a great many nontariff barriers (NTBs), such as inspecting each imported motor vehicle severely, continued until at least until 1983.

125. Between 1962 and 1973, the special depreciation allowance for automobiles at 13 percent was still judged to be well above the average.

126. Ogura and Yoshino 1988, 146–47.

127. The industry was only truly revived, as were so many other industries at the same time, by the special procurements of the U.S. forces engaged in the Korean conflict. The procurement of an estimated 7,079 trucks worth $13 million amounted to a great deal for both the industry and the country's foreign exchange reserves and also focused attention definitively on the auto parts industry.

128. Interview No. 6, Automobiles Division, Machinery and Information Industries Bureau, MITI, Tokyo, 1997.

129. Mutoh 1988, 312; Cusumano 1985, 19; U.S. Congress 1991, 246.

130. Interview No. 6, Automobiles Division, Machinery and Information Industries Bureau, MITI, Tokyo, 1997.

131. Interview No. 12, General Affairs Division, Minister's Secretariat, MITI, Tokyo, 1997.

132. Interview No. 4, Commercial Policy Division, Industrial Policy Bureau, MITI, Tokyo, 1997.

133. Interview No. 6, Automobiles Division, Machinery and Information Industries Bureau, MITI, Tokyo, 1997.

134. JAMA 1997, 26.

135. It is worth noting that the industry as a whole was reconfigured in the late 1990s due to domestic and foreign takeovers, and this may have had an effect on its political power and influence.

136. Interview No. 103, JAMA, Tokyo, 1998. Also confirmed via Interview No. 85, Automobiles Division, Machinery and Information Industries Bureau, MITI, Tokyo, 1997.

137. JAMA 1997, 19. Between 1989 and 1992, for example, there was a 6 percent tax levied on the purchase of all automobiles except minicars, and this was only brought down to the 3 percent tax level applied to all other goods and services in April 1994. Along with lobbying against fuel taxes and two national taxes (the Consumption Tax and the Tonnage Tax), the JAMA has been lobbying most strenuously against the municipal taxes, the Acquisition Tax, and the Automobile Tax, which apply to the private purchase and ownership of passenger cars and that potentially dampen demand for automobiles.

138. Interview No. 85, Automobiles Division, Machinery and Information Industries Bureau, MITI, Tokyo, 1997.

139. Interview No. 6, Automobiles Division, Machinery and Information Industries Bureau, MITI, Tokyo, 1997.

140. Interview No. 67, Automobiles Division, Machinery and Information Industries Bureau, MITI, Tokyo, 1997.

141. For the historical data and information on the prewar and postwar machine tool industry, extensive use is made of Friedman 1988, 37–125. By one count there are at least seventy-six different categories subclassified in this sector, ranging from hammers, screwdrivers, and nuts and bolts to construction and mining equipment, mills, and robots.

142. Although it was the most important channel of influence for the industry in the immediate postwar years as well as later, the *gyōkai* did not represent all interests. In 1955, it represented 55 firms out of a total of 264 industry firms. In 1981, it represented 113 firms out of a total of 1,928 firms. Despite this meager representation, the *gyōkai* members accounted for 75 percent of the total output in the machine tool industry until the late 1970s.

143. Vogel 1985, 69–74; Magaziner and Hout 1980, 93; USITC 1983, 141–47; Ogura and Yoshino 1988, 147–48. Whatever the problems with enforcing MITI's ideas of the market structure of the industry, the fact is that the historical dependency on imports lessened substantially. From 1960 to 1962, Japan imported over 30 percent of its total domestic consumption of machine tools. In 1963, imports dropped to 50 percent of their previous level, and in 1965 they dropped an additional 50 percent.

144. Tsuruta 1988, 53, 80–81. That both import substitution and export promotion were at play well into the 1970s was made more clear by the fact that while imports of machine tools increased from only $188 million in 1962 to $234 million in 1980, their exports increased from about $45 million to $1.7 billion over the same period, making Japan a net exporter in the meantime.

145. Friedman 1988, 105–7; Vernon, Spar, and Tobin 1991, 113–28. Very briefly, Houdaille Industries in the United States shut down after being unable to persuade

its own government that the Japanese government was unfairly supporting its own industries. In the Toshiba-Kongsberg affair, a subsidiary of Toshiba violated export control regulations by selling submarine-quieting technology to the USSR. Both of these cases seemed to confirm the view that MITI cared about precious little except its own economic advantage in the international marketplace. From the domestic point of support, however, these events showed how little influence MITI actually exerted in terms of disciplining the firms. At this stage, MITI restricted itself to enforcing the 5 to 20 percent rule (in which a firm would be barred from producing any category of product that amounted to less than 20 percent of the firm's final sale and less than 5 percent of the total market share) and pronouncing that firms should not encroach on other firms' specialty products. In large part this realization came from trying to coordinate the myriad firms in the industry, often to little avail in terms of rationalization efforts.

146. Interview No. 22, Machine Parts and Tooling Industry Division, Machinery and Information Industries Bureau, MITI, Tokyo, 1997.

147. Interview No. 4, Commercial Policy Division, Industrial Policy Bureau, MITI, Tokyo, 1997.

148. JMBTA 1996, 1.

149. Unless otherwise indicated, the following discussion draws heavily on Interview No. 13, Industrial Machinery Division, Machinery and Information Industries Bureau, MITI, Tokyo, 1997; and Interview No. 34, Machine Parts and Tooling Industries Division, Machinery and Information Industries Bureau, MITI, Tokyo, 1997.

150. Interview No. 28, Industrial Machinery Division, Machinery and Information Industries Bureau, MITI, Tokyo, 1997.

151. As one of the interviewees pointed out, overall concentration in the industry is weak, with Yamazaki Mazak holding about 20 percent of the internal Japanese market, followed by Mori Seki, Toyoda Machine Works, and Okuma with about 10 percent each, followed further by a lot of SMEs with 5–8 percent of the total.

152. JMBTA 1997. Hiroshima and Saitama are next in line with about seven to eight firms each.

153. Interview No. 22, Machine Parts and Tooling Industry Division, Machinery and Information Industries Bureau, MITI, Tokyo, 1997.

154. Interview No. 29, Industrial Machinery Division, Machinery and Information Industries Bureau, MITI, Tokyo, 1997.

155. Interview, Executive Director, Japan Machine Tools Builders Association, Tokyo, 1997.

156. For background, this section draws heavily on events and information in the works by Anchordoguy 1989; Fransman 1995; Calder 1993, 116–17; and Shinjo 1988, 341–54.

157. Kaplan 1972, 80; USITC 1983, 132.

158. Flamm 1988, 175–79, 197–200. Other key players included research labs that actually developed technology. The Electrotechnical Laboratory (ETL) was taken over by MITI in 1952, and the Electrical Communications Laboratories (ECL) was under NTT. Although MITI's ETL is widely regarded as playing a visible role in

shaping public policy toward high-technology industries, NTT's far less visible ECL has been no less important in pushing R&D in such industries.

159. Although most accounts discount the total amount of monetary aid to the computer industry, Anchordoguy 1989, 36, provides evidence that it was definitely significant in comparison to what the private firms themselves were investing in the industry. Her data suggest that in the 1960s government benefits in the form of taxes and subsidies came to $131.7 million, which was about 46 percent of what the private firms were investing in plants and equipment and R&D at the time. If government loans are added to the other benefits, then government support was about 188 percent of the firms' total investments. Additionally, the government was responsible for procuring over 25 percent of all domestic computers.

160. Itoh and Kiyono 1988, 160–61; Shinjo 1988, 364.

161. Anchordoguy 1989, 32–33; Tyson 1993, 76–82; U.S. Congress 1991, 273; Prestowitz 1989, 265–67. The most spectacular evidence for these charges came with the attempts of Cray Supercomputers to sell to Japanese public agencies in the early 1980s and the company's charge that Japanese public procurement practices favored domestic manufacturers covertly.

162. Shinjo 1988, 343–52; USITC 1983, 133–38; Fransman 1995, 183–88. This led to an emphasis on customized, not packaged, software.

163. Ogura and Yoshino 1988, 148.

164. Interview No. 43, Electrical Machinery and Consumer Electronics Division, Machinery and Information Industries Bureau, MITI, Tokyo, 1997.

165. Vogel 1985, 143.

166. Interview No. 7, Electronics Policy Division, Machinery and Information Industries Bureau, MITI, Tokyo, 1997.

167. Interview No. 14, Electronics Policy Division, Machinery and Information Industries Bureau, MITI, Tokyo, 1997.

168. Fransman 1995, 139. In 1956, IBM supplied over 70 percent of the value of the computers sold globally, and by 1957 its sales exceeded $1 billion. Although its major market was the United States, roughly 30 percent of its revenues came from foreign sources in 1964.

169. Shinjo 1988, 342.

170. Vogel 1985, 133; Anchordoguy 1989, 27. By the time that FONTAC was ready to test its large-scale computer, IBM had moved to the more advanced 360 series. Instead of conceding to IBM's superior technology, MITI bureaucrats deemed the situation a crisis rather than a failure and pushed forward with other research agendas deemed to be in the national economic interest. MITI did not allow IBM to produce its System 360 series in Japan until 1965—long after Fujitsu and NEC came out with their family series in late 1964. In fact, through various tactics, such as local content requirements and negotiations over limits to production, IBM started production of the 360 series in Japan only in February 1966.

171. Interview No. 37, Electronics Policy Division, Machinery and Information Industries Bureau, MITI, Tokyo, 1997.

172. Interview No. 43, Electrical Machinery and Consumer Electronics Division, Machinery and Information Industries Bureau, MITI, Tokyo, 1997.

173. Vogel 1985, 146; Fransman 1995, 130–31, 142, 182–83; Woronoff 1992, 123; Anchordoguy 1989, 165–66. IBM continued with its emphasis on large, centralized mainframes, and failed to see the explosive importance of personal computers (and the idea of networks of decentralized information processors) that, ironically enough, it had been the first to develop.

174. Interview No. 37, Electronics Policy Division, Machinery and Information Industries Bureau, MITI, Tokyo, 1997.

175. Interview No. 25, Industrial Electronics Division, Machinery and Information Industries Bureau, MITI, Tokyo, 1997.

176. Interview No. 52, Information Systems Development Division, Machinery and Information Industries Bureau, MITI, Tokyo, 1997.

177. Callon 1995, 25–30.

178. Interview No. 48, Information Services Industry Division, Machinery and Information Industries Bureau, MITI, Tokyo, 1997.

179. Interview No. 52, Information Systems Development Division, Machinery and Information Industries Bureau, MITI, Tokyo, 1997.

180. Interview No. 43, Electrical Machinery and Consumer Electronics Division, Machinery and Information Industries Bureau, MITI, Tokyo, 1997.

181. Interview No. 96, Agency of Industrial Science and Technology, MITI, Tokyo, 1997.

182. This section relies extensively on Borrus et al. 1983 and Fransman 1995 for the background and the data.

183. Okimoto 1989, 65.

184. By semiconductor technology is meant both the market for semiconductor memories (such as DRAM) and also microprocessors (computer on a chip).

185. Japan's formal trade barriers were not phased out until 1976, and its formal investment restrictions remained in place until 1978. As other OECD countries were quick to point out, Japan consistently had the lowest recorded proportion of foreign direct investment flows of almost any other industrial country, averaging a mere 1.3 percent well into the 1980s.

186. Okimoto 1984, 109. In comparison, the EU's tariff rate was at 17 percent and America's was at 10.1 percent until the end of the 1960s. The EU's tariff rate remained roughly at 17 percent throughout the 1980s, but Japan brought its tariff rate to equal America's in 1980, at 10.1 percent. By 1982, when there was no question that Japanese companies had become fully competitive in the international arena, Japan's rate was dropped to 4.2 percent.

187. Borrus et al. 1983, 203–4; Itoh and Kiyono 1988, 180. In 1964, TI applied to MITI for a license to produce semiconductors, specifically ICs for which it held the patents. MITI refused and then stalled until 1967 in order to give the infant domestic manufacturers a long chance to grow up, something they both wanted and requested. When approval finally came in 1972, it was on the condition that TI give control of 50 percent of the venture to Sony; license its IC patents to NEC, Hitachi, Mitsubishi, Toshiba, and Sony; and finally limit its future share of the Japanese semiconductor market to no more than 10 percent.

188. Flaherty and Itami 1984, 155.

189. Okimoto 1989, 82. MITI has internal funds, which come from bicycle racing and special energy tax revenues, over which the MOF has no control. It has disbursed some of these funds directly in support of high-tech R&D support. Estimates suggest that these sums are modest even at the aggregate level, a mere $8.5 million in 1982.

190. Fransman 1995, 161–64; Anchordoguy 1989, 138–41; USITC 1983, 149.

191. Basically, the project focused on the production and refinement of memory devices and logic circuits, such as placing one megabit of memory on a single chip.

192. Tyson 1992, 97; Fransman 1995, 164. Although MITI's VLSI project was prematurely terminated in 1979 due to intense American pressure, the Japanese firms themselves were so convinced of the benefits of the entire enterprise that they continued the project in the private sector without government help. Since 1994, MITI has internationalized its ambitions in terms of such projects, saying that it intended to invite domestic and foreign firms to participate in future ventures.

193. Uenohara, Sugano, Linvill, and Weinstein 1984, 19.

194. Tyson 1992, 97; Borrus et al. 1983, 207–11.

195. Interview No. 52, Information Systems Development Division, Machinery and Information Industries Bureau, MITI, Tokyo, 1997.

196. Interview No. 44, Electrical Machinery and Consumer Electronics Division, Machinery and Information Industries Bureau, MITI, Tokyo, 1997.

197. Interview No. 52, Information Systems Development Division, Machinery and Information Industries Bureau, MITI, Tokyo, 1997.

198. Interview No. 37, Electronics Policy Division, Machinery and Information Industries Bureau, MITI, Tokyo, 1997.

199. Interview No. 44, Electrical Machinery and Consumer Electronics Division, Machinery and Information Industries Bureau, MITI, Tokyo, 1997.

200. Fransman 1995 and Borrus et al. 1983 maintain essentially that, in the case of Japanese industry, it is more useful to think of telecommunications-computers-semiconductor producers rather than only semiconductor producers.

201. Howell, Bartlett, and Davis 1992, 57–58; Flaherty and Itami 1984, 159. One of the key features of the Japanese electronic industry is that roughly the same six to twelve companies compete across product lines such as televisions, computers, integrated circuits, etc. These include the familiar companies that produce for merchant markets, such as Hitachi, NEC, Fujitsu, Toshiba, Mitsubishi, and Oki. Estimates from the late 1970s suggest that, unlike their U.S. competitors in the high-volume IC market, Japanese firms such as NEC consumed 16 percent and Oki 44 percent of their own respective IC production. No less important are companies that generally focus on in-house developments such as Sony, Sharp, Sanyo, Matsushita, and Sumitomo Electric. Sony consumed 80 percent and Matsushita 57 percent of their respective IC production.

202. Fransman 1995, 424–25.

203. Even the push toward ICs is attributed to consumer electronics producers. In 1967, Sharp was the first company in Japan to use ICs in producing desktop calculators, after which they became a standard in commercial applications that would go on to devastate American producers.

204. Tsuru 1993, 199; Irwin 1996, 24–25; Fransman 1995, 128, 169–81. While Japanese companies became competitive in memory semiconductors, they did not achieve the same international status in microprocessors (the one truly revolutionary invention in terms of its impact on computer architecture and vision), which is still dominated by American firms.

205. Interview No. 37, Electronics Policy Division, Machinery and Information Industries Bureau, MITI, Tokyo, 1997.

206. The information on the lobbying processes in the industry draws on Interview No. 84, Director, Information Systems Development Office, EIAJ, Tokyo, 1997.

207. Interview No. 44, Electrical Machinery and Consumer Electronics Division, Machinery and Information Industries Bureau, MITI, Tokyo, 1997.

208. Interview No. 58, Industrial Electronics Division, Machinery and Information Industries Bureau, MITI, Tokyo, 1997.

209. This section relies extensively on both the prewar and postwar account of the Japanese aircraft sector by Samuels 1994 and by Samuels and Whipple 1989, 275–318.

210. Samuels and Whipple 1989, 284–85. By the end of the war, the industry, which had about eleven major firms, actively sought to have itself rationalized through MITI, with the result that the top four firms, namely Mitsubishi Heavy Industries, Kawasaki Heavy Industries, Fuji Heavy Industries, and Ishikawajima-Harima Heavy Industries, ended up accounting for more than 75 percent of sales in the early 1960s.

211. Mowery and Rosenberg 1985, 9.

212. USITC 1983, 126.

213. The companies participating in the consortium, Ishikawajima-Harima Heavy, Fuji Heavy, Fuji Precision, and Shin Mitsubishi, did produce the JO-1 engine in 1954, but it was never used in any airplane because of its poor quality.

214. The consortium included Mitsubishi Heavy Industries, Kawasaki Heavy Industries, Fuji Heavy Industries, Showa Aircraft, Japan Aircraft, and Shin Meiwa Industries.

215. Mowery and Rosenberg 1985, 10.

216. The JCTDC included Mitsubishi, Kawasaki, and Fuji Heavy Industries.

217. U.S. Congress 1991, 350.

218. Mowery and Rosenberg 1985, 17. In 1982, the JCTDC was turned into the JADC, which was charged with the task of developing another indigenous civil transport aircraft, the YXX, which never got off the ground. In keeping with an alternative strategy now pursued by the government, the JADC helps promote joint ventures (such as the 767, V2500, etc.) with the goal of acquiring expertise in all phases of aircraft design, manufacture, and sales.

219. Woronoff 1992, 183–84; Samuels 1994, 244–52.

220. Hazard 1994, 126–27.

221. Interview No. 8, Aircraft, Ordnance, and Space Industry Division, Machinery and Information Industries Bureau, MITI, Tokyo, 1997.

222. Prestowitz 1989, 5–58.

223. Tyson 1992, 157; Samuels 1994, 260. As a whole, the sector accounted for less than 1 percent of total machinery production in the 1960s. In the 1990s, the Japan-

ese industry remained small, with sales worth less than 0.7 percent and exports less than 10 percent of those of the United States. The entire industry itself is barely 10 percent of the production of Toyota motors alone and less than 2 percent of the production of the entire automobile industry. It does not even produce many completed airplanes, which are not, in any event, sought after in world markets.

224. Interview No. 8, Aircraft, Ordnance, and Space Industry Division, Machinery and Information Industries Bureau, MITI, Tokyo, 1997.

225. Interview No. 21, General Affairs Division, Industrial Policy Bureau, MITI, Tokyo, 1997.

226. MITI 1987/88, 4–5, 12. In the document, the emphasis is especially on "*gijūtsū hokyū kōka*," meaning extended technological effects. But government support is deemed essential not only because of this but also because, as a high-technology industry, the aircraft sector is deemed conducive to preserving national security, which is why various countries (United States, Holland, Indonesia, Brazil) seek to support it both directly and indirectly. While these criteria for selection certainly exist in official documents, it is open to debate whether MITI came up with them on its own or whether the industry in question (particularly the heavyweights, such as Mitsubishi Heavy Industries, Kawasaki Heavy Industries, Fuji Heavy Industries, and Ishikawajima-Harima Heavy Industries) brought them to the government's attention. As Samuels 1994 shows, these very same concerns were often brought to MITI through potential channels of influence such as Shingikai, industry associations, and the Defense Production Committee set up specifically within Keidanren by the end of 1953. Nevertheless, the point remains that these criteria played a key role in justifying TIPs to the sectors.

227. Interview No. 8, Aircraft, Ordnance, and Space Industry Division, Machinery and Information Industries Bureau, MITI, Tokyo, 1997.

228. Interview No. 65, Aircraft, Ordnance, and Space Industry Division, Machinery and Information Industries Bureau, MITI, Tokyo, 1997.

229. Interview No. 53, Aircraft, Ordnance, and Space Industry Division, Machinery and Information Industries Bureau, MITI, Tokyo, 1997.

230. *Financial Times* (16 September 1997), for example, pinpointed the source of Boeing's delays to the steepest production increases ever. At that point, output was planned to be increased from about 18.5 aircraft per month in 1996 to 43 aircraft per month by 1998.

231. Interview No. 65, Aircraft, Ordnance, and Space Industry Division, Machinery and Information Industries Bureau, MITI, Tokyo, 1997.

232. SJAC 1996b. Typically, the executives of the SJAC are industry heavyweights, with the chair usually from Kawasaki or Mitsubishi and so on. However, the secretariat is composed of government officials, with the president of the secretariat from MITI and vice presidents from the JDA. While the presence of the executives is required every once in a while, the secretariat members are there full-time to facilitate interactions with their home government agencies.

233. Interview, General Manager, SJAC, Tokyo, 1997.

234. Interview No. 8, Aircraft, Ordnance, and Space Industry Division, Machinery and Information Industries Bureau, MITI, Tokyo, 1997.

Chapter 5

1. For further background details, see Pekkanen 2001.

2. Basic terminology and facts concerning the global launch vehicles industry are from the American Institute of Aeronautics and Astronautics (AIAA) and, on space launch systems, the American National Standards Institute (ANSI), specifically ANSI/AIAAb 1994, ANSI/AIAAa 1999, and Isakowitz, Hopkins, and Hopkins 1999. For up-to-date information, extensive use was made of the official websites of all major private companies and government space agencies; the leading U.S. industry trade journal, *Aviation Week and Space Technology* (hereafter *AWST*); and the excellent online source http://www.space.com (hereafter *Space.com*, posted date).

3. Asker 1995a, 44–45. In terms of commercial applications, satellites are used for telecommunications, Internet access, broadcasting, and imaging, as well as other scientific and military applications.

4. Lenorovitz 1993, 83–86; Anselmo 1996, 87–89.

5. Anselmo 1996, 89.

6. Anselmo and Mecham 1997, 48–49.

7. Anselmo 1997, 51–53; Covault 1993, 83–84.

8. Anselmo 1996, 89.

9. Velocci 1995, 66. There was a great deal of disagreement over the many projected trends for market growth for launch vehicles because of the inclusion and/or exclusion of LEO, MEO, and GEO satellites.

10. The following discussion draws on Caceres 2000b, 151–52.

11. *Space.com*, 6 June 2001. After the original company's bankruptcy, in 2000 the Iridium system was bought out by Iridium Satellite, which signed a two-year $72 million contract with the Pentagon.

12. Dornheim 2000, 34, 51.

13. AST/COMSTAC 1999, iii; 2000, iii, 1. These estimates are for the GEO as well as LEO, MEO, and elliptical (ELI) orbits. Several factors may be affecting this flattening of demand in the GEO market. With respect to the non-GEO market, failures like the Iridium bankruptcy are likely to affect the increased skepticism regarding non-GEO launches in the short term as a whole.

14. Buskirk 2000.

15. U.S. launch service providers carried out thirteen launches, with the European ones carrying out an additional twenty-one. China and a multinational launcher carried out one each of the remaining two.

16. See http://www.arianespace.com for some of the basic information. GTO refers to an elliptical Earth orbit that is used to transfer a payload or spacecraft from LEO or flight trajectory to a GEO orbit.

17. Since 1996, Arianespace has also been a partner in the Starsem joint venture that commercializes Russian rockets Soyuz and Molinya. The French government now permits Russian rockets to launch from its facility in Kourou, Guiana, in an effort to compete head-on with U.S. EELVs by Boeing and Lockheed Martin. See *Aerospace Daily*, 12 June 1998, 407.

18. Part of the following draws on information at http://www.arianespace.com/news_features.htm for 7 January 2001, 10 January 2001.

19. Scott 1999, 36–38.

20. In addition, several performance improvements have been introduced in the second batch of Ariane 5s ordered in 2000 by Arianespace.

21. There was a four-month hiatus between 18 April and 18 August 2000 due to the unavailability of satellite payloads. *Space.com*, 10 January 2001, reported that the Arianespace launch consortium posted its first-ever net loss in 2000 of about $190 million due largely to its ability to operate two simultaneous launch pads but inability to launch the heaviest commercial satellites two at a time.

22. The most recent information on the company and its launch activities is from http://www.ils.com and also http://www.ilslaunch.com.

23. Lockheed Martin has also independently developed the Atlas V, but this launcher competes head to head with Boeing's Delta IV, which has already been contracted to launch the majority of U.S. military satellites in the near future. For this reason, the future commercial or government viability of the Atlas V, much less the Atlas V Heavy, is highly uncertain. See Caceres, 2001, 146.

24. See, for example, U.S. Congress 1995, esp. 2–3. Lockheed Martin and Orbital Sciences were responsible for developing the X-33 and X-34 suborbital test vehicles, respectively.

25. Halvorson 1998. The X-33 is about one-half the size, one-ninth the weight, and one-fourth the cost of VentureStar.

26. See *Space.com*, 26 August 1999, 27 August 1999, and 2 September 1999 for congressional criticisms and NASA's defense of the X-33 program's cost overruns at the end of 1999.

27. Dornheim 2000, 36, 41.

28. *Space.com*, 1 March 2001; Morring 2001a, 24.

29. Morring 200b1, 29.

30. *AWST*, 19 February 2001, 66. Given NASA's unsuccessful trajectory in the development of reusable launch vehicles, the birth of the SLI has not been welcomed at many levels. Representative Dana Rohrbacher (R-Calif.), chair of the space subcommittee of the U.S. House Science Committee, considers that the SLI is way off course in terms of its objectives of improving U.S. national launch capabilities in financial and human terms.

31. *Space.com*, 16 May 2001.

32. *Space.com*, 16 April 2001. Orbital Sciences was seeking similar funding from the U.S. Air Force for its equally stymied X-34 project.

33. Legally, ILS is owned by Lockheed Martin Commercial Launch Services (LMCLS) and the Lockheed Khrunichev Energia International (LKEI) joint venture.

34. All Angara flights are to be supervised by the Russian Aviation and Space Agency and will give Russian military or national satellites priority over commercial ones.

35. The most recent information on the company and its launch activities is from http://www.boeing.com and http://www.sea-launch.com.

36. The most recent information is from http://www.unitedspacealliance.com. USA was originally a joint venture between Rockwell and Lockheed Martin in

1995. However, Rockwell aerospace and defense businesses were sold in December 1996 to Boeing.

37. Boeing executives explicitly saw the heavy-lift Delta III competing directly with Lockheed Martin and foreign competitors in the "sweet spot" of the booming commercial launch market. See *Seattle Post-Intelligencer*, 21 August 1998.

38. *Seattle Post-Intelligencer*, 21 August 1998, 27 August 1998.

39. Covault 2000d, 48–49; 2000a 27–30. Hughes, as part of Boeing, booked eleven flights, Loral booked five, and the SkyBridge project booked two more.

40. In October 1998, the U.S. Air Force announced an order for nineteen Delta IV launches, valued at about $1.3 billion, for the EELV program. The first commercial Delta IV orders were announced in 1999, with launches planned for 2001. Note that there are two rockets, the Delta IV Medium and Medium Plus, both with a projected launch in 2001, and the Delta IV Heavy with a projected launch in 2003. It was not until 20 November 2002 that the Delta IV family of rockets actually made its inaugural launch.

41. Covault 2000a, 27. The statement is attributed to Phil Condit, chair and CEO, Boeing.

42. *Space.com*, 13 January 2000.

43. Up-to-date information is from the official website at http://www.sea-launch.com.

44. Moorer 1993, 51.

45. *Financial Times*, 3 September 1998.

46. Bruno 1998.

47. Smith 2000a, 36–37.

48. Smith 2000b, 47.

49. Although the baseline GTO payload weight capability for the system was 5,000 kg, it was increased specifically for the launch of the Thuraya-1 satellite built by Boeing Satellite Systems. The stated goal of Sea Launch is to increase payload weight capacity to 6,000 kg by the end of 2002. See *AWST*, 2 October 2000, 47.

50. See the comments by the Sea Launch vice president for marketing and sales at *Space.com*, 29 July 2000.

51. *Space.com*, 6 June 2001 and 8 June 2001.

52. Estimated launch prices are from Isakowitz, Hopkins, and Hopkins 1999 for each series of launch vehicles.

53. In the assessment of the geosynchronous orbit launch demand model, the AST/COMSTAC 2000 report points to the growing consensus that the weight of the commercial GEO satellites is growing.

54. Caceres 2000a, 135–36, points out that with just about 700 satellites forecast to be launched through 2005, there is insufficient business to sustain all these newer ventures since anything less than 1,000 satellite missions worldwide in the next five years represents a weak market.

55. *AWST*, 7 February 2000, 19; Taverna 2000a, 126–27.

56. Taggart 1999, 50–51.

57. Taverna 2000a, 127.

58. *Space.com*, 18 April 2001.

242 Notes to Chapter 5

59. Launch figure estimates are from Isakowitz, Hopkins, and Hopkins 1999.

60. Caceres 2001, 145.

61. Taverna 2001a, 35–36; 2001b, 36.

62. Some of the basic information is drawn from the official websites of Japan's National Aeronautics and Space Development (NASDA) at http://www.nasda.go.jp; Institute of Space and Astronautical Sciences (ISAS) of the Ministry of Education at http://www.isas.ac.jp; and the Space and Technology Agency (STA) operating out of the Prime Minister's Office at http://www.sta.go.jp.

63. SJAC 1996a, 3.

64. SJAC 1997, 13.

65. Wray 1991–92, 478–79.

66. The planned reforms, which are designed to strike at the heart of bureaucratic power and which should be completed by 2005, involve cutting twenty-three central government ministries and agencies to thirteen and in contracting the 128 ministerial secretariats and bureaus to 96.

67. *AWST*, 8 February 1999, 65.

68. See http://yyy.tksc.nasda.go.jp and http://www.isas.ac.jp for details.

69. Sekigawa 2000, 123–26. The string of visible failures has included the following. In 1996, a $500 million ETS-6 (Experimental Test Satellite) was lost in orbit. Also in 1996, the HYFLEX (Hypersonic Flight Experiment) minishuttle test vehicle was lost at sea. In 1997, a solar panel collapsed and destroyed the $1 billion Adeos-1 (Advanced Earth-Observation Satellite). In 1998, as discussed in more detail in the text later, a second-stage malfunction of the H-II launch vehicle delivered a $375 million COMETS tacking and data relay satellite in a useless orbit. In 1999, an H-II launcher had to be destroyed minutes into orbit because it was veering off course, and this also led to the destruction of a $97 million MTSAT satellite. In February 2000, an ISAS M-5 launcher failed, ruining a $108 million Astro-E X-ray satellite.

70. Interview No. 53, Aircraft and Defense Products Division, Machinery and Information Industries Bureau, MITI, Tokyo, 1997.

71. Interview No. 104, (anonymity requested), MEXT, Tokyo, 2002. ISAS has twice the space budget of MITI, and the Ministry of Transport has roughly the same budget as MITI.

72. STA 1996–97, 499–505.

73. Some of the basic information is from RSC's website at http://www.rocket-system.co.jp.

74. *AWST*, 9 March 1987, 132.

75. *AWST*, 14 February 2000, 61.

76. *Space.com*, 30 July 2002.

77. The historical overview draws on Harvey 2000, 6–33, 52–78, 97–101.

78. In the following section, specific information on the Japanese launch vehicles is from Isakowitz, Hopkins, and Hopkins 1999.

79. Winter 1990, 102–3.

80. The M-V was first launched in 1997 for government payloads and continues to be commercially unavailable.

81. Wray 1991–92, 478–79.

82. Harvey 2000, 29–32.

83. Komahashi 1988, 176.

84. According to a 1969 U.S.-Japan agreement, Japan was permitted access to U.S. technology but prohibited from using that technology for launches for third parties without U.S. consent. The autonomous development of the H-II would therefore allow Japan to throw off this legal shackle.

85. *Nihon Keizai Shinbun*, 19 August 1994, 20 August 1994; *Yomiuri Shinbun*, 28 August 1994.

86. Mecham 1994, 50.

87. Estimated launch costs for the H class launch vehicles are from Isakowitz, Hopkins, and Hopkins 1999. In large part the H-II was also expensive because few launches could be carried out due to the "fishermen's problem." An agreement with the fisherman's union means that the launch window opportunity is available only for about six-week periods in January–February and August–September. According to *Nihon Keizai Shinbun*, 17 August 1994, Japan had to get over the "high cost wall" in order to even enter the commercial launch arena. It showed how the launch costs of the H-II made the Japanese rocket a distinct outlier in comparison to other launchers in its class, such as the Delta, Ariane, and Titan in Europe and the United States.

88. *Yomiuri Shinbun*, 21 February 1998.

89. The Japanese press lambasted NASDA and even the emphasis on lowering costs as main culprits for the failure. It thereby also called into question the future of Japan's space program as a whole. See front-page coverage and editorials in *Yomiuri Shinbun*, 16 November 1999, 17 November 1999; *Nihon Keizai Shinbun*, 16 November 1999; *Asahi Shinbun* 16 November 1999; *Financial Times*, 18 November 1999.

90. *Space.com*, 27 June 2002.

91. Asker 2000, 127.

92. *Yomiuri Shinbun*, 5 December 1999.

93. *Asahi Shinbun*, 13 February 1996; *Yomiuri Shinbun*, 13 February 1996.

94. *Asahi Evening News*, 26 April 1998.

95. See "The 3rd Evaluation Report of Subcommittee for Space Transportation" (May 2000), appearing at http://yyy.tksc.nasda.go.jp/Home/Press.

96. These are identified by NASDA as H2A202, H2A2022, H2A2024, H2A212, and H2A222.

97. I am grateful to Paul Kallender for bringing this story to my attention.

98. Interview No. 87, Space Utilization Division, Research and Development Bureau, STA, Tokyo, 1997.

99. MITI 2000b, 2.

100. Interview No. 98, Aircraft, Ordnance, and Space Industry Division, Machinery and Information Industries Bureau, MITI, Tokyo, 1997.

101. STA 1996-97, 499–505. Comparable figures for the American space budget stood at a postwar high of 0.6 percent of GDP in 1967 and since then at about 0.2 percent of GDP. Space budgets in Germany, Italy, Canada, and England have individually averaged around 0.04 percent of GDP. In the early 1980s, the French space budget began to distinguish itself from its European counterparts, rising to about 0.15 percent of GDP as of 1993.

102. Interview No. 104, (anonymity requested), MEXT, Tokyo, 2002.

103. Interview No. 106, (anonymity requested), MEXT, Tokyo, 2002.

104. Interview No. 107, (anonymity requested), MEXT, Tokyo, 2002.

105. Interview No. 104, (anonymity requested), MEXT, Tokyo, 2002.

106. *Space.com*, 18 November 1999.

107. Wray 1991–92, 482–84.

108. Ibid., 487.

109. *New York Times*, 27 November 1996.

110. *Yomiuri Shinbun*, 25 May 2000; *Wall Street Journal*, 26 May 2000.

111. *Nikkei Weekly*, 7 August 2000.

112. Interview No. 105, IHI Aerospace, Tokyo, 2002.

113. Interview No. 65, Aircraft, Ordnance, and Space Industry Division, Machinery and Information Industries Bureau, MITI, Tokyo, 1997.

114. MITI 1997e, 169–70.

115. SAC 1996, 1–2.

116. SAC 2002, 2.

117. STA 1996–97, 18.

118. Interview No. 87, Space Utilization Division, Research and Development Bureau, STA, Tokyo, 1997.

119. NASDA 1997, 1.

120. MITI 1997e, 164.

121. MITI 2000a, 4–5.

122. MITI 1996, 1, 5.

123. SJAC 1996–97, 11.

124. Interview No. 65, Aircraft, Ordnance, and Space Industry Division, Machinery and Information Industries Bureau (previously Space Industry Division), MITI, Tokyo, 1997.

125. Interview No. 107, (anonymity requested), MEXT, Tokyo, 2002.

126. Green 1995, 3.

127. *Yomiuri Shinbun*, 5 November 1998; *Space.com*, 13 June, 2001; 9 April 2003. Japan successfully launched a pair of spy satellites in March 2003.

128. Interview No. 82, General Manager, Space Division, SJAC, Tokyo, 1997.

129. Interview No. 65, Aircraft, Ordnance, and Space Industry Division, Machinery and Information Industries Bureau, MITI, Tokyo, 1997.

130. Covault 2000d, 48. The Delta III also has hardware from France's Société Européenne de Propulsion (SEP), which makes missiles and rocket engines.

131. *Nikkei Weekly*, 7 August 2000. Lockheed Martin's Atlas vehicle, for example, shares a satellite mount with Russia's Proton.

132. http://yyy.tksc.nasda.go.jp/home/press.

133. See the editorial in *Nihon Keizai Shinbun*, 21 December 1999, which stresses the importance of cost competitiveness and risk reduction, factors that continue to be key in Japan's attempt to gain entry in the global commercial launch market.

134. *AWST*, 15 January 2001, 433; 12 March 2001, 68; *New York Times*, 8 May 2001. Under Secretary of Defense Donald Rumsfeld, military space issues are widely expected to be high on the Bush administration's priority list.

135. Interview No. 82, General Manager, Space Division, SJAC, Tokyo, 1997.

There is a wide-ranging perception in Japan that the Europeans are far more effective at securing foreign procurements through their governments than the United States and that the European model therefore is the one that Japan should actively follow.

136. SAC 2002, 3.

Chapter 6

1. Krugman, ed., 1986; Stegemann 1989, 73–100.
2. Bhagwati 1988, 65–71.
3. Milner and Yoffie 1989, 239–72.
4. Okimoto, Sugano, and Weinstein 1984; Johnson, Tyson, and Zysman 1989.
5. Borrus, Tyson, and Zysman 1986, 92.
6. As discussed more closely in Chapter 2, this has the advantage of making us pursue the answer more conscientiously and not merely stopping at one that conforms to some strongly held a priori beliefs or expectations.
7. In contemporaneous estimations, the danger is that selection can be a self-fulfilling prophecy in that the government grants TIPs to industries that are economically strategic, and these sectors are economically strategic potentially because they are selected and favored by the government. The evidence on the most-favored sectors established in the structured data analysis in Chapter 3 is a good check because it shows that, in any event, based on their economically strategic characteristics at time t-1, MITI was not favoring such sectors at time t consistently. In the econometric analysis, we can also do the same kind of thing by lagging the criteria for selection at time t-1 and seeing whether they have a "causal" effect on selection through TIPs at time t.
8. Interview No. 96, Agency of Industrial Science and Technology, MITI, Tokyo, 1997. The official explained that criteria such as "necessity" or "future potential," used in the past, were beginning to be deemed irrelevant and that the focus was shifting to a new "technology evaluation code" with an emphasis on quantitative criteria and trends.
9. The processed food sector is under the sole jurisdiction of the agricultural ministry. The evidence shows that it has been one of the most consistently favored sectors in postwar Japan, but here I concentrate only on MITI's selections.
10. The same idea of a basic industry applies to the chemicals industry, which has been one of the most consistently favored of all the most-favored sectors. The chemicals industry, however, has also been under split jurisdiction, between MITI, the agricultural ministry, and the health and welfare ministry, all of which stress the importance of futuristic niches within the industry, such as biotechnology, new materials, and microelectronics. All of them, of course, also lament the fact that the Japanese chemicals industry is nowhere near being globally competitive, like BASF, Hoechst (Aventis), or Dupont, for example. Although political pressures were certainly part of the story in the late 1970s and early 1980s after the first oil shock, today the continued-favored status of the chemicals industry as a whole stems from the keen interest of Japanese government officials in all of these ministries in its futuris-

tic niches such as biotechnology, genomics, new materials, and microelectronics, which are perceived as having immense spillover potential for the rest of the Japanese economy. What is also noticeable is the government officials' concern that the chemicals industry is the least globally competitive of Japanese industries in comparison to those of the West, which dominate the world market, and this is often said to be the most important reason for government intervention.

11. Murakami 1996, 387; Samuels 1994, esp. 319.

12. There are also potentially more important axes of conflict in the Japanese political economy, namely politicians, bureaucrats, and business against others such as consumers and labor.

13. Pempel and Muramatsu 1995, 37–40.

14. One study does just that. Rather than drawing polemical extremes about who rules, Kato 1994 offers a balanced and realistic picture of the extensive game of political coordination and bargaining between bureaucrats and politicians in the actual governmental policy-making environment in Japan. Additionally, in examining the Japanese case, Ramseyer 1994, esp. 743–46, has suggested the historical and cross-national possibility of differential control of agencies, bureaus, or courts by politicians depending on electoral advantage.

15. Johnson 1999, 48–49; Murakami 1996, 223, 226.

16. Interview No. 64, General Affairs, Consumer Goods Bureau, MITI, Tokyo, 1997. This official pointed out that MITI personnel may have one to two post changes per year and that over the course of their career the competitive "up or out" system at MITI ensured that they had an average of fifteen to twenty post rotations.

17. Top economists like Anne Krueger 1996, 2, who helped pioneer key parts of the new political economy, also conclude that there is little in the way of quantitative empirical evidence that repeatedly confirms the influence of political variables, such as employment, geographic concentration, and lobbying pressures back in the real world. The same kinds of variables in this study, such as potential votes and campaign contributions, are not overwhelmingly influential. Compared to the economic variables, their general effect is even weaker. To the extent that these variables capture political influence, we have to conclude that they have limited explanatory power in the real world or, more appropriately, we have to employ more process-oriented ways of assessing political influence as done here using case studies and interviews.

18. In a notable new work, Solis (forthcoming) also discusses institutions that prevented rent-seeking in one TIP, namely public foreign direct investment loans. She shows how features, such as budgetary rules and control over the mandate of government financial institutions, arose out of conflict between MOF and LDP politicians and were largely responsible for preventing rampant subsidization.

19. Muramatsu and Krauss 1987, 433; Komiya 1988, 11–13, 15–17; Stiglitz 1997, 112; Schwartz 1998, 58, 69. As of 1996, MITI had the largest number of *shingikai*, with a total of thirty-three.

20. In the context of Japanese industrial policy, Itoh et al. 1991, 64–65, argue that it is unrealistic to assume that even firms in oligopolistic industries, let alone governments, can acquire the kind of information needed to anticipate all the changes

resulting from general equilibrium effects. For such firms, the considerable costs of acquiring complete information regarding the conditions of (1) demand and supply and their interrelationships for all relevant industries, and (2) an accurate calculation of the ensuing quantitative effects depends *ex ante* on the expected profits from such an activity that remain unclear.

21. Grossman 1986, 66; Krugman 1983, 124.

22. Callon 1995, esp. 191–92, has underscored the importance of information in choosing industries for promotion and points out rightly that MITI made several catastrophic ventures with high-tech consortia in the 1980s largely because of unilateral initiatives that lacked corporate inputs.

23. Okimoto 1989, 115, 171–72.

24. Curtis 1999, 58–61. Curtis also points out that LDP backbenchers do not really have influence on the party leadership's policy positions, which, in turn, potentially reduces the influence of elections on policy.

25. Johnson 1987, 149–51.

26. Johnson 1982, 323; Muramatsu and Krauss 1987, 523; Pempel 1997, 349–58; 1998, 146–48.

27. Yamamura 1995, 110–14, 127–28; Gao 1997, esp. 14, 295–96.

28. Samuels 1994, 3, 33.

29. Yamamura and Streeck 2003.

30. Murakami 1996, 191, 225–26; Johnson 1982, 274.

31. The emphasis on deselection has surfaced in many works concerned with industrial development, especially in the East Asian context, but has not been systematically studied. Cumings 1984, 38, for example, points to remarkable similarities in the role of the states in Japan, Korea, and Taiwan and especially their flexible ability to move in and, more important, out of industrial sectors. In writing about the industrialization of South Korea more specifically, Amsden 1989, 8, 14–15, points to the extraordinary discipline of the state and especially what she calls its "cold-bloodedness" in deselecting firms with poor export performance. In fact, the general rule was that the more disciplined the firm, the lower its subsidies and protection. Haggard and Cheng 1987, 128, attribute the industrial competitiveness of Korea and Taiwan to "self-conscious" deselection after ten years of import substitution strategies. In marked contrast to these countries, they suggest that Mexico's lack of globally competitive industries can be attributed to the government's inability to deselect industries for support—or its general unwillingness to let go—which over time then created high political barriers against the very possibility of such a policy option.

32. Interview No. 5, General Coordination Division, Policy Planning Office, MITI, Tokyo, 1997.

33. Okita 1980, esp. 97–98.

34. Citing the role of MITI-authorized recession cartels in a few industry examples that ended up reinforcing inefficiencies, Katz 1998, 169–74, argues that broader patterns of deselection did not exist.

35. Interview No. 96, Agency of Industrial Science and Technology, MITI, Tokyo, 1998.

36. Pempel 1998, 159–61.

248 Notes to Chapter 6

37. Saxonhouse 1983 shows the limited nature of most Japanese TIPs that were singled out in the industrial policy literature. Additionally, Sakakibara 1993, 9, stresses the importance of firm independence and the feature of "excessive competition" as integral parts of the Japanese model of market economics—a feature that may also be conducive to the politics of deselection.

38. See Krugman 1983, 124–39, and Spencer 1986, 70–80, for discussions of some characteristics of industries appropriate for selection.

39. Some of these issues are raised and dealt with in Chapter 3.

40. Krugman and Smith 1994, 5–6.

41. Yamamura 1986, 201–2, agrees that essentially TIPs validated or hastened the market dictates in Japan. In other words, they were largely market conforming.

42. See also Okimoto 1986, 54, on this point.

43. Beason and Patterson 2002.

44. Woo-Cumings 1999, 31. In light of the new prevailing sense of triumph about America's rebounded economic preeminence, Krugman 1998 also suggests caution with respect to interpreting actual changes in the U.S. economy's fundamentals and thus the viability of American institutions that are potentially underwriting those changes. Moreover, he also points out that most of the fundamentals of the Japanese economy remain remarkably intact despite the present stagnation.

45. Even the idea of a monolithic Japanese government needs to be disaggregated. The present banking and financial crisis, for example, is under the jurisdiction of the finance ministry, not MITI.

46. While some, such as Krugman 1994c, esp. 73, rightly question the sustainability of the "Asian miracle," they also point to the viability of the Japanese one. In short, Japan will be back—if indeed it ever really went anywhere.

47. Nor has Japan's concern with promoting its own brand of development policy advice ended—a fact made more important by its huge aid interest and its position as the largest aid donor, especially in East Asia.

48. Okimoto 1989, 50–51. To some extent, these results suggest a reassessment of the idea that MITI's patterns of intervention were based on the industrial life-cycle. The overall evidence on TIPs suggests that MITI did not necessarily intervene at greater levels at the start or end of the industrial cycle across sectors.

49. Lincoln 2001, 148–49, 173, 181–85; Keller and Samuels 2002, 492–93.

50. SAC 2002, esp. 3.

51. See, for example, Nordwall 2000a and the National Defense Research Institute (NDRI) Pentagon briefing on a survey of the oncoming technology revolution appearing on http://www.rand.org/natsec/products/techrev.htm (accessed 31 August 2002).

52. Green 1995, 19, 157–58.

Bibliography

Amsden, Alice H. 1989. *Asia's Next Giant: South Korea and Late Industrialization*. New York: Oxford University Press.

Anchordoguy, Marie. 1989. *Computers Inc.: Japan's Challenge to IBM*. Cambridge: Harvard Council on East Asian Studies.

Anderson, Kym, and Robert E. Baldwin. 1981. "The Political Market for Protection in Industrial Countries: Empirical Evidence." World Bank Staff Working Paper No. 492. Washington, D.C.

Anselmo, Joseph C. 1996. "New Satellite Uses Spur Space Boom." *Aviation Week and Space Technology* (3 June): 87–89.

———. 1997. "Launch Upgrades Key to Milspace Evolution." *Aviation Week and Space Technology* (1 September): 48.

Anselmo, Joseph C., and Michael Mecham. 1997. "R&D Pipeline Shaping New Era for Satellites." *Aviation Week and Space Technology* (31 March): 48–49.

ANSI/AIAA (American National Standards Institute/American Institute of Aeronautics and Astronautics). 1994. *Guide to Terminology for Space Launch Systems*. Washington, D.C.: AIAA.

———. 1999. *Commercial Launch Safety*. Washington, D.C.: AIAA.

Asker, James R. 1995a. "Racing to Remake Space Economics." *Aviation Week and Space Technology* (3 April): 44–45.

———. 1995b. "X-34 to Be Acid Test for Space Commerce." *Aviation Week and Space Technology* (3 April): 44–53.

———. 2000. "Japanese Space Agency Cites Lessons of H-II Failure." *Aviation Week and Space Technology* (9 October): 127.

AST/COMSTAC (Federal Aviation Administration's Associate Administrator for Commercial Space Transportation/Commercial Space Transportation Advisory Committee). 1999. *1999 Commercial Space Transportation Forecasts*. Washington, D.C.: FAA.

———. 2000. *2000 Commercial Space Transportation Forecasts*. Washington, D.C.: FAA.

Baerwald, Hans J. 1986. *Party Politics in Japan*. Boston: Allen & Unwin.

Bates, Robert H. 1981. *Markets and States in Tropical Africa: The Political Basis of Agricultural Policies*. Berkeley: University of California Press.

———. 1988. *Toward a Political Economy of Development: A Rational Choice Perspective*. Berkeley: University of California Press.

Beason, Richard, and Dennis Patterson. 2002. "The Japan That Never Was." Paper presented at the annual meeting of the Association of Japanese Business Studies, St. Louis.

Beason, Richard, and David E. Weinstein. 1996. "Growth, Economies of Scale, and Targeting in Japan (1955–1990)." *Review of Economics and Statistics* (May): 106–15.

Beck, Nathaniel, and Jonathan N. Katz. 1995. "What to Do (and Not to Do) with Time-Series Cross-Section Data." *American Political Science Review* 89, no. 3 (September): 634–47.

Berk, Richard A., et al. 1979. "Estimation Procedures for Pooled Cross-Sectional and Time Series Data." *Evaluation Quarterly* 3, no. 3 (August): 385–410.

Bhagwati, Jagdish N . 1980. "Lobbying and Welfare." *Journal of Public Economics* (December): 355–63.

———. 1982. "Directly Unproductive Profit-Seeking (DUP) Activities." *Journal of Political Economy* 90, no. 5: 988–1002.

———. 1985. "Export Promotion as a Development Strategy." In *Essays in Honor of Saburo Okita*, edited by Toshio Shishdo and Ryuzo Sato. Boston: Auburn House.

———. 1987. "Export Promoting Trade Strategy: Issues and Evidence." Mimeo, World Bank, Washington, D.C. Revised version: *World Bank Research Observer* 3 (1988): 27–57.

———. 1988. *Protectionism*. The 1987 Ohlin Lectures. Cambridge: MIT Press.

Borrus, Michael, Laura D'Andrea Tyson, and John Zysman. 1986. "Creating Advantage: How Government Policies Shape International Trade in the Semiconductor Industry." In *Strategic Trade Policy and the New International Economics*, edited by Paul R. Krugman. Cambridge: MIT Press.

Borrus, Michael, James E. Millstein, and John Zysman. 1983. "Trade and Development in the Semiconductor Industry: Japanese Challenge and American Response." In *American Industry in International Competition: Government Policies and Corporate Strategies*, edited by John Zysman and Laura Tyson. Ithaca, N.Y.: Cornell University Press. Revised version: *U.S.-Japanese Competition in the Semiconductor Industry: A Study in International Trade and Technological Development*. Policy Papers in International Affairs No. 17. Berkeley: Institute of International Studies, University of California.

Brander, James A. 1986. "Rationales for Strategic Trade and Industrial Policy." In *Strategic Trade Policy and the New International Economics*, edited by Paul R. Krugman. Cambridge: MIT Press.

———. "Strategic Trade Policy." 1995. National Bureau of Economic Research Working Paper No. 5020: 1–76. Cambridge, Mass.

Brander, James A., and Barbara J. Spencer. 1985. "Export Subsidies and International Market Share Rivalry." *Journal of International Economics* 18, nos. 1/2 (February): 83–100.

———. 1995. "Tariff Protection and Imperfect Competition." In *Imperfect Competition and International Trade*, edited by Gene M. Grossman. Cambridge: MIT Press. (Originally published in *Monopolistic Competition and International Trade*, edited by H. Kierzkowski. Oxford: Oxford University Press, 1984).

Bresiz, Elise S., Paul R. Krugman, and Daniel Tsiddon. 1993. "Leapfrogging in International Competition: A Theory of Cycles in National Technological Leadership." *American Economic Review* 83, no. 5 (December): 1211–19.

Bruno, Antony. 1998. "Sea Launch Expects to Capitalize on Satellite Launch Business." *Business and Industry* 17 no. 30: 10.

Buchanan, James M., and Robert D. Tollison, eds. 1984. *The Theory of Public Choice II*. Ann Arbor: University of Michigan Press.

Buskirk, Howard. 2000. "Rocket Failures, Instability Slow Launch Market." *Military Space* 17, no. 4 (14 February).

Caceres, Marco A. 2000a. "Industry Faces Launcher Excess." *Aviation Week and Space Technology* (17 January): 135–36.

———. 2000b. "Satisfied Demand, Financing Woes Soften Satellite Market." *Aviation Week and Space Technology* (17 January): 151–52.

———. 2001. "Expendables Face Tough Market." *Aviation Week and Space Technology* (15 January): 145–46.

Calder, Kent E. 1988. "Japanese Foreign Economic Policy Formation: Explaining the Reactive State." *World Politics* 40, no. 4: 517–41.

———. 1990. "Welfare and the Developmental State: Postal Savings in Japan." *Journal of Japanese Studies* 16, no. 1: 31–59.

———. 1993. *Strategic Capitalism: Private Business and Public Purpose in Japanese Industrial Finance*. Princeton, N.J.: Princeton University Press.

Callon, Scott. 1995. *Divided Sun: MITI and the Breakdown of Japanese High-Tech Industrial Policy, 1975–1993*. Stanford, Calif.: Stanford University Press.

Clemons, Steven. 1994. "Letters." *National Interest* 37 (fall): 101–2.

Covault, Craig. 1993. "Ambitious Decade Ahead for Europe's Space Effort." *Aviation Week and Space Technology* (15 March): 88–89.

———. 2000a. "Boeing Sets Costly Delta III Flight Test." *Aviation Week and Space Technology* (19 June): 27–30.

———. 2000b. "Cape Gears for New Vehicles, Launch Surge." *Aviation Week and Space Technology* (13 March): 54–58.

———. 2000c. "Commercial Space Faces Rough Road." *Aviation Week and Space Technology* (16 October): 57–58.

———. 2000d. "Delta III Succeeds, But Will It Sell?" *Aviation Week and Space Technology* (28 August): 48–49.

Cowhey, Peter, and Matthew D. McCubbins. 1995. *Structure and Policy in Japan and the United States*. New York: Cambridge University Press.

Craib, B. Anne. 1994. "Japan As a Development Model: Promise or Problem?" In *Japan Economic Institute (JEI) Report No. 19A*, 1–10. Washington, D.C.: Japan Economic Institute.

Cumings, Bruce. 1984. "The Origins and Development of the Northeast Asian Political Economy: Industrial Sectors, Product Cycles, and Political Consequences." *International Organization* 38, no. 1: 1-40.

Curtis, Gerald L. 1971. *Election Campaigning Japanese Style*. Tokyo: Kodansha.

———. 1988. *The Japanese Way of Politics*. New York: Columbia University Press.

———. 1999. *The Logic of Japanese Politics: Leaders, Institutions, and the Limits of Change*. New York: Columbia University Press.

Cusumano, Michael A. 1985. *The Japanese Automobile Industry: Technology Management at Nissan and Toyota*. Cambridge: Harvard Council on East Asian Studies.

Department of State. 1946. *Administration of Coal Production in Japan*. Washington, D.C.: Office of Economic Security Policy, Interim Research and Planning Division.

Dielman, Terry E. 1989. *Pooled Cross Sectional and Time Series Data Analysis*. New York: Marcel Decker.

Dixit, Avinash K. 1986. "Trade Policy: An Agenda for Research." In *Strategic Trade Policy and the New International Economics*, edited by Paul R. Krugman. Cambridge: MIT Press.

Dixit, Avinash K., and Gene M. Grossman. 1986. "Targeted Export Promotion with Several Oligopolistic Industries." *Journal of International Economics* 21, nos. 3/4 (November): 233–49.

Dixit, Avinash K., and Albert S. Kyle. 1985. "The Use of Protection and Subsidies for Entry Promotion and Deterrence." *American Economic Review* 75, no. 1 (March): 139–52.

Dore, Ronald. 1983. *A Case Study of Technology in Japan: The Next Generation Base Technologies Development Programme*. London: Technical Change Centre.

———. 1986. *Flexible Rigidities: Industrial Policy and Structural Adjustment in the Japanese Economy 1970–1980*. Stanford, Calif.: Stanford University Press.

Dornheim, Michael A. 2000. "Iridium, Overcapacity Worry Space Industry." *Aviation Week and Space Technology* (10 April): 34, 51.

Dosi, Giovanni, Laura D'Andrea Tyson, and John Zysman. 1989. "Trade, Technologies, and Development: A Framework for Discussing Japan." In *Politics and Productivity*, edited by Chalmers Johnson, Laura D'Andrea Tyson, and John Zysman. New York: Harper Business.

Eckelmann, R. L., and L. A. Davis. 1983. *Japanese Industrial Policies and the Development of High Technology Industries: Computers and Aircraft*. Prepared for the Office of Trade and Investment Analysis, International Trade Administration, U.S. Department of Commerce. Washington, D.C.: Government Printing Office.

Fishlow, Albert, et al. 1994. *Miracle or Design? Lessons from the East Asian Experience*. Policy Essay No. 11. Washington, D.C.: Overseas Development Council.

Flaherty, M. Therese, and Hiroyuki Itami. 1984. "Finance." In *Competitive Edge: The Semiconductor Industry in the U.S. and Japan*, edited by Daniel I. Okimoto, Takuo Sugano, and Franklin B. Weinstein. Stanford, Calif.: Stanford University Press.

Flamm, Kenneth. 1988. *Creating the Computer: Government, Industry and High Technology*. Washington, D.C.: Brookings Institution.

Foust, Jeff. 2000. "Surviving the Launch Market Downturn." *www.Spaceviews.Com/2000/0515*.

Fransman, Martin. 1995. *Japan's Computer and Communications Industry: The Evolution of Industrial Giants and Global Competitiveness*. New York: Oxford University Press.

Friedman, David. 1983. "Beyond the Age of Ford: The Strategic Basis of the Japanese Success in Automobiles." In *American Industry in International Competition: Government Policies and Corporate Strategies*, edited by John Zysman and Laura Tyson. Ithaca, N.Y.: Cornell University Press.

————. 1988. *The Misunderstood Miracle: Industrial Development and Political Change in Japan*. Ithaca, N.Y.: Cornell University Press.

Fukukawa, Shinji. 1990. *Recent Development of Industrial Policy and Business Strategy in Japan*. Background Information BI-72. Tokyo: Ministry of International Trade and Industry.

Gao, Bai. 1994. "Arisawa Hiromi and his Theory for a Managed Economy." *Journal of Japanese Studies* 20, no. 1:115–53.

Gerschenkron, Alexander. 1962. *Economic Backwardness in Historical Perspective*. Cambridge: Harvard University Press.

Gao, Bai. *Economic Ideology and Japanese Industrial Policy: Developmentalism from 1931 to 1965*. New York: Cambridge University Press, 1997.

Goldberger, Arthur S. 1991. *A Course in Econometrics*. Cambridge: Harvard University Press.

Gownder, Joseph P., and Robert Pekkanen. 1996. "The End of Political Science? Rational Choice Analyses in Studies of Japanese Politics." *Journal of Japanese Studies* 22, no. 2: 363–384.

Green, Donald P., and Ian Shapiro. 1994. *Pathologies of Rational Choice Theory: A Critique of Applications in Political Science*. New Haven, Conn.: Yale University Press.

Green, Michael J. 1995. *Arming Japan: Defense Production, Alliance Politics, and the Postwar Search for Autonomy*. New York: Columbia University Press.

Greene, William H. 1993 [1990]. *Econometric Analysis*, 2nd ed. Englewood Cliffs, N.J.: Prentice-Hall.

Grindle, Merilee S. 1989. "The New Political Economy: Positive Economics and Negative Politics." World Bank Policy, Planning, and Research Department Working Paper: 3–21. Washington, D.C.

Grossman, Gene M. 1986. "Strategic Export Promotion: A Critique." In *Strategic Trade Policy and the New International Economics*, edited by Paul R. Krugman. Cambridge: MIT Press.

Grossman, Gene M., and Elhanan Helpman. 1994. "Protection for Sale." *American Economic Review* 84, no. 4 (September): 833–50.

Haggard, Stephan, and Tun-jen Cheng. 1987. "State and Foreign Capital in the East Asian NICs." In *The Political Economy of the New Asian Industrialism*, edited by Frederic C. Deyo. Ithaca, N.Y.: Cornell University Press.

Halvorson, Todd. 1998. "Space Coast Enters Intense Competition for New Launch Vehicles Business." *Florida Today* (11 January).

Harvey, Brian. 2000. *The Japanese and Indian Space Programmes: Two Roads into Space*. New York, N.Y.: Springer-Praxis.

Hazard, Heather A. 1994. "Comment." In *Empirical Studies of Strategic Trade Policy*, edited by Paul Krugman and Alasdair Smith. Chicago, IL.: University of Chicago Press for the National Bureau of Economic Research.

Hein, Laura E. 1994. "In Search of Peace and Democracy: Japanese Economic Debate in Political Context." *Journal of Asian Studies* 53, no. 3: 752–78.

Helpman, Elhanan, and Paul R. Krugman. 1989. *Trade Policy and Market Structure*. Cambridge: MIT Press.

Hicks, Alexander M. 1994. "Introduction to Pooling." In *The Comparative Political Economy of the Welfare State*, edited by Thomas Janoski and Alexander M. Hicks. New York: Cambridge University Press.

Hillman, Arye L. 1982. "Declining Industries and Political-Support Protectionist Motives." *American Economic Review* 72, no. 5 (December): 1180–87.

———. 1989. *The Political Economy of Protection*. Chur, Switzerland, and New York: Harwood Academic Publishers.

Hillman, Arye L., and Heinrich W. Ursprung. 1988. "Domestic Politics, Foreign Interests, and International Trade Policy." *American Economic Review* 78, no. 4 (September): 729-745.

Howell, Jeremy, and Ian Neary. 1991. "Science and Technology Policy in Japan: The Pharmaceutical Industry and New Technology." In *The Promotion and Regulation of Industry in Japan*, edited by Stephen Wilks and Maurice Wright. London: Macmillan.

Howell, Thomas R., Brent L. Bartlett, and Warren Davis. 1992. *Creating Advantage: Semiconductors and Government Industrial Policy in the 1990s*. Washington, D.C.: Semiconductor Industry Association and Dewey, Ballantine.

Irwin, Douglas A. 1996. "Trade Politics and the Semiconductor Industry." In *The Political Economy of American Trade Policy*, edited by Anne O. Krueger. Chicago: University of Chicago Press for the National Bureau of Economic Research.

Isakowitz, Steven J., Joseph P. Hopkins Jr., and Joshua B. Hopkins. 1999. *International Reference Guide to Space Launch Systems*. Washington, D.C.: American Institute of Aeronautics and Astronautics (AIAA).

ISIJ (Iron and Steel Institute of Japan). 1996–97. *Activity and Profile 1996–1997*. Tokyo: ISIJ.

Ito, Takatoshi. 1992. *The Japanese Economy*. Cambridge: MIT Press.

Itoh, Motoshige, and Kazuharu Kiyono. 1988. "Foreign Trade and Direct Investment." In *Industrial Policy of Japan*, edited by Ryutaro Komiya, Masahiro Okuno, and Kotaro Suzumura. Tokyo: Academic Press.

Itoh, Motoshige, Kazuharu Kiyono, Masahiro Okuno-Fujiwara, and Kotaro Suzumura. 1991. *Economic Analysis of Industrial Policy*. San Diego, Calif.: Academic Press.

JAMA (Japan Automobile Manufacturers Association). 1997. *The History of Japan's Automobile Industry: An Overview*. Tokyo: JAMA.

Japan Government. 1997. *Kokkai Binran: Heisei 9 Nen 2 Gatsu Shinpan* (Diet handbook, February 1997, new edition). Tokyo: Nihon Keizai Shinbunsha.

Jeffries, Francis M. 1987. *Understanding the Japanese Industrial Challenge: From Automobiles to Software*. Poolesville, MD.: Jeffries and Associates.

JISF (Japan Iron and Steel Federation). 1997. *The Steel Industry of Japan 1997*. Tokyo: JISF.

JMBTA (Japan Machine Tool Builders Association). 1996. *Nihon no Kōsaku Kikai Sangyō: Kikai Kōgyō no Hatten o Sasaeru Sangyō* (Japan's machine tool industry: Supporting the development of manufacturing industries). Tokyo: JMBTA.

———. 1997. "The Geographical Distribution of the JMBTA Member Builders' Factories." Handout. Tokyo: JMBTA.

Johnson, Chalmers. 1978. *Japan's Public Policy Companies*. Washington, D.C.:American Enterprise Institute.

———. 1982. *MITI and the Japanese Miracle: The Growth of Industrial Policy, 1925–1975*. Stanford, CA.: Stanford University Press.

———. 1987. "Political Institutions and Economic Performance: The Government-Business Relationship in Japan, South Korea, and Taiwan." In *The Political Economy of the New Asian Industrialism*, edited by Frederic C. Deyo. Ithaca, N.Y.: Cornell University Press.

———. 1989. "MITI, MPT and the Telecom Wars: How Japan Makes Policy for High Technology." In *Politics and Productivity: How Japan's Development Strategy Works*, edited by Johnson Chalmers, Laura D'Andrea Tyson, and John Zysman. New York: Harper Business.

———. 1995. *Japan: Who Governs? The Rise of the Developmental State*. New York: W. W. Norton.

———. 1999. "The Developmental State: Odyssey of a Concept." In *The Developmental State*, edited by Meredith Woo-Cumings. Ithaca, N.Y.: Cornell University Press.

Johnson, Chalmers, and E. B. Keehn. 1994a. "Rational Choice and Asian Studies." *National Interest* 36 (summer): 14–22.

———. 1994b. "Letters." *National Interest* 37 (fall): 14–22.

Johnson, Chalmers, Laura D'Andrea Tyson, and John Zysman, eds. 1989. *Politics and Productivity: How Japan's Development Strategy Works*. New York: Harper Business.

Kaplan, Eugene A. 1972. *Japan: The Government-Business Relationship: A Guide for the American Businessman*. Washington, D.C.: U.S. Department of Commerce.

Kato, Junko. 1994. *The Problem of Bureaucratic Rationality: Tax Politics in Japan*. Princeton, N.J.: Princeton University Press.

Katz, Richard. 1998. *Japan: The System that Soured*. Armonk, N.Y.: M. E. Sharpe.

Kawahito, Kiyoshi. 1972. *The Japanese Steel Industry with an Analysis of the U.S. Steel Import Problem*. New York: Praeger.

Keller, William W., and Richard J. Samuels, eds. 2002. *Crisis and Innovation in Asian Technology*. New York: Cambridge University Press.

Kernell, Samuel. 1991. "The Primacy of Politics in Economic Policy." In *Parallel Politics: Economic Policymaking in Japan and the United States*, edited by Samuel Kernell. Washington, D.C.: Brookings Institution.

Kim, Hyung-Ki, et al., eds. 1995. *The Japanese Civil Service and Economic Development: Catalysts of Change*. New York: Oxford University Press.

King, Gary, Robert O. Keohane, and Sidney Verba. 1994. *Designing Social Inquiry: Scientific Inference in Qualitative Research*. Princeton, N.J.: Princeton University Press.

Klepper, Gernot. 1994. "Industrial Policy in the Transport Aircraft Industry." In *Empirical Studies of Strategic Trade Policy*, edited by Paul Krugman and Alasdair Smith. Chicago: University of Chicago Press for the National Bureau of Economic Research and the Centre for Economic Policy Research.

Komahashi, Shizuka. 1988. *Nihon Kōkū Uchū Sangyō No Chōsen: FSX, H-II Roketto* (The Japanese industrial challenge: FSX and the H-II rocket). Tokyo: Nikkan Shobō.

Komiya, Ryutaro. 1988. "Introduction." In *Industrial Policy of Japan*, edited by Ryu-taro Komiya, Masahiro Okuno, and Kotaro Suzumura. Tokyo: Academic Press.

Komiya, Ryutaro, Masahiro Okuno, and Kotaro Suzumura, eds. 1988. *Industrial Policy of Japan*. Tokyo: Academic Press.

Komiya, Ryutaro, and Motoshige Itoh. 1988. "Japan's International Trade Policy, 1955-1984." In *The Political Economy of Japan: The Changing International Context*, edited by Takashi Inoguchi and Daniel I. Okimoto. Stanford, Calif.: Stanford University Press.

Kosai, Yutaka. 1988. "The Reconstruction Period." In *Industrial Policy of Japan*, edited by Ryutaro Komiya, Masahiro Okuno, and Kotaro Suzumura. Tokyo: Academic Press.

Krauss, Ellis S., and Jon Pierre. 1993. "Targeting Resources for Industrial Change." In *Do Institutions Matter? Government Capabilities in the United States and Abroad*, edited by R. Kent Weaver and Bert A. Rockman. Washington, D.C.: Brookings Institution.

Krueger, Anne O. 1974. "The Political Economy of the Rent-Seeking Society." *American Economic Review* 64: 291–303

———. 1993. *Political Economy of Policy Reform in Developing Countries*. Cambridge: MIT Press.

———, ed. 1996. *The Political Economy of American Trade Policy*. Chicago: University of Chicago Press for the National Bureau of Economic Research.

Krugman, Paul R. 1983. "Targeted Industrial Policies: Theory and Evidence." Presented at Conference on Structural Change in the U.S. Economy, Jackson Hole, Wyoming. Printed in *Industrial Change and Public Policy*. Federal Reserve Bank of Kansas City, MO. 123–55.

———. 1987a. "Strategic Sectors and International Competition." In *U.S. Trade Policies in a Changing World Economy*, edited by Robert M. Stern. Cambridge: MIT Press.

———. 1987b. "Is Free Trade Passé?" *Journal of Economic Perspectives* 1: 131–44.

———. 1990 [1984]. "Import Protection as Export Promotion: International Competition in the Presence of Oligopolies and Economies of Scale." In *Rethinking International Trade*, edited by Paul R. Krugman. Cambridge: MIT Press (Originally published in *Monopolistic Competition and International Trade*, edited by H. Kierzkowski. Oxford: Oxford University Press, 1984).

———. 1991. *Trade with Japan: Has the Door Opened Wider?* Chicago: University of Chicago Press for the National Bureau of Economic Research.

———. 1993. "The Narrow and Broad Arguments for Free Trade." *American Economic Review* 83, no. 2: 362–66.

———. 1994a. "Competitiveness: A Dangerous Obsession." *Foreign Affairs* 73, no. 2: 28–44.

———. 1994b. *Peddling Prosperity: Economic Sense and Nonsense in the Age of Diminished Expectation*. New York: W. W. Norton.

———. 1994c. "The Myth of Asia's Miracle." *Foreign Affairs* 73, no. 6: 62–78.

———. 1995. *Development, Geography, and Economic Theory*. Cambridge: MIT Press.

———. 1998. "America the Boastful." *Foreign Affairs* 77, no. 3: 32–45.

————, ed. 1986. *Strategic Trade Policy and the New International Economics.* Cambridge: MIT Press.

Krugman, Paul R., and Maurice Obstfeld. 1994. *International Economics: Theory and Policy*, 3rd ed. New York: HarperCollins College Publishers.

Krugman, Paul R., and Alasdair Smith, eds. 1994. *Empirical Studies of Strategic Trade Policy.* Chicago: University of Chicago Press for the National Bureau of Economic Research and the Centre for Economic Policy Research.

Lal, Deepak. 1985 [1983]. *The Poverty of "Development Economics."* Cambridge: Harvard University Press.

Lawrence, Robert Z., and Charles L. Schultze, eds. 1990. *An American Trade Strategy: Options for the 1990s.* Washington, D.C.: Brookings Institution.

Lenorovitz, Jeffrey M. 1993. "Steady Growth Seen for Commercial Space." *Aviation Week and Science Technology* (15 March): 83–87.

Lincoln, Edward J. 1984. *Japan's Industrial Policies: What Are They, Do They Matter and Are They Different from Those in the United States?* Washington, D.C.: Japan Economic Institute of America.

————. 2001. *Arthritic Japan: The Slow Pace of Economic Reform.* Washington, D.C.: Brookings Institution.

Magaziner, Ira C., and Thomas M. Hout. 1980. *Japanese Industrial Policy.* Policy Papers in International Affairs. Berkeley: Institute of International Studies, University of California.

Magee, Stephen P., William A. Brock, and Leslie Young. 1989. *Black Hole Tariffs and Endogenous Policy Theory: Political Economy in General Equilibrium.* Cambridge: Cambridge University Press.

Matsuura, Shinya. 1997. *H-II Roketto Jōushō: Kokusan ōgata Roketto Kaihatsu 12nen No Kiseki* (The rise of the H-II rocket: The twelve-year history of Japan's indigenous rocket). Tokyo: Nikkei BP.

McCubbins, Matthew D., and Gregory W. Noble. 1995. "Perception and Realities of Japanese Budgeting." In *Structure and Policy in Japan and the United States*, edited by Peter Cowhey and Matthew D. McCubbins. New York: Cambridge University Press.

McCubbins, Matthew D., and Frances M. Rosenbluth. 1995. "Party Provision for Personal Politics: Dividing the Vote in Japan." In *Structure and Policy in Japan and the United States*, edited by Peter Cowhey and Matthew D. McCubbins. New York: Cambridge University Press.

McCubbins, Matthew D., Roger G. Noll, and Barry R. Weingast. 1987. "Administrative Procedures as Instruments of Political Control." *Journal of Law, Economics, and Organization* 3: 243–77.

————. 1989. "Structure and Process, Politics and Policy: Administrative Arrangements and the Political Control of Agencies." *Virginia Law Review* 75: 431–82.

Mecham, Michael. 1994. "Japan Space Programs Keyed to H-2 Success." *Aviation Week and Space Technology* (31 January): 50.

Milner, Helen V., and David B. Yoffie. 1989. "Between Free Trade and Protectionism: Strategic Trade Policy and a Theory of Corporate Trade Demands." *International Organization* 43, no. 2: 239–72.

MITI (Sangyō Kozo Shingikai [Industry Structure Council]). 1971. *70-Nendai no Tsusho Sangyō Seisaku* (MITI's industrial policy for the 1970s). Tokyo: MITI.

————. 1974. *Sangyō Kozo no Chōki Bijon* (Long-term vision of the industrial structure). Tokyo: MITI.

————. 1980. *80-Nendai no Tsusho Sangyō Seisaku Bijon* (MITI's industrial policy vision for the 1980s). Tokyo: MITI.

————. 1987/88. *Kōkuki Sangyō no Genjō* (The present condition of the aircraft industry). Tokyo: MITI.

————. 1996. *Uchyū Sangyō Kihon Mondai Kondankai Hōkokusho: Uchyū Sangyō no Ririku e Mukete* (Report of the roundtable on the basic problems in the space industry: Towards a take-off of the space industry). Tokyo: MITI.

————. 1997a. "Coal Policy in Japan." Internal document, Agency of Natural Resources and Energy. Tokyo: MITI.

————. 1997b. *Kokunai Sekitan Kōgyō: Sekitan Kōgyō no Ayumi* (The domestic coal mining industry: The path of the coal industry). Tokyo: MITI.

————. 1997c. *Seni Sangyō no Ichizuke* (The position of the textile industry). Tokyo: MITI.

————. 1997d. *Shitsu no Takai Koyō o Sōsei Suru Kagaku Sangyō* (Creating high quality employment in the chemicals industry). Tokyo: MITI.

————. 1997e. *Kōkū Uchyū (Minjyu) Kanren Bunya* (Civilian demand in aircraft and space related fields). Internal document. Tokyo: MITI.

————. 2000a. "Challenge and Prospects for Economic and Industrial Policy in the 21st Century: Building a Competitive, Participatory Society." Internal document. Tokyo: MITI.

————. 2000b. "National Strategies for Industrial Technology." Tokyo: internal document, MITI.

Moe, Terry M. 1984. "The New Economics of Organization." *American Journal of Political Science* 28, no. 4: 739–77.

————. 1987. "An Assessment of the Positive Theory of 'Congressional Dominance.'" *Legislative Studies Quarterly* 12, no. 4 (November): 475–520.

Molony, Barbara. 1990. *Technology and Investment: The Prewar Japanese Chemical Industry*. Cambridge: Harvard Council on East Asian Studies.

Moorer, Thomas H. 1993. "Sea Launches Offer Commercial Benefits." *Aviation Week and Space Technology* (11 January): 51.

Morring, Frank, Jr. 2001a. "NASA Kills X-33, X-34, Trims Space Station." *Aviation Week and Space Technology* (5 March): 24–25.

————. 2001b. "NASA Tightens Reins on RLV Contractors." *Aviation Week and Space Technology* (12 March): 28–29.

Morris-Suzuki, Tessa. 1989. *A History of Japanese Economic Thought*. London: Routledge.

Morris-Suzuki, Tessa, et al. 1989. *Japanese Capitalism since 1945: Critical Perspectives*. Armonk, N.Y.: M. E. Sharpe.

MOT (Ministry of Transport). 1995–96. *Shipbuilding 1995–1996*. Tokyo: MOT.

Mowery, David C., and Nathan Rosenberg. 1985. "The Japanese Commercial Aircraft Industry since 1945: Government Policy, Technical Development, and Industrial Structure." Occasional Paper of the Northeast Asia–United States Forum on International Policy, Stanford University, Stanford, Calif.

Murakami, Yasusuke. 1996. *An Anticlassical Political-Economic Analysis: A Vision for the Next Century.* Translated by Kozo Yamamura. Stanford, Calif.: Stanford University Press.

Muramatsu, Michio, and Ellis S. Krauss. 1984. "Bureaucrats and Politicians in Policy-making: The Case of Japan." *American Political Science Review* 78, no. 1: 126–46.

———. 1987. "The Conservative Policy Line and the Development of Patterned Pluralism." In *The Political Economy of Japan: The Domestic Transformation*, edited by Yamamura Kozo and Yasuba Yasukichi. Stanford, Calif.: Stanford University Press.

Murata, Kiyoji, ed. 1980. *An Industrial Geography of Japan.* London: Bell and Hyman.

Mutoh, Hiromichi. 1988. "The Automotive Industry." In *Industrial Policy of Japan*, edited by Ryutaro Komiya, Masahiro Okuno, and Kotaro Suzumura. Tokyo: Academic Press.

NASDA (National Space Development Agency of Japan). 1997. *NASDA.* Tokyo: NASDA.

Nelson, Joan M., et al. 1989. *Fragile Coalitions: The Politics of Economic Adjustment.* U.S.–Third World Policy Perspectives No. 12. New Brunswick, N.J.: Transaction Books.

Nihon Choki Shinyō Ginkō Sangyō Kenkyū Kai [Japan Long Term Bank Industrial Research Division]. 1972. *Shuyō Sangyō Sengo 25-nen Shi* (A twenty-five year postwar history of principal industries). Tokyo: Sangyō to Keizai Kabushiki Kaisha.

Noble, Gregory. 1981. "The Japanese Industrial Policy Debate." In *Pacific Dynamics*, edited by Stephen Haggard and Chung-in Moon. Boulder, Colo.: Westview Press.

Nordwall, Bruce D. 2000a. "Nanotechnology Extending Materials Science Frontier." *Aviation Week and Science Technology* (4 September): 89–90.

———. 2000b. "Alaska Competes for Satellite Launches." *Aviation Week and Space Technology* (13 November): 77–79.

North, Douglass. 1990. *Institutions, Institutional Change, and Economic Performance.* New York: Cambridge University Press.

O'Connell, Philip J. 1994. "National Variation in the Fortunes of Labor: A Pooled and Cross-Sectional Analysis of the Impact of Economic Crisis in the Advanced Capitalist Nations." In *The Comparative Political Economy of the Welfare State*, edited by Thomas Janoski and Alexander M. Hicks. New York: Cambridge University Press.

Ogura, Seiritsu, and Naoyuki Yoshino. 1988. "The Tax System and the Fiscal Investment and Loan Program." In *Industrial Policy of Japan*, edited by Ryutaro Komiya, Masahiro Okuno, and Kotaro Suzumura. Tokyo: Academic Press.

Ohta, Fusae, Tanikawa Hiroya, Hiroshi Nagai, and Taisuke Ohtani. 1993. *Industrial Policies in Japan's Postwar Reconstruction Period: A Reevaluation of the Priority Production System, Industrial Rationalization and Automobile Industry Development Measures.* Studies in International Trade and Industry 13. Tokyo: MITI RI (Research Institute of International Trade and Industry).

Okimoto, Daniel I. 1983. "Pioneer and Pursuer: The Role of the State in the Evolution of the Japanese and American Semiconductor Industries." Occasional Paper
of the Northeast Asia–United States Forum on International Policy, Stanford
University, Stanford, Calif.

———. 1984. "Political Context." In *Competitive Edge: The Semiconductor Industry in
the U.S. and Japan*, edited by Daniel I. Okimoto, Takuo Sugano, and Franklin B.
Weinstein. Stanford, Calif.: Stanford University Press.

———. 1986. "Regime Characteristics of Japanese Industrial Policy." In *Japan's High
Technology Industries*, edited by Hugh Patrick. Seattle: University of Washington
Press.

———. 1989. *Between MITI and the Market: Japanese Industrial Policy for High Technology*. Stanford, Calif.: Stanford University Press.

Okimoto, Daniel I., Takuo Sugano, and Franklin B. Weinstein. 1984. *Competitive
Edge: The Semiconductor Industry in the U.S. and Japan*. Stanford, Calif.: Stanford
University Press.

Okita, Saburo. 1980. *The Developing Economies and Japan: Lessons in Growth*. Tokyo:
University of Tokyo Press.

Okuno-Fujiwara, Masahiro. 1991. "Industrial Policy in Japan: A Political Economy
View." In *Trade with Japan: Has the Door Opened Wider?* edited by Paul Krugman.
Chicago: University of Chicago Press for the National Bureau of Economic Re-
search.

Ostrom, Charles W., Jr. 1990 [1978]. *Time Series Analysis: Regression Techniques*. Sage
University Paper Series on Quantitative Applications in the Social Sciences, 07–
009, 2nd ed. Newbury Park, Calif.: Sage.

PAJ (Petroleum Association of Japan). 1996. *Petroleum Association of Japan Annual Review*. Tokyo: PAJ.

Paone, R. M. 1979. "Japan." In *Energy Policies of the World: India, Japan, Taiwan*, edited
by Gerard J. Mangome. New York: Elsevier.

Patrick, Hugh, and Henry Rosovsky. 1976. *Asia's New Giant: How the Japanese Economy Works*. Washington, D.C.: Brookings Institution.

Peck, Merton J., Richard C. Levin, and Akira Goto. 1987. "Picking Losers: Public
Policy Toward Declining Industries in Japan." *Journal of Japanese Studies* 13, no. 1:
79–123.

Pekkanen, Saadia M. 1996. "Picking Winners? TIPs from Postwar Japan." Ph.D. diss.,
Harvard University.

———. 2001. "The Global Commercial Space Launch Industry: Japan in Comparative Perspective." MIT-Japan Working Paper No. 10.01 (16 July): 1–37.

Peltzman, Sam. 1976. "Toward a Moral General Theory of Regulation." *Journal of
Law and Economics* 19: 211–40.

Pelzman, Joseph. 1984. "The Multifiber Arrangement and Its Effect on the Profit
Performance of the U.S. Textile Industry." In *The Structure and Evolution of Re-
cent U.S. Trade Policy*, edited by Robert E. Baldwin and Anne O. Krueger.
Chicago: University of Chicago Press for the National Bureau of Economic
Research.

Pempel, T. J. 1978. "Japanese Foreign Economic Policy: The Domestic Bases for International Behavior." In *Between Power and Plenty: Foreign Economic Policies of Ad-*

vanced Industrial States, edited by Peter J. Katzenstein. Madison: University of Wisconsin Press.

———. 1987. "The Unbundling of Japan, Inc.: The Changing Dynamics of Japanese Policy Formation." *Journal of Japanese Studies* 13, no. 2: 271–306.

———. 1997. "Regime Shift: Japanese Politics in a Changing World Economy." *Journal of Japanese Studies* 23, no. 2: 333–61.

———. 1998. *Regime Shift: Comparative Dynamics of the Japanese Political Economy.* Ithaca, N.Y.: Cornell University Press.

Pempel, T. J., and Michio Muramatsu. 1995. "The Japanese Bureaucracy and Economic Development: Structuring a Proactive Civil Service." In *The Japanese Civil Service and Economic Development: Catalysts of Change*, edited by Hyung-Ki Kim, Michio Muramatsu, T. J. Pempel, and Kozo Yamamura. New York: Oxford University Press.

Porges, Amelia. 1986. "U.S.-Japan Trade Negotiations: Paradigms Lost." In *Trade With Japan: Has the Door Opened Wider?* edited by Paul Krugman. Chicago: University of Chicago Press for the National Bureau of Economic Research.

Prestowitz, Clyde V. 1989 [1988]. *Trading Places: How We Are Giving Our Future to Japan and How to Reclaim It.* New York: Basic Books.

Ramseyer, J. Mark. 1994. "Letters." *National Interest* 37 (fall): 99–101.

———. 1995. "The Puzzling (In)Dependence of Courts: A Comparative Approach." *Journal of Legal Studies* 223, no. 2: 721–47.

Ramseyer, J. Mark, and Frances McCall Rosenbluth. 1993. *Japan's Political Marketplace.* Cambridge: Harvard University Press.

———. 1995. *The Politics of Oligarchy.* New York: Cambridge University Press.

SAC (Space Activities Commission [Uchyū Kaihatsu Iinkai]). 1996. *Uchyū Kaihatsu Seisaku Taikō* (Fundamental policy of space development). Tokyo: SAC.

———. 2002. *Wagakuni no Uchyū Riyō Suishin no Kihonteki Hōkō to Tōmen no Hōsaku* (Basic direction and present measures in Japan's space utilization promotion). Tokyo: SAC.

Sakakibara, Eisuke. 1993. *Beyond Capitalism: The Japanese Model of Market Economics.* Lanham, Md.: University Press of America for the Economic Strategy Institute.

Samuels, Richard J. 1987. *The Business of the Japanese State: Energy Markets in Comparative and Historical Perspective.* Ithaca, N.Y.: Cornell University Press.

———. 1994. *"Rich Nation, Strong Army": National Security and the Technological Transformation of Japan.* Ithaca, N.Y.: Cornell University Press.

Samuels, Richard J., and Benjamin C. Whipple. 1989. "Defense Production and Industrial Development: The Case of Japanese Aircraft." In *Politics and Productivity: How Japan's Development Strategy Works*, edited by Johnson Chalmers, Laura D'Andrea Tyson, and John Zysman. New York: Harper Business.

Saxonhouse, Gary. n.d. "Tampering with Comparative Advantage in Japan?" Ann Arbor: Department of Economics, University of Michigan.

———. 1983. "What's All This about Industrial Targeting in Japan?" *World Economy* 6: 253–73.

———. 1986. *Industrial Policy and Factor Markets: Biotechnology in Japan and the United States.* Australia-Japan Research Centre, Pacific Economic Papers No. 136. Canberra: Research School of Pacific Studies, Australian National University.

————. 1987. "Comment on 'Strategic Sectors and International Competition.'" In *U.S. Trade Policies in a Changing World Economy*, edited by Robert M. Stern. Cambridge: MIT Press.

Sayrs, Lois W. 1989. *Pooled Time Series Analysis*. Sage University Paper Series on Quantitative Applications in the Social Sciences, 07–070. Newbury Park, Calif.: Sage.

Schwartz, Frank. 1998. *Advice and Consent: The Politics of Consultation in Japan*. New York: Cambridge University Press.

Scitovsky, Tibor. 1954. "Two Concepts of External Economies." *Journal of Political Economy* 62: 143–51.

Scott, Phil. 1999. "Lots in Space." *Scientific American* (July): 36–38.

Sekigawa, Eiichiro. 2000. "M-5 Loss Prompts Consolidation Talks." *Aviation Week and Space Technology* (21 February): 123–26.

Shapiro, Helen, and Lance Taylor. 1990. "The State and Industrial Strategy." *World Development* 18, no. 6: 861–78.

Shinjo, Koji. 1988. "The Computer Industry." In *Industrial Policy of Japan*, edited by Ryutaro Komiya, Masahiro Okuno, and Kotaro Suzumura. Tokyo: Academic Press.

SJAC (Nihon Kōkū Uchyū Kōgyō Kai [Society for Japanese Aerospace Companies]). 1987. *Nihon no Kōkū Uchyū Kōgyō Sengoshi* (Postwar history of Japan's aerospace industry). Tokyo: SJAC.

————. 1996a. *Uchyū Sangyō Jittai Chōsa Hōkokushō* (Report on the actual conditions of the space industry). Tokyo: SJAC.

————. 1996b. *Organization and Activities*. Tokyo: SJAC.

————. 1996–97. *Kōkū Uchyū Kōgyō no Hatten o Suishin Suru: Soshiki to Katsudō* (Promoting the development of the aerospace industry: Organization and activities). Tokyo: SJAC

————. 1997. *Aerospace Industry in Japan*. Tokyo: SJAC.

Smith, Bruce A. 2000a. "Sea Launch Failure Stalls ICO Satellite Test Program." *Aviation Week and Space Technology* (20 March): 36–37.

————. 2000b. "Sea Launch Hones Mission Operation." *Aviation Week and Space Technology* (7 August): 47.

Solis, Mireya. Forthcoming. "The Politics of Self-Restraint: FDI Subsidies and Japanese Mercantilism." *World Economy*.

Spencer, Barbara J. 1986. "What Should Trade Policy Target?" In *Strategic Trade Policy and the New International Economics*, edited by Paul R. Krugman. Cambridge: MIT Press.

Spencer, Barbara J., and James A. Brander. 1983. "International R&D Rivalry and Industrial Strategy." *Review of Economic Studies* 50, no. 4 : 707–22.

Spero, Joan Edelman. 1990. *The Politics of International Economic Relations*. New York, N.Y.: St. Martin's.

Spindler, Andrew J. 1984. *The Politics of International Credit: Private Finance and Foreign Policy in Germany and Japan*. Washington, D.C.: Brookings Institution.

Srinavasan, T. N. 1985. "Neoclassical Political Economy: The State and Economic Development." *Asian Development Review* 3, 2: 38–58.

STA (Science and Technology Agency). 1996–97. *Shuyōkoku no Uchyū Kaihatsu Yosan no Suii* (Changes in space development budgets of principal countries). Tokyo: STA.

Stegemann, Klaus. 1989. "Policy Rivalry Among Industrial States: What Can We Learn from Models of Strategic Trade Policy?" *International Organization* 43, no. 1 (winter): 73–100.

Stigler, George. 1971. "The Theory of Economic Regulation." *Bell Journal of Economics and Management Science* 2, no. 1 (spring): 3–21.

Stiglitz, Joseph. 1997. "Looking Out for the National Interest: The Principles of the Council of Economic Advisors." *American Economic Association Papers and Proceedings* 87, no. 2: 109–13.

Stimson, James A. 1985. "Regression in Space and Time: A Statistical Essay." *American Journal of Political Science* 29: 914–47.

Sumiya, Miko, and Koji Taira, eds. 1979. *An Outline of Japanese Economic History, 1603–1940: Major Works and Research Findings.* Tokyo: University of Tokyo Press.

Suzumura, Kotara, and Masahiro Okuno-Fujiwara. 1987. "Japanese Industrial Policy: An Overview and Evaluations." In *Japan-U.S. Trade Friction and Economic Policy*, edited by R. Sato and P. Wactel. Cambridge: Cambridge University Press.

Taggart, Stewart. 1999. "Breathing Rarefied Air." *Asiaweek* (18 June): 50.

Taverna, Michael A. 2000a. "China, India Plan Launcher Upgrades." *Aviation Week and Space Technology* (9 October): 126–27.

———. 2000b. "Industry Bullish on Broadband, but Impact on Satellites in Doubt." *Aviation Week and Space Technology* (16 October): 55–57.

———. 2001a. "Europe Strives to Put RLV Effort on Track." *Aviation Week and Space Technology* (9 April): 35–36.

———. 2001b. "Industry Bullish on Broadband, but Impact on Satellites in Doubt." *Aviation Week and Space Technology* (9 April): 36.

Tilton, Mark. 1996. *Restrained Trade: Cartels in Japan's Basic Materials Industry.* Ithaca, N.Y.: Cornell University Press.

Tsuru, Shigeto. 1993. *Japan's Capitalism: Creative Defeat and Beyond.* New York: Cambridge University Press.

Tsuruta, Toshimasa. 1988. "The Rapid Growth Era." In *Industrial Policy of Japan*, edited by Ryutaro Komiya, Masahiro Okuno, and Kotaro Suzumura. Tokyo: Academic Press.

Tullock, Gordon. 1994. "Letters." *National Interest* 37 (fall): 99.

Tyson, Laura D'Andrea. 1990. "Managed Trade: Making the Best of Second Best." In *An American Trade Strategy: Options for the 1990s*, edited by Robert Z. Lawrence and Charles L. Schultze. Washington, D.C.: Brookings Institution.

———. 1991. "Comment." In *Trade With Japan: Has the Door Opened Wider?* edited by Paul Krugman. Chicago: University of Chicago Press for the National Bureau of Economic Research.

———. 1992. *Who's Bashing Whom? Trade Conflict in High Technology Industries.* Washington, D.C.: Institute for International Economics.

———. 1993. Statement on technology policy as chair, President's Council of Economic Advisers, before the Joint Economic Committee, U.S. Congress, 21 June.

Tyson, Laura, and John Zysman. 1983. "American Industry in International Competition" In *American Industry in International Competition: Government Policies and Corporate Strategies*, edited by John Zysman and Laura Tyson. Ithaca, N.Y.: Cornell University Press.

Tyson, Laura D'Andrea, and David B. Yoffie. 1991. "Semiconductors: From Manipulated to Managed Trade." Division of Research Working Paper 92–031. Cambridge: Harvard Business School.

Uenohara, Michiyuki, Takuo Sugano, John G. Linvill, and Franklin B. Weisntein. 1984. "Background." In *Competitive Edge: The Semiconductor Industry in the U.S. and Japan*, edited by Daniel I. Okimoto, Takuo Sugano, and Franklin B. Weinstein. Stanford, Calif.: Stanford University Press.

Upham, Frank. 1987. *Law and Social Change in Postwar Japan*. Cambridge: Harvard University Press.

Uriu, Robert M. 1996. *Troubled Industries: Confronting Economic Change in Japan*. Ithaca, N.Y.: Cornell University Press.

U.S. Congress, Office of Technology Assessment. 1991. *Competing Economies: America, Europe, and the Pacific Rim*. OTA-ITE-498. Washington, D.C.: Government Printing Office.

U.S. Congress. Senate. 1995. Committee on Commerce, Science, and Transportation, Subcommittee on Science, Technology, and Space. *Hearing on the NASA Space Shuttle and the Reusable Launch Vehicles Program*. 104th Cong., 1st sess.

USITC (U.S. International Trade Commission). 1983. *Foreign Industrial Targeting and Its Effect on U.S. Industries. Phase I: Japan*. USITC Publication 1437 (October). Washington, D.C. United States International Trade Commission.

Velocci Anthony L., Jr. 1995. "Launch Market Future Cloudy." *Aviation Week and Space Technology* (6 November): 66.

Vernon, Raymond, Debora L. Spar, and Glenn Tobin. 1991. *Iron Triangles and Revolving Doors: Cases in U.S. Foreign Economic Policymaking*. New York: Praeger.

Vogel, Ezra F. 1985. *Comeback Case by Case: Building the Resurgence of American Business*. New York: Simon and Schuster.

Wade, Robert. 1990. *Governing the Market: Economic Theory and the Role of the Government in East Asian Industrialization*. Princeton, N.J.: Princeton University Press.

Wakiyama, Takashi. 1987. "The Implementation and Effectiveness of MITI's Administrative Guidance." In *Comparative Government-Industry Relations: Western Europe, the United States, and Japan*, edited by Stephen Wilks and Maurice Wright. New York: Oxford University Press.

Weingast, Barry R., and Mark J. Moran. 1983. "Bureaucratic Discretion or Congressional Control? Regulatory Policymaking by the Federal Trade Commission." *Journal of Political Economy* 91, no. 51: 765–800.

Weinstein, David E. 1993. "Administrative Guidance and Cartels in Japan (1957–1990): Did MITI Really Coordinate Japanese Industry?" Harvard Institute of Economic Research, Discussion Paper No. 1628: 1–25.

Wheeler, Jimmy W., Merit E. Janow, and Thomas Pepper, with Midori Yamamoto. 1982. *Japanese Industrial Development Policies in the 1980s: Implications for U.S. Trade and Investment*. Croton-on-Hudson, N.Y.: Hudson Institute.

Wilks, Stephen, and Maurice Wright, eds. 1991. *The Promotion and Regulation of Industry in Japan*. London: MacMillan.

Winter, Frank H. 1990. *Rockets into Space*. Cambridge: Harvard University Press.

Woo-Cumings, Meredith. 1999. "Introduction: Chalmers Johnson and the Politics of Nationalism and Development." In *The Developmental State*, edited by Meredith Woo-Cumings. Ithaca, N.Y.: Cornell University Press.

World Bank. 1993. *The East Asian Miracle*. New York: Oxford University Press.

Woronoff, Jon. 1992. *Japanese Targeting: Successes, Failures and Lessons*. London: MacMillan.

Wray, William D. 1991–92. "Japanese Space Enterprise: The Problem of Autonomous Development." *Pacific Affairs* 64, no. 4: 463–88.

Yamamoto, S., and M. Murakami. 1980. "Iron and Steel." In *An Industrial Geography of Japan*, edited by Kiyoji Murata. London: Bell and Hyman.

Yamamura, Kozo. 1986. "Caveat Emptor: The Industrial Policy of Japan." In *Strategic Trade Policy and the New International Economics*, edited by Paul Krugman. Cambridge: MIT Press.

————. 1995. "The Role of Government in Japan's 'Catch-up' Industrialization: A Neoinstitutionalist Perspective." In *The Japanese Civil Service and Economic Development: Catalysts of Change*, edited by Hyung-Ki Kim, Michio Muramatsu, T. J. Pempel, and Kozo Yamamura. New York: Oxford University Press.

Yamamura, Kozo, and Wolfgang Streeck. 2003. *The End of Diversity? Prospects for German and Japanese Capitalism*. Ithaca, N.Y.: Cornell University Press.

Yamawaki, Hideki. 1988. "The Steel Industry." In *Industrial Policy of Japan*, edited by Ryutaro Komiya, Masahiro Okuno, and Kotaro Suzumura. Tokyo: Academic Press.

Yamazawa, Ippei. 1988. "The Textile Industry." In *Industrial Policy of Japan*, edited by Ryutaro Komiya, Masahiro Okuno, and Kotaro Suzumura. Tokyo: Academic Press.

Yonezawa, Yoshie. 1988. "The Shipbuilding Industry." In *Industrial Policy of Japan*, edited by Ryutaro Komiya, Masahiro Okuno, and Kotaro Suzumura. Tokyo: Academic Press.

Young, Michael K. 1991. "Structural Adjustment of Mature Industries in Japan: Legal Institutions, Industry Associations and Bargaining." In *The Promotion and Regulation of Industry in Japan*, edited by Stephen Wilks and Maurice Wright. London: MacMillan.

Zellner, A. 1962. "An Efficient Method of Estimating Seemingly Unrelated Regressions and Tests for Aggregation Bias." *Journal of the American Statistical Association* 57: 348–68.

Zysman, John. 1983. *Government Markets and Growth: Financial Systems and the Politics of Industrial Change*. Ithaca, N.Y.: Cornell University Press.

Zysman, John, and Laura Tyson, eds. 1983. *American Industry in International Competition: Government Policies and Corporate Strategies*. Ithaca, N.Y.: Cornell University Press.

Index

Tables are identified by (t) following the page number.

Ceramics (CE): *dantai*, 95; growth rates, 87; JDB Loans, 68; lobbying power function, 97; net subsidies, 65, 66; net transfers, 66, 67; quotas, 70; subsidized borrowing, 69; tariffs, 69; tax rates, 67; value-added levels, 88; votes (variable), 91; wage levels, 88

Chemicals (CH): *amakudari*, 96; competitors of, 245n10; *dantai*, 95; favored sectors, 83, 98; future of, 245n10; growth rates, 87; industrial selection (1960), 99; JDB Loans, 68; lobbying power function, 96, 97; as most-favored sector, 80–81; most favored sectors, 245n10; need for deselection in, 210; net subsidies, 66; net transfers, 66; quotas, 70; R&D expenditures, 89; R&D Subsidies, 70, 71; subsidized borrowing, 69; support from MITI, 82; tariffs, 69; tax rates, 67; TIPs rankings, 78; value-added levels, 88; votes (variable), 91; wage levels, 88

China: catch-up mode with, 185; as emerging space competitor, 113; France and, 156; as global space competitor, 179, 239n15; progress in space launch industry, 169–70; space militarization possibility, 184

China Great Wall Industry Corporation, 169

Chirac, Jacques, 156

choice-theoretical principle, 10; rationality and, 4

classical trade theory, 10

clientalism, 26

coal industry: competition from oil, 119; demise of, 226n19; employment levels in, 119–20; political influence of, 119, 120, 226n25; in postwar era, 117–18; in postwar Japan, 226n15, 226n17; prices of, 121; production levels of, 119, 226n24; as reindustrialization key, 118; as strategic economic sector, 118; structural adjustments of, 119, 121; structural decline of, 121, 226n27; structural trend of, 120

Coal Industry Rationalization Council, 120

coal mine closures, 119, 120

Coal Mine Rehabilitation Corporation, 120

Coal Mining Council, 121

Coal Mining Rationalization Law (1956), 120

Cochrane-Orcutt procedure: defined, 41; JDB Loans, 48, 49; quotas, 51, 52; R&D

Subsidies, 52; for serial correlations, 41; subsidized Borrowing, 49; tariffs, 50–51

commercial space launch industry, 28

Commercial Space Transportation Advisory Committee (COMSTAC), 163

commercialization, 184, 208

committees (*iinka*), 38

comparative advantage: and automobiles lack of, 137; government created, 11, 16; and steel's lack of, 122; in textiles, 109, 125

competition: in aircraft industry, 154; for industry's support by politicians, 20; international oligopolistic, 12; by launch vehicles, 162; of space launch industry, 161; in space launch industry, 163–64; for TIPs among industries, 20; of TX (Textiles), 126

computer industry (*see also* IBM): as basic technology, 146; competition in, 234n161; as EM (Electrical Machinery) component, 82; favored by MITI, 82; industry leaders in, 147, 234n170; jurisdiction battles, 144; linkages, 149; as strategic economic sectors, 146; tariff levels on, 145; technological externalities, 149; technological spillovers or linkage, 145; TIPs to, 234n159

COMSTAC. *See* Commercial Space Transportation Advisory Committee

consensus building, 117

constant-coefficient model, 46

Consumer Goods Industries Bureau, 115

core beliefs about technology, 7

core ideological consensus, 6

corruption, 24, 202, 205, 219n46

cost-consciousness, 179

Cray Supercomputer industry, 234n161

criteria: for 1955–1959, 99–103; for 1961–1965, 103–4; for 1967–1971, 104–5; for 1973–1977, 105–6; for 1979–1983, 106; for 1985–19893, 107; assumptions about, 16; and historial perspective, 112–40; of industrial selection, 9; for industrial selection, 100–102(t), 158–59(t), 192–96; knowledge gap about, 114–15; for most-favored sectors, 28; period comparisons, 99–104; regression analysis of, 27; for selection, patterns to, 125

criteria-endowed sectors, 99

criteria for selection: Japanese space launch

SCAP. *See* Supreme Commander of Allied Powers
Science and Technology Agency (STA): case study interviews, 115; Japanese administrative reforms, 171; lobbied directly by industry, 156; on R&D in Japanese space launch industry, 179; selection criteria of, 180; space budgets of, 242*n*72; steel R&D, 124
Science and Technology Basic Plan, 177
SDO Yuzhnove/PO Yuzhmash, 167
Sea Launch, 167–69, 241*n*49
sector analysis, 39
sectoral level employment, 35, 38
sectoral pressures, 9
sectors (*see also* most-favored sectors; specific sectors, e.g., chemicals): econometric characteristics of, 83–90; main trends of, 83–89, 91–97; of manufacturing industry, 39; political characteristics of, 90–91
selection: criteria for, 83–98; determinants for, 79; examining, 63; failure of, 220*n*65; identifying, 79–80; of strategic industries, 16, 23
selection criteria: high value-added and spillovers or linkage, 197; for independent variables, 36–37(t); of NASDA (National Space Development Agency of Japan), 180; of SAC (Space Activities Commission), 180; of STA (Science and Technology Agency), 180
selection decisions, 98
self-interest (utility maximization of the actors), 21
semiconductors industry: American industry's fortune in, 147; barriers to entry in, 235*n*187; competition between Japanese firms, 152; as EM (Electrical Machinery) component, 82; favored by MITI, 82; industry leaders in, 235*n*187; inhouse consumption of, 236*n*201; Japanese development of, 149; JDB Loans, 150; JECC, 150; national projects, 150; NTT (Nippon Telegraph and Telephone), 150; political influence of, 152; preferential procurement practices, 150; private industry development of, 149, 151; selection of, 149; Sony Corporation, 149; technological development in, 151–52; TIPs, 150; VSLI projects, 150

serial correlations, 41, 43
shingikai (advisory bodies), 205, 221*n*12, 246*n*19
Shipbuilding Bureau (of MOT), 129
shipbuilding industry (*see also* Transport Equipment): captive market for, 229*n*85; cartels for, 129, 229*n*82; case study interviews for, 130; employment levels of, 130–31; excess capacity problem, 129; foreign exchange earnings, 130; industry association of, 131; industry leaders of, 131; linkages, 130; loans to, 129, 229*n*79; oil shock (1973), 130; Planned Shipbuilding Program (1947), 129, 229*n*85; in post war Japan, 129; strategic economic sectors, 132; structural adjustments to, 130, 229*n*81
single non-transferrable vote (SNTV), 128, 143
Single Stage to Orbit (SSTO), 165
SJAC. *See* Society of Japanese Aerospace Companies
SLI. *See* Space Launch Initiative), 165, 184
Small and Medium Enterprise Agency, 128, 139
Small and Medium-sized Enterprises (SME), 128, 131, 132, 143
Small Business Finance Corporation (SBFC), 137, 141
SMEs. *See* small and medium sized enterprises
SNTV. *See* single non-transferrable vote
social concerns, 127
social stability, 143
Society of Japanese Aerospace Companies (SJAC), 156, 181, 182, 238*n*232
soft landings, 120
software, 147
Sony Corporation, 149
South Korea, 297*n*31
Space Activities Commission (SAC), 171, 180
space industry, 156–57
space launch industry (*see also* Japanese space launch industry; launch vehicles; NASA; satellites): Arianespace, 163–64; barriers to entry, 169; Boeing, 166–69, 240*n*36; budgets, 243*n*101; case study of, 113; China, 169[-}70; competition, 113, 161, 163–64, 184; failures of, 167, 168; future trajectories of, 183–85; global competitors, 163–

70; global context of, 162–70; government TIPs, 177–80; India, 169[-}70; industry leaders in, 169; information sources, 239*n*2; joint ventures, 239*n*17, 240*n*33; launch forecasts, 163; launch prices, 169, 170; Lockheed Martin, 164–66; 240*n*36; major projects in, 162; market forecast, 241*n*54; mergers, 240*n*36; national security, 162; Rockwell, 240*n*36; sales volume, 163, 166, 167; spillover and linkages, 162; timeline of, 185–91; TIPs and criteria for selection of, 176–83; TIPs to, 162
Space Launch Initiative (SLI), 165, 184
space policies in Japan, 170–76
Space Shuttle, 165
Special Committee on Coal Policy, 119
special interest groups, 19, 20, 21, 22
Spencer, Barbara J., 215*n*3
spillover and linkages: aircraft industry, 155; space launch industry, 162
spillover potential (econometric variable), 46–48, 50–54
spillovers, 12, 17
spy satellites, 181, 182
SSTO. *See* Single Stage to Orbit
STA. *See* Science and Technology Agency (STA)
stabilization law (1978), 129
Standard Industrial Trade Classification (SITC), 30
state-centric theories, 14–15
statist approach, 15, 16, 23
steel industry: as cultural icon, 122; early support of, 122; economies of scale in, 123; as favored sector, 124; future of, 124–25, 227*n*47; industry mergers, 123; political influence of, 123; as strategic economic sector, 122, 123; TIPs to, 124
Steel Subcommittee on Industrial Funds, 122
strategic, defined, 215*n*1
strategic economic sector: coal, 118; petrochemicals, 133; steel, 122, 123
strategic sectors: aircraft industry, 154; basis for identifying, 209; computers, 146; criteria for identifying, 216*n*4; determination of, 17; economic benefit of, 194; extensiveness of uses, 17; most economical of, 84–87(t), 89; politically influential, 92–95(t); technological change, 17
strategic trade policy, 218*n*31

strategic trade policy literature, 3, 13, 89, 192, 194, 215*n*3
strategic trade theory, 195
structural adjustments: benefits of, 229*n*98; of coal, 119, 120, 121; to declining sectors, 224*n*9; from oil shocks, 105, 108, 225*n*13; of petrochemicals, 82, 107, 110; to shipbuilding, 130, 229*n*81; of textiles, 126; TIPs as tool for, 226*n*32
structural decline of coal, 121, 226*n*27
structural depression, 230*n*106; petrochemicals in, 135
structured data analysis: benefits from, 30; industrial aggregation levels, 196, 197; limitations of, 224*n*6; for most-favored sectors, 28, 63; TIPs in, 197
subsidized borrowing (BOR): Cochrane-Orcutt procedure, 49; *dantai* (econometric variable), 49, 50; high-growth (variable), 49, 50; high-value added (variable), 49, 50; lobbying contributions (variable), 51; after oil shock, 69; panel corrected standard errors, 49; wages (variable), 50
Sumitomo Heavy Industries, 131
Sumitomo Petrochemical, 133
summary impact, 53–54
sunset provisions, 207, 208
Super-301 investigation, 178
supertankers, 130
Supreme Commander of Allied Powers (SCAP): aircraft and rockets ban, 173; on automobile production, 136; ban on aircraft production, 153; on economic recovery, 118; reparation payments, 140; support for textiles, 125
Switzerland, 142
systems integrator, 168, 173

Taepodong-I missile, 181–82
Taiwan, 247*n*31
tangible TIPs: demise of, 108, 110; in deselection, 124; in economic hypothesis, 64, 197; for Japanese space industry, 179; measures of, 36; for petrochemicals, 133; statistics of, 225*n*9
tariff levels, 145
tariff rates, 149, 235*n*186
tariffs (TAR), 50–51, 69, 129, 195
tax incentives: petrochemicals, 133; as TIPs, 150, 152

tax rates, 46, 47, 48, 67
taxes, 223n4
TE. *See* transport equipment
technological change, 17
technological spillovers or linkage, 200;
  Japanese space industry, 181, 184
technonational ideology, 16, 17
telecommunications, 146, 162, 163
Temporary Measures for Electronics and
  Machinery Industries Law (1971), 149
Temporary Measures for Machinery and Information Industries Law (1978), 149
Temporary Measures Law for the Promotion of Specified Electronics and Information Industries (1978), 145
Temporary Measures Law on the Promotion
  of Specified Electronics and Machine Industries (1971), 145
Temporary Special Measures Law on Promoting the Machine Industries (1956), 137
TEPCO. *See* Tokyo Electric Power Company
Texas Instruments (TI), 149, 235n187
textile industry: administrative guidance in,
  228n55; *amakudari*, 96; cartels for, 125;
  comparative advantage in, 109, 125; competition of, 126; *dantai*, 91, 95; deselection
  of, 126, 198; employment of, 127, 128–29;
  export earnings from, 125, 126; growth
  rate of, 83; growth rates, 83, 87; JDB
  Loans, 68; linkage lacking, 126; net transfers, 66, 67; political influence of, 103, 128;
  in postwar period, 125; quotas, 70; sales
  level in, 228n64; structural adjustments of,
  126; tariffs, 69, 70, 125; tax rates, 67; TIPs
  rankings, 78; value-added levels, 88; votes
  (variable), 91
theories: of bureaucracies, 21; classic trade,
  10; of endogenous policy, 3, 19, 21, 24,
  193; of industrial selection, 4; international
  trade, 194; neoclassical trade, 18; of new
  international economics, 14; new trade,
  195; political economic, 6, 204; principal-
  agent, 24, 25, 26, 202; public choice, 21;
  state-centric, 14; strategic trade, 3, 19, 195
third-ware industries, 181
Thuraya-I (satellite), 241n49
time-series cross-sectional (TSCS) regression analysis, 27, 30
timeline for Japanese Space Program, 185(t)

TIPs. *See* Trade and Industrial Policies
Titan (launch vehicle), 164
Tokyo Electric Power Company (TEPCA),
  149
Tokyo Round (1973–79), 35(t)
Toshiba, 148, 150
Toshiba-Kongsberg affair, 141, 233n145
"total" import protection, 70
Toyota, 137
Trade and Industrial Policies (TIPs) (*see also*
  nontariff barrier; quotas; tangible TIPs;
  tariffs): analysis intervals, 72; analysis of,
  33; and causal effect, 245n7; to computer
  industry, 234n159; criteria for selection,
  98, 176–83, 222n26; at cross purposes, 72;
  debates over, 195; defined, 3; as dependent
  variables, 33, 34–35(t); depreciation ratios
  as, 137; disbursement of, 215n2; distortion
  brought by, 19; econometric evidence for,
  45(t); effect on development timing,
  248n41; effects of, 211; estimations for, 55–
  62(t); export promotion, 144; finding of
  Japanese government use of, 32; implications of, 204–11; import controls and restrictions, 144; inconsistency in distribution of, 78; and industrial growth, 210;
  initial selection of, 116; Japanese space
  launch industry, 177; lagged data modeling, 42; in market allocation of capital, 26;
  as mercantilism, 215n3; and MITI vision,
  movement of, 80; motivating principle
  for, 142; national projects as, 150, 152;
  overall movement across sectors, 63, 64;
  pattern of allocation, 99; from postwar
  Japan, 192–213; preferential procurement
  practices, 150; ranked distributions of, 65,
  74–78(t); and rival hypotheses, 98–107;
  for shipbuilding, 129; significance of, 25–
  26; soft measures of, 33; as source of corruption, 219n46; to space launch industry,
  162; to steel, 124; in structured data analysis, 197; sunset provisions for, 207, 208; tax
  incentives as, 150; time lagged, 98; TIP
  model, 32, 43; as tool for structural adjustments, 226n32; types of, 64; in unselected
  sectors, 224n7; weighting of, 72
trade barriers, 231n121, 235n185
trade disputes, 177, 178, 194
trade liberalization, 106, 141, 145, 149
trade policy, 2, 70, 194, 220n67